Spooks

To the memory of
Harry George Thomas
1947-1993

omnia vincit amor

Spooks

The Unofficial History of MI5 from M to Miss X 1909-39

Thomas Hennessey
& Claire Thomas

AMBERLEY

Acknowledgements

The authors which to thank a number of people without whose assistance this book would have taken considerably longer to complete: in particular the staff of The National Archives of the United Kingdom; the Imperial War Museum; the Northern Ireland Political Collection, the Linen Hall Library, Belfast; and to the Security Service for permission to use material from their website. We would also like to thank Linda Herviel, Elizabeth Cantello, Janet Allen and Su Bradley; particular thanks go to Kate Marsh and Simon Mills; Lesley Clay; Marion and Derek Hall; and Ross Gower of Nineteen80 Design and Illustration. Finally thanks to Emma, Susannah, Sam and John for putting it all in persprective.

This edition first publis

Amberley Publishing Pl
Cirencester Road, Chal
Stroud, Gloucestershire
www.amberley-books.c

© Thomas Hennessey &

LONDON BOROUGH TOWER HAMLETS	
910 000 00228283	
HJ	20-Aug-2010
327.124	£9.99
THISCA	

British Library Cataloguing in Publication Data.
A catalogue record for this book is available from the British Library.

ISBN 978 1 84868 526 0

Typesetting and Origination by Amberley Publishing.
Printed in Great Britain.

Contents

Introduction
A Matter of Life & Death

Every morning hundreds of thousands of commuters make their way into the city of London on their way to work. This morning appeared no different to all the others except, perhaps, that only the day before, 6 July 2005, London had beaten Paris in its bid to host the 2012 Olympic Games. There was a feel good factor in the capital. It was the peak of the morning rush hour, and London's iconic Underground and red bus system was coping well. But this was not going to be like any other morning on the Tube. It was the morning of 7 July and nothing was going to be the same again for hundreds of commuters, their families and, indeed, the Government itself.

At 8.51 a.m., a bomb tore through the carriage of a Circle Line train 100 yards inside a tunnel between Liverpool Street and Aldgate stations. There were around 700 passengers on this train. The first thing that Michael Henning, aged thirty-nine, a City worker from Kensington, knew about the explosion was 'silver travelling through the air, which was glass, and a yellow flash'. Then 'I was getting twisted and thrown down on the ground. The blast just twisted and turned me.' He was in the next carriage from the blast but within 10ft of where the bomb went off. There was a stunned silence. 'It was very dark all around us,' Michael recalled. 'People panicked and were screaming and a few of us were telling them to calm down. The girls were the calmest and they got things under control quickly. We tried to open the side doors, we were trying to pull them. The London Underground drivers were trying to get them open from the outside but they weren't moving. There was a lot of dust and smoke. There was no communication, no Tannoy, no feedback.' Michael, like many others, had been injured: he had glass in one eye and dozens of cuts and scratches over his face. As people tried to get out of the Tube train he noticed: 'There was part of the side wall missing. Some of the seats were missing. People were still in their seats and they were screaming with pain and were covered in blood down one side of their body. There were other people that were trapped and they were just left there.'[1]

Four minutes after the bomb at Aldgate, a second bomb exploded on a Piccadilly Line train just south of King's Cross station. Twenty-one people were to be killed by this bomb. Hundreds were injured. Helen Long, a station assistant for London Underground held the hand of a commuter for almost two hours after he was rescued from the train at King's Cross. The man, an insurance broker aged thirty-five called Paul, was inside the carriage which exploded and later had part of his left leg amputated. She talked to him to keep him awake while paramedics treated his injuries, trying to distract him from a young girl dying nearby. 'The tube driver,' recalled Helen, 'used Paul's own belt to stem the blood that was streaming from his injury. I'm sure that saved his life. We had a laugh and a joke and he asked me to say the Lord's Prayer at one stage. He had a joke about the 2012 Olympic Games and said he would be the first paraplegic to take part. The bottom of his left leg was missing. He explained that his sister was pregnant and was expecting a baby near Christmas and I told him to do the same exercises that pregnant women do by breathing in small pants. Every time he fell off to sleep I kept him awake. I had his hand in my hand and I kept squeezing it. He asked me lots of times to promise that he would not die. It was horrific but all the staff were calm and brilliant, even though some were in total shock. They helped out even though they themselves were traumatised.'[2]

At 9.47 a.m., in Tavistock Square, Joe Bor and Vicki Dokas, were standing twenty yards from a No.30 bus as it slowed down: 'Nothing was really moving, and there was a lot of traffic, a lot of people like us who had started walking from Euston or King's Cross to try and get to work,' Bor recalled. 'As I put the mobile phone down, I heard a massive bang and I felt this enormous power hit me in the face. All I could see was white smoke and then the top of a bus, which was opened up like a tin can. I didn't know what to do. I froze, but my girlfriend shouted out, "Run".' Bor ran and looked back to grab his girlfriend's hand. What he saw was horrifying: 'As the smoke died down, there were bodies everywhere. Everyone I could see in front of me looked dead. Suddenly, after all the noise of people trying to get to work, it was very, very silent. There was blood splattered everywhere, but strangely people seemed quite calm... I wanted to take a photo, to document it, but then I didn't want to, because it seemed wrong. Then people started crying, my girlfriend was hugging a woman who was very distraught. Many people started to shelter in doorways, I don't really know why. We tried to, but the doorways were full up, so we just walked away.'[3]

On the bus, a nurse, only known as Josephine, was returning from a hospital night shift. She was sitting on the upper deck of the bus when she heard a huge explosion and was knocked out. When she came round, she saw the man next to her was dead. Josephine had to climb over the man's body to escape the bus. 'I struggled to walk due to the shards of glass in my feet,' she said. The bus driver, George Psaradakis aged forty-nine, thought a tyre had blown. He looked up to see the entire top half of the bus missing.[4]

Dr Ann Somerville, thirty-seven, was in her Honda, driving to the British Medical Association, where she was head of ethics. The BMA was located right beside where the explosion occurred and Dr Somerville was in the car nearest the bus when the bomb went off. 'There was a loud explosion and the roof peeled off the bus like a banana skin. You could hear cries. There were plumes of smoke and lumps of debris flying everywhere at all angles... I was just amazed. I couldn't work out whether to get out of the car and run and help, or move my vehicle out of the way of the emergency services. I decided to do a three-point turn and clear out of the way.' Blood was splattered up the walls of the BMA's offices. A blue plaque nearby declaring that the building had once been home to Charles Dickens was pockmarked with shrapnel. Dr Sam Everington was inside the BMA's headquarters when he heard the blast. He knew, straight away that it was a bomb and ran downstairs to see bodies scattered across the pavement. With six other doctors he immediately began trying to save the lives of the casualties. 'The majority of casualties were all over the road but there was one person alive on the bus. He was Chinese, and we were worried about a neck injury so a passer by helped us by holding his head in the right position for quite a long time, until the fireman got him out. Next time I saw him he was in BMA House, seriously injured. I don't know what happened to him.' The doctors had to try and resuscitate the victims with whatever equipment they could. Dishcloths, tea towels and tablecloths were used to try and stem the enormous blood losses. 'Much of the work was simply about stopping bleeding. A bit later, we had access to fluids and oxygen, but it took quite a long time for the emergency services to arrive because this was the last bomb blast and most of them were at the other sites and couldn't get through easily,' Everington said. Some had lost limbs; a tourniquet had to be used to save one person who lost the lower part of a leg. Another person died as the doctors worked. 'It was simply about trying to stop the bleeding, keeping the airway open, and dealing with chest injuries.'[5]

Sergeant Steve Betts of the British Transport police was one of the first rescuers to reach the Piccadilly line train between King's Cross and Russell Square on Thursday: 'It was pitch black and we had torches. The tunnel where the train was was about 150 metres down the track round a corner and there were still a few wounded coming towards us as we approached. As I walked down the track, I heard someone cry out for help but I could not see them. I called out back and looked around but it was very smoky and dusty and they did not answer.' Sergeant Betts got into the train 'and it was quite obvious that this was something horrendous. There were people with limbs missing, huge open wounds with their organs showing and people were crying out and moaning and asking for help.' He thought: 'This is the worst thing I have ever seen. I am not very good in enclosed spaces at the best of times and we had to climb over bodies and body parts to try to help people and see who was still alive. I thought this is the end of the world, right here in this carriage, but you have to do your job.' Sergeant Betts found a man and his leg had been blown off below the knee; there was another body next to him. 'There was also what I thought was a pile of clothes but as I passed to try and get to the man, it moaned and asked me for help. It was a woman. She had all her limbs blown off. I think she died on the concourse.'

The rescuers had not yet got into the carriage where the bomb had exploded. When they did it was a scene Sergeant Betts found difficult to describe. 'The roof had collapsed and we had to almost crawl in. There were body parts everywhere, there was not one bit as far as I could see that was not covered with organs or blood or bits of body. I was squashed in by chairs and dead bodies as we searched for anyone alive. I could not help standing on things but I had to carry on and do my job. It was like collecting a lot of shop dummies and then cutting them up, pouring black paint over them, and filling the carriage.' After a couple of hours, he came back up to the surface. 'The station was pretty quiet by now but someone asked me for directions which made me smile and that made me feel more human. But, as I stood there I felt lonelier than I thought was possible, I just wanted to see a friend or somebody new and give them a hug.'[6]

The 7 July bombers were identified as Mohammed Siddeque Khan, (thirty), Hasib Hussein (eighteen), Shazad Tanweer (twenty-two), and Jermaine Lindsay (nineteen). All apart from Jermaine Lindsay were British nationals of Pakistani origin, born and brought up in the UK, and at the time of the bombings based in West Yorkshire. Lindsay was a British national of West Indian origin, born in Jamaica and based in Aylesbury prior to the attacks. He was a convert to Islam. On the day of the attacks the group assembled at Luton train station and travelled together to King's Cross from where they dispersed to conduct their near simultaneous explosions. The fourth bomber, Hasib Hussein, stopped to buy batteries before boarding the bus suggesting that he had difficulty setting off his device. Homemade organic peroxide-based devices, packed into rucksacks, caused the explosions. This was dangerous to manufacture because of its instability but it did not require a great deal of expertise and could be made using readily available materials and domestic equipment. Some small homemade devices were left in the car at Luton railway station.[7]

On 1 September 2005 a video message from Siddeque Khan was aired on Al Jazeera in which he said:

> I and thousands like me are forsaking everything for what we believe. Our driving motivation doesn't come from tangible commodities that this world has to offer. Our religion is Islam – obedience to the one true God, Allah, and following the footsteps of the final prophet and messenger Muhammad... Your democratically elected governments continuously perpetuate atrocities against my people all over the world. And your support of them makes you directly responsible, just as I am directly responsible for protecting and avenging my Muslim brothers and sisters. Until we feel security, you will be our targets. And until you stop the bombing, gassing, imprisonment and torture of my people we will not stop this fight. We are at war and I am a soldier.

The video message went on to praise the leaders of Al Qaeda, Osama Bin Laden and Ayman al-Zawaheri, as heroes, although no indication was given that they had directed the attacks. Ayman al-Zawaheri appeared on the same tape in a separate recording and praised the 'blessed battle' which had transferred to the 'enemy's land'. In a later videotaped message, aired on Al Jazeera on 19 September, al-Zawaheri claimed responsibility for the attacks although this claim was not supported by any firm evidence.[8]

In the forefront of the battle against terrorism in the United Kingdom stood the Security Service – popularly known as MI5. It was MI5's task to protect British citizens and British interests from attack. Clearly, on 7 July 2005, the Security Service had failed to do this. Once the identities of the bombers were confirmed, the Security Service and the other Agencies initiated reviews of their records to establish whether they had come across any of the individuals before 7 July, whether they had had any prior intelligence of the attacks, or whether the attacks made the meaning of any existing intelligence clearer.[9] It came as a shock to many when it was revealed that, in February 2004, MI5 operatives had, at one stage, two of the bombers under watch while investigating another bomb plot. It was decided not to maintain a watch. The two men went on to cause death and destruction on 7 July 2005. The decision of MI5, in 2004, not to focus more closely on these two men showed that, sometimes, the decisions made by the Security Service can be that of life and death.

1

The Army Game
Vernon Kell & the Origins of MI5

The birth of MI5 is intrinsically bound up with one man. Vernon George Waldegrave Kell was born on 21 November 1873 in Great Yarmouth, where his mother was enjoying a seaside holiday. He would later jokingly describe himself as a 'Yarmouth Bloater'[1] At the time of Vernon's birth his parents lived in Gorleston, Norfolk where his father was serving as a Lieutenant in the South Staffordshire Regiment.[2] Although the family had a peripatetic life-style moving from one posting to another, Vernon grew up in a cosmopolitan environment as his mother was half Polish; her father, Count Konarska had fled Poland during the mid-nineteenth century, married an English girl and settled down to an 'uneventful country life' in England.[3] Count Konarska had various friends and relatives across Europe and the young Vernon Kell regularly visited them. By the age of fourteen, not only was he a seasoned traveller, he was also fluent in German, French, Polish and Italian[4] and clearly possessed a natural talent for languages, which he would later develop further. It is likely that the travelling was also for health reasons; from the age of eight, Vernon suffered from chronic asthma, sometimes severely, which was controllable 'except in certain localities'; in Victorian Britain a chest infection could easily be a death sentence and throughout his life, Vernon's chronic asthma was 'always the thing he dreaded and had to fight against.'[5].

Vernon's father, Major Waldegrave Kell started his army career serving in the Connaught Rangers in Ireland; he travelled to South Africa with his regiment at the outbreak of the Zulu War as an infantry officer. Heavy casualties and illness amongst the officers meant that he ended up being put in command of a battery of artillery; a challenge which he eagerly met, so successfully that he was Mentioned in Despatches and was promoted. He was also responsible for bringing home for burial the body of Louis Napoleon, the Prince Imperial, who had been ambushed and killed by Zulus; a death that was deeply felt back in Britain, notably by Queen Victoria. On his return from South Africa, Waldegrave Kell was promoted to the rank of Captain in the South Staffordshire Regiment and was posted to Lichfield with his family. This did not please Mrs Kell, who was tired of moving from one married quarters to another and she persuaded him to retire.[6] Mrs Kell had some money, which enabled them to buy Ruckley Grange, a 400 acre estate in Shropshire, originally the site of a twelfth century abbey, which included a large house, built in 1820, three lakes and a trout stream.[7] Vernon developed a keen interest in fishing which was to continue throughout his life; fishing was always his favourite sport and in his final years he would enjoy fishing in the sluggish river Ouse.[8]

Vernon was privately educated, with the intention that he would enter the diplomatic service. For reasons unknown, Waldegrave Kell suddenly abandoned this idea and decided that his son should join the army. There was no margin for error; aged eighteen, Vernon was under considerable pressure as he had only one chance to pass the entrance exam before he exceeded the age limit. He was sent to a crammer to quickly get up to speed for the competitive examination for entry to Sandhurst, which he did successfully, going to Sandhurst in 1892. He was 'very happy' during his two years there, especially as he was entirely free from asthma. During his second year he became friends with another cadet who had quite a reputation for being 'irrepressible... [and]... individualistic and purposeful'. These personality characteristics meant he had to suffer some 'pretty drastic ragging', which had absolutely no effect as 'nothing could get him down'. This association would prove to be very significant throughout Vernon Kell's life and he would 'see much more of this'; for his future path would cross with that of Winston Churchill's many times.

On finishing his studies at Sandhurst, Vernon took some leave and went to London to stay with his father at his house in Clarges Street. His mother had eventually found life in the country no better than life as the wife of an army major and had left his father Waldegrave Kell had remarried an American woman, who was 'a very charming hostess' and of whom Vernon was very fond. Vernon enjoyed the company of his father and stepmother very much, but liked to travel to France whenever possible, to visit his relations in the south of France and Paris. His mother's two sisters lived in the ancient town of Saint Germaine en Laye, the birthplace of Louis XIV, situated in the leafy Paris suburbs. Countess Marie Konarska and Countess Emma MacSwiney lived in a 'lovely house' and, despite their pronounced accents, were well known locally as 'the English ladies'. Countess Emma had married a wealthy banker; she was a haughty, artistic woman who loved horses and had her own dressage school. She loved antiques and her home 'resembled a museum... surrounded by glass cases, cabinets, statues of all sorts and no comfort anywhere'. This was at odds with her sister Countess Marie who 'loved her creature comforts'. Vernon loved to visit his aunts, along with his many cousins who lived in France.[9]

Following this breathing space of leave in France, in October 1894, Vernon joined his father's old regiment, the First Battalion South

Staffords, in Lichfield. For the next four years he lived the typical subaltern life, with plenty of hunting, shooting and parties.[10] But this was not enough for him and he was determined to 'strike out on his own and make use of his languages'.[11] He applied to travel to Russia to study so that he might become a Russian interpretator and, while awaiting the outcome of his application, effortlessly passed the exams to become an interpretator of French and German. Vernon was granted permission to sit the preliminary Russian exam, which he passed with flying colours and was granted leave to travel to Moscow to learn the language fluently, setting off in 1898.

In Moscow, Vernon lodged with the von Kotsk family, who were 'interesting, amusing, most artistic and lively'. Madame von Kotsk, an excellent teacher, specialised in boarders who were British officers studying for the Russian interpretership. One of Vernon's fellow pupils was a Captain Lindsay, whose wife and daughter had come with him to Moscow; their little girl was a great favourite with Madame von Kotsk's boarders and a constant companion of Vernon's. Everyone was very concerned when she developed scarlet fever, which Vernon unfortunately caught. In the absence of anywhere else to send him, Vernon was packed off to the primitive Fever Hospital, which catered only for the poor and destitute. With a raging fever, the seriously ill Vernon was driven there in a one horse tumbledown vehicle with all the windows broken. On arrival a nurse unsuccessfully tried to bathe him using a 'coarse wisp of straw' as would be used on a horse and a 'sort of piece of circular metal to scrape him with'. Conditions on the ward were positively medieval; Vernon was put to bed on a straw mattress, which stuck to his raw and inflamed skin and to further add to his agony, his asthma had flared up again. He was able to speak enough Russian to convince the Matron that he had the means to pay for a proper mattress and pillow, which she sent for. During the five weeks he spent in the hospital, Matron and the nurses became very fond of Vernon and, on discovering that he was learning Russian, did their utmost to help him, by reading and chatting to him. Vernon's stay in hospital also gave him an insight into the lives of the Russian people, who were, on the whole, 'very poor'; he found them 'simple kindly people with the most trusting and childlike outlook on life, their ignorance quite astounding but their cheeriness most infectious'. Vernon greatly appreciated this time convalescing in the hospital and it is testament to his linguistic gift that, by the time he was discharged from the hospital, he was fluent in Russian.

When recovered, he returned to the von Kotsk household for the rest of the winter. The time passed quickly and gave him an 'insight into the brightness and light-heartedness of life in the Moscow of those days. The sunshine, the snow, the sleighs and their lovely teams of horses with jingling harness driven by fat drivers sitting perched up high and muffled to the ears'. But, all too quickly, his leave was up and he returned to London to sit his exam, which, of course, he flew through. He then rejoined his regiment at Spike Island in Cork Harbour, Ireland.

It was here that Vernon met Constance Rawdon Scott, the daughter of a local landowner. Constance's father, James William Scott, was 'well known and much beloved in that part of Ireland'. Her family were extremely musical which appealed to Vernon, who, amongst his other talents, was an accomplished pianist. During his time in Russia, he had 'brought back some lovely Russian folk songs' which the Scott family loved to sing along to when gathered around the piano.[12] Despite his contentment in Cork and his ever-growing close bond to the Scott family, Vernon became restless and sought another posting abroad. This time, he decided, he would apply to go to China to try for a Chinese interpretership. His application was successful and he made plans to go to Shanghai. However, fate intervened in the form of the Jameson raid in South Africa, which would lead to the South African War and Vernon desperately wanted to go to the Cape with his regiment. This was refused, despite Vernon appealing personally to Major General Sir John Ardagh. Although sympathetic, Sir John would not revoke the decision to send Vernon to China, telling Vernon that he would not be surprised if 'some active service might not be in store for him in the Far East'. Vernon was bitterly disappointed and returned to Spike Island in the spring of 1900. A small consolation was that he had agreed to act as correspondent for the *Daily Telegraph* while in China.[13]

By now Vernon had fallen deeply in love with Constance Rawdon Scott and wondered if she would go to China with him, which would mean an immediate wedding. He talked it over with her; Constance was thrilled and thought it was 'just wonderful'. This was to set a precedent; throughout his career Vernon would always discuss decisions and problems with his wife. Constance's parents, however, were alarmed at the prospect of their daughter going to China for two years. But her father relented and on 5 April 1900, Constance and Vernon were married at the parish church in Queenstown; the groom was twenty-seven years of age and his bride was just twenty.

The couple travelled to Dublin for a few days' honeymoon, which coincided with what was to be Queen Victoria's first and last visit to Ireland. The streets were 'crowded and beflagged' and Constance noted that the Queen looked 'pleased and happy' and surprised at her 'spontaneous welcome'. The newly-wed Kells left Dublin on 12 April to join the *Teutonic*, one of the 'fastest ships of the White Star Line';[14] it would take them to New York for the first leg of the long journey to China, which was to take over a month.[15] The young couple felt apprehensive, as they had 'taken a big step and wondered what lay in front of us'. Constance's parents came to see them off; in an emotional farewell, her mother 'looked very white and strained' while her father, putting on a brave face, tried to be as 'gay as possible'.

The voyage was not as straightforward as anticipated, for a heavy storm brewed up in the Atlantic, which delayed arrival in New York by a whole day. On landing the newly-wed couple were overwhelmed by the city, with its tall buildings, sidewalks, streetcars and 'strange sights'. They were not, however, as impressed with their first experience of Chinese cuisine, sampling 'Chop Sue' [sic], which they 'were not especially pleased with'. Vernon's step-mother's sister, Mrs Thomas, visited them in New York and invited the couple to visit her family in Troy for a few days. Constance enjoyed this glimpse of American family life and especially liked talking to the Thomas's Irish maid, who, like Constance, was finding her feet in her new environment and 'felt as strange as I did… having left Ireland only recently'. The Thomas's took the Kells to Albany to see the Capitol building where they met Theodore Roosevelt and were 'astonished at his friendliness'.

The Kells continued their journey across North America, travelling by train, through the Rocky Mountain range and the vast prairies. As they boarded the train at Toronto, the other passengers stared at the amount of hand luggage the Kells had brought; Constance later wryly recalled that they had not yet 'learned to travel light' as they were both 'used to more spacious accommodation' and they were forced to stow their vast amount of luggage in their tiny sleeping compartment, which made for a rather uncomfortable journey. The Kells eventually arrived in Vancouver and were sorry to get off the train as they had greatly enjoyed the journey, especially the beauty of the scenery and meeting native Americans at Moose Jaw and Medicine Hat, although Constance noted sadly that the Indians seemed to prize all things European; one 'friendly fellow shook Vernon warmly by the hand, and then asked for five cents for the pleasure of doing so'. The weather in Vancouver was wet, which caused Vernon's asthma to rear its head, luckily for only a short while and Constance celebrated her twenty-first birthday. On 8 May the Kells joined the *Empress of China* for the final leg of their journey, which was fairly 'monotonous', with the exception of a near miss when, in heavy fog, the ship grazed some rocks on the Japanese coast.[16]

In Japan, the Kells visited Yokohama, Kobe and Nagasaki and watched a performance at a Kobe theatre, where the audience all turned and stared, more interested in the appearance of the Europeans than in what was happening on stage. The Kells eventually arrived in Shanghai in May and settled into a boarding house run by an English woman. Vernon began studying for the Chinese interpretership, a process that he found very trying at first; the complex Chinese characters were totally unlike anything he had ever encountered before. He was very relieved that the Chinese name, 'Ko Lu', bestowed on him by his tutor meant 'capable of blessing', as he had heard anecdotes of Europeans being given names which 'when translated into verbal terms would mean something appalling'. Vernon was especially impressed with the Chinese custom of bowing, which he considered to be 'certainly more hygienic' than the European handshake. Constance busied herself learning about Chinese porcelain and bronze works of art, as she hoped to eventually become an expert.[17]

But trouble lay ahead. For months in China there had been whispers of a Chinese uprising against the 'foreign devils' and the activities of a Chinese society called the I Ho Chuan (or 'Big Sword Society') became more evident. Vernon noted that information 'from various sources' suggested that the society had coalesced under a 'very powerful and influential leader, who claimed miraculous powers of immortality' and was against 'foreigners in general and Christians in particular'. In July 1900, these whispers developed into the Boxer Rebellion.

On hearing that his fellow Briton, Colonel Dorward, was being dispatched to Tientsin to command the besieged garrison there, Vernon immediately wired a telegram: 'Here I am, take me' and offered his services in any capacity. Dorwood replied, 'Come up by the next boat.' Vernon was thrilled at the prospect of active service, especially after the 'mortification' of seeing his regiment off to active service in the Boer War. He spent the next couple of days gathering equipment and putting together a 'motley kind of half civilian kit' and joined the last ship to leave Shanghai for the north, which was also inhabited by legions of cockroaches. Poor Constance was left to her own devices; to Vernon the 'only fly in the ointment' was that he had to leave his wife behind in the hope that she would later be able to join him. The ship arrived at Tientsin on 4 July 1900, sailing up the Pei Ho River, which was a nasty mud colour, with the bodies of dead Chinese floating at intervals. Vernon was pleasantly surprised to discover that by coincidence Sidney Barton (who would eventually become First Minister for Abyssinia), a friend of his cousins, was employed by Dorwood as a Chinese interpreter; when he left England, Vernon's cousins had told him to look out for Barton, which he thought 'rather a tall order' considering the size of China.

For the next two years, Vernon was on active service, seeing action within his first few days in Tientsin when shelling hit the main staircase of the (rather conspicuous in Vernon's opinion) British Headquarters. Vernon considered it a narrow escape and had an even more hair-raising experience a few days later when a shell landed on the dinner table but did not explode. Following this, Colonel Dorwood took up the offer of alternative premises and the five staff officers shared a large room, sleeping on the floor together.[18]

Left behind in Shanghai, Constance was extremely worried and had deep misgivings; rumours of the rebels and their tortures and brutalities were rife and she was terrified of what could happen to her husband. She was equally concerned that he had no sun-hat with him and, that as well as suffering a horrific torturous death at the hands of the rebels, Vernon might get sunstroke. Within a few days of Vernon's departure, Constance, with great relief, for 'the situation was very strained and tense [and] guns were trained in the direction of foreign settlements', went to stay with the sister in law of Colonel Bowers, travelling to the island of Liu Kun Tao with Mrs Bowers and her young baby in July. Unbeknown to Constance, who was carrying the baby, restrictions on landing were in place and she later found out that she only managed to get ashore because the authorities assumed that she was the baby's nanny. When Vernon did eventually get some leave to see his wife in September, it was, to her disappointment, because he had dysentery (which he would sporadically suffer from throughout his stay in China) and he was eventually hospitalised for nearly a week. Constance, a self-proclaimed 'Irish rebel' found the rules and regulations of the hospital rather tedious and they were both relieved when Vernon was discharged and they were finally able to spend some time together.[19]

The Boxer Rebellion was successfully crushed, but chaos reigned in its wake. Eight nations had sent contingents to the international relief force, which was set up to deal with its aftermath. Vernon's linguistic skills came into their own with this situation and he was appointed as Intelligence Officer on the staff of General Lorne Campbell (who had taken over as commanding officer of the British Forces) at Tientsin, where Constance was able to join him. As part of his remit he travelled widely, participating in a small expedition to the north. He worked for a short while as a railway Staff Officer where his languages were in constant demand[20] and, in July 1901, he was transferred to Shanghaikuan. This was a remote, but strategically important outpost where the Great Wall of China meets the sea, and also the junction of the British and Russian controlled sections of the railway. His wife considered that it was here that Vernon learned his diplomatic skills by having to work with the Chinese stationmaster, a Russian railway Staff Officer and the displaced British stationmaster, Mr Ricketts.

Constance found Captain Ignatieff, the Russian Staff Officer 'a curious friendly sort of a person, quick to take offence, rather self important [and who] possessed none of the charm of the Russian officers we had met who came from St Petersburg under the Tsarist influence'. Mr Ricketts and his wife, to whom 'nothing seemed too much trouble' were to become close friends of the Kells; Mrs Ricketts kindly offered Constance the use of her bathroom, and, when Constance was covered in flea bites from sleeping in the station waiting room 'laughed heartily saying I could certainly not [sleep there] until it had been cleared of fleas'. Vernon and Constance moved into a converted railway outbuilding, situated next to the railway points; their home was known as the 'Domtchik', or 'small house' in Russian. They were still living in the Domtchik when their first child, was born, although Vernon encouraged Constance to go to Tientsin for the birth of their baby and was storing up his leave in order to visit her as soon as possible.

Constance and Vernon could not afford a hotel for her to stay in during her confinement, and the hospital that she intended to go to informed her that they would not take her. Her doctor's wife offered her their home as a sanctuary. However, Constance, by chance, met a woman who had heard of her situation and invited her to come and stay. Constance was overwhelmed: 'I could hardly credit such generosity from anyone, let alone from someone I had never met before, but such is the hospitality and kindness you meet when people are very far away from home and they have difficulties and dangers to face in common.' Constance and her newborn son – baby James – moved into the Domtchik and, despite their unusual circumstances, settled in well finding life 'quite gay... we settled in happily to this up-country life'. Vernon found it easy to be on the platform at the required times of midnight and 4 a.m. as baby James 'preferred to be awake at night, often very noisily, and his Amah let him do exactly as he pleased!'

The winter brought heavy snows and ice-skating with the Russian contingent, at which Vernon excelled. Although Constance found the Siberian Russians 'uncouth', Vernon, probably due to his fluency in their language, found it easy to enter into their thoughts and outlook. In the spring, the Kells and baby James moved into a little house that belonged to one of the railway officials, which they jokingly referred to as 'the meat safe'. The winter and early spring weather caused Vernon to suffer from several bouts of asthma, but this did 'not affect his cheerfulness and he made very light of it'. When the railway official who owned the house that the Kells were living in returned, Mrs Ricketts came to their aid, finding them a 'really lovely house' which had been the residence of a local Chinese official. Vernon was, at last, able to have a study.[21] On Sundays, Vernon organised a 'little church service' for the British expatriates, borrowing Mrs Rickett's harmonium and leading the responses himself, with Constance taking on the role of chief chorister. Eventually a little church was built in the Ricketts' garden, which was to host a wedding, a christening and also a funeral, when a young army doctor met with a tragic accident.

Through the course of his work, Vernon met a variety of interesting personalities, such as General Marchand, who had 'long ago cut across British interests in Africa', causing a 'good deal of unpleasantness' between the British and the French – when he planted the French flag in the Sudan which nearly led to war with Britain – and the 'famous old Chinese statesman' Li Hung Chan who, although he had lost his influence, was still held in eminent respect by the representatives of the various nations represented in Peking. Constance and Vernon treasured the friendship of the Ricketts and spent many happily nostalgic musical evenings with them, where they 'dished up the favourite tunes time after time… they seemed, somehow, to bring us closer to the joys of home'.

In September 1902, it was decided to put the station under Chinese control and Vernon participated in a bizarre ceremony at Shanghaikuan involving various British, Russian and Chinese ceremonies. Vernon had been presented with a 'large silver bowl and tray of very ornate, but very beautiful design' from Baron von der Ropp, who was in charge of Russian operations and belonged to the courtly circles in St Petersburg that Constance was more inclined to, unlike the rough and ready Siberians she had encountered. Vernon 'felt quite sad at giving up what had become an interesting job' as he knew that he would now have to reluctantly return to his interpretership studies.[22]

The Kells travelled to Peking the following spring, as guests of the Italian Legation and Vernon sat his exams. By now feeling homesick, Constance dreaded the thought of him failing, putting aside 'the rather awful thought that we should have to stay yet another year in China unless he succeeded at the first effort'. Vernon was 'feeling very depressed' and was convinced that he would fail his exams. On the final day, Constance went for a walk along the Great Wall of China, with the then wife of the Italian Minister and suddenly saw a smiling figure rush along the Wall. Vernon had passed and the Kells could travel home to London via Siberia, Russia, Poland and Germany, a journey that would take seventeen days in total. Vernon decided that they should break their journey in Moscow to visit his old haunts.

The Kells bid an emotional farewell to the Ricketts and their other friends at a raucous dinner party and attended an evening hosted by the local Chinese magistrate's wife (who, to Constance's fascination, had traditionally bound feet), the climax of which was a Chinese traditional play, none of which the Kells understood. Constance noted that, although their hostess had gone to considerable trouble, European eating customs were not really understood, as a motley selection of rusty cutlery was presented to the guests and mutton cutlets were served in dainty Chinese bowls. The dinner became an ordeal as the guests tried to keep the cutlets from falling out of the bowls and on to the floor while the Chinese guests who were present were shocked at the mischievous behaviour of the Ricketts' children.[23]

The Kells invited the magistrate's wife for tea a few days later. She arrived, bringing her own food, her entourage of lady attendants and her nine-year-old son. The Chinese ladies were entranced with the blonde-haired and blue-eyed baby James Kell, despite his crib being dressed in white silk and muslin: that was, for the Chinese, the colour of mourning. They were equally as impressed with the Kell's bed and the magistrate's wife spent some time 'rolling backwards and forwards on it saying "hao, pu hao", "good, very good".' The Kells attended several farewell parties held in their honour, but the one that stood out for Constance was their final social evening held at the Ricketts' house; during the dessert course as the wine flowed freely, the Ricketts' house boy came in with a telegram addressed to Vernon, instructing him to take up another appointment. Constance 'could see the official form and Vernon's look of surprise' and as her 'heart sank' she feared for her husband's health: 'it seemed a shattering blow' and she felt 'pretty miserable.' The telegram, however, turned out to be a joke played by the Ricketts and the Kells thoroughly enjoyed the rest of the evening, which Constance remembered as 'the gayest of all our goodbyes'.[24]

Although the Kells had thoroughly enjoyed their time in China, they had been horrified by the fearful poverty and suffering they encountered. Constance described how, when out for a walk one bitterly cold winter's day in sub-zero temperatures, she and Vernon encountered a small boy, aged around nine, wearing no clothes, with 'just a wretched piece of sacking to protect him from that dreadful wind'. The horrified Kells tried unsuccessfully to help the little boy by approaching a local missionary and were devastated to realise 'the relentless forces of ignorance and cruelty that we were up against'. Constance also witnessed a beggar, who had placed next to him, his severed frozen feet, lost through frostbite: she 'could not look at him, it was so horrible'. After the relatively sheltered world at Shanghaikuan, where there were few unpleasant incidents these forays into the real early twentieth century China came as an unpleasant and unpalatable shock.[25]

The Kells and baby James now travelled via Mukden to Harbin to join the Trans-Siberian Railway. They were initially glad to find the carriages well heated, but, on trying to obtain a breath of fresh air, found that, on opening the windows, bits of glowing cinders from burnt wood used as fuel, were blown into the carriage, to the indignation of their fellow passengers. The Kells had to resign themselves to breathing the 'really lovely exhilarating air' of Siberia when the train pulled into a station. Vernon's fluent Russian meant that the Kell's needs were met during the journey and they enjoyed the company of some Russian officers who pushed aside the tables in the dining car to play with baby James. One evening the Kells were alarmed to notice the train rocking violently from side to side; Vernon was despatched to question the officials on board and was told that the train driver was 'exceedingly drunk'. The Kells arrived in Moscow, where they broke their journey for a week, and Vernon was able to show off his wife and baby to his old friend Madame von Kotsk, who was able to find a trustworthy person to care for baby James while his parents went sightseeing, visiting the Kremlin and several cathedrals. They also saw the famous Tenor Chaliapin at the Opera House and were 'spellbound'. In later years, Constance recalled how she and Vernon treasured this visit to Russia 'before all the sorrows and troubles had overwhelmed it'. The Kells boarded yet another train, travelling through Warsaw and on to the Hook of Holland. Constance's mother and Vernon's father had arranged to meet them London from where they all set off for the Curzon Hotel; Vernon's father and step-mother were moving from Clarges Street to Hertfort Street, so everyone stayed at the hotel and made a 'very hilarious party'.[26]

Present at the Birth

After a few days leave, Vernon reported to the War Office and was astounded to be told that he should be in India; the telegram instructing him to rejoin his regiment had been delivered in Shanghaikuan after the Kells had boarded the train to leave. It seemed that by a cruel twist of fate – and the War Office – the Ricketts' practical joke had become a reality. Constance was terribly upset and concerned and 'begged him to seek an exchange with another officer'. Fortunately he was able to, starting work at the War Office as a Staff Captain in the German section. Thus fortune smiled upon Kell for this marked the beginning of a career, which, 'with various twists and turns' kept Vernon at the War Office for the rest of his service and meant the Kells would live in or around London. The Kells had, by now, sent baby James to Constance's family in Ireland and rented some rooms in Brompton Square, from an unpleasant landlady.

Constance had no experience at housekeeping or cooking, having relied on servants and, faced with having to shop for provisions, was distraught. The Kells started house hunting, renting a furnished house in the green-belt London hinterland of Weybridge, Surrey, where Constance's cousins lived. The house had a nice garden, which made up for the 'abominably hideous furniture'. Vernon commuted into London on the train, joining the crowds of other 'daily breaders' all bound for the metropolis in the morning. Although Vernon was involved in intelligence work, it was at that time 'not particularly interesting'. But when baby James was brought back from Ireland with his Swiss nursemaid, the Kells felt settled and were happy. Their joy was increased when their daughter, Margaret was born.

Soon Vernon's linguistic talent and experience were attracting attention and interest at work: General Sir Fraser Davies, the Assistant Director of Military Operations, was on the look out for someone to undertake an intelligence job. In later years, Vernon would describe General Davies (who was affectionately known as Frankie or Joe) as the 'father of the work', for he enthusiastically backed Vernon and used his influence to help him in his career. However, the man who 'always claimed to have picked Vernon out for this intensely important job' was Colonel James Edmondes, who was to become a great friend of the Kells. In later years, Constance recalled Edmondes saying quietly to her: 'what was it that led me to pick out Vernon Kell for this job, which was so urgently needed for the safety of the country? How did I know that he was the best man to deal with it?' He 'smiled thoughtfully and looked penetratingly' at her 'evidently feeling that his inspiration had proved correct'.[27] The respected Edmonds, (whose skills had earned him the nickname 'Archimedes' from school contemporaries who included Douglas Haig and Edmund Allenby[28]), believed that the French failure in the Franco-Prussian War of 1870 'was largely due to want of Secret Service'. It bothered Edmonds that Britain had no 'official' counter-espionage system in place; he complained to the Director of Military Operations (DMO): 'We have only casual assistance from members of police and [the] Post Office.' He went on to give examples; recently, in the *Daily Mail*, a Territorial Officer had told of how a 'certain German Officer' had told him that every German Officer had a 'district' which was 'a part of England to know thoroughly'. To reinforce this, an 'English Lady', married to a German Officer, had 'repeatedly told Lieutenant Colonel H.B. Williams that her husband's "district" is part of Yorkshire'.[29] To Edmonds, these and other incidents put a different slant on the media hype and frenzy and confirmed what he suspected: that the threat of German espionage was real and Britain was 'in the position of the

French in 1870: our enemy is "training" for the conflict [and] we are not'.[30]

At this stage there was only a rather pathetic effort at a serious counter-espionage service: it existed in the form of an extraordinary Irishman – William Melville. The Kerryman embodied many of the contradictions that constituted Ireland's relationship with Britain: Roman Catholic, Home Ruler and former hurley player, he had joined the Metropolitan Police and was instrumental, as part of the Special Irish Branch, in combating Fenian terrorism. In 1893 Melville became Superintendent of Scotland Yard's Special Branch. Towards the end of October 1903, Melville was on annual leave when Colonel Trotter, of the War Office, wrote asking him to call upon him as soon as he could. When Melville called upon him the Colonel explained that he had heard that the policeman had completed his time in the Met to enable him to claim a full pension, and, if so, 'would I leave the police and take up duty at the War Office?…I replied that this was quite correct, but that there was no necessity for me to retire from the police. However, if I got a suitable offer, I would consider it. We soon arranged matters, with the result that I took up duty with the War Office on the 1st December, 1903.' Melville started work in two rooms at 25 Victoria Street, London, SW, with the name 'W MORGAN, General Agent' on the door. He chose the offices especially for the reason that while the public entrance in Victoria Street showed almost innumerable offices in the building, immediately around the corner was another entrance: 'Thus, in case of necessity, I used either door – a great asset.'

'Few men at this time (1903),' recalled Melville, 'were better known in London than I was, yet, strange to say, during the five years I was there and although only about 400 yards from Scotland Yard, I never met any person in or coming out who knew me. This could only obtain in London.' Colonel Sir Francis Davies was Melville's first War Office chief: 'My duties were rather vague, but were generally to enquire into suspicious cases which might be given to me; to report all cases of suspicious Germans which might come to my notice; and foreigners generally; to obtain suitable men to go abroad and obtain information; to be in touch with competent operators to keep observation on suspected persons when necessary.' There was much to be done, in the aftermath of the Boer War, with an incessant stream of South African suspects arriving in Britain: 'The Boers when arrived in London were most difficult to observe; they saw detectives everywhere. It was a great relief when they had passed, say, a week in London – by that time they much relaxed in their surveillance.'

Melville had to travel to all parts of the country to make enquiries regarding suspected persons: 'In these duties I found the police, whether in London or the provinces – absolutely useless. Their invariable estimate of a suspect was his apparent respectability and position. Just as though only blackguards would be chosen for espionage. But the fact was the police could not understand such matters. The idea was foreign to them.' The following case was typical: there was at one time a strong suspicion that the Germans intended to blow up railway tunnels leading to London in the event of war. In this connection, Melville learned that a German photographer had resided at Merstham, Surrey, where there was a very long tunnel. He went there, but found the German had already disappeared. Melville recalled: 'It must be remembered that in those days I was absolutely forbidden to mention the word "spy." All sorts of pretexts had therefore to be resorted to, even with the police.'

Melville found that a constable of the Surrey police was living in the same street as the German suspect – in fact, opposite to him. 'I called on this officer and told him who I was. He knew of me well and became most willing to assist. In reply to my questions, he said he knew the German well, yes, he was a splendid photographer he did not care for taking photographs of people, he went in for landscapes.' The German had shown many photos to the constable, and the latter said they were 'marvellously good. I then spoke to the officer for some time on the fact that the times were strange, and that we all should take stock of those foreigners and have our suspicions of them, etc., etc. "Yes Sir," he said, "I am sure you are right; I believe these fellows are the authors of nearly all the burglaries we have around the country." Thus my eloquence was absolutely thrown away.' Melville subsequently learned that this German had made a photographic survey of the whole of the country around Merstham and Surrey generally. He also found that the man the German lodged with was a general sort of handyman at Merstham Railway Station. In carrying out his duties, he had to travel through and examine the tunnel twice a week at least. In those walks he was frequently accompanied by his lodger, the German photographer, who, of course, went out of 'mere curiosity', so the handyman thought. Altogether, concluded Melville, 'this German was clever at his work'.

Melville found that the supposed occupations in vogue with German agents were: poultry farming; the teaching of foreign languages; learning agriculture; commercial travelling; selling marine lamps in various shipping centres; hotel waitering; 'and many other callings'. Besides this, there were the rich, independent Germans who bought land and houses and the well-to-do German shopkeepers, who were looked up to in their respective localities and, of course, beyond suspicion. To get 'behind these people' was a difficult matter, necessitating weary months of enquiry and almost indefinite patience. 'And this at a time when the Post Office was sealed against us and, as stated already, the police were useless.' As with the latter, 'so also with the public, not to one in a thousand did the idea occur that Germans might be here on espionage'.

In 1905 there was news of a German student farmer staying with a substantial farmer named Smith, living about six miles from Ipswich. Melville went there and interviewed Smith. The German had already left. Smith said the latter came to him as a student recommended by the Vice President of the Royal Agricultural Society. Smith stated:

> the initial part was done plain and above board. Before the German was here many days, I could see he knew quite as much about farming as I did. I drive to Ipswich every morning, and the German invariably went with me. He never ceased asking me questions on the way, such as, 'Who lives in that house? What does he do? Is he wealthy? Where does that road take you to? How many miles is it to such a town? How many inhabitants there? Who keeps that forge? Is he a good blacksmith? Where does the next blacksmith live? How many cattle and horses are there in this county?'

All the answers were carefully written down by the German, his pretext being that he wished to be able to talk about the countryside. Smith and his visitor were always back home for luncheon, after which the German invariably retired to his room to write, so he said, and he was not again seen until dinner time. The German paid several trips on his own to Felixstowe and Harwich with his camera, which he always carried. He spoke to Smith about the forts he had seen at the above places. After about four months the German went back to his home in Schleswig-Holstein. He informed Smith his father had been in the Franco-German War of 1870, and that he was himself an officer in the German Cavalry. Melville asked Smith whether he had any suspicion of the man while staying with him:

> Not in the slightest were my suspicions aroused in this way. I saw a report [in the local papers] of a sermon preached by the Rev. Mr. KENNEDY, of Woodbridge, who was Chaplain to the Volunteers at Felixstowe for the Summer Manoeuvres, just as they were returning to their homes. In that sermon the clergyman told the Volunteers that when they were back in their fields and lanes, they should be suspicious of foreigners asking them questions about the country. At once, I read it to my wife and we both of us came to the conclusion that

our late visitor was a spy. What else could he be? Although paying a good fee, he did not trouble about farming, nor learning English, which he spoke very fairly. And then he had every afternoon till 7 p.m. in his room, where no doubt he was busy drawing maps, etc.

Melville went to Woodbridge, and interviewed the Reverend Kennedy, with a view to learning if he had any particular reason for preaching the sermon in question to the Volunteers at Felixstowe. Kennedy told Melville that prior to coming into the Church, he had been an officer in the Guards. In this capacity he had made the acquaintance of an officer in the German Army. During his holidays the previous summer he found himself in Berlin, and looked up his military friend, with whom he had got on well, and had a high position in connection with a military college in Berlin. His friend invited him to the college to look round. Kennedy continued:

We entered brusquely into a class room, and I was dumbfounded when I saw what the students were doing. On a black-board in front of them was this series of questions: 'Having landed an army of 50,000 men in Hastings, (England), describe the route you would take to get to London. What food would be available? What number of horses could be obtained? What roads could carry artillery? The principal towns en route, and the number of inhabitants in each?' Knowing German thoroughly I read this very carefully while my German friend was at first visibly embarrassed, and subsequently affected to laugh at it by saying 'We give these young men all sorts of rubbish to write' and led me from the room. This was the reason, which prompted me to preach the sermon in question to the Volunteers as they were on the eve of going home.

In this case the alleged German spy had written to the President of the Royal Agricultural Society asking to be favoured with the addresses of some good farmers, preferably on the east coast, who would take in an agricultural pupil. In due course, the name of Smith was sent to the German. 'Thus the German started under good auspices,' noted Melville.

Early in 1906 an anonymous letter was received at the War Office stating that a 'foreign-looking man' had been seen taking photographs of a disused fort close to Epping, and Melville went to the latter place and made enquiries. He found that the man referred to was one of seven or eight Germans, who had been, for some months, residing in Epping. These men were living in a large furnished house on the fringe of Epping Forest, just outside the town of Epping. A woman went to the house every morning, did the cleaning, and then left. Sometimes the men did their own cooking, or had their food at the Forest Gate Inn, kept by a German named Speiglhalter, which was close by. Frequently, there were as many as thirteen Germans staying together at Epping. They all had either cycles or motor-cycles, and invariably carried cameras. They also carried field glasses. They had, apparently, plenty of money. These men aroused no suspicion whatever in the minds of the inhabitants, nor did the local police take any interest in them. Melville recalled:

> And yet, any casual observer could see they were not there for pleasure. As a fact, they worked hard. They left home regularly every morning at 9.o'clock, irrespective of the weather, on their bicycles or motorcycles, and armed with cameras. All took different routes. No information could be obtained as to their destination, for the reason, as I have said, that no person took any notice of them. However, through frequent visits to the place, and asking questions, I succeeded in getting a few persons to interest themselves in the strangers. In the result, some people chatted with them. All said they were on holidays. It was learned that these Germans went for long trips to the seacoast; also, that immediately a man had completed three months at Epping, he left and another German took his place. At times the Germans were not discreet, as when enquiries were made as to what had become of so and so (one of the men who had left), the answer came, 'oh, he has gone back to Germany to join his regiment'.

While at Epping these Germans sometimes bought horses and traps. Finally, they melted away from Epping, and Melville traced four of them to Newport Pagnell, in Bucks. Here he found they had hired a furnished house at the village of Milton Keynes, about four or five miles from Newport Pagnell. Melville learned that they were living on the same lines as at Epping. He brought them under the notice of the local police, who appeared to take little notice of them.

> Ultimately, I believe, all these Germans went to other parts of England, and we heard no more of them. Needless to say, they were under no supervision of any kind in this country. I mentioned to the Superintendent of Police at Epping that the Germans might be spies; he laughed at the idea as being ridiculous, adding, 'Spies! what could they spy here?' Argument was useless. The fact remains that undoubtedly they were spies, and their business, I should say, was to become thoroughly conversant with the routes from the sea coast to London, and thus be able to guide a German army landed in this country. These Germans frequently, to the surprise

of some Epping people, told the number of miles even to very remote places on the sea coast. They knew the geography of the country by heart. They were all of the non-commissioned officer type. There was also the fact that when a man completed three months at Epping, he was transferred to other parts.

Owing to the 'almost continuous enquiries on the Eastern coast re suspected Germans, alleged staff rides by Germans, etc.' Melville submitted reports to the War Office outlining a scheme of surveillance on all suspected foreigners around the country. In this he suggested the utilisation of the police, the Postal authorities, and the Coast Guard service. 'This,' he later recalled, 'could have been carried out at that time with very little cost, if any, and I now feel confident it would have resulted in collecting a large and valuable amount of information respecting foreigners in this country.' In particular, Melville suggested that, in the first place, a circular should be sent from the Home Office to all the Chief Constables in England, drawing their attention to the growing menace of espionage, and directing that steps be taken to obtain particulars of all foreigners possibly so employed. Melville understood later that the Home Office declined to move in the matter, on the ground that the police were not fitted for such duties.[31]

But the mood of complacency was changing. As the decade ended, the British public had been whipped into a state of paranoid frenzy by the media, who claimed that the country was awash with German spies lurking behind lamp-posts and eaves-dropping on conversations everywhere. The press regularly predicted a German conquest of London, after which Teutonic soldiers would march down Pall Mall and seize supremacy. Britain and Germany were engaged in a naval arms race and were competing against one another to gain technological superiority for their fleets, a rivalry that was reflected in sensational newspaper coverage of German espionage activity, with numerous (and much exaggerated) reports of spies and invasion plots. The *Weekly News*, for instance, offered £10 to readers to provide information on German agents to its 'Spy Editor' and received hundreds of letters naming and shaming alleged German spies. These fears were not only confined to the paranoia of the British public and media sensationalism: in 1908, Field Marshal Earl Roberts VC, the Commander-in-Chief of British forces during the Boer War and a national hero, made a widely publicised speech, calling for increased armed forces as a German invasion was imminent. This was not a hysterical outburst, but a considered and measured assessment. In 1909 the press, particularly the *Daily Mail*, constantly ran stories about espionage, claiming that many German barbers and waiters in Britain were actually spies. This caused such an outcry that the Government were forced to formally deny to Parliament that 66,000 German soldiers were in hiding in Britain, waiting for the call to arm themselves. Speculation around Zeppelins and invaders became prolific; 'things which are being said and done in England these days strike us Germans as magnificent material for farce and comedy' commented one German newspaper.[32]

Even so, within the War Office, the possibility of German infiltration, leading to an attack had been taken very seriously. Kell, working in the German Section of the War Office, heard constant discussions of this nature. Lord Haldane, for whom Kell had the greatest admiration, warned forebodingly of the work of the German General Staff. Kell was offered a post on the Imperial Defence Committee but this did not stop the Kells employing a German nanny for their children – after they bought a house in Weybridge – as they wanted them to become as proficient in foreign languages as their father. Around this time, Vernon's favourite cousin also married a German, though her family were not enamoured of the idea, feeling uneasy at the 'continual sabre rattling' in Berlin. By now, one of the questions constantly coming under review at the meetings of the Imperial Defence Committee was the need to form a system of counter-espionage.[33]

In 1909 the Committee of Imperial Defence made a deep study of Britain's defences against a German threat: in the early twentieth century, Germany was a growing nation and was being watched, with a wary eye, by Britain. The Committee had been set up after the South African War and was considered to be 'the least formal and the most effective' of the Government branches. It had influence over Cabinet and the power to make and approve decisions fast. Although the Committee had no formal power over the Armed Forces or the Government, the calibre and reputation of its members meant that it was taken extremely seriously.[34] Colonel Edmonds, pointing out that strategic information could only be got through agents, pushed for the formation of a secret service organisation and was backed up by General Ewart, who impressed that, in the current climate, no legal action could be taken against German spying in Britain. Ewart suggested that the solution would be to, with the help of the Civil Departments, track down and make a note of German agents in England. In any time of national emergency these agents could be immediately seized and incarcerated, and stopped from 'executing demolitions and furnishing information to the enemy'. Ewart also thought that, by monitoring German agents in peacetime, their geographical areas of interest could be discovered, to pre-empt where they might strike in a time of war. The problem was there were absolutely no resources, in terms of manpower, or otherwise, to carry out this task. Ewart contrasted the situation with that of the Continent, where 'one cannot get a bed at an hotel without the Police being informed'. He also mentioned a recent report in

La France Militaire, where a German had rented a house and some land just above an important railway tunnel. The French were suspicious and expelled him. Yet the Germans, the year before, had 'paid particular attention' to the new railway junction at Hither Green in south-east London. Of course no action could be taken in the latter case.

Ewart also told the Chief of the General Staff that 'a third bureau, to deal with England, has been added to the Nachrichten bureau (Secret Service) of the German General Staff. The service is worked from Brussels and we have recently had cause to believe partly from New York. The bureau was not in existence in 1899.' It was impossible to trace the movements and record the residences of German agents unless, as on the Continent, the police, General Post Office (GPO), Customs and other departments of State co-operated with one another. German agents in Britain corresponded with one another by post 'in the most open fashion'; while in France agents had to communicate personally and were therefore more easily detected. Some of the Chief Constables – as ex-army officers – had, when asked, 'made enquiries for us' but strictly on an *ad hoc* basis:

> they have made us understand that it is not their business... last week we were very anxious to trace the doings of the head of the German Secret Service at Brussels, who was, we were warned, coming to England via Ostend. We asked the head of the Criminal Investigation Department to let his men at Dover watch for the man among the arrivals by boat. He was compelled to refuse as the man was not a criminal and if the matter had leaked out there might have been tiresome questions in Parliament. It would have been most useful to have learnt with whom the man communicated with over here. We were told he was coming to interview certain new (British) agents.

The Post Office, Ewart explained, had also always refused to give assistance, except concerning certain addresses. Postmasters were not allowed to inform the authorities as to which new foreigners came into a neighbourhood – 'which their postmen must know at once' – nor to tell the authorities if certain foreigners were regularly cashing remittances from abroad. Even in war time – such as during the Boer War of 1899–1902 – a special Home Office warrant was required before the letters of suspected foreigners could be examined. Customs had been approached privately with a view to special vigilance at places like Lowestoft and Great Yarmouth, but they evidently thought the matter should be done officially and were not interested in intervening. However, officials of all of these departments indicated that they would be prepared to help if some form of official sanction was given. They had assisted greatly in the matter of preparation for cable censorship in war, which was dealt with by an interdepartmental conference, and the matter had remained a secret. But Ewart wanted to go much further, extending this co-operation to peacetime and he proposed that the reference for an interdepartmental conference should be: 'How far can the civil departments of the State assist the Admiralty and War Office in tracing and ascertaining the residences and vocations of foreigners in the coast districts and vicinity of London.' The Foreign Office should be represented although no foreign Powers 'can object even if proper measures are taken by us, as we can plead "reciprocity".' Ewart echoed Edmonds, in warning that: 'The matter is one which I consider is of vital national importance; Germany is now taking in England the same measures as she took in France in 1866–1870.' There was, of course, no objection under international law to the expulsion of undesirable aliens 'but apparently we have no municipal law to effect it'.[35]

Soon afterwards, Edmonds quietly turned to Kell and asked him to jointly head any counter-espionage machine. Kell, according to Constance, 'was amazed to hear his name put forward'. He had to think very fast, being all too aware that, should he accept the post, 'he would be running a great risk. He might be a failure, and what then?' Kell consulted Constance, who had 'not the slightest doubt that he would make a success of it'.[36] He formally accepted the job on 19 September with the reply: 'I shall be glad to accept the billet you have been good enough to offer me'.[37] Thus the Special Intelligence Bureau (SIB) – but also unofficially known as the Secret Service Bureau (SSB) – was born. Vernon Kell ultimately held responsibility for counter-espionage within the British Isles, while the flamboyant Captain Mansfield Cumming of the Royal Navy, was selected by the Admiralty and, ultimately, held responsibility for gathering intelligence overseas. The two men were polar opposites in character: a colleague later described Cumming as 'the cheeriest fellow I have ever met, full of the most amusing yarns' while Kell was 'quieter, more studied and tactful... perhaps more bureaucratically wily'. Another colleague reflected on how Kell would 'scheme quietly and with the use of exceptional charm, get his way'.[38] Kell, it was clear had a 'wonderful flair for organising, coupled with the gift of making people work together happily and smoothly'; his wife later described how he was 'diplomatic and tactful to an unusual degree'.[39] Kell and Cumming were both to report to George Macdonogh (later Lieutenant General Sir George Macdonogh), who was Head of Mo5, the section of the War Office's Intelligence Department that was created in 1907 for special duties, including protective security, ciphers and the censorship of post and telegraphs.[40]

Both Cumming and Kell had to build up their organisations from scratch; initially Kell had only a room, a desk and a filing cabinet at his disposal in his office – Melville's office located at 64, Victoria Street, SW. The office was rented from Messrs Hammond by Mr Drew a retired inspector of the Metropolitan Police, who sublet several rooms to the Bureau. Drew conducted a private detective agency; he was paid £500 per annum for the rooms and the use of his name as a screen; and undertook work for the Bureau when required on payment of his usual charges. He was, however, never entrusted with 'anything of importance', although he was employed on one occasion to trace a 'suspected German' to Charlottenburg. Cunningham and Kelly were the names by which Cummings and Kell were known in Drew's office. The office, though, was soon found to have great drawbacks. Its position opposite the Army and Navy Stores led on more than one occasion to awkward meetings with inquisitive friends; and Captain Cumming (usually known as C or MC) soon ceased to use it. He took a flat at Ashley Mansions, Vauxhall Bridge Road which he used as a residence, and the flat opposite to it on the same floor which formed his office. Kell (K or VK) continued to use the office in Victoria Street.[41]

With no clerk to assist him, he had the use of a typing pool, but decided that the sensitive nature of his work rendered this inappropriate. Cumming and Kell were eventually offered an annual sum of £150 to procure the services of a clerk to share between them, but Cumming declared that he had no use for one, while Kell asked for someone he knew to be appointed.[42] In March 1910, Mr Westmacott, formerly a soldier-clerk in the War Office, was engaged as clerk to Kell.[43] It was not until 1911 when Captain F.L. Stanley Clark joined as Kell's assistant on 1 January at a salary of £400 per annum with a three year guarantee of work, that Kell had permanent staff to assist him. Lieutenant E.J. Chisom, joined too, as an assistant on probation for twelve months, tasked with the collection of information in the ports along the East Coast.[44] In May 1911, B. J. Ohlson, RNR (codenamed 'O') was posted to K's branch as 'Marine Assistant'. In April 1911, K moved into an office at 3 Paper Buildings, Temple. His staff was increased by the addition of Mr Strong and two lady clerks as well as a detective named Regan (codenamed 'R'). In April, 1912 Captain R.J. Drake joined K. C left Ashley Mansions in 1911, and moved into 2, Whitehall Court, flat no. 54.[45]

But the key man was already in place – William Melville (codenamed 'M'). Here was a meeting of minds. The older Melville was the man with the experience; the younger Kell was the man with the drive and clout within the War Office to get things done. Together they were a perfect partnership. Upon his retirement from Secret Service work, in

1917, Melville recalled:

> In Colonel [as he had become in 1917] Kell I had a remarkable
> chief, who was always enthusiastic for work, and ever encourag-
> ing. He quickly saw the necessity of doing things in a logical way.
> We were frequently at variance as to how certain matters should
> be dealt with, but after a friendly discussion – to which he was
> always open and indeed invited, the difficulties invariably melted
> away and we were of entire accord.[46]

Kell's relationship with 'C' could not have been more different. From
the very start, Cumming was insecure and felt undermined by Kell,
who, at thirty-six was not only fourteen years younger than him,
but was also already firmly established in the War Office. When first
approached by Rear Admiral, the Honourable A.E. Bethell, Director of
Naval Intelligence (DNI), Cumming had the impression that he alone
would be running the Secret Service Bureau, having 'charge of all the
Agents employed by him and by the War Department' and that there
would be a 'junior colleague'. He was soon disappointed, however, 'to
find that I was not to be Chief' but was to share it with a "War Office
representative" with whom he would work on equal terms.'[47]

Cumming disliked sharing an office with Kell, complaining that the
location of the Victoria Street office meant he was constantly bumping
into people he knew. Cumming would have preferred to work from a
flat, where he could meet agents, with a servant to answer his calls.[48]
Nor did he feel that the War Office was 'disposed to give me their confidence or to make use of me in the same way as their colleague [Kell who
was] their representative'; he thought that he had 'been put on one side
in favour of my colleague' and feared that 'if this attitude is maintained
I shall have to take a very second place in the Department.' Although
he recognised Kell's attainments and linguistic talents, he saw him as 'a
much younger man than I and… very junior to me in the Service', and
did not think it appropriate that he 'be asked to work as his subordinate either nominally or in practice'. Cumming was upset that Melville
seemed to favour Kell and was insulted to find that when Kell was taking
leave Melville said that he would personally cover for him. Cumming
'could see plainly – only too plainly – that Col M [Melville] gives all his
confidence to K and does not really want me at all'[49] Kell, it seems, was
unfazed by Cumming and does not, at this stage, appear to have picked
up on Cumming's resentments; his wife (in whom he confided) mentioned nothing of any tensions between the two colleagues. C's feelings,
however, would continue to simmer away.

2

Filing Systems & First Blood
1909–1914

In the first four months, after taking his new job, Kell sat in his office, searching through files and making notes,[1] which, at first, he found was 'very uphill work, for it took much time and patience'.[2] Kell worked swiftly and thoroughly: between the 15 October 1909 and the 1 March 1910, he waded through the previous history of counter-espionage as shown in the War Office files and familiarised himself with the various aspects of the work. In his second General Report, set out between March and October 1910, Kell concluded that:

> [if] I were asked to give my opinion on the success or otherwise of the counter-espionage section of the Bureau, I should find it exceedingly difficult to do so. I have no hesitation on saying, from my year's experience of the work, that this section of the Bureau has justified its institution. Hitherto it had been found impossible to devote the necessary time and attention to this kind of work, and in many cases important clues had been lost by not being able to follow them up at the moment of their being reported. But when we come to discuss the <u>success</u> of this section, we are brought face to face with two great obstacles:
> 1. Lack of funds, and consequently an insufficient staff.
> 2. Inefficiency of the present legislature.

Counter-espionage work in peacetime should, Kell thought, be divided between 'Passive Operations' and 'Active Operations'. Passive operations involved the locating and noting of all useful details regarding known spies and other suspected aliens and traitors; and the compilation of handwritings, description-returns and photographs of all suspects for immediate transmission to the Post Office and Police. Also, information should be collected in home ports from captains of merchant ships, who could be counted upon to give reliable information about an enemy's fleet, or any unusual activity in foreign ports; and MO5 agents in the coastal counties should be trained to act behind the enemy's lines in case of invasion. Active operations should involve shadowing known spies or highly suspected persons, seeing whom they associated with and thereby 'getting on the track of traitors'. Kell also advocated the dissemination of false or useless information at places that foreigners frequented, such as ports.[3]

In order to remedy the situation he found, Kell set about establishing contact with the Chief Constables of England; his old friend from schooldays, Winston Churchill, was now Home Secretary and he authorised a letter of introduction:

> The bearer of this letter is Captain Kell, who is attached to the Intelligence Department of the War Office and is employed by General Ewart in making enquiries regarding the many alleged instances of foreign espionage and other suspicious incidents which are brought to the notice of that Department. Mr Churchill desires... to say that he will be obliged if you will give Captain Kell the necessary facilities for his work.[4]

Kell had also managed to obtain a letter of introduction to the Scottish Office and to the Chief Inspector of Constabulary for Scotland. Ireland was covered through contact with the Inspector-General of the Royal Irish Constabulary.

Kell 'moved cautiously: he was aiming at building up gradually the channels by which a network at the centre could be created.'[5] He contacted Captain Grant RN, the Head of the Coast Guard, and also Colonel Lexham in charge of the Naval Works at Rosyth. Visiting the north and west of England Chief Constables, Kell found that several had foreigners under suspicion. But, towards the end of July 1910, the Secretary to the Admiral commanding the Coast Guards informed Kell that the Admiralty had issued orders that they were not to communicate with Kell directly, as heretofore, but were to send any information through the usual channels. As it was a matter of the greatest importance that all information should reach Kell with as little delay as possible, he visited the Director of Naval Intelligence and convinced him that the order should be rescinded. This bureaucracy, it was later noted, was 'a typical case of how certain red-tape officials attempted to frustrate delicate work by imposing impossible rules.'[6]

Kell's primary aim, at this stage, was to establish an unofficial register of aliens resident in the United Kingdom. The register that emerged formed one of the special Series of Cards and its importance was of critical importance for no work 'requires more close attention to detail than the records of a Counter-Espionage Bureau'. It was necessary not only that every document received should be serially numbered, recorded and filed in such a manner as to be easily found, but also that all names, places and subjects mentioned in the documents should be minutely indexed in order to enable new information to be readily linked up with that already recorded. Kell regarded the following as essential 'even to the smallest office':

Register of Documents
A Register, by their serial numbers of all Documents received or sent out. This is most conveniently kept on a series of cards; one card being allotted as the counterfoil or history sheet of the disposal of each Document.

Name Card Index
A General Card Index of the names of all Persons mentioned in documents received or sent out. Each card should also show clearly sufficient particulars of the person dealt with to distinguish him from others of similar name and initials, as well as containing references to all papers in which he is referred to. These cards are maintained in strictly alphabetical order.

Place Card Index
A card index of the names of all Places, Ships and Aircraft, with references to the serial numbers of all the documents in the Bureau in which that place &c. is mentioned. It is impossible to lay down a more general rule than that every place, ship or aircraft should have at least one separate card. In some cases it may even be necessary to have a separate card for every street in a certain town, or even for a single building such as a large Hotel &c.

Subject Card Index.
A card index of all Subjects referred to in the Bureau records. This should resemble exactly the index of a well indexed book, the references on the cards being to the serial numbers of the Bureau documents in which that subject is mentioned.

Personal Files
A series of foolscap Files or Dossiers, each containing full copies of or extracts from all papers relating to a particular person or firm, whose credentials or circumstances come under investigation or correspondence. This series should be the principal repository of the Bureau documents, since the basis of all counter-espionage work is the individual Suspect.

Subject Files
A series of Files, each containing papers dealing with a particular Subject in a general sense. Such files should contain a cross index to all papers relating to the same subject but of which the originals are put away in personal files.

Officials Files

A series of Files, each containing general correspondence with other offices or individuals upon strictly service matters connected with the working of the Bureau, which cannot be put away in personal or subject files. These, like the subject files, should be cross-indexed when necessary, and should be labelled by the name of the Office or Official (not the personal) title of the correspondence.

Rules for Filing

The general rule for filing any documents should be to put it away in a personal file if possible. If this is not possible to put it in a subject file, reserving the official files for papers which cannot conveniently be put away in either of the other classes.

Other records, which Kell considered could be required as the work of the Bureau increased, were:

Classification Cards

Special cards for classifying such matters as registers of aliens under nationalities or localities, or 'Black Lists' of names classified according to the nature of the offences committed or suspected. To each of these cards is allotted a serial number according to the number of instances arising in each class and they are filed in serial and not in alphabetical order, reference being made by means of the general card index mentioned in 2 above. The reason for adopting this method is that the total number and the latest instance of each Class can thus be ascertained at a glance.

Photographs and Handwritings

Books containing photographs and specimens of handwritings. These should be kept on a 'loose leaf' system arranged by classes rather than by the alphabetical order of the names of those concerned, ready comparison of new examples with those already filed being the essential feature.

By using this system 'the records of any person, place, ship or subject could be traced from the card series'.

Kell believed that the organisation and scope of counter-espionage work had to vary according to local conditions, and even to different conditions prevailing in different areas of the same locality. Thus, while in one locality the work might be confined to the detection and presentation of the unauthorised acquisition and transmission of naval and military information, it might in another be more intimately connected with seditious movements amongst subject races. In time of war, it could involve the close observation of peace propaganda and industrial disputes for or implicated in such movements. A counter-espionage bureau should, by providing a link between the naval, military and civil authorities, enable a Government to decide what concerted measures were necessary to prevent the betrayal to an enemy, (whether actual or potential), of vital national interests. The extent of these measures, depending as it did on local conditions, was a matter for the decision of the local authorities. It followed also that, provided the Bureau maintained close touch with all the departments concerned in its work, local conditions would determine the particular department to which it was most closely affiliated. An essential point in the work of such a Bureau was that, while it might exchange information with organisations devoted to the acquisition, either by secret or open means, of naval and military information regarding the enemy, it had to be kept absolutely distinct from them. The duties of a counter-espionage bureau comprised:

1. Prevention: The prevention or at least the obstruction of espionage by precautionary legislation and such other means as can be openly enforced by the uniformed police and other Government officials for facilitating personal identification and for the control of the sections of potential suspects in the mass.
2. Detection: The detection of espionage by means of the detective police force, supplemented by and co-operating with a small number of agents specially trained for counter-espionage work, who are under the direct control of the Bureau; and the preparation of such evidence and exhibits as can appear in court to enable the law officers to secure the conviction and punishment of offenders without publicly disclosing the processes by which the crime has been detected.
3. Control: The examination of the credentials and the control of travellers passing through the seaports, across the frontiers, or circulating within the country; including the circulation of warnings and descriptions of suspects to the officials at the ports and frontiers.
4. Records: The compilation of records and interchange of information with British and allied Officials.
5. Organisation: The internal organisation and administration of the Bureau, including financial and secretarial duties, and the registration, indexing, filing and custody of documents.

Where a counter-espionage bureau included two or more officers, the above group of duties should be divided among them in the manner most suitable to local conditions. Generally speaking the duties numbered 1, 4 and 5 might conveniently be grouped together as the work of one officer, while those numbered 2 and 3 might form the work of the second. The methods adopted by the Bureau and the means whereby the activities of enemy agents were watched or frustrated could only be developed as the outcome of long experience and specialization and depended on local circumstances and individual astuteness, combined with close observation and the judicious and intelligent co-operation of all the official servants of the local authorities. Where compulsory Registration of Aliens (i.e. others than British subjects) were not enforced by legislation, and where the personnel at the disposal of the Government admitted to such action being taken, it was desirable that an unofficial register of all aliens should be 'made and maintained quietly'. Such a register should form one of the special Series of Cards.[7]

Every letter entering or emanating from the Bureau was entered in a schedule, where it was given a Bureau (or B) number. This was a general number. Any letter emanating from the office was always entered in red ink. When a case had been thoroughly gone into it was placed in a jacket, which in turn was placed in the 'Cases File', and was given a Cases File number (C number). Persons who were of 'distinctly suspicious habits' were noted in the Bureau Black List. This consisted of a file and an album. At the beginning of the former was a note explaining how fresh pages, files, etc., could be procured, and the name in which they were to be ordered. In the file were noted certain particulars regarding the various persons concerned. Each of these persons was given a Black List (BL) number, which was the one standing immediately before his name. Miscellaneous papers of no great interest were placed in a Miscellaneous File. The Black List album contained specimens of hand-writing, and these were numbered to correspond with the numbers in the List. A photograph file was a companion to the Black List, but was also used for individuals not on that list. All letters to or from the General Post Office were placed in the GPO File, and received a file number. The 'Outgoing' and 'Incoming Letters' Files were used for letters of special importance: outgoing letters of trivial importance were entered in precis in the schedule.

Personal Index Cards were in the left hand drawer in a safe. Subject Index Cards were in the right hand drawer in the safe. County Index Cards were in a red cupboard. The first card in this index was a key card. All cards were filled in accordance with this key card. The remarks were on the backs of the cards. The top card in each county sheaf showed the last serial number allotted in the county. These serial numbers were those given by Kell to individuals reported by the police. Their names were sent in to Kell by the Chief Constables of counties, and the numbers allotted to them were notified by him to the Chief Constable concerned. The County Files were placed on the shelf in the safe. They were pink in colour. Copies of all important information were made by Kell were placed in the Chief Constables File. These copies were then sent or handed to the Chief Constables concerned as convenient. Finally, there was a 'Watching File' and all cases that wanted periodical watching were entered in it.[8]

To arrive at this level of organisation, by the outbreak of war in 1914, was, probably, Kell's greatest achievement. In many cases Chief Constables had at least one personal interview with Kell, who explained his methods and the purpose of his work, and the ways in which the police could assist in it. At first Kell had to work hard to establish a working relationship with the Chief Constables; so the possibility of a general registration of aliens, even in the coastal districts, was tactfully not mentioned by Kell when he was present for the first time, on 2 June 1910, at a meeting of the Chief Constables' Club in London.[9] Kell recalled that his position was greatly strengthened by the fact that Sir Edward Troup, the senior civil servant in the Home Office, was present, for a short time, during the meeting. Troup said that 'although the meeting was entirely a private one – and had not been convened by the Home Office – he had the authority of the Home Secretary to say that the work was being carried out with the approval of Mr Churchill and that he appreciated the assistance which the Chief Constables had given to Captain Kell'. The hint was taken and Kell recorded: 'I think I may say that the meeting was a very satisfactory one. It helped to clear up a few difficulties and to prepare the way for further action.'[10]

Kell's 'softly, softly' approach now began to pay off; by October 1910, details of over 500 aliens had been registered. The inquiries on which the Aliens Returns were based had to be conducted quietly and confidentially, and while particulars were, ultimately, obtained about almost 30,000 persons, the Home Office received only two complaints on the subject.[11] At a further meeting, which was held on 29 April 1911, Kell and the Chief Constables approved a scheme whereby the police sent in quarterly reports on 'possible suspects' chosen by Kell out of the general lists of aliens received from each county. By the autumn of 1912, when the Quarterly Report Scheme had been working for about a year, valuable data had been collected about 391 Germans and Austrians, amongst whom the 'probably dangerous' were now distinguishable from the 'harmless'.[12] From this information, Kell compiled a list of persons who should be: 1. Arrested and detained; 2. Searched, both as to papers, premises and every person found thereon, and arrested if any thing of a suspicious nature is found; 3. Carefully watched. This list was to be kept up to date, ready for instant despatch to Chief Constables in the event of a national emergency. Kell and SIB believed they now had the names and addresses of seventeen German agents in Britain and five agents abroad, who were connected with or engaged in espionage work.[13] Kell was confident that he was in a position to strike at the heart of the German espionage network should war become a reality.

But setting up a counter-espionage organisation was not all that Kell had to contend with: because of a shortage of manpower he also had to had to investigate 'some interesting and curious matters'; of these the Frant and Rusper cases stand out.[14] In his report on 'The Rusper Case', Kell purposely omitted all personal names. In 1910, Kell, in the first of his regular six-monthly reports to his superiors, considered that the cases:

> in themselves, constitute strong supplementary and confirmatory evidence to the existence, in this country of an organised system of a German espionage. As in the majority of cases dealt with, there are a good many links missing in the chain of circumstances, but it does not require a very great stretch of imagination to insert connecting links of one's own forging, thus producing a pretty strong chain of evidence, all emanating from the same source viz: Germany, and ending in the same objective: 'the spying out of the land'.

He reported how, in January of 1910, a 'lady of high social standing' in Surrey and Sussex and living close to the boundary line of these two counties, 'actuated by patriotic motives', reported the following facts to a friend of hers, a General Officer on the active lists. She was in the local Post Office one day and found there two foreigners; Herr A. and Herr B. having a discussion with the village Post-master about a foreign money-order which they were wanting to cash. Being herself a good linguist, she offered to assist them out of any difficulty. In doing so, this lady noticed that the money order was made payable to a Polish-German name, and that the sender appeared also to be a Pole; and also that the place of despatch was a town in the south of France. Her interest and suspicions were aroused, and after making some enquiries in the neighbourhood, she discovered that these two foreigners were living a few miles from her home; they had no visible occupation. Her report was then sent on to the Bureau to investigate.

This led to the following facts being established: Herr A. had arrived about the middle of November 1909, and applied straight for rooms at a Mr X's in the village, professing to have travelled straight through from Monte Carlo, and to have been recommended to Mr X, by a certain Polish baroness, whom Mr X. declared he had never heard of. Two months later, in January, Herr B. arrived from Nice – professedly and also recommended by the same baroness. Herrs A. and B. 'pretended' not to have known each other before, but they became very quickly on intimate terms, and appeared to know all about each other's previous careers and private affairs. Herr A. became visibly disturbed on the arrival of a Mr.Y. – Melville sent down by the Bureau to investigate – and cross-questioned the landlord 'very severely' about the newcomer, especially anxious to know if the latter understood or spoke any foreign language; they were visibly relieved when Mr. Y. assured him of his ignorance of French and German. Herr A. received registered letters from Germany, and Herr B. was in continuous correspondence with the baroness. After the arrival of Melville, Herrs A. and B. quarrelled – 'evidently a put up job' – and refused to speak to each other during the remainder of Mr Y's. stay there. These foreigners 'were constantly motoring between the south coast and Rusper, and appeared to time the various distances very carefully. One day they succeeded in doing the run from Brighton to Rusper in 55 minutes, (a distance of just under 30 miles).'

Kell noted that it was hardly necessary to draw attention to the fact that a knowledge of the country lying on and between the North and South Downs, including as it did the important heights of Hindhead, Box Hill and the Towers of Holmbush, Rusper Church and Lyne House, would be of the greatest value to an invading force advancing from the direction of the coastline lying between Dover and Portsmouth as would an intimate acquaintance with the railway lines leading to the Guildford, Dorking and Tunbridge junctions from the Coast. Kell continued: 'If you carry your eyes eastwards, along practically the same line of natural defences, you come to FRANT, where another centre of German Intelligence would appear to have been established, as the following facts will demonstrate.'[15]

Bartley Mill, a mile and a half from Frant Station, on the Camden Estate, had been let, in July 1909, to a Mr H., who first arrived with his wife, friend and maid, all four of them being unmistakably German. Herr H. let it be understood in the neighbourhood that he was a man of independent means, but was in some way connected with a particular trade in London. However, he was always extremely vague when referring to his business. His visits to town were, from all accounts not very frequent, and he spent most of his time at Frant. The Mill stood in a hollow, at crossroads some distance from any other habitation, and it was interesting to note that it was easy to reach the house by any of the roads leading to it from the south, west or east, without being seen from any spot on the other roads. Therefore to keep observation on the house, it was practically necessary to stand at the gate. 'They never have any but German guests at the house,' noted Kell. Herr H. was 'the typical "Feldwebel" in mufti; this was especially apparent in the way he takes his seat on the driving-box, and gathers up the reins in the manner peculiar to artillery or cavalry-drilled Germans. Although he is breeding a few ducks, Herr H. cannot be deriving any income from the farm; the mill is idle, and he is ignorant of the mere rudiments of farming and poultry-breeding.'

Kell established that visitors at the Mill, 'who are always Germans, are regularly relieved by two's and three's'. The German, who arrived with Mr H. in the first instance, moved over to Yalding in August 1909, and in January 1910 he left very suddenly, without giving any notice. He spent most of his time driving about the country, received foreign friends, and seldom, if ever, went to town. 'The principal point to be borne in mind is that nobody knew where he came from, he never alluded to any business, and disappeared just as mysteriously and unexpectedly as he had come, evidently intending not to leave any traces behind him. He appears to have been well supplied with money, and was generous. He sold a horse and trap he had bought at Frant, to a local farmer.' Melville was duly sent down to investigate. He reported that:

There were two newcomers the day I was there. I met them on the road on motorcycles and tri-cars. These two fresh arrivals are entirely superior men to those I had seen so far connected with the Mill. I have had considerable experience of all classes of Germans, in their own country, and I believe I can confidently state that, judging from general appearances, I cannot be mistaken in putting these newcomers down as German officers.

It is also worth mentioning, that although the visitors change, the motorcycles used are always the same. Mr.H. let out, when I was talking to him, that he does not understand motorcycles, and that they belonged to his friends. Who are then, in reality, the mysterious proprietors of these cycles and tri-cars? I found out also that these two new-comers posted some letters at Frant Green, why post there, which is some distance off, when their nearest post-office is at Frant Station, which they probably passed on the way![16]

In the Frant case the name given by the German under suspicion was de Corina who, in MI5's internal history, was described as a 'typical German' and it was 'quite obvious' that he could not be making his living from the proceeds of the farm. Although nothing was ever discovered which could definitely connect this man with espionage the whole circumstances of the case were 'very peculiar and suspicious' and the extremely secluded position chosen for the scene of their operations as well as the difficulty of watching it 'lends colour to the belief that it was used as a centre for espionage.'[17]

Kell considered it interesting to note that, whether in connection or not with the cases of Frant and Rusper, there was a German cavalry officer staying at the vicarage at East Horsley, (which lay about 10 miles from Rusper and about 30 miles from Frant). This officer professed to be there for the purpose of studying the language, 'but one of our officers who happened to meet him out at a dinner a few weeks ago, reported that his English was perfect'. From these two cases, and others, Kell reached three conclusions. The first was that the Bureau 'has justified its institution.' The experience gained had proved that it was essential, to the effective working of the counter-espionage section of the Secret Service Bureau, that all information coming within its province should be sent to and exclusively dealt with by the Bureau. It had been found that a 'more hearty' co-operation with outside departments and individuals had ensued since it had become known that questions involving secrecy and tact were being dealt with thought by one and the same person. Secondly, for the effective working of the counter-espionage branch, it was essential to ensure the co-operation of the Chief Constables: 'Those who had already been approached by me in this matter were willing to help in every way.' Thirdly, there was, at present, 'no power to complete one's evidence by preliminary search on suspicion, although search warrants are freely granted in trivial cases of larceny: i.e. under the Army Act 1861 Sect.156. Subsect.5. a magistrate may grant a search-warrant upon reasonable cause for suspicion that anyone has in his possession the property of a comrade (e.g. a blanket!), and yet in cases involving the safety of the Empire, there is no such power which the Chief Constables could avail themselves of.' If a clause were added to the Official Secrets Act of 1889 empowering any magistrate to grant a search warrant on the application of a Chief Constable showing reasonable ground for suspicion, the proper working of the counter-espionage branch would be ensured. Moreover, there was no direct law dealing with cases of photographing, planning, or sketching of forts and unless damage to property had been committed, any action came merely under the common law of trespass, in which case the punishment was in most cases a small fine 'which for our purposes is useless as a deterrent.'[18]

Kell complained at the lack of police support, the level of which depended on whatever the Metropolitan and County police could spare at the time; the County police in particular had very few plain-clothes men at their disposal, and some of the Chief Constables themselves had acknowledged that however excellent their men's work might be as regards to crime, 'they have not all got the necessary degree of tact to carry out such delicate enquiries'. Kell was, therefore, forced to rely upon the services of Melville, 'who in view of his age and standing can hardly be expected to perform such work as the shadowing by night and day, a duty which in any case is quite impossible for one man alone'. Melville had on occasions been able to enlist the services of one of two ex-police officers of his acquaintance, but they were not always available when their services were required. Moreover, 'the system of employing odd men for our kind of work is obviously undesirable, besides being very costly. [It is very difficult to get private detectives to work for less than a guinea a day, plus all out of pocket expenses].' Kell requested the services of two detectives who should be ex-officers from the Metropolitan Police who had recently retired with a pension.[19] In November 1911, Kell got his second detective on the staff and engaged him in keeping suspected persons under observation. The employment of another clerk and one officer had also been approved.[20]

Just how ineffective the existing law could be was demonstrated in September 1910. On the fifth day of the month a telegram arrived at SIB from the General Officer Commanding (GOC) Portsmouth Defences to say that some of his officers had arrested a Lieutenant Helm of the 31st Pioneers (German Army) in the act of sketching Fort Widley. The next day Captain Bonham Carter came up with all the necessary evidence concerning Helm's alleged espionage. Then the unsatisfactory state of the law under the Official Secrets Act of 1889 was demonstrated. The Public Prosecutor gave it as his opinion that the necessary evidence was at hand to apply for the Attorney General to prosecute Helm. As, however, the Attorney General was away on the continent it was necessary to wire for his authority to carry out the arrest. In consequence it was necessary to detain Helm in military custody until 4 p.m. on 7 September by which time he was handed over to the Civil Power. The German officer was eventually tried and was bound over in his own recognizances of £250, to come up for trial if called upon to do so. In fact the fort he was sketching had been long out of no military use and could be of no possible interest to Germany, but the case highlighted the difficulty of taking proceedings against a suspected spy.

For Kell and SIB the inadequacy of the law was also demonstrated when two British officers, Captain Trench and Captain Stewart, were arrested, tried and condemned in Germany for attempts at spying in the neighbourhood of Borkum. Kell, during a visit to Plymouth, was informed by the Admiral there that a hairdresser in the town, employed at a firm with the German name of Schneider, had remarked to him about the capture of these two officers giving the names of their ships. The hairdresser also stated that Trench had told Schneider before he left that he was just off to Denmark to learn the language but that he intended going on to Borkum and the other islands to see what he could discover. Kell pointed out that there was nothing to prevent Schneider informing the German authorities of Trench's intentions and 'it is difficult to credit such an indiscretion, but it is useful in drawing attention to the necessity of absolute silence and secrecy in all such matters'.[21]

The odd spy, however, was caught and prosecuted under the Official Secrets Act 1889. Dr Philip Max Schulz was a German with a degree of Doctor of Philology from Berlin University. He settled at Plymouth in 1911 as a teacher of languages and early in May hired the house-boat *Egret* which was moored on the River Yealm. He appeared to have plenty of money, which was supplied in notes from abroad and was accompanied by a young German student, named Ahlers. Shulz would send wires to a Tobler Ostend, asking for money and a meeting. Dr Shulz also consulted Mr Duff, a solicitor in Plymouth, offering him employment as correspondent for a German newspaper 'like the *Times* with a salary up to £1,000 a year. He explained that his duty was to send the latest news about British naval and military matters and enquired whether Duff could procure such news from his naval friends. Pending a meeting with the head of the (supposed) newspaper syndicate, Duff signed an agreement to act for one month as naval and military correspondent for the south coast of England on behalf of the 'Depot de Correspondence pour le Continent' at a salary of £60 a month. This agreement, along with a letter from Schulz in a sealed envelope addressed to a G. Neumann, London, was given to Duff to post; but instead he took it to the Police, whom he had wisely contacted.

Schulz had also engaged a Mr Tarren for the same purpose. Tarren was employed by the National Cash Register and had access to the

Royal Dockyard. As with Duff, Schulz asked him to supply news for a Continental newspaper 'like the *Times*'. He unsuccessfully tried to convince Tarren to go to Portsmouth, and also enquired whether he could get into the Woolwich Arsenal. Tarren signed an agreement, which was also addressed to Neumann, from whom Tarren was to receive £50 a month. The General Staff Officer, South Western Coast Defences, drew SIB's attention to Schulz and forwarded a report received through the Admiral's office from the Chief Constable of Plymouth. SIB went to the Home Office and discovered through the police that Schulz received about £250 in monthly cheques from Germany.

Checks were placed on the correspondence of those concerned and SIB took up the direction of the case, guiding the action of the police and the two informers; Duff and Tarren were instructed to accept payment from Schulz; to make any journeys required; to keep a record of any work done for him; to note all the addresses to which he sent letters; and to submit all the questions asked by him to SIB, who would supply suitable answers. The evidence gathered against Schulz was laid before the Director of Public Prosecutions, who decided that it was necessary to establish the following points before he could be prosecuted: 1. That Schulz had asked Duff for some definite information on naval or military affairs, which it would be undesirable for a foreign power to be in possession of; 2. That Duff had become possessed of that information and had wilfully communicated it to Schulz; 3. That Schulz intended to communicate it to a foreign power. Schulz was sent pertinent questions by Tobler (his employer) to ask Duff and Tarren, and also received £110 in notes to pay for the answers – which were supplied by SIB. The questions asked referred to naval matters of a secret and highly confidential nature. Duff and Tarren went on board the *Egret* several times to hand in their answers to the questions, and received various sums in return. In the meantime the required evidence was being collected by SIB and, on 16 August, it was laid before the Attorney General and his fiat obtained for the arrest of Schulz on the grounds that he did unlawfully incite, counsel and attempt to procure one Samuel Hugh Duff, to commit an offence against sub-section 2 of Section 1 of the Official Secrets Act, 1889.

In order for Schulz to be arrested on the *Egret* there was a field that had to be crossed, in which a flock of sheep were grazing. Shultz who was, by now, aware that he was under suspicion, had engaged a solicitor. Just as Kell and the police were approaching the boat, they saw the solicitor approaching the *Egret* from the opposite direction. The sheep rushed away from Kell and the police and became 'thoroughly mixed up' with the solicitor. Shulz, on being arrested, merely 'smiled sadly at the baffled solicitor'.[22]

A search of the *Egret* produced documents, letters and the key of a cipher code. Schulz was brought up before the Mayor of Plymouth and remanded, and he and his solicitor wired to Tobler for help but no response was received. The case was tried on 3 November 1911 at Exeter. The witnesses, Duff and Tarren, were supported by a letter from Tobler and evidence of the receipt of registered packets from abroad. Schulz was found guilty and sentenced to twenty-one months imprisonment. At the same time as Schulz was arrested a writ of subpoena was taken out for Neumann the intermediary to whom the various letters had been addressed. His house produced no incriminating documents and he denied all knowledge of the letters, which he said had been forwarded by his wife.[23] Immediately after the arrest of Schulz, Chief Constables were warned to pay special heed to and report at once any change of address made by aliens in their districts, for it was thought the guilty would try and leave places where their activities might have been observed.

A day or so later (22 August 1911) the new Officials Secrets Act was passed which made a criminal offence of practically every form of spying; it also gave the authorities the right to search and detain on suspicion. Churchill, as Home Secretary, did all he could to push the Act through.[24] In May 1911 a report had been drawn up for Lord Haldane, at his request, to help him in getting the Official Secrets Bill through Parliament on some twenty-two cases of suspected espionage, which could not be properly followed up owing to the inefficiency of the old Act. Most of these cases occurred in Kent, Essex, and the East Anglian counties. As a result it was believed that the German General staff now had knowledge of these areas and had compiled a 2½ inch map and a gazetteer giving details as to the number and location of carts and draught animals, position and maximum capacity of bake-houses, and many other matters of importance to an invading army. The following example was typical of the twenty-two suspected cases:

Herr STEPHAN. Dover 1910. The following are extracts from letters written by the Garrison Adjutant, Dover in December 1910:–
I am writing by order of Colonel Bittlestone, Comdg, S.E.Coast Defences. I am the Garrison Adjutant, Dover.
  Today some officers of the R.Berks Regt. detained a German who was acting suspiciously, making notes round Fort Burgoyne and other obsolete works at Dover. I interviewed the man, talking German to him. He said he was called STEPHAN and was a schoolteacher. He said he was observing birds. He had in his

possession a number of notes regarding the songs of birds and also a book in German about how to recognise different birds by their songs. His observations concerned starlings, thrushes, sparrows and other common birds that exist in Germany – and which it is not necessary to come to England to observe.

The Detectives have found out that the man spends his time tramping about the country and the cliffs. He has no heavy luggage and is leaving for London – Cannon St. – tomorrow afternoon.

By direction of Colonel Bittlestone, who saw the man, he was let go, as he was not searched and we could not keep him in custody on any specific charge.

Description: – Height 5ft 10in, ruddy complexion, fair moustache, square and thickset, wears pince-nez – talks English well but pretends not – looks drilled and well set up – carries a green canvas knapsack on his shoulders – Age between 40 and 45.

I know enough German and ornithology to know that he was lying freely to me.

It now appears 'from information received' that in October last he was often seen in the neighbourhood of Fort LANGDON here, one of the modern works, armed with 9.2 and 6 inch guns. He then had maps in his pocket and was taking notes. It is a pity he was not run in then but, unfortunately, he was on a public footpath, running by the fence round the fort, and the person who observed him could not say anything definite against him.

On December 29th Mr STEPHAN told me what he was going to do on Dec 30th. Being suspicious, I had him shadowed by detectives, with the result that he, of course, did exactly opposite to what he said he would do.

It was ascertained yesterday that he was very flush of money and cashed a draft for a large amount on Dec. 30th.[25]

Even if this suspect was a German spy the 1889 law did not permit an immediate arrest and search. As it was, nothing could be done until after the fiat of the Attorney General had been obtained, which might mean a delay of days or weeks if he happened to be away from London at the time. At the end of such a delay, 'the suspect, if really a spy, would probably have disappeared altogether, or at any rate he could have sent off his notes and photographs and concealed all traces of his handiwork'. A new Act was therefore urgently needed and rapidly passed into law. The Official Secrets Bill was introduced in the House of Lords on 17 July 1911, and was sent down to the Commons, after the third reading, on 2 August. It was read in the House of Commons for the first time on 17 August, and for the second and third time on the following day. The Royal Assent was given on 22 August.[26] The 1911 Act was the basis of all subsequent counter-espionage legislation.[27] Clause 1 of the new Act stated that:

> any person shall be guilty of felony, and shall be liable to penal servitude (3 to 7 years), if, for any purpose prejudicial to the safety of the State, he (a) enters, approaches or is in the neighbourhood of any 'prohibited place'; or (b) makes any sketch, plan, model or note which is calculated to be or might be or is intended to be directly or indirectly useful to an enemy; or (c) obtains or communicates to any other person any sketch, plan, model, article or note, or other document or information which is calculated to be or might be or is intended to be directly or indirectly useful to an enemy.

It was not now necessary to show that the accused had been guilty of any particular act. The *onus probandi* was thus thrown on the accused person to prove his innocence and not on the prosecution to prove guilt.[28] In September, a memorandum on the new Official Secrets Act was drawn up and sent out by the Army Council to General Officers Commanding-in-Chief throughout Britain. It was also circulated, with copies of the Act itself, to Chief Constables throughout the Kingdom.[29]

Kell noted, with satisfaction, that with the new Official Secrets Act now law 'the work of counter-espionage is thereby greatly facilitated'.[30] He was soon proved right. Heinrich Grosse was one of the first Germans to fall foul of the Act. Grosse had established himself at Portsmouth during the Anglo-German crisis over Morocco in 1911 and passed under the name of Captain Grant. SIB noted how he endeavoured to get into touch with men of the navy and ex-naval men, with the intention of acquiring information under the following headings: '1. Our Naval Coal Reserve; 2. Details of construction and armament of our battle fleet; 3. Preparations made or contemplated for the arming of our mercantile marine in time of war.'

As a result of a report from an ex-naval petty officer with whom he had contacted, an observation was kept upon Grosse's movements; he was arrested on 4 December 1911, and a long cipher letter found on him. By means of 'an ingenious catch phrase', which formed the key to the code, he was able to carry the key in his head. Nevertheless, he was brought to trial at Winchester and convicted of espionage and sentenced to three years penal servitude.

Armgaard Karl Graves also fell foul of the new law. Graves was a German claiming to be a doctor and passing as an Australian under the name of Stafford; thus he had drawn attention to himself in the early part of January 1910. He made Glasgow and Edinburgh his head-quarters for the purpose of examining the progress of the naval works at Rosyth in Scotland. He paid particular attention to Cromarty and the private yards of Beardmore & Scott on the Clyde, in which some of the Royal Navy's latest Dreadnoughts were being built. In view of the importance of Cromarty as a naval base in any war with a Great Power bordering on the North Sea – for example Germany – and of the fact that Messrs Beardmore & Scott had been conducting experiments in connection with a new large calibre gun, SIB noted it was significant that, on Graves, when he was arrested on 14 April 1912, were found a note referring to new guns being made by Beardmore, and an extensive code of considerable ingenuity. This code contained groups of figures by which reference could be made 'to all our naval ports and harbours, as well as to all phases of naval activity.'

Graves was convicted of espionage at Edinburgh on 23 July, 1912 and sentenced to eighteen months imprisonment.[31] It was while Kell was investigating this case that the excitement of chasing spies paled in significance – albeit temporarily – when set against a tragedy of international proportions: the *Titanic* went down, in April 1912, with a large loss of life. The Kells were shocked and upset: Constance's father was the agent for the White Star Line to which the *Titanic* belonged, and had 'only a day or two before' shaken hands with the captain. Many family friends were aboard when the ship went down, and even years later, Constance still felt 'the horror'.[32]

By now considerable progress had been made in compiling the register of aliens. By May 1911 all the Chief Constables of England and Wales had been approached and communicated with. Returns of aliens had been made for a total of eighteen counties – with the result that details concerning 4,500 aliens had been registered. The work of the Bureau had been especially studied with reference to the Home Defence Scheme, and a general map of England had been prepared showing all places which required special guarding, such as docks, wireless stations, cable-landing places, magazines, both inland and on the coast. It also showed the number of Germans resident in the vicinity of these places, excluding the Metropolis, boroughs and cities.

Alongside this, the principal foreign institutions in London were being enquired into 'as far as possible as to locality, members and staff'.[33] An influx of German miners into Kent, at the beginning of 1911, had also been investigated and a considerable number of their names had been registered; the registration of Germans and Austrians living close to vulnerable points on the London & South Western, Great Eastern and South Eastern Railways was under consideration; a telegraphic address had been registered for the Bureau; and a three weeks walking tour was undertaken by SIB's Captain Clarke – along the coast of Essex and Suffolk.[34] By June instructions had been issued by the Admiralty with a view to registering the names and details concerning all aliens employed in all Government Establishments under the Controller of the navy. SIB's agent at the ports – 'O' – was now doing regular work at ports and through him the Bureau already had the names of six merchant skippers of ships playing between London and the Continent, 'who are discreet and willing to keep their eyes open and report any useful information that comes to their notice. Other names will be collected as time goes on. 'O' has also been able to bring in a certain amount of information which is being passed on to 'O' as soon as it is received.' The case of a suspicious schooner *Helena* had shown Kell 'that we can rely on the co-operation of the Chief Constables of Counties with regard to watching suspicious vessels – as well as suspicious persons'. There was now a new detective on the staff, who was engaged in keeping suspected persons under observation. The Bureau was to be informed in the event of secret manoeuvres, or mobilization of defences taking place, and given all necessary data, 'so that we may, in future, arrange to have men on the watch for suspicious persons'; and a map showing the position of all vulnerable points in England and Wales, and the number of Germans and Austrians resident in their vicinity (by counties) had also been completed.[35]

The Bureau were aware of a number of agents operating in the country but, owing to the fact that a trial in open court would, in most cases, result in disclosures which would force the German Secret Service to adopt methods even more difficult of detection, action had not been taken against these individuals. Action could, however, be taken at any moment – e.g. when their activities threaten to result in serious danger to the State or at a time of grave emergency. The agents that fell into this category were as follows:

London.
1. E.G. Believed to be merely a collecting & forwarding agent for information collected by agents – also distributes pay.
2. K.O. Same as 1, except as regards pay. Came under notice prominently in connection with Case 28 (q.v. supra.), and since fled the country.
3. O.A. Same as 1 above, and also distributes pay.

4. <u>K.A.</u> Same as 1 above, and also distributes pay.

5. <u>B.R.</u> Has offered his services to this country, no doubt with a view to playing a double game.

Naval Port No. 1.

1. <u>G.F.</u> Passes as an Australian and speaks English fluently, but is undoubtedly a German. Good grounds exist for believing that he has serving British naval men in his pay. Established by the German Secret Service as licensee of a public house much frequented by soldiers and sailors. Has a son in the Royal Engineers – doubtless for the purpose of espionage – Steps have been taken to render the latter's efforts innocuous and he will be got rid of as soon as he gives an opportunity.

2. <u>H.P.</u> A photographer established in the port for many years. His whole family appear to be engaged in espionage.

3. <u>R.H.</u> Married daughter of the above. Known to have direct dealings with a high officer of the German Secret Service.

Naval Port No. 2

1. <u>W.H.</u> An artist. Appears to disappoint his employers to some extent, but since a local colleague was tried and sentenced, no doubt he finds it necessary to be very circumspect.

Naval Port No. 3

1. <u>S.J.</u> Coal contractor, chiefly engaged in observing the arrival and departure of our warships, the maintenance of naval stores at the port and other kindred matters.

Coast Defences No. 1.

1. <u>H.G.</u> A teacher of languages, who furthers his work under the pretence of fostering Anglo-German friendship. Much interested in the local submarine and destroyer base, has reported fully on important dockworks recently completed and sends comprehensive and detailed reports on items of local naval and military intelligence, such as mine-laying experiments, manning of the defences, coaling facilities, local storage of coal, supplies, personnel, etc., etc.,

In addition to those listed, there were also distributed about the country some seventy-five or more German residents whose actions had brought them under suspicion, and whose proximity to important works, dockyards, signal stations, and other centres of naval or military interest 'justifies the presumption that they are so situated for ulterior motives'.[36]

As Kell pieced together a picture of the enemy, he also identified his adversary in the Great Game: Georg Steinhauer had become, at some date unknown, head of the German Secret Service section directed against the United Kingdom.[37] SIB did not know much about him. He was said to have spent some years in America and to speak English fluently. He had started his working life as a sailor and had been one of the crew on the Kaiser's yacht, *Hohenzollern*. Then he entered the police and passed into the Secret Service, becoming at some date unknown the head of the section directed against Britain. Steinhauer used to come to Britain in the Kaiser's suite and was nominally in charge of the protection of the Emperor's person. In 1903, Melville had met Steinhauer and had been struck by his intimate knowledge of the doings of Captain Stewart Stephens, formerly a French agent and afterwards employed in the British Secret Service.[38] Melville recalled how the 'notorious German', had come to Britain several times with other police officers, supposedly for the protection of the Kaiser when visiting England:

> The Kaiser himself asked me one day at Windsor whether I knew STEINHAUER, and on my answering in the affirmative, he told me with gusto, and a wealth of detail how a Captain in the German Army had sold secrets to the French and absconded to Brussels. STEINHAUER was sent to the latter place, where he remained for six months, succeeded in becoming fast friends with the Captain, and finally by a trick succeeded in luring him to Herbestal, the frontier town, where he was arrested and was ultimately sentenced to 20 years' penal servitude. 'Yes,' said the Kaiser, 'STEINHAUER is a splendid fellow.' The latter, having been many years in America, spoke English fluently. He was in correspondence with many German spies in this country; he also travelled England as a Commercial man and visited his agents. On one occasion he had an exceedingly narrow escape of arrest in London. He did not venture to come here again.[39]

Intercepted specimens of the work of German Secret Service agents at work in Britain revealed where German interests lay:

> 1. Portland: Records of movements of 3rd Division Home Fleet and Atlantic Fleet and of probable arrival of 2nd Division Home Fleet. Reports of amount of naval coal in store.
> 2. North Sea: A full report of manoeuvres of torpedo flotilla in North Sea and steam trials, with sketch of system of attack adopted by our torpedo boats, details as to coal consumption, coal capacity, armament, ammunition storage, and speed.

3. Scotland: Detailed report of military preparations in SCOTLAND (chiefly Territorial Force). Details of works undertaken, or in contemplation at CROMARTY Dingwall, number of workmen employed – details of railway construction, armament.

4. Firth of Forth: Report of fleet movements and concentration, victualling arrangements. coal contracts; Promises reports on latest type of submarine.

5. Humber: Report on: (a) manning and exercise of HUMBER COAST DEFENCES; (b) alteration of the navigable channel, owing to construction of new Immingham Docks; (c) Proposed new Admiralty Pier and installation of oil tanks for fleet use; (d) Shortage of coal, owing to deficiency of rolling stock and serious consequences on naval mobilisation thereby entailed.

6. Humber: Further report on 5(a) with details regarding mines and mine-laying cruisers in the same locality.

7. Humber: Full report on the Immingham Dock and proposed new Admiralty Pier at KILLINGHOLME, giving structural details, soundings, extracts of opinions and objections of HUMBER Conservancy Board on the proposed pier, delimitation of area controlled by Admiralty Piermaster. Report on East Yorkshire Territorials.

8. Humber: Report on mine sweeping arrangements and vessels used for that purpose.

9. Chatham & Medway: Reports on preparation for naval manoeuvres – shortage of naval personnel, number of men on Naval Establishment in the port. Report on naval aeroplanes and hydroplanes.

10. Chatham: General narrative of Naval Manoeuvres, 1912. Report on arrangements for distribution of orders by Admiralty. Specimens of information, etc., which German Secret Service Agents have been instructed to obtain.

BOOKS &c.

1. Torpedo Manuals.

2. Annual Report of progress Torpedo School.

3. Books on Wireless Telegraphy.

4. Submarine Manuals.

5. Mining and mine laying manuals.

6. Signal Book.

INFORMATION.

Naval.

1. Exact names and titles of confidential books on Wireless

Telegraphy, Torpedoes & Submarines.

2. Details of armour of newest ships.

3. Details of bulkhead construction.

4. Height of double bottom.

5. Displacement.

6. Details of torpedo tubes, number, position, etc.

7. Mine Defences, position, number of mines, where stored in peace.

8. Boom defences, construction, position and where stored in peace.

9. As to probability of formation of a new submarine station and preparations in connection therewith – possibility of its being also a destroyer base – date of its being completed.

10. Movements of warships, especially submarines.

11. Details of Naval Manoeuvres.

Military.

1. Details of new 4.n° Field Howitzer, especially ammunition supply; and extent of issue of this gun to the troops.

2. Progress with regard to introduction of an Automatic Rifle.

3. Training and efficiency of Territorial Force Field Artillery.

4. Details of Army Mobilisation – the likelihood of its being carried out by divisions, simultaneously or otherwise.

Political & General.

1. Popular feeling towards Germany, especially in the Fleet. Opinions of high Officers especially to be gathered.

2. Opinion of Officers and men of British Fleet as to chances of success in a war with Germany. Are they sure of success or not?

3. Does anyone think of converting Naval Manoeuvres* into actual war with Germany ?

4. Does the idea mentioned in (3) originate from responsible quarters and is it at all generally discussed?

Report quickly.[40]

Post Boxes or Intermediaries played a crucial part in the general system of the German espionage system as it was through these individuals that Steinhauer carried on his activities. The Intermediary acted as a protection to both the German agent in the United Kingdom and the German Central authority abroad. If the spymaster's name and address were unknown to the agent he could not be indiscreet about it; if on the other hand the agent received letters from and wrote letters to merely British addresses he would not be suspected. The complete system involved the use of two Intermediaries: one for incoming letters and pay, the other for out-going reports. After the early days of its initial inception this system was not rigidly kept up. For out-going reports, foreign addresses e.g. in Denmark and Belgium were much used. Besides posting letters and registering and forwarding the pay of agents, Intermediaries had to keep the Germans supplied with British stationery and stamps; to forward press cuttings of interesting events; and to undertake enquiries. Intercepted letters showed that eventually the German Government scrutinised the out-of-pocket expenses of their agents in Britain and of Steinhauer himself most carefully and sometimes insisted on their being reduced. An intermediary's ordinary pay was £1 a month but they could make something extra on these side issues, as the letter below demonstrates:[41]

Dover

January den 20te

1912

Dear Sir

Re your enquiry about the tunnels, there would be very little trouble in stopping all communication through these.

The Folkestone-Dover can be blocked by blowing up the cliffs and effectively stopped.

The Chatham-Dover tunnel as you call it would have to be blown up, there is no difficulty about this, as the access is very easy from Chatham end.

I cannot answer the question about the depth of the water under the Fourth Bridge will obtain the charts.

I saw Hauptman vl.s/d. he told me he has obtained the knowledge you wished for about Harwich.

I have sent you phograf [sic] of the plans of superbD [sic] at the price you offered me.

I am going to… to find out about the Naval guns I expect this will not be very easy.

The white lines are only the signs of the different aquadrons, if you wish to know what 1 line 2 lines. etc mean I will give it to you for m100.

I have now complete drawings of Rosyth d. h. as far as it is possible to have them for these I want m2000 extra those of D. were not easy

I want some money now for expenses.

Aufwiedersehen

Primo (in Little Lotlod. W.C.) [42]

The check on Steinhauer's correspondence brought the name of Walter Reimann, of Hull, to SIB's notice as a German agent engaged particularly in obtaining information about the Humber Defences. In January 1912, Mr Cox, the private secretary to the editor of *The Standard*, informed the police – and afterwards had an interview with Kell – regarding certain questions that Fred M. Manasse, a German Jew and journalist, had asked about the Scott Fire Director, which the German Naval Authorities were taking a great interest in. He was kept under special observation for some time. At the end of January, letters were intercepted showing that 'undoubtedly' one Wagener was a German agent and during the year investigation and enquiry into this case, and also the case of Klare at Portsmouth took place.

In February, a Second Class Stoker in the navy, by the name of Ireland, who had previously come under suspicion, once again attracted SIB's attention. It was known that his uncle, Kruger, was a German agent residing in the UK and it was discovered that Ireland was endeavouring to acquire information about certain 'secret experiments' that were being conducted with the object of communicating it to a member of the German Secret Service. He was arrested on 21 February and summarily dismissed from the navy as it was decided that it would be inadvisable to place him on trial owing to the nature of the correspondence, which would have to be produced in court. Kruger, his uncle, who had played an important part in this affair, at first fled the country, but later returned; he was kept under close observation and his correspondence was intercepted and examined.[43]

On 28 June 1913, W. Klare of Portsmouth, was sentenced three to five years penal servitude for attempting to obtain a secret naval work. Karl Hentschel, was remanded on 24 October 1913, on his own confession, for inciting the commission of offences against the Official Secrets Act by ex-Gunner George Charles Parrott, now undergoing four years penal servitude. The activities of foreign agents had been directed particularly to naval affairs and towards ascertaining the strength, efficiency, and powers of mobilisation of the Territorial Force. In the former connection 'wholesale attempts have been made to seduce naval officers & men from their duty by means of letters purporting to come from a foreign publishing firm, addressed to them by name. The writer asks for information on naval matters and promises high rates of pay for such information. It is significant that in nearly every case the persons so approached have been technical experts in Gunnery or torpedo work.' The letters were at first sent 'as usual through the ordinary channels, intercepted by us, and so prevented from reaching the addressees.' Later, however, they were sent direct to the addressees from abroad. Consequently it became necessary for an Admiralty order to be issued to the effect that officers and men were to make no reply to the writer, and the letters were to be handed to the Officer Commanding. 'As a result some 130 original letters are now in our possession.' Particular attention had been paid by German agents to the Cromarty and Humber defences as well as to contractor's ship building yards. Kell noted: 'I have still to report that no agents other than those of German nationality have come within our cognizance.'

Some investigation had been made into the various German clubs and societies in London. Though these were doubtless in most cases genuine institutions founded for purely social reasons, 'the fact that several of their officials have come under our suspicions points to the possibility of danger from these sources in time of war'. Similarly the fact that letters were addressed to a German agent at a German Seamen's' Home in Hull directed attention to these institutions which had been established in various ports. It had been ascertained that in 1912 some 4,000 German seamen lodged in these Homes, while the total number frequenting them during the same period was about 40,000.

A revised scheme for the control of Wireless Telegraphy had been entered into in conjunction with the G.P.O. and the Constabulary forces of the United Kingdom. By this scheme the responsibility for establishing the bonâ-fides of foreign applicants rested on the Bureau, while Chief Constables were responsible for seeing that no installations were erected without a licence – the G.P.O. to grant or withhold the licence. Two police sergeants had been detailed for special duty in connection with the safeguarding the Admiralty Coalfields in South Wales. While they were, for disciplinary purposes, under the Chief Constable of Cardiff and formed part of his force, they were paid by the Admiralty, and were at all times available for work under the Bureau in connection with counter-espionage in that district.[44]

On 3 March 1914 at a meeting of the Committee of Imperial Defence, at 2 Whitehall Gardens, a presentation of the work and records of the Bureau was given by Kell, which was also attended by Captain Holt-Wilson, K's number 2. Kell's audience included the Prime Minister, Churchill (First Lord of the Admiralty), Colonel Seely the Secretary of State for War and the Lord Privy Seal. Captain Hankey the Secretary to the C.I.D. was also present. Kell presented exhibits, and a list of persons arrested as Foreign Agents, and of prosecutions undertaken.[45] For Kell it was a crowning moment.

3

Shot at Dawn
How a Little Lemon Juice Could be Bad for a Spy's Health – MO5 at War 1914–1915

Sir

I feel it my duty as a German officer to express my sincere thanks and appreciation towards the staff of officers and men who were in charge of my person during my enforcement.

Their kind and considered treatment has called my highest esteem and admiration as regards good fellowship even towards the enemy and if I may be permitted, I would thank you for make [sic] this known to them.

I am, Sir, with profound respect

Carl Hans Lody

Senior Lieutenant Imperial German Naval Res[erve].

[Carl Lody: shot at dawn for spying in November 1914, the first person to be executed at the Tower of London for 150 years.] The pre-war policy of the SIB was framed with the principal object of paralysing the German spy-system, in case of war, 'by one powerful blow'. In implementing this policy, 'the Detective Branch acted on the maxim that a bird in the hand is worth two in the bush', and refrained from arresting known enemy agents whenever this course could be followed without immediate danger to the safety of the country. Instead, spies' correspondence was intercepted, and sent on as a rule, with or without emendations, to their post-boxes on the Continent. In this way, the SIB became aware of the whole existing military secret service organisation constructed by Germany in the United Kingdom, and was able, it claimed within twenty-four hours of the declaration of war, to arrest practically every member of the organisation. The success of the policy was, it was believed, proved by the fact (disclosed in a German Army Order) that on 21 August 1914, the German military commanders were still ignorant of the despatch and movements of the British Expeditionary Force, although these had been known for many days to a large number of people in the UK.[1]

The identification of each individual had been left to the Police. The real difficulty of identifying a suspect did not ordinarily arise until a state of war had caused the 'construction of controls' to avoid which the intending spy found it convenient to pretend to be someone else.

As with the known enemy agents, no steps were taken in peace time (apart from censoring their correspondence) to control the persons classified as dangerous or doubtful. It was thought better to leave them alone as far as possible – except for the quarterly reports confidentially collected by the police – until the precautionary period was declared on 3 August 1914. Arrangements were made, however, to ensure that action, when taken, should be sudden, and completely effective. In May 1913, all County Chief Constables were informed that, in case a national emergency should arise, they would receive a warning letter containing the names of all persons within their jurisdiction who had been classified either: (a) for immediate arrest; (b) for search, both as to premises and every person found thereon, and arrest if anything suspicious were found or (c) for careful watch.

At the end of 1913, similar information was sent to the Chief Constables of all Cities and Boroughs in which there were persons on the 'possible suspect' list; but it was not thought worth while to arouse the attention of Borough Chief Constables unless it was known that special action would be required of them in the event of war. The warning letter – which was actually despatched to the appropriate Chief Constables, on 29, 30 and 31 July 1914 – was submitted in draft to the Public Prosecutor (Sir Charles Mathews) and to Sir Edward Troup at the Home Office, both of whom approved it. The letter gave lists of persons for: (a) arrest; (b) search and (c) careful watch. It was intended merely to ensure that the police were in possession of the necessary information to enable them to act on the shortest notice. The actual arrest or search was to be carried out with all possible speed on the receipt of a telegram, the wording of which was given in the warning letter to prevent mistakes. The letter went on to specify the legal authority on which the action could be taken.[2] Chief Constables were requested, in the same letter, to take action against anyone not on the lists if there was sufficient evidence against them.

The telegrams were sent out on the afternoon of 4 August, after the British ultimatum but before the declaration of war, which followed at once on the expiry of the ultimatum at 11 p.m. the same night. Twenty-one persons were arrested in pursuance of these instructions. It was claimed that one man on list (a) got away, as he happened to leave the country a few days before the warning went out. Another fifty-six persons on list (b) were searched, but without the production of further incriminating evidence. Many of them were detained later on and transferred to military custody as enemy aliens likely to be dangerous to the safety of the realm, or as enemy reservists still liable for naval or military service. There were 155 other persons named on list (c) who were put under 'special observation' on the outbreak of war. These were not necessarily suspected of espionage, but were chiefly ex-officers and men of enemy nationality whose movements required, and received, close supervision during the early days of war. Many were afterwards interned as enemy reservists.[3]

This episode subsequently went down in MI5 history as a masterstroke against the German espionage network in Britain, and Kell lived off the tale for the remainder of his career; except that he was not telling the truth. There was no German espionage 'network' to speak of. Kell had warned, in July 1914, of sabotage by hundreds of resident German agents, to coincide with a possible German invasion. Because the threat did not exist, in the words of one historian, 'The great spy round-up of August 1914 never took place.' On the outbreak of war, Kell's Special Watch Arrest List did include twenty-two suspects – but this was not the one (of several) that was later released to the public as proof of the SIB's effectiveness. The real SWL Arrest List showed that Kell thought that only fifteen of those on it were living in Britain. In four cases the addresses he gave the police were wrong, and as a result the code telegram of 4 August 1914 produced only eight arrests under the Official Secrets Act. The police eventually detained eleven of those on the SWL Arrest List, with only one, who had British citizenship, facing a public trial. The Official Secrets Act charges against the other ten were quietly dropped but they were rearrested under the Aliens Restriction Act and 'detained pending deportation' – which was illegal. Many of the twenty-one arrested from the later list were done so by police without any direction from Kell. The myth of the 'one powerful blow' seems to have become a – perhaps – necessary 'lie' on the part of Kell to save his organisation from savage post-war expenditure cuts.[4] But a lie it was.

The Lody Case

The Special Intelligence Bureau was instituted as a military measure to defend the Services and the country against attempts being made by the German Secret Service to obtain intelligence. Prior to August 1914 there was no Directorate of Military Intelligence, the functions of intelligence being included under the Directorate of Military Operations which was divided into six sections. Of these Mo5 was responsible for policy in connection with a variety of matters including censorship, aliens and the civilian population in war, and legislation affecting the General Staff. On the outbreak of war in August 1914 there was a rapid expansion in the Directorate of Military Operations the most important being in Mo5 on account of the wide variety of its duties which included responsibility for all Secret Service work. On 17 August

1914, Mo5 was divided into eight sub-sections of which Mo5g came under (now) Major Kell who was responsible for counter-espionage, aliens and control of civilian traffic overseas.[5] The success MO5g had in disrupting the German espionage system directed against the United Kingdom illustrated how these methods worked in practice.

On 6 November 1914, Carl Hans Lody, the first spy to be tried by Court-Martial since the outbreak of war, was shot at the Tower of London. Lody was a Lieutenant in the 2nd German Naval Reserve known as the Seewehr and a travelling agent employed by the Hamburg-Amerika Line. He used the cover of a genuine American Emergency Passport belonging to Charles A. Inglis who had deposited it for a visa at the Berlin Foreign Office, where it disappeared. Lody came to Britain via Denmark and Bergen, procuring there a certificate of American nationality. Arriving at Newcastle on 27 August, he went straight to Edinburgh where he stayed a month with the odd absence at night. One of these trips was to London, another to Peebles. From Edinburgh he went to Liverpool and then crossed to Ireland. He was arrested in Killarney. In the course of his travels he managed to dispose of a small handbag which was never traced. Lody carried about £200 in bank notes, English gold and German gold. Some of the notes were traced to a South American named Kinkelin who left England on 1 August. Besides sending reports to his German masters, Lody collected quantities of newspapers representing different opinions and classes of the community. Twenty-two different journals were represented in his collection. Generally speaking he seems to have protected himself by cultivating chance acquaintances and making trips in their company. Lody communicated with a spy centre in Stockholm in a telegraphic code and sent under cover to the same address letters in German containing spy reports en clair and directed to Stammer, Courbierestrasse, Berlin and also to other addresses. He used the signatures: Charles, Lody and Nazi. His mission seems to have been a general one but he was to stay in Britain until after the first major battle when he was to report British naval losses and then proceed to America.

The counter-espionage system put in place with the recommendation of the SIB proved its worth in the Lody case. Since 4 August all mails from the United Kingdom to Norway and Sweden had been brought to London and examined there for letters to certain suspect addresses. Lody wired to the spy address at Stockholm on 30 August and having to endorse the telegram with his name wrote 'Charles Inglis'. His first letter, posted on 4 September was intercepted, read, photographed and forwarded; others that followed were similarly treated in the hope of learning more. Eventually a letter came through addressed to Charles A. Inglis c/o Thomas Cook, Edinburgh, dated 8 September. 'Charles Inglis' never called to collect it. At what precise moment the traveller Inglis was connected with the writer of the letters was not clear, but two long reports signed 'Nazi' of 27 and 30 September respectively were retained and orders issued for Lody's arrest, which took place on 2 October. Various addresses and a telegram were found on him. At the trial it was learned that seemingly innocuous words as 'shall' and 'leave' had coded meanings. As a result of the trial special enquiries were made at King's Lynn as to the steps taken to guard against the arrival of undesirable aliens. Some uncorroborated evidence was adduced to the effect that Lody had been there in June and in the early part of July and had received telegrams under the name of Inglis and of Sideface. Through enquiries made by MO6 the name of the agent in Stockholm with whom Lody was in communication – Leipziger – was established.[6]

The Lody case was the first time in centuries that someone had stood trial for treason in Britain, and presented a number of unique problems for the authorities as, initially, the true identity of Lody remained hidden in the guise of Charles A Inglis. Kell, as MO5g's Director General, had handed over the details of the case on the afternoon of 7 October to Major Byrne, of the War Office. He consulted the Treasury Solicitor regarding the evidence who concluded the evidence was sufficient to warrant proceedings taking place.[7] Charles A Inglis had then been arrested on suspicion of spying. The question was what to do with him. There was some suspicion that Inglis might not be who he said he was and might, in fact, be a German. If he was then the case would be relatively clear-cut – as Haldane, the Lord Chancellor, pointed out: if an alien belligerent was caught in Britain spying or otherwise waging war 'he may in my opinion be court-martialled and executed'. The key principle was one of nationality: 'When war breaks out an alien becomes *prima facie* an outlaw... and if he is a spy or takes up arms... he becomes a person without legal rights. By international law he must have a trial before punishment but this trial may be by court-martial. He cannot invoke the jurisdiction of the Civil Courts.'[8] The Cabinet decided that, although Inglis was not subject to military law, he should be tried by General Court Martial. The offence was considered to be of such a serious nature – a War Crime – that the proceedings should be based on the Defence of the Realm Regulations.[9]

Sir John Simon, the Attorney-General saw a problem: 'There is a good deal of doubt whether Inglis is not an American citizen: and there is no evidence that he is not a German. This would be no difficulty, of course, if he were tried in the ordinary way before judge and jury; for anyone of any nationality who avails himself of the protection and hospitality of this country can be guilty of high treason.' But neither the Manual of Military Law nor the Cabinet's decision covered Inglis's case if he was tried by court martial and the prosecution failed to prove he was an 'enemy civilian'. Inglis was 'alive to this point'; he held a passport granted to him as an American citizen and he had seen the American Vice-Consul. If the Manual of Military Law was to be followed it would appear necessary to charge Inglis with being an enemy civilian: 'The evidence could not support this.' If, however, Inglis was tried for treason, in a criminal court, the American authorities could not complain if one of their subjects was dealt with by judge and jury. This would mean, if found guilty, that Inglis would hang rather than be shot.[10] Haldane agreed that Inglis should be tried by a Civil Court for high treason even though the 'avoidance of a case with the United States is of course of great importance'.[11] Under Article 17 of The Hague Convention a neutral could not claim the benefit of neutrality if he: (a) committed hostile acts against a belligerent; or (b) if he committed acts in favour of a belligerent.[12] Consequently, the Cabinet decided to try Inglis for treason in the Civil Courts.[13] Inglis was duly transferred from military custody to the care of the police.[14]

Lody then sprung a surprise by candidly admitting his true identity. He seems to have been moved to do so by what, to him, were noble motives. As his defence counsel at his subsequent trial stated Lody admitted to be being a spy because he would 'rather go down to his final fate as a brave man, as an honest man, as an openhearted man… refusing to tell… anything where it clashed with his word of honour as an officer and a gentleman'.[15] When Lody admitted in his statement that he was a German subject, it was decided to try him by General Court Martial.[16]

Guarded by soldiers with fixed bayonets, Lody stood on trial at the Guildhall, Westminster on 30 October. The President of the Court Martial, Lord Cheylesmore, dressed in his Major General's uniform, occupied a raised oak-canopied chair, and situated to his right and left, all in khaki, were the other officers constituting the court. According to one observer Lody, in the dock, appeared: 'Pale, clean-shaven, with black hair cut close, compressed lips, and an intelligent face, he had the typical appearance of a naval officer.' Much of the evidence 'appeared to bore the prisoner, who gazed around at the oil paintings of Middlesex worthies which adorn the walls, at the stone and oak carving, at counsel and others, finally resting his eyes and remaining quite passive for long intervals. When the Court rose he bowed three times before going down the dock steps.'[17]

When giving evidence Lody admitted to the Court Martial that he was a senior Lieutenant in the German Navy, that was to say, in the second division of the Navy Reserve. He was educated in Germany and afterwards went to sea in the mercantile marine. He had served in

German, Norwegian, British and American ships. In 1900 he entered the service of the German Navy. He served only one year and was then put in the reserve. In 1912, Lody married in the United States an American woman of German descent. Consequently he was casting off his ties with Germany and was looking forward to making his home in the United States and becoming a naturalised American citizen and would have done so had not his marriage broken down. Subsequently he dissolved the marriage and returned to Germany. During his marriage, Lody had been transferred from the first to the second German Naval Reserve. While in the United States, Lody had been employed in the Hamburg Amerika Line as a shipping or tourist agent. Back in Germany this made him a suitable candidate for spying since Lody was an invalid – during an operation for an internal abscess two ribs were removed leaving him with a weak left arm – and unfit for active service; he also had failing eyesight. But he was approached and asked if he would travel to England there:

> to give notice of my safe arrival in England, to remain until the first [naval] encounter had taken place between the two Powers [Britain and Germany], and to send accurate information as the actual losses of the British Fleet... I should observe what was going on with regard to movements here in England – movements of the Fleet, but I was warned not to spy around. I was to go and have a look round and see as much as any traveller could see... I felt I was not a fit man for a job of that kind. I was so well known to so many people and so accustomed to be called by my own name that I felt I would make a blunder with the first man I met... There was no pressure in that sense of the word. But there was an understanding – as when a suggestion is made to you that you feel obliged to obey. I have never been a coward in my life, and certainly I won't be a shirker.[18]

This testimony sealed his fate, as he must have known it would. On 2 November the Court Martial announced its verdict: Lody was guilty and sentenced 'to suffer death by being shot'. The sentence was confirmed by the King on 4 November and was carried out at 7 a.m. on 6 November at the Tower of London.[19] In meeting his fate with dignity and honour, Charles Lody became what he had always wanted to be: an officer and a gentleman.

The Cases of Kuepferle, Muller and Hahn

On 26 January 1915, a Belgian refugee living at Rotterdam wrote to the

War Office stating that F. Leibacher of 1 Zwaanensteeg, Rotterdam, was a German agent who received letters containing messages in secret ink and forwarded them to their proper quarters. In the course of February three men – Kuepferle, Muller and Hahn – were found to be in communication with this address. Anton Kuepferle, alias Anthony Copperlee, was a German who became a naturalised American in 1912. He had been educated in the United States. At the end of 1911 he was said to have set up as a woollen draper at 1665 de Kalb Avenue, Brooklyn, New York, but the business failed in 1913. He was employed as a salesman by two clothing firms between 1907 and 1913. From passages in a letter and his last confession he would seem to have served at the Front between August 1914 and January 1915, as a German officer. On 14 January 1915, he received 100 dollars, an American passport was issued to him on the 25th, and he sailed for Liverpool on the 4th February.[20]

A check had been placed on correspondence to Laibacher, in Rotterdam, on 30 January 1915. It was understood that German agents were communicating with this address in invisible ink by messages written in lemon juice, inscribed between the lines of an ordinary communication. On 17 February MO5g received, from the Censor, a communication to this address which contained information written in invisible ink – probably lemon juice – as to the position of British fleet units and troops. This letter was posted in Liverpool, at 12.45 p.m. 15 February, and was on business notepaper with the heading of:

A. Keupferle & Co.,
Importers of Woollens,
1665 de Kalb Avenue,
Brooklyn, N.Y.

It was addressed to 'Dear Friend Frans' and was signed 'Anthony Keupferle'.[21] On 17 and 18 February, two more letters were intercepted addressed to Leibacher. These letters contained messages in secret ink.[22] The following was inscribed in invisible writing:

At present two ships in harbour – Engadine and Collingwood. When passing in to the Irish Channel on the Irish Coast two large cruisers and one battleship – one about two miles behind the other, lying at anchor. On the east lay six torpedoes, behind each other, and one emergency cruiser among them.

As regards land troops AES Lancashire fully equipped for field, apparently for 15th. Guns which arrived from America, also ammunition and rifles to the value of 7,000,000 dollars.

Also 72 (or 12) motorcars on the boat.
Infantry Territorials M Regiment and Irish Kings not known
unit T.196.
Up to now I have been stopped twice for my pass and have
rest – tomorrow in Dublin.'[23]

The last line led to telegraphic enquires being made, between the
Chief Constable, Liverpool, the Royal Irish Constabulary and
the Commissioner of Police, Dublin, as to whether there was any
trace of Kuepferle. At 10.53 p.m. on the evening of 17 February
the Commissioner of Police, Dublin, replied to the effect that one
A. Kuepferle, of New York, arrived at the Grosvenor Hotel on 15
February and left Kingstown by the mail boat for Holyhead on the
morning of 17 February, bearing an American passport, and was
believed to be returning to the United States via Liverpool. On the
morning of 18 February the second letter was intercepted, written on the same business notepaper, addressed to the same address
in Rotterdam. It was signed in visible writing 'A Thom'; in invisible
writing it was signed 'A or H Keupferel.' As before it contained an
innocent message in the visible part, and information as to the movement of troops and other details of naval or military importance in
the invisible part:[24]

Two ships – Ajax and Louis are lying at anchor in Liverpool.
Saw 150 Marine Artillery leaving from Liverpool ACA. At Holyhead
there were 250 men ready to receive uniform for field service.
In English: I found only soldiers on guard, estimated amount of
3,000 in all. Tomorrow in Queenstown.
In German. Other information verbally, Opinion is favourable
towards Germany.[25]

The description and name of Kuepferle were circulated to the relevant
ports and to the Chief Constable of Liverpool with instructions to
arrest.[26] Although it was thought that Kuepferle might still be in Ireland,
in order to cover the possibility of him having returned to England special arrangements were made with the Special Branch and the Criminal
Investigation Department to make enquires at the hotels in the neighbourhood of Euston, as it was thought there was some possibility that
Kuepferle might have been put up there, having come to London after
his long journey from Dublin. As a result of these enquires it was ascertained that a man of that name, and answering the description, had
stayed in a hotel in the area on the night of 17 February but had left

the premises about ten minutes before the officer arrived, when he had made enquires at the American Consulate, and asked for direction to Victoria Station as he was going to proceed to the Continent.[27] But, unfortunately for Kuepferle he was unable to complete his journey on the 18th, for the boats for Flushing had been held up owing to the German blockade.[28]

On the morning of 19 February a third letter was intercepted on the same business paper signed by Kuepferle and addressed to the same address in Rotterdam. It announced his arrival in London and asked for money. It also contained in invisible writing, information as to the movements of troops and transports and other information of naval and military importance. Enclosed was a card from the Wilton Hotel on which was written Kuepferle's name and the number of his room, 215. CID was at once informed and Kuepferle's arrest was carried out at about midday on 19 February. In a search of Kuepferle's room, carried out by Sergeant Magrath, three lemons were found, bearing a small hole, apparently like a pen nib. In a pocket book on Kuepferle's person, the same officer discovered a steel nib and the metal part of a pen-holder which appeared to have been used, not in ink, but in some sticky substance like a lemon.[29]

On 20 February a small phial was found in Kuepferle's room; it was half full of formalin. This, it was believed was used for mixing with lemon juice to write in invisible characters.[30] In the inner part of his coat was a bone handle of a pen, the metal of a pen and a steel pen nib. When examined it was found that between the nib and the holder was some cellular matter such as that came from a lemon and, when the nib was examined with distilled water, there were distinct traces still on the nib that were of the sort of acid which would be found in a lemon. The cut lemon had been tested by what was called the Prussian blue test. If the fluid had not been touched by something made of iron or steel, the test would not produce any specific results; but if the lemon had something pressed into it, such as the steel nib of a pen, a clear indication was obtained that iron or steel had touched the lemon because it turned a blue colour. In order to prove the case against Kuepferle it would have to be proved that the three letters containing messages in invisible ink, and their respective envelopes, had been sent through the post; that they had reached the Postal Censor's Office and had been opened in the usual course of examination; that the three letters were in the same handwriting; that correct translations of German were procured; and that the handwriting of the visible and invisible should be proved to be in the same handwriting.[31] Evidence of Kuepferle's connection with Leibacher was found at Dublin and in London as well as materials for secret writing. Kuepferle's movements were traced in Liverpool. The information he had sent abroad was found to be mostly incorrect. Enquiries were set on foot in America to ascertain his nationality and business and the American Consulate were kept informed as to the case.[32]

On 22 February the General Officer Commanding London District was asked to take Kuepferle, now being held at Cannon Row police station, into military custody 'on a serious charge of espionage'. It was deemed 'essential that this individual should be carefully guarded and that he should not be allowed to have any communication with unauthorised persons'. The GOC was informed that counsel for the prosecution was being briefed by the Director of Public Prosecutions who would inform the GOC as to the arrangements which it would be necessary to make regarding the taking of the Summary of Evidence. As soon as the Summary of Evidence had been taken a decision would be given as to whether Kuepferle would be charged with: (a) a convention of the Defence of the Realm Regulations (court martial); (b) War Treason (court martial); or (c) Treason (Civil Court). It was advisable that the preliminary proceedings should be kept, as far as possible, secret with a view to preventing any information regarding Kuepferle's arrest being communicated to Germany.[33]

A postbox connection between the case of Kuepferle and that of Muller and Hahn was discovered. John Hahn, a British subject, was the son of a German who naturalised as a British subject in 1897 and returned to Germany about 1905 to end his days there. Hahn spent the two years from 1901 to 1903 learning his trade as a baker and confectioner in Germany. From 1903 until 1910, he worked as a journeyman baker in London and Dublin where he spent two years. In September 1910 he bought a baker's shop at 111 High St. Deptford, became a bankrupt at the end of 1913, and leased the shop to his wife in January 1914. The shop was raided by an anti-German mob in November and the business failed utterly in consequence of the war. Hahn had married, in May 1912, Christine, daughter of Richard Dorst, a German residing at 4 Osy Straat, Antwerp. C.F.H. Muller, a Russian said to have been born at Libau of German parents, had lived at Antwerp for at least eleven years. He occupied a room in the house of Richard Dorst, combining the occupation of check-weigher of cargoes on German steamers with other employment. For six months he worked in Kattendyke's Engineering Works, Antwerp and following this, was an agent for a German firm dealing in motor-winches. Before the siege of Antwerp, Richard Dorst left with his family for Holland; Muller stayed behind and took charge of Dorst's property. Muller had a daughter who was said to have lived in Hamburg and Bremen, who was married to a German who perished in the battle of the Falkland Islands. By his own admission Muller was on friendly terms with German officers at Antwerp. He arrived at Sunderland on the 12 January 1915, carrying Russian papers and claiming that he had just been released from a German prison, where he had been brutally treated. He called at the house of some English people with whom he had a slight acquaintance. They did what they could for him but Sunderland was at that time a Prohibited Area to all aliens and the police expelled him. He came to London to 38 Guildford Street, on the 13th and immediately got into touch with Hahn. On the 17th he left, returning to Guildford Street on the 21st. He went away almost immediately but returned on the 28th, having been at Rotterdam and Roosendaal on the Belgian frontier. On 5 February he again went to Rotterdam, procured there a fresh passport, and returned to Guildford Street on the 13th. On 15 February he was signalled from Rotterdam as a German agent for the German GOC, Brussels. He was said to be receiving letters in London either from *Poste Restante* or a Post Office Box addressed to the name of Leidec.[34]

Meanwhile, under the check on F. Leibacher (other forms Laibacher and Laybaker) a letter had been intercepted on 3 and 4 February containing interlinear secret messages referring to military matters, signed A.E.111 and posted in the WC District of London. The signature seemed to confirm previous reports received by MO5g of a book containing the record of German agents directed against Britain in which each agent was entered by a number corresponding to the order of his enrolment. On the receipt of the first letter enquires were made at the address given in the *en clair* message, but without result. As, however, the handwriting faintly resembled that of a German who lived at the address, it was resolved to search the house for further evidence. Before this could be done, a second letter containing a different name and address was intercepted. On receipt of the message incriminating Muller the police went to call at Guilford Street. Muller was interviewed on 15 February without much result. A check was put on the name Leidec. This resulted in the intercepting of two letters dated 20 and 21 February and addressed to Mr Lybecq, Postbox 447, Rotterdam, again posted in the WC district. Each contained a secret message signed A.E.111 written on the back of the letter, the writer mentioned that he was shortly going to Sunderland. The letter of the 21st was written on a peculiar kind of paper and the en clair message was in another hand. MO5g deduced that A.E.111 was probably living in the Bloomsbury district as he always used a 2½p stamp. Stamps of this value were issued to a branch office and were specifically marked, and enquiries with regard to the notepaper were conducted on foot in the district. Then came a letter dated 24 February written on the same kind of notepaper as the fourth, containing a secret message beginning: 'In the absence of A.E.111' signed Hahn. The letter was posted in Deptford. MO5g concluded that this second agent would be using his own name and posting in his own district. Reference to the Aliens Register brought to light the existence of John Hahn. His shop was raided and evidence connecting Hahn with the writing of the last two letters was found. Hahn was arrested on 24 February and, when questioned, made reference to Muller. The next day Hahn's wife called at Scotland Yard, gave Muller's address, and said he might be connected with the trouble. Muller had also been arrested on 24 February with incriminating evidence found in his rooms. Four of the marked stamps were found on him.

In May, Hahn made a written confession that was of some value to MO5g. Muller, he said, had received a fortnight's instruction at Antwerp; using photographs he had been taught to recognise the silhouettes of British ships, and he had to learn his code by heart. His chief object in coming to Britain was to obtain precise details of Lord Kitchener's New Armies being raised for the Front. His repeated visits to Rotterdam were made with a view to learning the course followed by steamers, and to give information concerning, for example, the ships he met with at sea. Muller's cover was business in the tinned goods line; he had asked Hahn to write two letters so that his own handwriting did not appear too frequently. He offered Hahn a post in the German service and told Hahn that the password 'have you seen Matilda?' would get him past any sentry in the German Army. Muller had been promised German nationality; he had received 2,000 francs for some special service; and his life had been insured for 16,000 marks. MO5g subsequently ascertained that Muller had sent abroad information that was correct, on the whole, and applied to no fewer than eight different authorities for testimony as to the value of his information.

The arrest of the three German agents had been carried out within a space of six days. In order to suppress all notice of the arrests the Cable Censor was warned to stop any mention of them in the press cables to America, and the British Press received similar warnings. On 1 March, it was arranged to transfer the three prisoners to the Tower of London for greater secrecy. But the question of how to try the cases caused difficulty. At first it was decided to try them by Court Martial. But the nationality of Kuepferle, an American, and of Hahn, technically British and with the 'immemorial rights of a British subject', caused difficulty, political in the one case, judicial in the other. And the case of Muller could not be separated from that of Hahn.[35] Lord Haldane felt that it would be wisest to take it as an instruction that whenever an offender pleaded a foreign nationality the preferable tribunal should be civil and not military and that in every case where an American nationality was pleaded the tribunal should be civil unless the plea could be easily disposed of.[36] The Attorney General, Sir John Simon, did not think such nuances really mattered in this instance: 'These are very plain cases. I cannot doubt that a jury would convict: my own view is that a jury would be very eager to do so.'[37] Lord Kitchener, however, insisted that Kuepferle should be tried by Court Martial. Sir Reginald Brade, of the War Office, had taken it upon himself to contact the American Embassy and found that they knew all about the Kuepferle affair but 'were not much interested in the man, who... was a recently naturalised American' although 'they considered that the attendance of a representative of the Embassy would be useful in the event of questions being raised in the future. Arrangements are accordingly being commenced for a Court Martial'.[38] The Director of Public Prosecutions, however, overruled the interfering War Office and decided to try Kuepferle at the Central Criminal Court before the Lord Chief Justice of England under an Act of Parliament passed the previous week.[39] On 16 March the Defence of the Realm Act had been amended so as (1) to give the Civil Court power to inflict such punishment as might have been inflicted had the case been tried by Court Martial; and (2) to recognise the right of a British subject to trial by jury. And, on 23 March, Regulation 56A was issued giving effect to the amendment. The three prisoners were therefore treated as British subjects and tried in the Civil Court under Defence of the Realm Regulation 56A. The charge against all three was that of attempting to communicate information with a view to helping the enemy. Part of the evidence was taken in camera but the cases generally were tried and the sentences were by law promulgated in open court.[40] The American Ambassador was to be represented at the trial by the Office of the Consul-General.[41]

Kuepferle's defence was that he had been asked by an American named Reihly (real name Ruehle) to collect information for the press and to forward it to Leibacher. An attempt had been made to get Leibacher and Ruehle to come over and give evidence in Kuepferle's favour but, unsurprisingly, they refused. Instead, three affidavits attesting to Kuepferle's innocence were received from Holland including one from Leibacher. Kuepferle was tried on the 18 and 19 May.[42] His own actions made his fate certain. When arrested, Kuepferle had insisted on giving a statement even though he was cautioned that this could incriminate him. The statement he made was in the same handwriting as the many signatures used by the man who had stayed in the various hotels it was claimed that Kuepferle had visited, and found in the visible and invisible writings in the letters. Kuepferle compounded this mistake while in Brixton Prison: the prisoner had, as of right, access to writing paper. Kuepferle used this paper to write a communication that he hoped to hand to some fellow prisoners, who were apparently housed in an adjoining cell. Part of it read: 'Dear Friend, – After my study today I cannot refrain from writing a few words again… [referring to Belgium] Here is the true appearance of that deceitful friendship. The English refuse credit to her so-called best friend; so I suppose the fact that Belgium is now in our hands has nothing to do with that state of things.' This was reproduced in court and Sir John Simon, prosecuting, asked how it came to be that an American citizen should talk about Belgium being 'in our hands?' Kuepferle went on in the letter to refer to the Battle of Ypres: 'I believe Ypres and neighbourhood have now fallen. If I could only see the day when the whole English trickery is exposed and her preparation, England's shame must be known, otherwise there can be no justice. Oh, if I could only be at the Front again for half an hour!'[43] This seemed to be an admission that Kuepferle had served at the Front.

For two days Kuepferle stood in the dock before three judges – the Lord Chief Justice, Mr Justice Avory and Mr Justice Lush – and a jury. When the Court adjourned, Kuepferle, having given his evidence and submitted himself to cross-examination at the hands of the Attorney General, was taken back to Brixton Prison. Despite being kept under almost continuous observation, Kuepferle managed to take his own life in the early hours of the morning while the warder was visiting other cells. Warder Perry had seen Kuepferle in his cell at 4.15 a.m. but a quarter of an hour later, on looking through the spyhole, the official failed to obtain a view of him. Knocking elicited no response; the warder alerted his superior officer, Richard Cooke. Together they entered the cell and found Kuepferle with his shirt, trousers and socks on, hanging from the ventilator in the corner of the room. He had committed suicide by attaching to the ventilator the black and white scarf which he worn throughout his trial and fastening it around his neck. His feet were six to nine inches from the ground and a thick book which had been provided to him from the prison library suggested how he hoisted himself. Despite his body still being warm, artificial respiration proved futile. Kuepferle left a message, written on a slate. Written in broken English it read:

> To whom it may concern. My name is Kuepferle, born at Solingen… I am a soldier with the rank which I do not desire to mention.
>
> In regard on my behalf lately, I can say I have a fair trial of the United Kingdom, but I am unable to stand the strain much longer, and take the law into my own hands. I fought many battles, and death is the only saviour for me. I would have preferred death to be shot, but do not wish to ascend the scaffold and hope that the Almighty Architect of this Universe will lead me in the unknown land in the East. I am not dying as a spy, but as a soldier. My fate I stood as a man, but cannot be a liar and purger [sic] myself… What I have done I have done for my country. I shall express my thanks and the Lord bless yours all.[44]

Muller and Hahn were tried on 2 June. Hahn was condemned to seven years' penal servitude. Muller was sentenced to be shot. His appeal was dismissed and the judges upheld the sentence which was carried out on 22 June. Mrs Hahn was not allowed to leave the country until December 1915. Although the names of the prisoners were known to the world, and subsequently the sentences, MO5g believed that Muller – being a common German name – was not identified initially by the Germans as having been executed for at least one attempt was made later on, from America, to ascertain clearly which Muller had suffered the penalty.[45]

German Espionage and MO5g Counter-Measures

During 1915, MO5g learned of the existence of a German spy school operating out of Rotterdam and The Hague in neutral Holland: the Dierks Recruiting Agency was the cover. Hilmar Dierks, who was also known as Richard Sanderson, was said to have 150 agents working in Britain by July 1915. He sent all his recruits to the Antwerp Admiralstab Zweigstelle, 38 Chaussée de Malines there to be trained and to receive their instructions. Through counter-espionage successes and the treachery of some of the Dutch agents employed, a good deal of information was acquired about the personnel and methods of the spy bureau. The confession of one spy, Melin, revealed the existence of another bureau at Wesel, which acted independently of, and it would seem in rivalry with, the bureau at Antwerp. In April 1915 a Dutch source reported that spies were using double passports; and that fifty or sixty German firms were doing business in London and sending information in false business telegrams piecemeal to different centres to be afterwards patched together and forwarded to Antwerp. Already in December 1914 sources had reported that Belgian women were being sent via Folkestone to spy in France, and MO5g ensured that an order was issued that such persons were to be allowed to enter but not to leave the United Kingdom. With the object of destroying Admiralty coalmines, the Germans were reported to be intending to send over spies disguised as Belgian miners and to be stealing Belgian miners' books to provide identity papers for the purpose. Soon after this, a report came that stated that Germans were being brought in as coal heavers.

Rumours of espionage abounded and were brought to the attention of British Intelligence. In April 1915, the Germans were said to be buying the services of Dutch agents who were to live in London and Paris and report from there. The British Consul at Rotterdam stated that not only were a number of Dutchmen coming to England, but also that many Germans were being encouraged to spend the summer in Holland. From Washington came a report that stated that Germans were taking situations with shipping companies in the United States and Canada, to enable them to warn the U-boats of vessels carrying important stores for the Allies. A British ship's captain learned from a Belgian pilot of a scheme by which Belgians in England joined their army in France, then deserted, went as stowaways on a cheese-boat to Rotterdam and there consorted with Germans. A German named Carl Haasters, head of a firm exploiting iron ores in Holland, required his manager to sign a certificate to the effect that a person, whose name he refused to give, proceeding from Spain but at that moment in Holland and known to the North German Lloyd people at Amsterdam, was a representative of the Iron Ore Company. As this company had in former years had dealings with the Gas Light & Coke Company, the manager believed that Haasters intended to send over a hostile agent under guise of doing business with the British company and accordingly informed a representative of Scotland Yard. British ports were also warned. From Lausanne came a warning that about twenty young persons claiming Polish nationality and with papers in order were coming from Switzerland to England, and then to America as Russian ballet dancers. The ports were again warned – Washington also – and in February 1916 the Russian troupe, numbering seventy-three members, arrived at Washington. Nothing further transpired.[46]

With each new scrap of intelligence MO5g sought to enhance their preventative intelligence counter-measures. Owing to the delays occasioned by postal censorship the practice grew up of firms sending their correspondence abroad by a clerk who travelled regularly to and fro. An officer at Tilbury reported that an immense traffic of this kind was in progress and that one courier would carry as many as 100 letters. The captains of neutral ships were entitled to carry 'ship-owner's' letters and the same officer at Tilbury sent in a report incriminating the director and an officer of the Zeeland S.S.Company. This complaint echoed one sent in by 'a traveller' in February 1915, who declared the measures taken with regard to travellers at Whitehall, Victoria and the ports to be insufficient; letters and telegrams could be sent from the steamers, clerks and journalists carrying letters for their principals were not supervised, and no control was exercised over the crews of neutral vessels although there was much German capital invested in Dutch liners. As a result the Zeeland S.S. Company was specially warned against including private correspondence in the Captain's box, a measure which had some effect, for in August 1915, illicit carrying by small trading vessels was far commoner than by ordinary passenger boat. This traffic was conducted by the simple expedient of addressing letters to persons on board the ship lying in port.

During 1915, the system of Port Control was gradually elaborated. The influx of 'undesirables' and the persistent illegal carrying of letters caused MO5g to both make a formal complaint about the divided responsibilities at the ports, and also to procure the appointment of special representatives at Hull, Newcastle, Liverpool, Bergen and Rotterdam to watch the traffic carefully and suggest improvements in applying preventive methods. These officers had no executive powers so it rested with the Aliens Officers to prevent an undesirable from landing or to admit him and with the police to arrest and search him; accordingly circulars indicating the line of action required in the case of an individual were issued by MO5g's E Branch at the request of the Investigating Branch to the Home Office as well as to the Port Officer. But the Port Officer also acted as general adviser and supervisor in these cases. By means of this control the Investigating Branch could arrange for an undesirable to be kept out or admitted; to be most carefully searched and watched; his papers sent to Scotland Yard for investigation; or to have the man arrested and sent up to Scotland Yard. Equally important was the work done in stopping an undesirable from leaving the country or from making too frequent journeys to and from the continent.[47]

On 6 February 1915, Richard Sanderson, alias Hilmar Dierks, had come to the attention of MO5g: among a number of Dutch post-boxes used by German agents in England, the following were reported:

'Richard SANDERSON, Post-box 417, Rotterdam and Dr. Brandt, Dordrecht'.

The addresses were put 'on check' on 9 February. On the 27th of that month it was reported from Holland that a Mrs Schwartz, of 32 Coptic Street, London, and a Mrs Wertheim, Hampstead, address unknown, had lodged German agents and on 10 May it was said that Mrs Wertheim was visiting Mrs Schwartz. Therefore a connection was established between the two women. On 28 May, the British Consul General at Rotterdam, forwarded to the Foreign Office a report supplied by the French Military Attaché coupling Sanderson, of 72 Provenierstraat, Rotterdam with a M. Blanken Wolfshoek, 7b Rotterdam and Brandwijk & Co, of 106a Bingley Straat, Rotterdam. Sanderson, who represented the tea merchants Bjarks and Leming, was engaging young Dutchmen to travel in tea and sending them to Southampton and London, Cardiff and Hull to obtain news of the sailings of ships. Letters were to be addressed to Blanken and to Brandwijk in Rotterdam, and wires were to be sent in a code. Brandwijk's connection with Sanderson was confirmed by Hoogendyk, a Dutch sailor, on 10 October 1915, who gave the address Ipers Schiedamschedyk 33, as the post-box for letters. As a result of this information and subsequent interceptions to these addresses a number of German agents were arrested in Britain.[48]

Janssen and Roos

Haicke Marinus Petrus Janssen, aged thirty-two, landed at Hull on the 13 May 1915.[49] He was detected as a result of a wire of 25 May sent to Dierks & Co, in The Hague. He was associated with Wilhelm Johannes Roos who was confirmed as a spy as a result of a search of wires at Edinburgh again implicating Dierks.[50] Janssen carried a passport that had been issued on 1 April. On arrival he wired to Dierks for funds. He spent a week in Hull, then went to London and on the 23rd arrived at Southampton, whence he despatched five telegrams, purporting to order different kinds of cigars but in reality conveying information regarding the movements of ships, to Dierks & Co, from 24 to 28 May. After Janssen's arrest it was discovered that he had come to England in February to receive at Liverpool a medal for lifesaving at sea, and that he had visited Cardiff, Hull and Edinburgh.

Roos, a sailor who had served in the Dutch Navy, landed at Tilbury on 14 May with a passport dated 13 April. He travelled to Newcastle on the 15th, and then went on to Edinburgh. He wired to Dierks & Co from Edinburgh on 17, 18 and 25 May. Orders were issued for his arrest; he was traced to Aberdeen and Inverness and arrested in London on 2 June. A search of telegraphic money orders brought to light payments of £10 and £20 made to Janssen on 19 and 27 May respectively and of £25 made to W.J. Roos on 25 May, the remitter in each case being Dierks & Co. In a search of Janssen's room various telegrams to and from Dierks & Co were found as well as other items from the firm – such as green and white trade cards issued by the firm; a descriptive trade-book of Dierks & Co; a price list of the brands of cigars supplied by Dierks & Co containing some letters and figures which were interpreted as code; a copy of Jane's Fighting Ships 1915; samples of different brands of cigars; Eau de Cologne and custard powder and a bottle of liquid gum. Various pens, nibs and a mapping pen were also discovered, as well as a list of the addresses of various firms of tobacconists in Southsea and Portsmouth supplied by Stubbs & Co Mercantile Offices, Gresham Street and a letter from the same firm introducing Janssen to their branch at Plymouth.

A search of Roos's effects yielded the following: a cigar Stock List, signed Dierks & Co; a cigar stock list with the printed heading 'Louis Dobbelmann, 106 Hoogstraat, Rotterdam'; a number of plain memorandums and letter headings printed in the name of Dierks & Co; a copy of Pearson's Magazine for May 1915 containing an article by Fred. T. Jane, illustrated with photographs of different types of British warships and the names of several of His Majesty's ships written in pencil on the margin; various hotel bills showing the itinerary of Roos; a box of custard powders; a pen and seven nibs; a few cigars but no samples of different brands; and a communication from Janssen giving the address of the hotel at Hull from which Janssen was writing. A comparison of the two cigar lists supplied by Dierks & Co to Janssen and Roos respectively showed that they were practically identical except that the one in the possession of Roos was more detailed: it contained under the heading 'Mexico', code letters for a number of British ports on the Eastern and North-Eastern coasts. These were appropriately missing in Janssen's code.

The pretext given by both men was that they were travelling for a firm of cigar merchants. It was ascertained that neither of them had called on any tobacconists in the places where they had stayed. Roos, in registering as an alien, had declared that he was travelling for the firm of Mr L. Dobbelmann, cigar merchants of Rotterdam, which was a genuine firm. During interrogation, however, he did not mention the firm of Dobbelmann, but stated that he was in the employ of Dierks & Co, cigar and provision merchants, who gave him £25 to come to England. He admitted knowing Janssen quite well, but said that he had no connection with Dierks. Janssen, on the other hand, stated that he was the only traveller employed by Dierks, and denied that he knew Roos: but on being confronted with Roos he partially changed his story. The papers found on the men were submitted for testing to a chemical expert, whose tests revealed secret writing on the cigar lists. These had an odour of scent and the writing flashed up in a manner characteristic of scent. Gradually the expert conducting the tests reached the conviction that a fixative in the form of talc powder had been used with the scent.

Janssen was tried on the charge of having collected and communicated on various dates to Dierks & Co at The Hague information regarding the disposition of certain of His Majesty's ships and the movement of certain of His Majesty's forces at or from Southampton. Roos was tried on the charge of having collected and communicated information of a like nature, regarding ships and forces respectively lying in the Firth of Forth and stationed near Edinburgh. From MO5g, Major Drake gave evidence as to the code, and interpretation of the telegrams. The evidence of experts in the cigar trade proved that Dierks & Co's price lists were unintelligible or at least unusual. Per contra, expert naval evidence proved that the information sent abroad by both men was approximately correct and most valuable to the enemy. They were found guilty and sentenced to be shot. After the Court Martial and before the sentence had been confirmed, Janssen volunteered some information with regard to spy methods. However, all the addresses that he gave were already known to MO5g. He stated that the British had failed to discover two of the codes and that telegrams and letters of interest passed the Censor daily. Furthermore, he said that one method of smuggling messages was by slipping them down the back of a book between the binding and the leaves. If he thought that this might have had some favourable bearing on his fate, he was sadly mistaken: Janssen and Roos were both shot by firing squad on 30 July 1915.[51]

Breckow

Reginald Rowland's real name was George Breckow (or Breeckow). Born in Germany in 1884, the son of a Russian landowner who had gone to live at Stettin, Breckow at some time served in the Cuirassiers. For three years he was employed in a major export business, before travelling to America where he earned a living as a pianist. He never became naturalised in America and in June 1914 he returned to Germany. In March 1915, he was engaged by the German Naval Intelligence Bureau at Antwerp to act as Imperial Courier between Germany and America, but he was sent first to England with messages. A Captain Schnitzer (or Schmitzer) gave him a forged passport made

out in the name of Reginald Rowland from the particulars of the passport belonging to a man of that name. The real Reginald Rowland
had in March deposited his passport for a few hours with the police
in Berlin. Breckow was given an address for his correspondence and
told to sign his letters George T. Parker. He was sent to Holland and
there Dierks supplied him with papers and cards of the firm of Norton
B. Smith, New York. A genuine firm dealing in scrap iron and other
metals existed at New York under the name of Morton B. Smith.
Breckow received, besides £45 for delivery to a Mrs Wertheim, a letter
from Mrs Rohwedell, the wife of a photographer in Stettin, for delivery
to Robert Carter, an Englishman, residing at Southampton. Rowland
landed at Tilbury on 11 May, travelled to London and contacted Mrs
Wertheim. On the 20th he went to Southampton and saw Carter and
tried to induce him to return to Germany apparently under cover of an
American passport. Both Carter and his landlady suspected Rowland's
motives and after some exchange of letters Carter broke off relations. Rowland then joined Mrs Wertheim and together they stayed
at Bournemouth from 22 to 25 May. He went to Ramsgate with a Dr
Tullidge from the 28th to the 31st. From Bournemouth and Ramsgate
he sent information to the Germans. Under a check on Dierks & Co
the Censor forwarded from Holland a telegram of 30 May, 1915,
announcing the despatch to Reginald Rowland, c/o Société Générale,
Regent St., London, of £30 on account of Norton B. Smith & Co, New
York. Rowland was arrested on 4 June.

Not surprisingly with his German accent he had aroused suspicion
on two occasions; owing to his handwriting and correspondence,
his letters were stopped by the Postal Censor who submitted a letter,
dated 25 May and a second dated 2 June, to MO5g on the grounds
that they appeared to emanate from a German who wished to live on
the coast and to take photographs. The letters were signed George T.
Parker and posted in London. After Rowland's arrest they were identified by the handwriting as being his work. They were then tested and
found to contain naval and military information, some of it concerning Scotland, references to Bournemouth, to a lady accomplice and
to 'Lizzie' – all in secret writing. A batch of newspapers which was
intercepted after Rowland's arrest contained a reference to a journey
in the North. Among other articles in Rowland's possession there
was found a receipt for a registered letter addressed to L. Wertheim,
Inverness. This, apparently on 9 June, was connected with the references to 'Lizzie' which had at first been interpreted as a code name
for the Queen Elizabeth. The Chief Constable of Inverness was wired
to – he had already sent in a report regarding the woman in question

to the Metropolitan Police – and he replied that she had returned to London. She was arrested on the evening of 9 June. Among Rowland's effects hotel bills were found, which established some of his movements, along with cards of Norton B. Smith and a letter showing that he represented the firm and a copy of *Jane's Fleets of the World, 1915*. He was also found to have in his possession a phial of lemon-juice; pens and a tin of talcum powder; as well as a code resembling in its general features that used by Janssen and Roos. This code was written on a sheet of rice paper and concealed in the case of Rowland's shaving brush. He explained the lemon juice by saying that he used it after shaving. Rowland, it was concluded, had received £110 in total from the Germans.

The woman known as 'Lizzie' was Louise Emily Wertheim, by birth a German Pole whose maiden name was Klitzke. By her marriage to Bruno Wertheim she became a British subject. Separated from her husband for three years, she was in Britain when war broke out and, with the aid of a relative at Hampstead and of a local doctor, managed to obtain a passport to enable her to visit her mother in Berlin. She did not, however, leave until October 1914 when she went to Amsterdam and where she met an old friend named Dr Brandt. She returned to London in November and put up in Coptic Street. In December, Mrs Wertheim went again to Amsterdam to nurse the wife of an old friend named Moritz Lietzau. While there she arranged with Dr Brandt to correspond with him in a form of family code. She returned to London at the end of January and introduced herself to Miss Gertrude Elizabeth Brandes, the sister of Mrs Lietzau, of 62 Hammersmith Road, and thenceforward made her headquarters at that house. But she would frequently go away for two or three days together without giving an address. Subsequently it was ascertained that she had visited Folkestone, Margate, the Isle of Man, Fishguard and probably Ireland and Holland during these absences.

At Whitsuntide she called on an American lady named Miss Knowles-Macy at 33 Regent's Park Road, and persuaded her to accompany her to Scotland. They arrived in Edinburgh on 28 May and Miss Knowles, having no passport, was told to get one, so she returned for good to London. Wertheim went to Dundee from the 28th to the 31st, and on the 30th drove in a motor to Carnoustie and Arbroath. She spent the 1st to 3rd June in Inverness, arousing suspicion by ordering a motor to drive her to Cromarty. The Chief Constable was warned and he called at the hotel. Noting irregularities in Wertheim's signature, he interviewed her and practically obliged her to return to London. He clearly felt uneasy and, on 3 June, reported the matter to the Metropolitan

Police. Wertheim returned on the 3rd and next day deposited her Scottish luggage with Miss Knowles. On the 7th Miss Brandes turned Wertheim out and she then went to Miss Knowles for two nights. She was arrested in Miss Knowles's house. When the police went to search her room, she entered the maid's room, tore up a letter from George T. Parker and threw it out of the window. Among her papers, besides evidence showing that she had been recently in Berlin and had been communicating with German prisoners of war, there were found the address of Netta, wife of Dr Brandt; an Althuis, of 166 Loosduinsche-Kade and letters of 7 and 16 May, signed 'Mother' and 'Suzette' but written from Loosduische-Kade and by the same hand, which was that of Dr Brandt. There were also letters from George T. Parker; an envelope addressed to R. Rowland; an Irish railway guide and Irish money; £115 in banknotes; and a letter, attached to Rowland's visiting card, showing that she had applied to a Mrs Ausems for £50 to be sent in the name of her mother, which seemed to have been used as a letter of introduction. She was also found to have in her possession a bottle of scent and a tin of talcum powder. An examination of telegrams showed that on 1 May Wertheim had sent a conventional message to a known spy address in Holland.

In examination Rowland lied freely. He denied that he had ever been in the army 'but sprang to attention at the word of command'. Eventually he made some sort of confession. In preparing the prosecution case it was discovered by chemical examination that his passport was forged and a photograph of the genuine passport was obtained from America. The Germans had altered the age to suit Breckow's appearance. Enquiries were made in America with regard to the firm of Morton B. Smith which denied all knowledge of Rowland. The news forwarded to Holland by Rowland was verified and that sent to him by Wertheim was carefully verified in its relation to her movements and the actual facts. The information of Rowland and of Wertheim was found to be correct. The enquiry involved a great deal of correspondence with Chief Constables in Scotland. Wertheim's movements were fully proved but Rowland was never traced in Scotland; it seemed unlikely that he had ever been there. Rowland and Wertheim were tried together in the Civil Court as Wertheim claimed her rights as a British subject. They were both found guilty; Rowland was sentenced to death. He appealed, but the sentence was upheld and he was shot in October. Wertheim was sentenced to a long term of penal servitude.[52]

'The German Intelligence Attack on the United Kingdom' The Highpoint of German Espionage 1915

Buschman

Fernando Buschman was a Brazilian subject of German origin; his mother lived in Vienna and his wife in Dresden. He had been in partnership with a man named Marcelino Bello in Las Palmas. The firm Buschman & Bello traded as General Merchants and Importers. Buschman, who was an engineer, dealt with the engineering branch of the trade. At some time not specified, but presumably on the outbreak of war, Buschman severed his connection with the firm, which then became known as M. Bello & Co. On 26 August 1914, Buschman left Las Palmas, travelling via Barcelona and Genoa to Dresden and then on to Hamburg. He wrote to Bello from Hamburg, returned to Genoa, writing to Bello on 18 March to request money. He wired again, from Barcelona on 26 March and was sent a small sum, which he promised to repay as he had obtained a post at the Brazilian Legation in London. Buschman landed at Folkestone on 14 April 1915. His passport, which had been issued at the Brazilian Consulate in June 1912, bore the following visas: Las Palmas 26-8-14; Barcelona 5-9-14; Madrid 3-4-15; Paris 13-4-15; Boulogne 13-4-15.

There were no traces of his journey to Dresden and Hamburg, which became known of only through a letter from the British Bank of West Africa dated 6 July 1915. In London, Buschman stayed at various hotels. He rapidly established a friendship with a naturalised British subject of Romanian origin named Emile Franco, with whom he proposed to set up a commission agency for the sale of cheese, butter in tins, cotton blankets and soft soap to be imported from Holland, where Buschman stated that he had business. He also proposed to import cloth for the French armies from Spain. While in London, Buschman visited various firms with the ostensible object of renewing trade relations with the firm of M. Bello. He explained the change of style as necessary owing to loss of trade occasioned by the false belief that he, Buschman, was a German. Entries in Buschman's diary showed that on 23 and 24 April he went to Southampton returning by Portsmouth. Emile Franco saw him buy his ticket; Franco and the Head Porter at the Piccadilly Hotel also deposed that Buschman had intended to visit firms of Banana Importers at Liverpool. On 5 May, Buschman crossed to Rotterdam, visited various towns in Holland and returned on the 16th. Soon after he went to live with Emile Franco and the two men took a flat together in Harrington Gardens.

Immediately after Buschman's first landing in England he had entered into telegraphic communication with H. Flores, Dierks's partner in Rotterdam, to whom he wired repeatedly for money. The money was sent at least twice through the Brazilian Legation in London. Buschman had also wired Bello in Las Palmas asking for money. On 4 June a telegram from Dierks asking Buschman to return and confer with Flores was intercepted and Buschman was arrested. He was interviewed and denied involvement in any business with Dierks, against whom he had been put on his guard by von Staa, of the firm of Ivers and von Staa. He stated that Flores was engaged in selling guns to the French and he, Buschman, was dealing in picric acid, rifles and cloth. The investigation that followed showed that Buschman had concluded no business in England, 'and that on the other hand he was well equipped to act as a spy. He was a first rate mechanic, possessed a French authorisation to use the aviation ground at Issy, issued in 1910; and he carried a French passport issued in Madrid, on 9 April 1915.' His papers, newspapers, and music were covered with minute figures in secret ink and on a telegraph form there was a microscopic map in the same medium giving the positions of the headquarters of the British armies, corps, and divisions in France during April 1915. A search of his papers and of old telegraph forms at the GPO proved Buschman's connection with Flores, with an address formerly occupied by Colonel von Ostertag, German Military Attaché at The Hague, and a leader in espionage, and also with a man named H.Grund who had written to Buschman making an appointment for a meeting in Holland. A letter signed 'Chr. J. Mulder' referring to deals in cheese and chirurgical rubber wares, which was thought to be in code, also contained a reference to Grund – 'and a promising deal in bananas'.

However, the case against Buschman proved difficult. As the telegram of 4 June had not been delivered, it could not be produced in evidence, and corroborative evidence of the visits to Southampton and Portsmouth could not be obtained. There was no proof that the secret writing, which Buschman denied absolutely, had been done by him and the map was apparently also an unsatisfactory piece of evidence. On the other hand there was abundant proof that Buschman had been in the pay of Flores, who was well known from the evidence of other spy cases. In addition to the earlier evidence, the Financial Manager of the American Express Company had received on 2 July, an order to pay Buschman £50 on account of H. Flores. For the purposes of prosecution it was important to establish the identity of Grund. During July 1915, MO5g obtained some evidence of proof that Grund was a German agent; it was certain that another spy – Augusto Roggen – had written to him from Scotland. Enquiries made in Holland showed that Grund was a German, an inspector of a German navigation company who had no fixed address but lived on a tramp steamer in the harbour, and received his letters at the office of Ivers and von Staa. Von Staa was an officer of the German Reserve. The Summary of Evidence was taken on 18 August. Buschman was tried by Court Martial on 28 September. He was charged on four counts under DRR48; he was found guilty of three of the charges: of committing preparatory acts to collecting and communicating information in contravention of DRR18. The charge of attempting to elicit information was not proved. He was sentenced to death and was shot on 19 October 1915.[1]

Roggen

Alfredo Augusto Roggen, a Uruguayan, whose permanent residence was stated to be Montevideo, landed at Gravesend on 30 May 1915, and travelled to London, sending a telegram to Flores in Rotterdam asking for funds. Roggen travelled as a farmer and approached a London firm with a view to buying horses to the value of £3,600, and a firm in Lincoln on the subject of agricultural machinery for importation into Uruguay after the war. But he had no letters of introduction and did not pursue the business after his one call. He was in Lincoln on the night of 4 June; on the 5th he reached Edinburgh and put up at the Carlton Hotel, where Mrs Wertheim had been on 28 May. He went to the police to register on 6 June, spent the whole of Monday touring the Trossachs, and completed his registration at Edinburgh on 8 June. He went to the Tarbet Hotel on the 9th meaning to stay for eight or nine days, his excuse being his health and a desire for quiet fishing. Tarbet lay within two miles of Loch Long, which was then in use as a torpedo station and a prohibited area. On the evening of 8 June, Roggen posted two cards in Edinburgh, one addressed to Flores, the other to Grund. He announced that he had found a pretty place for fishing and walking in the mountains and to Grund he gave his address as Tarbet Hotel, Loch Lomond. Each card contained a message for 'his girl'. The cards were intercepted and Roggen was arrested five hours after reaching Tarbet. He was interviewed and gave an unsatisfactory account of his relations with Flores, whom he described as a friend of his partner in South America.

The addresses found in Roggen's notebook showed 'refinements of precaution': 127 Binnemveg was half crossed out and written so close beneath the words Consulado del Uruguay as to seem to be the address of the Consulate in Amsterdam. The incorrect form Ipers and von Staa was written immediately below a bogus address in Gainsborough. On a sheet of blotting paper was found a partly legible name which was taken to be 'G. BRECK(O)W.' A connection between Breckow and Roggen was never established but it was noted that Roggen had stayed at the Bonnington Hotel and within easy reach of Breckow, who was then at the Ivanhoe Hotel, London; and in Edinburgh, Roggen had put up in the hotel visited by Mrs Wertheim. A scent bottle and antiseptic talcum powder were found among Roggen's effects and secret writing was developed on several of his papers. But the most important discovery of all was a map of the North Sea torn from a Dutch railway guide, on which some minute characters, words and figures were detected, as well as stains of oil. The tester, however, pointed out the difficulty of obtaining results that would satisfy the untrained eye that such marks were anything else than stains in the fibre and added that the Germans had probably relied upon this effect in choosing the method. But to satisfy the strictest requirements of proof the expert carried out his test in the presence of other witnesses, and also carried out negative tests that proved similar reactions would not be obtained by treating the unmarked fibre of the paper in the same manner.[2]

Roggen was tried by Court Martial. He faced four charges, all under DDR 48: the first two related to 'Doing an act preparatory to the commission of an act prohibited by these regulations, namely – an act preparatory to collecting and recording without lawful authority, information which might be useful to the enemy...' on or about 30 May and 9 June 1915; the second two charges referred to 'Doing an act preparatory... to communicating without lawful authority information intended to be communicated to the enemy' on 8 June and being in the possession of the address of H. Flores and A Grund, both persons 'concerned in the communication of information to the enemy'.[3] After the prosecution and defence counsels had pleaded their cases, Roggen realised the desperate position he was in. He wrote to the Court Martial claiming that he had only found out from his solicitor, at the end of the proceedings, that 'there were no evidences against me and that I just as well not go to the witness box... It was a mistake that I did not speak, because I thought my solicitor was still going to speak'. The alleged spy used his letter to contest some of the evidence presented to the court, adding: 'There are so many agents for Germany in Holland... it is hard luck for me to have been in communication with [one of them in] Holland.'[4]

The Court Martial, however, found Roggen 'guilty of all the charges' and, by a sentence signed on 20 August 1915, sentenced him to suffer 'death by being shot'. The King confirmed the sentence.[5] Roggen was removed from Wandsworth Detention Barrack to the Tower of London early on the morning of 9 September. The sentence was to be carried out early on the morning of 10 September.[6] But this was not the end of the matter, for Roggen fought an increasingly desperate campaign to avoid death. When the Uruguayan Minister in London was informed by Sir Arthur Nicolson, of the Foreign Office, of the outcome of the trial he pleaded, on behalf of the prisoner, with Lord Kitchener, for clemency:

> The life of a man is at stake; I do not permit myself to doubt for one instant the legality or the correctness of the sentence that has been passed; on the other hand, from the reading, which only now I have been able to make, of the proceedings, it appears beyond doubt that Roggen had been sentenced to the capital punishment merely on suspicions. Indeed if your Excellency takes the trouble to read the… declarations made by the witnesses for the prosecution, your Excellency will see that there is not a single one of them, not one, which formulates a concrete charge. And your Excellency will also see that they are all of absolute vacuity. Neither the detectives nor the witnesses say aught that is not either a vulgarity or a suspicion without the support of any proof whatsoever… As there is no proof whatever, and only conjectures, is it not a cruel and excessive punishment to apply the death penalty merely on suspicion? I have the highest idea of the rectitude of English judges and I would never venture to question their opinions.
>
> Only the impression of the present moment, of the cruelty that is in the atmosphere in which we live today can have brought about the irrevocable penalty for mere suspicions.
>
> Where is the proof to be found? It does not appear from anything in the proceedings. No neutral foreigner who may happen to come from Holland, from Spain, or from any other nation, can have failed to come in contact, in any of those nations, with enemies of the Allies, who swarm everywhere, be they Germans or Dutch or Spaniards. But, if such meetings may lend themselves to suspicion, they do not in themselves constitute crime if they are not accompanied by acts which prove that spying is being carried on or prohibited information being transmitted … Sir, an honourable family would suffer the shame of seeing one of its member condemned to death, to a debasing penalty, without single proof to justify such a terrible sentence. The last penalty should only be applied, according to Spanish legislation, when the proofs are 'as clear as the light of day'… A penalty of

military prison would be sufficient for a case of suspicion and that is what I ask for a special mercy for the undeniable rectitude and high minded criterion of the judges of His Britannic Majesty in these cruel circumstances.[7]

Kitchener rejected the Minister's plea. Instead, the diplomat was informed by the War Office that Roggen had arrived in Britain with 'a fictitious address in the sense that it was an address which was not entitled to use' and the use of which was 'suspicious and unnatural'. He had given explanations of his business in Britain that were 'in many respects contradictory and none of which were supported in evidence'. His movements were 'extremely suspicious' and culminated in a visit to a restricted area. Roggen, it was pointed out, was in correspondence 'on terms of intimacy' with two known German agents whom he was careful to keep informed of his movements; his explanation of his relationship with these agents was 'inadequate, highly improbable, sometimes contradictory, and unsupported by evidence documentary or oral'; if the prisoner had been able to furnish an explanation to the these facts 'he would have done so.'[8]

Roggen made one last desperate and pathetic attempt to save his life, writing another letter stating: 'I like the English character and the soldiers specifically.'[9] It was, of course, to no avail. The sentence of death was now to be carried out on 17 September.[10] On that day the GOC London District informed Lord Kitchener that 'the sentence of death passed upon AUGUSTO ALFREDO ROGGEN was carried out at 6am... death was instantaneous'.[11] There was now little sympathy from the Minister of Uruguay who knew members of the rich and well-esteemed family of the Roggens back home, but who did not know Alfredo Augusto, and declared that both he himself and the Roggens thought Alfredo Augusto a thief and a liar.[12]

Hurwitz y Zender

Ludovic Hurwitz y Zender, a Peruvian, went in December 1914 from Peru to New York, sailing for Christiania on 18 February 1915. He landed at Newcastle on 11 April, reached Glasgow on the 12th, and on the 13th took up residence at Duncan's Temperance Hotel. On the 20th he spent the night at Aberdeen and from the 21st to the 24th, stayed at Inverness returning to Glasgow on 24 April. On 25 May he left Glasgow and sailed for Bergen from Newcastle on the 28th. In Glasgow he reportedly led a quiet life, walking the golf links with the manager of the hotel and going twice down the Clyde on a Sunday, but not appearing to have any business or friends. Early in June, MO5g asked for a scrutiny to be made of all telegrams sent during May from certain ports in the Kingdom. Five telegrams sent by Ludovic Hurwitz, from Glasgow, between 15 and 24 May to August Brockner (or Brochner) of 11 Todboldgatan, Christiania, attracted the notice of code experts. Ostensibly they were orders for different classes of tinned fish goods, but the wording of the messages varied suspiciously and they were written in a manner that resembled the arbitrary codes used by Roos and Janssen. From the Chief Constable of Glasgow it was learned that Hurwitz y Zender had left the country meaning to return in a few weeks.[13]

MO5g, having obtained a description of Hurwitz y Zender, circulated it to the ports with orders for his arrest and rigorous search, impressing that it was essential that the utmost secrecy should be observed. Neither the public nor press were to know of any arrest. On 2 July, Hurwitz attempted to land at Newcastle, was arrested and brought to Scotland Yard. Among other papers was a hotel bill showing that he had been to Copenhagen and a catalogue and price list of tinned fish and several tins of samples of these goods. He carried £84 in notes and £5 in gold and had, among other objects, twelve new handkerchiefs and a bottle of medicine. Hurwitz declared he was travelling for the firm of T. Vidal, General Importers of Lima, and that through the General Agent, August Brockner, he had bought fish on their behalf. He was to have purchased handkerchiefs at Glasgow and various kinds of goods at Sheffield yet he had done no business in Britain owing to the lack of specific instructions, which he had expected but had not received by post. An agent from Cumming's Secret Intelligence Service (SIS) – which was now solely responsible for overseas intelligence gathering and espionage – was sent to Christiania to ascertain the facts about Brockner, shadowed the man and saw him deliver a large envelope at the private house of the German Ambassador. Brockner was also said to be in daily touch with the German Consulate and to be organising German counter-espionage in Christiania. The firm of T. Vidal, Lima, did exist but it had no standing or credit and was connected with the Germans. It imported goods through travellers from Manchester and the Continent. Eventually, the whole correspondence between Hurwitz and Brockner was obtained, as were five earlier telegrams sent from Glasgow to Aberdeen in April and early May. This correspondence was submitted to an expert in the fish trade. Hurwitz was ordering and Brockner transmitting his orders for fish out of season and in wrong quantities and packings. A summary of evidence had been taken in August but the trial was delayed owing to the necessity of getting documents from Peru.

Hurwitz was tried by Court Martial during 20, 21 and 22 March 1916, and was condemned to death on four charges under DRR section

48: of having twice committed a preparatory act in coming to Britain on 11 April and 2 July and of having twice attempted to communicate information by sending a telegram on 15 and on 20 May. These two telegrams, when deciphered, were found to contain accurate information with regard to ships in the Firth of Forth. Hurwitz was shot on 11 April 1916. Three points were worth noticing: Brockner, the General Agent, had only one type of goods in his office at Christiania, which was ties; Hurwitz carried one dozen new handkerchiefs and a bottle of medicine which was afterwards found to be Protargol. During 1916, it was discovered that Protargol was a medium for secret writing and that ties and handkerchiefs were being used by the Germans as vehicles for these mediums.[14]

Ries

The true identity of the spy who was arrested and executed under the name of Irving Guy Ries was not satisfactorily cleared up until after his sentence. The real person of that name received a passport from the Department of State, Washington on 10 March 1915; he was to visit Holland, Austria, Germany, Switzerland, Italy, France and Great Britain. His mission was to take photographs for the Newspaper Enterprise Association in Chicago. Ries was impersonated by a man named Paul Hensel who landed at Liverpool on 4 July with a forged passport dated 20 March to travel in Holland and Denmark; his ostensible mission was to collect new clients in Great Britain and elsewhere for three American firms, two of which dealt in hay and corn. He registered at Liverpool, stating he was going to London. However, he initially bypassed the capital and travelled to Newcastle, Glasgow and Edinburgh, returning to Liverpool and arriving in London on 28 July. Between the 28th and 31st he went to Brighton, returning afterwards to town. On his tour in the North, he visited only three or four firms, and he approached a few others by letter after leaving the localities in which they were situated. In no case did he do any business. On 8 August, he booked a passage from Hull to Copenhagen and approached the American Consulate for a visa to get his permit. The American Consulate discovered the forgery and impounded the passport. Ries seems to have destroyed incriminating documents in expectation of his arrest, which took place on 10 August.

Meanwhile, he had been the object of enquiry since 5 August. On the 3rd the GPO had reported that he had received £20 by Telegraphic Money Order from Madame Cleton, Rotterdam and the sum was suspect. This report was followed by news from Rotterdam that a telephone message passing between German GHQ Wesel and the German Consulate Rotterdam had been tapped and decoded. It conveyed instructions to pay Madame Cleton, 72 Provenierstraat, Rotterdam, certain sums of money for the mission of Irwin Guy Ries, Hotel Cecil, and to continue to pay a tenth of this sum weekly. 72 Provenierstraat was a known address of Sanderson/Dierks and had been on check since May 1915. Madame Cleton was a name assumed by Sanderson's wife when her husband was taken into custody by the Dutch. No doubt existed as to Ries's connections and the wording of the message induced the belief that he was responsible for the destruction of Ardeer Factory, which blew up on the 30/31 July, 1915 (this was afterwards proved not to be the work of an enemy agent, but an accident).[15] The telephone interception and the other details were not revealed at the subsequent Court Martial.

After Ries's arrest MO5g traced his connections in the United States. Of the three firms mentioned by him two were genuine but he did not represent either of them although he had applied to do so. A partner in one of these firms 'seemed nervous' when he was interviewed. The third firm of Wackerow-Belcher did not exist but a man named Richard Wackerow was traced. This man stated that he had been an American Consul in Austria for eleven years and admitted knowing Ries, who was in the grain, wheat and flour business in Chicago, but refused to say more and avoided an office interview, which he himself had arranged. Money Orders received by and for Ries were as follows:

10th July: £40.
31st July: £20. Before arrest.
3rd Aug: £20.
16th Aug: £40.
21st Aug: £30. After arrest.
21st Aug: £39 10s.

Ries was charged with committing an act preparatory to spying and collecting information without lawful authority; of having been in communication with a spy; of having being found in possession of a false passport; and having falsely represented himself to be a person to whom a passport had been duly issued.[16] After he was arrested Ries was interrogated by Major Drake from MO5g, Basil Thompson, the Assistant Chief Constable of the Metropolitan Police, Captain Hall RN and Lord Herschell. He mysteriously admitted that 'Irving Guy Ries is not my correct name. I cannot say what my name is as my people on the other side are respectable and I would like to give them away.' He claimed that he was an American of Dutch and Scottish descent, and explained his false passport: 'You can buy false forged American passports in the streets in New York. I was standing in a bar of a saloon in New York one day, when two fellows approached me. I got into conversation with them, and they were boasting that they had been on the Continent travelling with false passports. There were four of us present, and the outcome of our conversation was that a wager was made that one of us should travel on the Continent with a false passport, and we tossed up and I had to go.' He also admitted knowledge of a man in Rotterdam – Cleton – that he called his friend; he accepted that a money order had been sent to him in the name of Madame Cleton but added: 'If you think that I am a German spy you must have got scared.'[17]

Later Ries, having thought over the matter, wrote out a paper in which he stated: 'The reason of my travelling under a false passport is that the Police of the United States of America are wanting me, and therefore I had to dock out from under, but I have never done any spying.' He claimed not to know why the police wanted him; but claimed that he was no spy and was unofficially representing a number of firms in the corn trade. However, the prosecution at the subsequent Court Martial observed: 'It was a curious thing, if this is a genuine story, that these firms, if they knew it, should have allowed themselves to be represented here by a man with a false name, with a forged passport, who admitted that he was a fugitive from justice, but for what offence he did not know.' By the opening of the Court Martial, Ries was argu-ing: 'I am guilty, but not guilty with a view to assist the enemy,' and stating that he had only been evasive because he was connected with diamond smugglers in the United States – Cleton was, in fact, involved in this illegal trade. His defence counsel argued that, although Cleton was believed to be spy, and there was no doubt that Ries had received money from Cleton, there was 'not a tittle of evidence' – as Major Drake had admitted to the court; furthermore, there was not any cor-respondence in the form of letters, or information being conveyed to Cleton from Ries or from Cleton to Ries beyond the money sent.

The problem for Ries was that the Defence of the Realm Regulations placed the onus on him to prove his innocence and not the prosecu-tion to prove his guilt. The relevant regulation did not say that for a person to be guilty of this offence the prosecution had to prove that he had known that the address was that of a spy but, on the contrary, it stated: 'A person shall, unless he proves to the contrary, be deemed to be in communication with a spy if the name or address, or any other information regarding a spy is found in his possession.' That is 'the onus that is cast on him, to satisfy the Court he did not know that this was the address of a spy that he was communicating with.'[18] Given this, and a not very convincing cover story, it was no surprise that the Court Martial found Ries 'guilty of all the charges'. He was tried by Court Martial and sentenced to death on 5 October. He was shot on 27 October.[19]

Rosenthal

The third group of spies dealt with by MO5g, in 1915, consisted of a number of agents who were sent out apparently by either the Berlin Centre, or by another centre, which was not identified. The first of these was Robert Rosenthal, a German, who made three journeys to Britain on behalf of Captain von Prieger, Chief of the Admiralty Secret Service in Berlin. It is very probable that this was the same Berger whose presence became known to MO5g owing to their enquiry as to cheques paid into German banks, still based in Britain, from abroad. In the middle of November 1914 he came to London via The Hague and Folkestone with orders to go to Plymouth, Portsmouth, Weymouth, Dover, Grimsby and Newcastle. He sent telegrams from London on 19 and 23 November, which gave information about ships at Edinburgh and Portsmouth. He embarked for Holland at Folkestone on 11 December after staying at Portsmouth from 4 to 7 December, 1914. On 9 January 1915, he arrived at Hull from Copenhagen, wiring on the 9th and 11th news about His Majesty's ships. From Hull he went to Newcastle and Liverpool, where he embarked on the 16th and went via Cardiff to Spain and Italy, and so to Germany. For these two journeys he used the cover address: George Haeffner, Christiania, Kirkegatan. 20.

A third journey took place in mid April again via Copenhagen and Hull. He went to London, Birmingham, Glasgow and Edinburgh sending wires to: Salomon, Vestervoldgade 10, Copenhagen, from those cities on 22 April, 5 May and 11 May respectively and letters on 9, 10 and 11 May.

The story of Rosenthal's passports was complicated. From 1908 to 1913 Rosenthal was in the USA having left Germany on account of forgery. He returned to Germany in November 1913. In June 1914 Rosenthal had urgent reasons for wishing to leave Germany and with the connivance of a friend in Hamburg he had managed to obtain a consular certificate of American nationality. With this he was able to successfully apply for an emergency passport in Berlin, where for a time he worked for the Relief Commission. In October he was sent to The Hague to get a genuine American passport, but he was given instead a consular certificate and an affidavit to say he had lost his passport. In Berlin he was given a new emergency passport. With this he made his two first journeys to Britain but on the second occasion it seems to have aroused suspicion at Newcastle and he was frightened enough to leave Britain. For the third journey he obtained a passport issued at Washington on 26 January 1915. Von Prieger had shown him apparatus for fabricating American documents and had offered him a passport and a birth certificate, but these he had refused. Rosenthal's ostensible reason for coming in November and January was to dispose of a patent with regard to smoking. His arrest on the third journey was due to a 'happy accident'.

On 8 April, Rosenthal wrote from the Hotel Bristol, Copenhagen, to Franz Kulbe, Berlin Schöneberg, Belzigerstrasse 10, sending him a letter containing a secret message to the effect that he was going to start work in England under pretext of selling a patent gas lighter. He signed his letter 'Robert Rosenthal'. The letter somehow ended up in England, where the censor thought the *en clair* message suspicious, tested it and found the secret message. The letter was submitted to MO5, the head of which section handed it on to MO5g on 3 May. The address of Franz Kulbe was already known as that of Captain von Prieger, and orders were at once issued for the arrest of any traveller in a patent gas lighter. Late at night on 11 May, Rosenthal was arrested when he tried to embark at Newcastle for Bergen. On being interrogated and led to admit the facts of his passage at Copenhagen, Rosenthal was then confronted with his letter when he immediately gave up the fight and confessed his true nationality and mission. Among Rosenthal's effects were found *Fleets of the World 1915*, a new map of Glasgow, a Scottish road book, field glasses, some flags, Eau de Cologne and Violet Powder. He had been given 2,500 marks to last until the middle of May. Of this £100 was in gold. Five of Rosenthal's telegrams dated 19, 23 November, 9 & 11 January and 16 April, were produced in evidence and proved to contain substantially accurate information of value to the enemy. He was Court-Martialed on 6 July, found guilty, and was hanged on the 16th.[20]

Marks

Josef Marks carried an American emergency passport, which had been issued in Berlin on 1 February 1915, without the production of any identification papers but on the personal identification of American Consul Thompson and Vice-Consul Heinrich Guadflieg both of Aix-la-Chapelle. The passport bore the following visas:

Aachen Police 12-2-15.
Rotterdam, German Consulate 15-6-15.
Object: journey to England.
The Hague, American Legation 21-6-15.
Object: journey to England.
The Hague, British Consulate 15-7-15.
Object: business with the Safety Chemical Co., 1 Eagle St. High
Holborn.

The American Minister at The Hague believed the passport to be a forgery and warned the British Consulate; on 25 June, SIS in Rotterdam reported that Marks was coming to England as an independent spy sent out by GHQ Berlin. Orders were issued to the ports for his arrest, search and conveyance to Scotland Yard. He was signalled as crossing on 15 July. When recognised and accosted on the boat by police constable Billett he at once asked to see an Intelligence Officer to whom he said he would give important information. He added that he was being shadowed by a German agent. In various interviews he gave the following story: he was born in Germany but was educated in the States and became an American citizen. He returned to Germany, married and set up in business there. In August 1914 he and his wife were arrested by the Germans and after pressure he entered the German Secret Service. He was trained by the Antwerp Bureau, had to make two trial trips to Holland and then was allowed a short holiday in Germany. He was coming to England to find out about munitions, was to use a book of stamps as code and received £45 for the trip. He decided to give information to the British authorities and on the way over wrote a letter to the Minister of Munitions. The letter was actually written on the ship's notepaper and was delivered up by Marks. The code book and about £37 and letters that he had written from prison in Germany to the military authorities to complain of his treatment were found, as well as a registration certificate proving that he was born at Munich and was a civil engineer. Investigation proved that Marks was in all probability a German subject, as he had once possessed American citizenship but had allowed it to lapse. Moreover, he was identified as Multerer, the former fraudulent managing director of the Safety Chemical Company, who had lived in England as a German subject from 1911 to about June 1913 and had left owing many debts. While in residence in Britain, Multerer had business notepaper printed for his wife under the name of Marks, and had visited Germany two or three times a year.

Marks was charged under DRR18 and 48, with an act preparatory to committing an offence, i.e. embarking upon and voyaging to Tilbury in the ship with intention to act as a spy. The question was, at what precise moment had he abandoned that intention and how sincere was he in confessing? During his detention Marks once more asked to see an Intelligence Officer. Two officers went to the prison but Marks then refused to give any information. A month later he offered to obtain the formulae for a new gas and its reagent now being used by the Germans at the Front. Yet there was still some doubt as to his willingness in his spying enterprise, which probably spared him from paying the ultimate penalty. He was tried by Court Martial on 28 September 1915 and was sentenced to five years' penal servitude. In December 1919 he was deported.[21]

Melin

Ernest Waldemar Melin, a Swede, and the son of a former managing owner of the Thule Steamship Company had been for many years manager of that company. He left it in 1906 and after 'some years of idleness' obtained a post at Nikolaieff, which he was forced to leave on account of the war. He went to Hamburg, was recruited for the German Secret Service by Dierks and was engaged by the Antwerp Centre. Melin came to Britain about 12 January 1915, spent a fortnight in London and returned to Holland on 29 January. The Antwerp Bureau insisted that he should make the round of the English and Scottish ports but this he refused to do. He was then taken on by the Wesel Bureau at a salary of £50 a month. He was sent to London on or about 26 February with instructions to report to a Katie Smith, Huize St Joseph, Lent near Nijmegen. His reports were made on the fifth page of a newspaper. Between 2 March and 12 June, he sent off twenty-nine such reports. Melin had also a telegraphic code in which the names of Dutch banks stood for various classes of ships, which he had had to learn by heart. His salary was paid by cheques forwarded by Schwedersky & Co and drawn on the Union of London and Smith's Bank, on the strength of an advice letter from the Rotterdamsche Bank-vereeniging. These cheques were dated 15 March, 12 April, 22 May. Other cheques dated 15 June and 12 July were paid by the Banque Belge pour l'Etranger, acting for S. van Dantzig. The three first cheques were cashed by the British and Northern Shipping Agency at the request of Melin.

On 16 March, MO5g were told, via an informant, that E.W. Melin, 23 Upper Parkway, Hampstead, was attached to the German Secret Service. The check put on his name resulted in the intercepting of Schwedersky's cheque on 15 April. Enquiries were then made at Melin's address and it was ascertained that he was living at a boarding house, was fond of drink, went to the City every day, and spent the afternoons at the Café Monico. On 12 June, two envelopes, which had been posted at Tilbury, were intercepted and found to contain three letters signed 'Kate' and addressed to Melin. In secret writing, hidden between the lines of these seemingly affectionate family letters were pertinent questions about British ships. The house was searched: a bottle of lemon juice, a pen and tooth-picks were found as well as a Baedeker guide, with the names of various British ports and hotels marked in pencil. Also between the pages of an English and Swedish dictionary was a slip of paper bearing the name of some regiments and other military terms. Besides these, Melin had four other dictionaries.

Melin was arrested on 14 June and was interviewed on the 15th. He acknowledged having received money through Schwedersky of Rotterdam. Schwedersky was already known to MO5g as a German agent. Efforts were made to trace Melin at the ports but without avail; he declared he had never left London. The letters of 12 June had not been delivered to him, but it was important that he should acknowledge they were for him. On 26 July, he was shown the envelopes of the letters containing the cheques of 15 June and 12 July. He asserted that he was expecting a cheque from Rotterdam. Melin was then shown the envelopes and the signature of the three letters containing secret writing; these also he acknowledged as being meant for him. The letters were then unfolded and the secret writing, which had been developed, stood revealed. Melin confessed his connection with the German Secret Service. He signed a receipt for the cheques and the money was impounded by the War Office.[22] During his interrogation he gave an insight into how, after losing his employment in Germany due to the war, he ended up as a spy:

I had to go to Hamburg. I have had friends at Hamburg for years. I went there and was at Hamburg for 2 months, left at the end of December [1914]. I could not get employment. All my friends had left. My father always helped me… My father then said – you shall not look forward to further help. One day at the end of December I got a letter from an old friend of mine asking me asking me if I could come and have lunch, which I accepted. There was another gentleman there… That gentleman said – I hear you have nothing to do. I am a friend of your old friend. I cannot tell you his name… He does not always go under the same name always. I think he was introduced as Diercks. He said I cannot talk to you about it here. He went to his office and into his private room. He said… I live at Rotterdam and work for the German Secret Service… I have been over to Sweden and I want to try and find someone, and I now hear from my relations you have nothing to do. Will you entertain this?

I was first perplexed. My father had refused me money. I said I will let you know the next day. I did not know what to do. I said to him he shall call on me where I live and I stated I accept... and we went together to Antwerp... to their branch office and then everything was fixed I should go to London... I wrote to my father the first time I went. I told him I left Hamburg and had an offer from an old friend of mine to look after some private things in England. I told him I came back and had a second offer, which I did not want to accept, but I wanted to go home and asked my father to send me money... He refused money: wrote a postcard to say that he had done what he could and I must help myself.

Then I accepted the second offer... At last I telegraphed to Dierks and said I accepted the work. He wrote, your letter just received, come to Wesel and I will have the money there... I... went to Wessel. Then people say I hear you have been working for the Antwerp people, it is better to work with us. You will go to London and live in London only if you wish. They gave me money for the trip and for the first month... Then he said to me you must have a code if you need to telegraph. The code only contains how many ships in the harbour or going to leave the harbour. So they gave me a code. I had to learn it by heart... About this code. They say to me, I shall buy a Baedaker, which I bought. If you have seen the Baedaker have you noticed anything about it.[sic] You have noticed marks on the index, spots, etc; if you refer in the Baedaker about different ports and places[,] hotels are mentioned. You notice there are two spots to 5 ports, because they said to me these five ports were of special interest. The code is made up – did you see that small note book, did you notice something about bankers A and R [sic] A = Amsterdam and R = Rotterdam, four bankers under each of them.[sic]

Those in the 1st row mean Dreadnoughts; 2nd row mean Pre-Dreadnoughts; 3rd row mean Cruisers and 4th row mean Transports.

and if, I, for instance, telegraphed to them – Please pay at your convenience, for example £50 to Y Potteramache first row, £100 to Y Amaterdamache 4th row, payment £40 Rotterdamache and £60 Rotterdamache must be effectuated latest (date) all correspondence to – hotel.

The name of the hotel refers to the port; at your convenience means lies

£50 = five Dreadnoughts – £100 = ten transports
Payment must be effectuated, etc, means 4 Dreadnoughts and 6
Cruisers leaving the harbour on the date given...

I do not know anything else to tell you. I can't understand,
I know nothing about Naval matters. I hope you will consider
and not make it too difficult for me. I went into the whole thing
to make a living and to send harmless things... My brother is a
Colonel in the Swedish Army. Although he is an officer I know
nothing about military things, I could not tell you the difference
between a Dreadnought and a Cruiser – I haven't the slightest
idea.[23]

Melin was tried on the charges of having twice come to England with
intent to collect information, of having in his possession lemon juice for
the purpose of unlawful communication of naval and military information, and of having attempted to collect information by recording
the names of units of His Majesty's Forces. The Summary of Evidence
was taken on 4 August; tried by Court Martial on 20 and 21 August,
Melin was found guilty and was shot on 10 September 1915.[24]

Meyer

At the end of June 1915 the Censor 'took exception' to a note written
on one side of the sheet and referring vaguely to business and a journey that might take place in a fortnight's time. Posted in London, this
letter was addressed to Mrs Goedhardt, 147 von Blankenburgestraat,
The Hague. The Censor ironed the back and discovered a secret message conveying information about the Thames Defences, Chatham
Dockyard and so forth. A 'first' letter was also referred to. The address
was put on check for letters and telegrams on 2 July and was circulated
to all ports, with instructions to arrest any traveller on whom it was
found. On 13 July, a postcard containing another secret message and
addressed to the same street and house but to the name Niendecker,
(spelt also Niendieker and Niendikker), was intercepted. It was signed
Lopez. The signatures of the first letter, e.g. 'van Nordensund' and 'Sven
Person' were interpreted as: 'Your worker from the north' and MO5g's
investigation started on the theory that the writer was a Scandinavian
sailor. At the same time enquiries in Holland established the existence
at the address of a man named T. Niendiker, and that Goedhardt was
an alias. The clue of the signature proved to some extent false, but on
the 20th another letter in the same handwriting and also containing
information was intercepted. It was signed 'Belmonte' and bore the
address 28 Greek Street. Both signature and address were false. Finally

a type-written letter, headed 1 Margaret Street, and signed 'Tommy' begging for a remittance of £50 resulted in tracing the writer. The police called at the address, discovered that a man and his wife lodging there had not yet filled up their registration form, gained access to the room and identified the handwriting on a label as that of the writer of the letters. Albert Meyer and Katherine, his wife, were arrested on 30 August.

Meyer, by turn a hotel waiter, cook, tailor, commercial traveller, was in all probability a German. He claimed to have been born in Constantinople of Danish parents, but the Danish Embassy subsequently could find no trace of his birth. Everything about Meyer was false; in business and in the lodging he used the alias Marcelle, and for business purposes he gave 96 Shaftesbury Avenue, as an address and received post there. Among his papers, testimonials of his work as a waiter, dating from September 1910 to August 1914 were discovered, but these did not agree with the records of his movements recorded in the books of the Geneva Association, of which he was a member. From these records, it would appear that Meyer came to Britain from Hamburg on 25 August, 1911, went on 14 March 1912 to Harrogate and returned on 22 August to London. On 17 October he took his membership book saying he was going to Spain and returned to London on 6 June 1914, claiming he had come from Nice. On 24 July he took his book saying he was going to India, but it would appear he went instead to Blackpool. On 10 August he brought his book back but fetched it away again on 20 March 1915, saying he was going to Copenhagen. The testimonials in Meyer's possession contained no reference to his first visit to England but showed that he had been in Seville, Spain, from October 1911 to June 1913, and in Pamplona from July 1913 to May 1914.

Only these facts were certain: early in August, Meyer was stopped at Folkestone as he was trying to embark and detained as a German. He was interned until 25 or 29 September when he succeeded in convincing the authorities that he was an Ottoman subject. He came to London and with Katherine Gray took a room at 40 Albany Street. He stated then that he was receiving thirty shillings a week from his father. In March he applied for a permit to go to work with his father who owned, he said, the Hotel Bristol, Copenhagen. He produced a birth certificate and the application was granted. But he never got further than Holland, from where he wrote postcards to Katherine Gray asking her to collect some correspondence from an address in the Haymarket. She wrote to him on 14 April asking him to return. He came back on 13 May, married her on the 20th and was turned out of his lodging owing to their joint misconduct on the 26th. He then moved to 134 Albany Street, although he had stated he was going to Edinburgh as a waiter. On 20 July, the Meyers moved to 1 Margaret Street.

Meyer had registered under the National Registration Act giving his occupation as a traveller. Various items were found to be in his possession: a letter of appointment as a picture vendor made out to J.Smit by a genuine firm of printers in Amsterdam; a letter of appointment as a cigar vendor together with other letters from the Amsterdamsche Sigarenfabrick of van Hulst; a letter from Siegfried Meyer, who purported to be his father, from the Hotel Bristol, Copenhagen; a catalogue of various brands of cigars; blotting paper which seemed to have been that used in writing the letter signed Tommy; and scent, three pens, and a small bottle of green ink with a small brush. A search of receipts for money orders disclosed the fact that on 23 July, Meyer had received £10 by telegraphic order from van Yselmuide, 13 Sleephellingstr., The Hague; after his arrest sums of £40, £10 and £50 were sent by Niendiker. Meyer was charged on 5 November with having attempted to communicate information; with having used secret ink; and with having attempted to communicate with a spy. At the trial, evidence was given that Meyer had sent correct information and that F. Niendiker was a wholesale tobacconist at Nieuwe Haven, Rotterdam, who resided at 147 van Blankenburgstraat, The Hague, and was in touch with The Hague Secret Service. As regarded secret writing it would seem that Meyer confined himself to the use of lemon juice, but that he had the materials for developing another process, which was doubtless the one in use by his employers. He was found guilty of all charges and was sentenced to death. He was shot on 2 December 1915. There was no evidence against Katherine Meyer, 'but she was a woman of bad morals' and it was thought that Meyer had obtained some of his information through her associations. She had been released from prison before Meyer's trial, but as she failed to notify her change of address she was again arrested and sentenced to three weeks imprisonment; in December she was recommended for internment. The order was made in January 1916, and upheld by the Advisory Committee. Eventually she was removed to a lunatic asylum.[25]

German Methods, Organisation and Agents

As MO5g reviewed their spy cases, a number of patterns appeared. It seems that Mrs Wertheim was the first spy sent out by the German's Admiralstab Zweigstelle spy centre at Antwerp. Mrs Wertheim's connection with Miss Brandes formed a link between the pre-war and the war organisation of the German Secret Service, for in February

1912, Miss Brandes had been in close touch with Heddy Glauer, wife of Heinrich Grosse; Glauer, in making this confession, insinuated that Miss Brandes and her sister Mrs. Claassen were at that time engaged in work for espionage purposes. In 1915, however, MO5g knew nothing of such contacts, but they rightly esteemed Miss Brandes to be a dangerous agent. Miss Brandes was then working for Baron Bruno von Schroeder in connection with his charitable efforts. Other agents of the Antwerp Branch who came early to England were Melin and Janssen. Melin afterwards transferred to the Wesel Branch, but Janssen's visit was especially interesting since it seemed to have marked a turning point in the development of German methods.

Up until May 1915, Lizzie Wertheim worked for Dr Brandt who was reported as living at Dordrecht, and concerning whom nothing more seems to be known except that early in May, he wrote to her from 166 Loosduinschekade, The Hague, which connected him with characters such as Dierks, Grund, Hochenholz, van Brandwijk, Vollrath and Ritzkey. Of these men only four, e.g. Heinrich Grund, German, Carl Ritzkey, Russian and van Brandwijk, Dutch and Henrich Flores, German, appeared on the Antwerp List of German agents, which had been secured by British Intelligence. They were respectively agents A1; A19; A51 and A68. Sanderson/Dierks might possibly have been connected with agent A2 viz: C. Shroeder, a German agent in Hamburg, who was described as very intelligent, energetic and the introducer of many agents and confidential agents.

Hilmar Dierks's part was to recruit and equip the agents sent out and to maintain correspondence with them. From early April 1915 onwards, telegraphic money orders seem to have been sent by Dierks. Dierks was arrested by the Dutch Government in June 1915 and his wife carried on the work of paymaster under the name of Madame Cleton. In May, Flores seems to have joined the business. He was a teacher in the German School at Rotterdam, a war invalid who had returned to his pre-war occupation. Later on he was said to have taken the alias Frank and to have lived at Zwaardecroonstraat. He was in daily touch with the German Consulate at Rotterdam. Heinrich Grund became known to MO5g through his connection with the spies Buschman and Roggen. Grund, who had lived in Antwerp before the war, was entered on the Antwerp roll as A1 with the note that he was a very reliable, successful and clever worker. His special mission was to place his agents on ships coming to Britain and to examine them as to what they had seen on the journey. He also kept watch on the shipping in Rotterdam harbour and reported the movements of shipping off the Dutch coast by wireless to Hamburg. He was said by this means to have brought about the capture of the S.S. *Brussels* by the Germans. In 1916, Grund moved to Utrecht and opened a motor business there. Hochenholz was another German agent also interested in shipping and he was known to Janssen. His name did not appear on the Antwerp roll but possibly he was identical with A21 i.e. 'GLEICHMANN Emil, engaged in Enquiry Service in Rotterdam, Captain in the Mercantile Marine, educated, reliable and very capable'. Jan van Brandwijk was entered in the List as A51; he was a Dutch casual labourer who had met with an accident and had been compensated by the Dutch Government. His entry on the roll gave the following note: 'Enquiry Service at Rotterdam. Uneducated but very diligent. Good connections in shipping circles, mostly among the employees. Very pro-German.'

The Dierks 'gang' was broken up by the Dutch Government in the autumn of 1915. Dierks, who in August had been acquitted of the charge of endangering Dutch neutrality by inciting young men to do espionage and other services for the German Army and Navy, was in October found guilty by the Court of Appeal at The Hague and sentenced to one year's imprisonment; but in the meantime he had disappeared from Holland. In June 1917, it was reported that he was coming regularly to the United Kingdom on behalf of Germany, and this was signalled to the Ports for arrest, but nothing further was heard of him. De Snoek (alias Patent alias Schwacbach) succeeded Dierks. De Snoek had been in partnership with a man named Haasbroeck in the business of German counter-espionage and Haasbroeck, an 'underling' of Dierks, engaged the spies Schell and Pierre Verdun, of whom it was said, the one that had a share in the Lusitania outrage, the other in the torpedoeing of the Aboukir, Cressy and Hogue. Haasbroeck betrayed the Belgian spy Rotheudt, who was working for the Germans, to the French and lost the confidence of the Germans around July 1915.[26]

The Antwerp Branch directed the work of spies coming to Britain from America and Holland, and it was probable that German agents who communicated with Norway were also Dierks's men, as they certainly used his methods. The spies' itineraries were arranged so as to ensure that spies should pass through important places in regular succession. Roos, Wertheim and Roggen, passed through Edinburgh between 15 May and 8 June, and were possibly to be succeeded by Rowland, who was to leave town when Wertheim returned. Buschman, Rowland and Janssen passed through Southampton between 13 April and 20 May. Between the visits of Buschman and Rowland it was probable that other agents had gone there.

On arrival in England the spy wired to his base giving his address and asking for funds. Wherever possible a spy tried to get into some private house: Muller, Wertheim and Roos either scraped an acquaintance or used a pre-war acquaintance as cover, the obvious reason being to avoid hotel registration. As regards the Aliens Registration Order, all the spies conformed. Others of the spies tried to settle down with a companion in a flat or furnished rooms: Buschman forced a rapid friendship with Emile Franco, Breckow meant to establish himself with Wertheim. Meyer, who had a companion, married her. The fixed quarters and companion, whether accomplice or not, enabled a person to escape notice, to get their letters regularly, and if need be to have a companion for their excursions. This, it was clear from Breckow's letters, the agent considered important but the German employer sometimes objected to on the score of expense. As regards Breckow it seems clear that he was to occupy an 'outstanding position': he brought money and orders to Mrs Wertheim; was to work with her and to forward her reports; was to recruit a fixed agent at Southampton; and probably was to keep in touch with Roggen.

As for payment, Dierks seems to have sent it by telegraphic money-order and by telegraphic orders to banks. Berlin seems to have paid by cheque or to have supplied funds to the spy before his departure. The regular paraphernalia for a German agent's equipment consisted in two kinds of materials for secret writing, e.g. lemon juice, and scent used with powder as a fixative, and very fine pens; a book to help them identify types of men-of-war; and business documents purporting to establish their bona fides. In connection with this there was an evolution in passing from the bogus names of firms to names closely resembling those of genuine businesses and finally to genuine businesses and addresses as in the case of Meyer. In the use of their business cover the spies were 'remarkably ineffective'. Janssen and Ries collected the names of firms to call on in Britain but Janssen went no further and Ries merely wrote to the firms. Buschman also collected names of firms at Liverpool but never went there. In no case was any business concluded and it was often a simple matter to prove by means of experts that the travellers had no understanding of the business they were engaged upon. Rowland, indeed, was so sensitive of this that he proposed to drop his agency and revert to his own profession as a pianist under cover of which he could visit the places he needed to see. Another spy, de Rysbach, was a music-hall artist and in this 'struck a fresh note'.[27]

Generally speaking the spy adapted his communication to his supposed business but in some cases there were alternative codes. By the end of the summer the codes had multiplied. In addition to the four codes known to have been used by German agents before the war, the following codes seem to have been in use at various dates between

November 1914 and December 1915:

> A German agent in Copenhagen wiring to a centre in the United
> Kingdom a message to be forwarded to the Minister of Marine
> in Berlin used surnames or Christian names to indicate the names
> of countries, towns, bays, channels, etc., mention of illness, etc.
> to indicate operations, and prices to indicate dates.
>
> In February a German communicating with Rotterdam and
> the German Consul at Rotterdam were using Family Codes;
> relationships indicated military or naval units (e.g. Father =
> Dreadnought), names of towns indicated harbours; numbers of
> ships were indicated either by terms of endearment, or by alpha-
> betical Christian name code; latitude and longitude by names of
> Dutch Towns; a nation by some special Christian name.
>
> In the Corset Code supplied by German Headquarters at
> Antwerp to an agent in England, places in the United Kingdom
> were indicated by prices; places on the Continent by business
> terms; countries by colours; military and naval terms by descrip-
> tive words.

In April 1915, Dutchmen sent to England communicated with
Rotterdam in commercial cipher and code: a three figure group indicated warships of different tonnage; a two figure group merchant
vessels; one figure indicated transports. The place mentioned in the
telegram indicated the port of departure and the date was ascertained
by deducting two days from the date mentioned in the body of the
telegram. Rosenthal used a telegraphic code which the Germans
thought could not be paraphrased and also a postal stamp code; Roos
and Janssen a cigar code in which names of foreign ports and brands
of cigars indicated vessels and ports of the United Kingdom; Rowland
used a musical code in which ships and ports were indicated by the
name of some selection or piece, the two first letters or else some pun-
ning meaning indicating the word intended e.g. Carmen Selection =
Calais. Popular Hits = Artillery.

Secret signs were also in use in letters sent through the Esperanto
Association and on maps of microscopic dimensions carried by spies.
Roggen used a fruit code in which the words 'potatoes' and 'bananas'
were supposed to indicate various types of ship. Another code consisted
of pin holes, dots and tears on printed documents. Communications
were also made by means of advertisements in the public press.
Another spy, Van Ekeren, supplied further particulars about methods
in use at Antwerp. He mentioned two codes somewhat resembling

some already known and a cypher. This was founded on a combination of letters to indicate military units and numbers. A.B.C.D., the first four letters of the alphabet, stood for Artillery, Cavalry, Infantry, Mixed Troops. A cypher of four figures stood for the numbers of each unit, each number in decoding had to be multiplied by 3000. Thus: 1284 represented: 1 = 3,000 Artillery, 2 = 6,000 Cavalry. 8 = 24,000 Infantry. 4 = 12,000 Mixed Troops.

Telegrams were signed with the true name, letters with a false named registered at Antwerp. Messages were also written in lemon juice on the inside of envelopes or between the lines of satirical postcards about the Kaiser; letter-groups would be marked in an *en clair* message, but so faintly as not to damage the fibre of the paper. Copies of the code were sent to the Chief Censor with the request that all such telegrams should be forwarded to MO5g without previous reference to the sender. To communicate with Antwerp and Wesel, Melin used a banking code in which classes of ships were indicated by the names of well-known Dutch banks; the number of ships by a sum of money in pounds, which sum had to be divided by five; the names of ports by the names of Dutch hotels; the dates and nature of movement by commercial phrases. The Wesel Bureau would occasionally vary the names of the firms and hotels. The increase in the use or detection of code appeared in the fact that whereas fifteen cases, mostly harmless, were reported in April, seventy-three were reported in August 1915. To sum up: use was made, in turn or in combination of Christian names, surnames, terms of relationship, names of countries, cities and firms, dates, prices, figures, and every kind of merchandise, coupled with ordinary words and word combinations to which a conventional meaning was attached. On 10 June 1915, DRR 22A prohibiting the use, unlawful possession of, or refusal to disclose the key of any cypher or code or other means adapted for secretly communicating naval, military or air force information was issued.[28]

As time went by it became clear that there was little evidence of espionage by another Power during the war: in the view of an internal post-war assessment, the experience of MI5 between 1909 and 1918 showed that 'there was but one really active enemy, viz, the Germans and that their conception of espionage embraced the whole life of the State: naval, military economic, political and social information and even details of the conduct and fortune of private citizens were of interest to them'. During the later years of the war, owing partly to the disruptive and deterrent work of MI5 acting in Britain, and MII6 (C's SIS organisation) acting abroad, and partly to the progress of hostilities ashore and afloat, the Germans seem to have laid even greater stress upon sabotage and the fomenting of discontent and revolution; fewer agents were sent into the country for espionage proper since Britain's armies were for the most part abroad, and naval espionage was carried on chiefly by seamen and travellers on board neutral merchant vessels. Throughout the war, the Germans attached considerable importance to the voyage of their agents, who were cross-examined by competent persons as to the ships, mines, etc. which they had seen at sea. The results achieved by air-raids, the effects upon the popular morale of such 'terrorist acts' and of the stress of submarine warfare, the question as to whether hospital ships carried munitions of war, the anti-recruiting and peace propaganda campaign, were questions and methods peculiar to the state of war. But speaking generally, the difference between the methods and aims of German espionage in peace and war was one of degree and emphasis rather than of quality. Its elements were 'so various and inclusive that in legislation the wider term, "German agent" is now substituted for that of spy, and similarly the expression "Defence Security Intelligence" of larger connotation than "counter-espionage" has been adopted to express more adequately the work done by MI5'.

The 'unity of the attack' was demonstrated in the long line of spy cases from 1911 to 1917; these cases were related to one another by one or more common factors, such as a spy address, or a method or knowledge of new developments and often the relation was so close that one more case would throw a flood of light upon another. This was so true that it was possible to discern one at least of the links between the pre-war and wartime organisations. That link was Miss Brandos, once Secretary to Baron Bruno von Schroeder and his agent in charitable work. Each spy case was 'indeed an entity, the details of which required mastering for itself; but each spy case was also only one link in a long chain and its details had to be mastered and called to mind in dealing with all other cases'. From these considerations 'one law emerges: success in investigation depends upon mastery of detail; and the corollary of this is that no one can foretell what detail will not prove to be of primary importance either in the case itself or in some later one'.[29]

Prevention & Cure
The Art of Catching Spies in War

Prevention

As noted, until the beginning of the war, the SIB was responsible to the Colonel commanding MO5, who acted as both its paymaster and military chief; but on 5 August, Kell's Bureau became a sub-section of MO5, known as MO5g.[1] Prior to August 1914, MO5 had been responsible for all Secret Service work, but on Colonel Macdonagh's departure for France it was decided that the Chief of the Secret Service in London should correspond directly with him at General Headquarters, France. This system continued until the beginning of October 1914, when, owing to a serious accident to the Chief of the Secret Service, Cummings, which incapacitated him for some months, the Secret Service organisation in London commenced to work under MO5 and General Headquarters instituted its own independent service in France. As the volume of work continued to increase it became more and more difficult for the DMO to keep in touch with so wide a range of interests outside the operations of his work, which alone would have been enough for one man. It was decided to divide up the work.

The original plan was to make three sub-directorates of Military Operations: one to deal with the purely 'operations' questions; a second for I.(A) work i.e. active intelligence of the enemy's plans from every source; and a third for I.(B) work or security intelligence work i.e. all the security services designed to prevent the enemy from gaining information. They were to be the sub-sections of the Military Operations with a brigadier-general at the head of each, who could relieve the DMO of all routine and detailed work, leaving him free to help the Chief of the Imperial General Staff in the work of advising the Secretary of State and the Government. In actual fact only the third of these sub-directorates was to be created by expanding MO5 into a sub-directorate with the title of 'Special Intelligence'. Brigadier-General Cockerill was the Director of Special Intelligence; Kell was promoted from Major to Lieutenant-Colonel, General Staff Officer 1st Grade (GOS1) as head of MO5; MO5g and Major R.J. Drake retained control of counter-espionage. MO5 was reorganised on 15 November 1915 and the duties redistributed. military port control officers were included in the section and a new sub-section was formed to deal with the selection of candidates for all intelligence appointments.[2]

As war approached, on 30 July 1914, the staff of the Secret Intelligence Bureau consisted of five officers and seven clerks. By 4 August, it had increased to seven officers and ten clerks; by early November 1914 it sprung up to twenty-two officers and about sixteen clerks, besides agents, chauffeurs, orderlies, and so on. In December, it grew again to twenty-four officers and about twenty-seven clerks. This rapid increase carried with it the necessity of organising MO5g on a more complex basis than had hitherto been possible or desirable. Until the summer of 1915, MO5g, considered as a department of the War Office, remained, as before the war, a single and indivisible sub-section of the Directorate of Military Operations; however, for purposes of purely internal organisation, the staff and duties of MO5g were subdivided at the end of September 1914 into three branches, corresponding to the three categories into which the Bureau's work could already be analysed before the war, those namely of detection, prevention and administration.

Up until September 1914 there had been only two branches, dealing respectively with 'detection' and 'registration'. The officers who came into the Bureau (as it was still affectionately called) in the first two months of the war joined one or the other of these two branches as their services were required. The work was 'increasing by leaps and bounds, and it was not easy to tell from day to day where the next rush would come'. But at the end of September 1914 a more definite arrangement was come to, and the administrative work of the Bureau, which up to that time had been performed by the aliens or 'registration' branch, was taken over by a third branch, which eventually grew to be far larger than any other branch contained entirely in the Bureau itself, including as it did the Registry which had charge of the vast and perennially increasing mass of counter-espionage records.

At the stage of 'full development', i.e., the last two years of the war, the SIB contained five branches (a sixth was added in April 1917). During 1915, from a single War Office sub-section – MO5g – the Bureau had been enlarged into the four sub-sections: MO5E, F, G and H. Of these, the three last were the departments above mentioned (detection, prevention and administration respectively), while the first, MO5E, was created during May – June 1915, to take over from the preventive branch the rapidly growing work of organising and administering the control of ports and frontiers, including the establishment of permit offices at home and abroad, and (eventually) the provision of a special corps of Military Foot Police for duty with the Military Control Officers at home ports. At the end of 1915, the old Military Operations Directorate was split up.[3] With the appointment of a Field Marshal Commander-in-Chief, Home Forces, and the transfer to General Headquarters, Home Forces, and of certain duties hitherto allotted to the Directorates of

Home Defence and Military Training, the General Staff was reorganised in December 1915. On 23 December a Military Intelligence Directorate, in addition to the Military Operations Directorate, was formed under the Chief of the Imperial General Staff, General Sir William Robertson. Major General C.E. Callwell became Director of Military Operations; he was succeeded by Major General Macdonogh in January 1916. MO5 became part of the Directorate of Military Intelligence and simply altered its title to MI retaining its old number. And MI5 was born.[4]

MO5E, F, G and H joined the new Military Intelligence Directorate as MI5E, F, G and H respectively. A fifth branch MI5D was added before the end of 1916 to develop the overseas connection of Special Intelligence work (Ireland, the Dominions, India and the Orient). The sixth branch, which completed the SIB's organisation during the War, was entitled MI5A and dealt with work (originally performed by the SIB's preventive branch, and then for a time – taken over by the Ministry of Munitions) connected with the registration and control of aliens on war work in the United Kingdom. Thus the final organisation of the SIB's duties neglecting minor sub-divisions, was as follows during the latter part of the war:

MI5 Special Intelligence – General.
MI5A Aliens on War Service.
MI5D Overseas Special Intelligence.
MI5E Control of Ports & Frontiers.
MI5F Preventive Branch.
MI5G Detective Branch.
MI5H Administrative Branch (Office & Records).

By Armistice Day, following a series of confusing restructures, the staff of the Bureau consisted of 133 officers, 300 clerks (the large majority women) and 274 ports police.[5] The Military Intelligence Directorate remained part of the General Staff division of the War Office. There were two separate halves of the MI Directorate, the first under the Director of Military Intelligence's immediate command, but the second under the Sub-Director of Military Intelligence (whose other name used to be the Director of Special Intelligence). The second half, MI5 to 9, and MIR, were almost exclusively engaged upon preventive duties. There were considerable changes in the grouping of the sections and sub-sections of the Directorate from time to time: for example, C's SIS organisation, engaged in intelligence gathering outside British territory was MI1C – whereas the original MI6 was less glamorous and concerned with cables war trade. MI7 was concerned with press censorship; MI8 with cable censorship; and MI9 with postal censorship.[6] Only MI5 retained a consistent association with its wartime role.

The two most important sections were the Preventive and Detective Branches of MO5/MI5. Before the war the work of the Preventive Branch was conducted by the same officer as the detective work – that officer being then, with a single clerk after the first six months, Vernon Kell. It was not finally separated, organically speaking, from the 'office and records' branch until September 1914. The preventive work in the pre-war period included also the preparation of schemes for the protection of vulnerable points from possible attack by enemy intelligence agents, and the provision of military advice on matters connected with Emergency Legislation and the Official Secrets Act. At the outset of the war, the duties of the Preventive Branch, or 'B' Branch as it was then called, were as follows:

> Co-ordination of general policy of Government Departments in dealing with Aliens. Registration of Aliens. Foreign Communities. Applications of Alien Enemies to leave the United Kingdom. Records of Alien soldiers, sailors and police in the United Kingdom. Records of Alien Enemies permitted to reside in Prohibited Areas. Co-ordination of Police methods in dealing with Aliens. Questions arising out of the Defence of the Realm Act and Aliens Restriction Act. Correspondence on the above subjects. Investigations connected with technical naval and military questions.

Before the war was many weeks old, the mass of administrative and co-ordinative work which came in made it necessary to break up the Preventive Branch's work into four divisions, besides the duties that were still carried out by the head of the Branch, who also held the position of Assistant Director in the SIB as a whole. To these four divisions, there was soon added a fifth, which consisted of one officer acting as deputy and assistant to the head of the Branch. This organisation, complete in November 1914, was carried on without much alteration during the early part of the following year. The sub-divisions of staff and duties were:

> B1. One Officer: Alien Intelligence.
> B2. One Officer: Prevention of Military Espionage and B3 Prevention of Naval Espionage.
> B4. Two officers, one an attached officer, a Belgian Army colonel with a position of 'Auditaire Militaire Belge'. Special measures for supervision and control of Belgian refugees, investigation of credentials of Belgian residents, lists of firms employing Belgian

workmen.

B5. General duties 'B' Branch including assisting the head of branch.

As the distribution of staff would suggest, the most urgent problems which arose early in the war were connected with the surveillance of Belgian refugees, 'amongst whom it seems reasonable to suspect that a certain number of enemy agents may have gained entry into the United Kingdom'. As to B1, B2 and B3, the second and third of these divisions dealt with the credentials of aliens serving in or employed by the army and navy, with 'alien resorts' favoured by military and naval personnel and with lists of Vulnerable Points, (military and naval) and so forth; while the first, B1, was responsible for Black Lists. In the latter part of the war, the Preventive Branch (now known as MI5F) was organised in a somewhat different way from that just described; the head of the Branch continued to deal with general matters of policy and with new legislation with the co-ordination of Special Intelligence work. The sub-divisions and their duties, as arranged during the year 1917, were as follows:

F1: Co-operation with the civil authorities regarding personal credentials of Aliens and others.

F2: Co-operation with the Naval and Military Authorities regarding personal credentials.

F3: Disposal and supervision of suspects and undesirables, otherwise than by prosecution, i.e. mainly by internment and other restrictions imposed under War Emergency Legislation.

F4: Records and classification of measures for the prevention of espionage.

F5: Legal procedure.

Starting from the three fundamental principles of Identification, Classification and Control, each particular portion of the Branch's work could be classified according to the purpose it was designed to fulfil.[7] The essential components of a Preventive Intelligence system were set out in ten Cardinal Principles:

CARDINAL PRINCIPLES.

(a) Information.

(b) Communication.

(c) Records.

(d) Counter-action.

(e) Examination.

(f) Identification.
(g) Classification.
(h) Control.
(i) Censorship.
(j) Protection.[8]

As part of this a system of preventive intelligence 'examining posts' had been established through which all travellers had to pass, or at which all persons seeking facilities which were restricted or controlled for reasons of military security had to call or pass under examination, either in person or by correspondence, in order to receive permission or qualified permission to pursue their affairs. These examination posts included not only Military Control Offices at ports and permit or passport offices, but also police stations, hotels and other places where particulars were registered by aliens; and military civilian posts where applications were received for war facilities of various kinds, such as permission to enter specially protected areas or munitions works.[9] Control could then be applied, on the one hand, to all persons where it was desired to protect a given area (say the whole United Kingdom or a specific area such as the Isle of Sheppey) from a particular kind of activity which was open to everyone, and on the other to selected and classified individuals or groups of individuals, where there was reason to think them likely to be dangerous but where there was not enough information for a prosecution on a charge of espionage or something less serious. Counter-action applied only in particular cases where there was a definite suspicion of espionage.[10]

Personal identification was the essential preliminary to the examination of a person and the classification of his credentials for preventive intelligence purposes. It was usually followed by classification which was the process that decided, first, whether a given person was actually a friend or a foe; and secondly, if a foe, in what particular forms and to what degree his hostility was likely to be translated into action prejudicial to military security. Upon the results of this classification depended the decision regarding the degree of Control.[11] Three distinct kinds of Classification existed for war purposes. Of these, two were military and were assessed by Special Intelligence, while the third was civilian and was made by the police and immigration authorities. The civilian classification was the simple one of nationality, whether British, allied, neutral or enemy. Special Intelligence took up the process of classification where the civil authorities left it and carried it on to the two further stages, those of the General Military (SI) Classification as friendly or hostile, and of the Special SI Sub-Classifications into one or more of eleven 'Black List Classes'. These last were applied only to suspects and between them exhausted all the possible kinds of actively hostile persons recognised as deserving inclusion in the SIB's Black List. The eleven classes were numbered alphabetically from A to K, and had catchwords by which they might be readily committed to memory:

Class SI/BL

A: 'Antecedents' in a civil, police or judicial sense so bad that patriotism may not be the dominant factor and sympathies not incorruptible.

B: 'Banished' during the war from or forbidden to enter one or more of the Allied States.

C: 'Courier' letter carrier, intermediary or auxiliary to enemy agents.

D: 'Detained', interned or prevented from leaving an Allied State for SI reasons.

E: 'Espion'. Enemy spy or agent engaged in active mischief, (not necessarily confined to espionage).

F: 'False' or irregular papers of identity or credential.

G: 'Guarded', suspected, under special surveillance and not yet otherwise classified.

H: 'Hawker' hostile by reason of trade or commerce with or for the enemy.

I: 'Instigator' of hostile, pacifist, seditious or dangerous propaganda.

J: 'Junction' wanted. The person or information concerning him wanted urgently by SI or an Allied SI.

K: 'Kaiser's' man. Enemy officer or official or ex-officer or official.

For War Purposes, this classification was adopted as the standard one, (omitting classes J & K.) by the French and other Allied services represented at the Bureau Centrale Interallier in Paris.

The fact that a person's name appeared in the Black List was not usually enough in itself to enable the SIB to come to a decision about the degree of control to be imposed on a suspect. It was essential to know under what class or classes his name was contained, and it was best where possible to have the whole dossier to study. The Black List, however, served up in tabloid form all the really vital information that was contained in the dossier, and should in most cases have enabled an Intelligence Officer who had no time for consulting the SIB itself to reach a fairly sound conclusion. It may be noted in passing that 'suspect' was far too vague a term to have even the smallest value in Special Intelligence work. An Intelligence Officer had to know of what the suspect was suspected, and on whose authority, before making up his mind about a course of action. Accordingly the person concerned might be considered 'friendly' or 'hostile' – the 'General Military (SI) Classification'; these terms referred not to the person's technical nationality but to the actual state of his national sympathies, as revealed in his words and deeds and (lacking much definite evidence) as shown to be likely by his origin or associations. The purpose of this classification was principally to prepare lists of persons of enemy connection for restrictive action in case of emergency. Such action might consist in (a) internment, (b) close restrictions or (c) ordinary restrictions. The General Military (SI) Classifications were divided into the following six classes:

Class: Military:
1. AA: True personal sympathies are believed to be 'Absolutely Anglicized' or Allied and undoubtedly Friendly.
2. A: 'Anglicized' or Allied and Friendly.
3. AB: 'Anglo-Boche', Friendly.
4. BA: Doubtful, probably Hostile.
5. B: 'Boche' and Hostile.
6. BB: 'Bad Boche' and undoubtedly Hostile.
Emergency restrictions would be imposed on these military classes in the following manner:
(a) class Restrictions on Military Classes BB or B.
(b) class Restrictions on Military Classes B or BA.
(c) class Restrictions on Military Classes BA.

Military Classes A and AA, being entirely composed of persons with friendly sentiments, would naturally be exempted from restrictions: 'It is by no means the least valuable of the Bureau's services that its investigations enable the authorities to concentrate their attention on those enemy descended persons who have retained the love of the land of their fathers, while allowing such as have true loyalty to the British Crown to remain unmolested, except indeed by the more despicable and thoughtless sections of the British Press and Public.' A person of British, Allied or Neutral <u>civil</u> classification might receive any of the six <u>military</u> classifications, from AA to BB. For instance, the military class of a 'Civil British Subject' was often BB in the case of naturalised enemy subjects who retained their enemy sympathies.[12]

Cure

According to a post-war MI5 assessment of counter-espionage, the qualities required of the investigator were:

> mental alertness, elasticity, knowledge of men, intuition, an accurate and powerful memory combined with imagination, judgment to choose the right method of handling a case and the moment to strike. His attainments should include besides the special knowledge of counter-espionage legislation and preventive measures, some knowledge of law, legal procedure and the laws of evidence. He should also know one or two languages thoroughly.

Whether in peace or war, the investigator should work under cover and use both 'ordinary and special machinery'. The ordinary machinery consisted of other government departments working in their ordinary routine but set in motion at the request of the investigator. The special machinery consisted of methods peculiar to counter-espionage but carried out by ordinary government departments in time of peace, and by departments specially conceived and constituted in time of war. The aim of the investigator was: 1. to discover enemy agents; 2. to collect evidence against such persons; and 3. to bring them to justice or to nullify their efforts. These were the three stages of an investigation. Two main classes of spy were deemed to exist: the foreigner, whether resident or on a mission; and the traitor, whether of British or alien origin. Detections might come either through the action of the Bureau or it might follow on information received from some outside source. The sources varied in peace and in war. Sources of detection in peace were:

> Inside [the SIB]: (1) The Precautionary Index, (2) Home Office Warrant, (3) Spy contacts established in pursuing an investigation.
> Outside [the SIB]: (1) Private informer, (2) Military or Naval, (3) Government Offices, (4) Police, (5) Chance: Returned Letter or a letter picked up and submitted, a conversation overheard and reported.

Sources of detection in time of war were:

> Inside: General check on the transmission of money, orders, telegraphic orders, cheques, drafts. General check on telegrams. General check on passenger traffic at ports and certain areas. H[ome].O[ffice]. Warrants and special checks. British Intelligence

Services at home and abroad. Foreign Office.
Outside: Special Departments: (1) Censorship, (2) Passport
Office, (3) Military Permit Office, (4) Allied Services, (5) Police.
(6) Private Informers, both British and Foreign.

In terms of the Inside Sources, the first of these – a general check on the
transmission of money – did not seem to have led to the detection of any
proved spy during the war. The second – checks on telegrams – and third
– checks on passenger traffic – were sources that frequently overlapped;
but the second was the most important source of detection in time of
peace. In time of war, of the Outside Sources, by far the most important
were the agents employed by British officials in touch with SIS.

After intelligence had been received, the action taken depended upon
the class of spy and the source and nature of the information received. If
it was a case of information lodged against an alien or civilian by a private person the first step was probably verification of the details through
police enquiry; if the accused was a Serviceman or a government official
the enquiry would begin in the department to which he belonged. If the
existence of a spy was known but his identity in doubt, the first step would
be identification. The means of identification most successfully used was
the comparison of handwriting. The best way of procuring a specimen of
handwriting was by securing from the local post office a receipt signed by
the suspect, but this pre-supposed that the enquiry had reached a point at
which suspicion was directed against a definite person.

The second stage of investigation, i.e. the collection of evidence,
showed important differences in peace and war. In peace it might be a
long and tedious process, involving the repeated shadowing of an agent
and the postponement of arrest until by a series of measures elaborated
between the Bureau, police and the Post Office, it became known that
incriminating documents would be found on the agent or in his house.
In war, the spy's movements might be known beforehand; he would be
invited or taken to Scotland Yard on arrival, duly cautioned and interrogated, and if he failed to extricate himself, he would be arrested. His
interrogation might be put in evidence against him. This difference of
procedure was due to the difference in the authority sanctioning proceedings: in time of peace it was in the hands of the Legal Officers of the
Crown; in time of war it was in the hands of the Competent Military
Authority. There were thus two stages in the collection of evidence: 1.
before and to justify arrest; and 2. after arrest and to prepare the case.
Both stages consisted of a series of verifications: the man's civil status,
movements, business, money affairs and receipts, communications,
friends and associations, both in Britain and abroad, formed the object

of enquiry. In addition, in every spy case in which information was sent to the enemy, verification of its truth and value was given in court.

The preparation of the case took place under legal direction. One principle governed both in peace and war: secrecy. In peace, the trial took place in open court and was fully reported – therefore it was essential to conceal counter-espionage methods; both for this reason and for reasons of evidence much damning information against 'the criminal' could be produced in court. In time of war, with control of the press and trial by Court Martial, there was less risk of exposing the methods of counter-espionage; moreover the special preventive measures were necessarily known to the enemy. Secrecy therefore bore upon another aspect of the case: 'the enemy must be kept in the dark as long as possible as to the arrest of his agent and the nature of the charge'. There was, however, one difficulty in war time: the spies may be neutrals and as a matter of courtesy and prudence, an official, whether of the embassy or consulate of that neutral country was present at the trial. He was of course held to secrecy – although presumably he furnished a report to his government. By whatever means, whether by a process of inference or by leakage, the record of the spy cases during the war showed that the Germans arrived at pretty accurate results as to the fate of their spies and the weak points in the tactics which led to their arrest; in searching for fresh methods 'they laid bare the weak points of our defence'. It was the business of the investigator to note these results and to offer suggestions for strengthening prevention to those persons who dealt with that side of counter-espionage.[13]

As has been already noted, the declaration of war immediately increased the work and activity of all sections of the SIB but particularly the Preventive or B Section of MO5. Initially the staff consisted of the Director of Intelligence Police, three Assistant Directors (these were Captain Drake, Captain Holt Wilson and Captain Haldane) and two Intelligence Officers. But, in November 1914, when the Preventive, or B Section, and the Detective, or A Section, were reorganised as separate branches the latter came under the Assistant Director, Drake (who had been promoted to the rank of Major), supported by the Branch Secretary, Miss Holmes; the work was carried out by four Staff Officers, assisted by three secretaries. The Branch was divided into four sections as follows:

A1: Captain J.F.G.Carter, Assistant Secretary, Miss Haldane.
A2: Major F.M.Peters, Assistant Secretary, Miss Robson.
A3: Commander F.B.Henderson, CMG, DSO, RN, Assistant Secretary, Miss Robson.

A4: A.Nathan Esq., Assistant Secretary, Miss Tunningley.

The duties of the Branch were defined generally as:

Investigation of cases of espionage.
Correspondence regarding suspected persons.
Action on intercepted correspondence.
Correspondence with D[irector of].P[ublic].P[rosecutions]. and A[ttorney].G[eneral].
Activities of foreign agents and measures to counteract them.

The following, more detailed definition of duties, showed the developments in countering the war activities of German agents:

Action on intercepted cables, telegrams, and letters.
Investigation of espionage, including uses of homing pigeons, wireless telegraphy, signalling, aircraft, etc.
Investigation of cases of outrage and sabotage.
Visé of Prisoners' letters and those of Prisoners of War.

The Distribution of Duties took place on a geographical principle:

A1: Cases arising in the Metropolitan Area and City of London.
A2: Cases arising in England south of a line drawn from the Bristol Channel to the Wash and comprising the counties of Gloucestershire, Oxfordshire, Northamptonshire, Cambridgeshire and Norfolk; also the Channel Islands.
A3: Cases arising in England north of the area allotted to A2, in Wales and the Isle of Man.
A4: Cases arising in Scotland, including the Orkneys, Shetlands and Hebrides.

This distribution of cases by geographical area held only with reference to the place where the case started; it was a principle of the work that the section which began a case should carry it right through to the end. In the main the work of investigation was carried on by the same methods as before the war. The chief agents continued to be the Police, officials of the Post Office and special agents employed by the Bureau. Owing to the great increase in the number of suspected persons, there was a noticeable increase in the number of Home Office Warrants (HOW's) taken out. In his report for November and December 1914, Major Drake mentioned various types of investigation as follows:

> General Inquiries with regard to:
> Bonafides of persons who had been and continued to be in receipt
> of regular payments through German Banks in this country with
> a view to detecting possible agents; search of all telegrams sent to
> certain countries since the outbreak of war.
> Special Inquiries with regard to:
> Records obtained and action taken with regard to certain persons
> holding commissions who were unfit for such posts; bonafides
> of certain Belgians; foreign business firms and a hotel supposed
> to be under German management; attempts to re-establish the
> German spy organisation.

Other enquiries related to German business firms and cases of suspected
espionage. The two General Enquiries mentioned above illustrated the
enlargement of scope conferred upon the Bureau by the war. The investigation of bank accounts and the search of telegrams were pre-war
methods used in individual cases but now raised to universal application
and carried out either by specially appointed persons as in the case of
the banks, or by the ordinary channel of a great Public Service.[14] Crucial
to the work of MO5g was the role played by the Central Censorship.
On the outbreak of war the Central Censorship was established for
the examination of mails between the United Kingdom and Germany
with Austria-Hungary; it was extended to mails with Turkey when that
Power came into the war. But experience soon proved that such scope
was insufficient and the system was extended as follows:

> 29-8-14 – To mails to and from Holland, Denmark and Norway.
> 19-9-14 – To mails to and from Sweden.
> 14-10-14 – To mails to and from Switzerland.
> 7-11-14 – To mails to and from Italy.
> 17-12-14 – To mails to and from Spain, Portugal and Romania.

Home Office Warrants had, however, been issued to the Censorship
on the outbreak of war for checking all correspondence to certain
addresses in neutral and Allied countries. The examination of parcels
to neutral countries was begun at the end of November 1914. Letters
to Prisoners of War were despatched in separate bags through the
Dutch Postal Administration. Letters were sorted into four categories
with sub-divisions as follows:

1. Dangerous:
containing definite political, naval or military information
addressed to persons on the Black List
offering service to the enemy
containing ciphers and codes.
2. Suspicious:
indicating unusual relations between persons resident in the UK
and abroad
indicating payments made to or demanded by persons in the UK
without mention of corresponding business
expressing intention of Germans to join the British Red Cross or
similar organisations.
3. Indiscreet: expressing pessimistic views.
4. Letters from or concerning Germans or Austrians liable to
military service.

All letters and telegrams to or from neutral countries in connection
with trading with enemy countries and ordinary trade telegrams from
and to any place were submitted to the Home Office and duplicates
were sent to the Foreign Office; all letters and telegrams other than
those above mentioned and especially those connected with diplomatic, consular, political, military and naval arrangements were sent
to MO5g. In addition to the Central Censorship, the Competent
Military Authority of a district had the power to ask the Postmaster
to stop specific letters and telegrams; and at the ports, papers carried
by passengers might be seized by officers stationed there by MO5g. In
examining letters submitted: 1. by the Censor; 2. by the Port Officers,
and 3. advertisements in the agony columns of the newspapers – three
codes which were supposed to have been used by enemy agents were
found to have been employed here. Special arrangements were made in
the Branch to carry out the work and a plant was established for testing letters by chemical means.[15]

Very soon methods of evading the Censorship became known to
MO5g: for example, censor labels were removed from old envelopes
and posted on to fresh ones; messages were sent abroad in bundles of
newspapers; and letters were carried by smugglers to and from enemy-
occupied territory or posted via intermediaries in neutral countries. The
methods of the Censor, in turn, developed with experience aided by the
suggestions of MO5g. Thus in December 1914, Major Drake reported
that it was known that German agents were sending information out of
the country written in invisible ink on the margins of newspapers, magazines and pamphlets; however, no specific instance had come to light

and it was desirable to take action with regard to printed matter passing through the post. An order was issued that printed matter addressed to neutral countries should be delayed for forty-eight hours unless it were despatched by newsagents or publishers. In April 1915, the sending of all such matter to enemy countries was prohibited to all but certain publishers and newsagents, and by July private individuals had been forbidden to post newspapers to Holland and a delay of a fortnight was imposed on press matter addressed to other neutral countries.

Early in January 1915, Drake requested that the Censorship should cover all mails to countries within five days journey of the United Kingdom. This was carried out in May 1915 when mails to Bulgaria and Greece were censored. At the same time a warrant for censoring northern and southern continental American mail was obtained and put into force, intermittently at first. In April 1915, all mails in transit through the UK were made subject to Censorship. A weak point was found in the system of submitting to MO5g a précis only of interesting letters for, owing to this, evidence that would have served to convict a German agent was allowed to go through. The system was therefore altered; letters of interest were submitted attached to the précis of contents and MO5g made special arrangements for dealing with these letters. Eight foreign businesses and one hotel, the Ritz-Carlton, came under suspicion either of trading with the enemy or of being concerned in espionage. The establishment of Siemens & Co was searched on several occasions and special examination made for wireless, and for some time a police officer was established on the premises to keep check.[16]

In addition to the use of Censorship as a counter-espionage measure, during the first three months of the war MO5g laboured at improving war legislation, and on 28 November 1914, the Defence of the Realm Regulations were issued in consolidated form. The provisions which were of chief interest to the Investigation Branch of MO5g were:

D.R.R.14
Conferring on the Competent Naval or Military Authority power to remove suspects from a specified area.
D.R.R.18
Prohibiting the collection, recording of, publication, communication, or attempt to elicit any information regarding the forces etc. of His Majesty or His Majesty's Allies, or of plans of naval or military operations, or of fortifications or any other information intended to be communicated to the enemy, and prohibiting also the unlawful possession of any document containing any such information.

D.R.R.19

Prohibiting the making of photographs, sketches of certain places and things, or the possession of a camera in the neighbourhood of certain places, or the making of photographs or sketches of any place or thing with intent to assist the enemy, or the unlawful possession of any representation of a prohibited object.

D.R.R.20

Prohibiting tampering with telegraphic or telephonic apparatus and the possession of apparatus for tapping wireless (if perpetrated by an enemy agent).

D.R.R.21

Prohibiting the possession of carrier pigeons unless by special permit.

D.R.R.22

Prohibiting possession of wireless telegraph apparatus etc.

D.R.R.23

Conferring power to prevent embarkation of persons suspected of communicating with the enemy.

D.R.R.24

Prohibiting non-postal communications to and from the United Kingdom – which specially interested the Censor was also of great value to 'G' Branch.

D.R.R.25

Prohibiting signalling.

D.R.R.27

Prohibiting the spread of false or prejudicial reports and prejudicial performances or exhibitions (in the case of enemy or alien agency or when the offence was committed by word of mouth).

D.R.R.45

Prohibiting false statements, whether verbally or in writing, in any return, declaration or application with intent to deceive.

D.R.R.51

Conferring on the Competent Military or Naval Authority power to search premises. (In making use of this power MO5g would conceal its identity beneath that of the Competent Military Authority of the locality concerned.)

In this early stage of the war DRR18, 19 and 51, were the chief new legal weapons in the hands of the investigating branch.[17] Armed with these powers, the SIB was a formidable counter-espionage service.

To accommodate the growth in work another re-organisation of the Special Intelligence Bureau took place again in August 1915 when the name of the Detective Branch was changed from A to G with the work of the Branch being expanded to include co-operating with the Allies' counter-espionage services in counter-espionage. Such an increase of duties involved an increase of staff. The Detective Branch retained this title known until the end of the war. In October 1915, G Branch was instructed to expand its duties to include: 1. 'investigation of all cases of suspected fomentation of strikes and sabotage, and dissemination of peace propaganda' and; 2. 'recommendation for amendments to legislation and regulations for the purpose of preventing espionage, sedition or treachery, or of impeding the activities of naval and military spies and agents'.[18]

6

The 'Hush Hush' Show
MI5 Victorious 1916-1918

During the winter of 1915–1916, various methods of conveying information out of the country came to light; spies were sending messages in invisible ink enclosed in envelopes addressed to Belgian and British POWs and marked in some way recognizable by the German Censor who forwarded them to the proper quarter. The British Postal Censor was asked to test letters addressed to British prisoners of war in Germany with the same stringency as was applied to ordinary correspondence. It was reported from an 'unguaranteed source' that letters of a harmless nature would be posted in England for the United States of America, there steamed open, fresh messages inserted, and the envelopes posted back to the original sender. In 1917 the Censor carefully examined all returned letters from the United States of America. Parcels of suspiciously marked magazines were being sent to prisoners of war and the opinion was expressed that old books should not be allowed through to enemy countries without careful enquiry into the bona-fides of the senders, as documents and papers of an undesirable nature were being sent abroad. From a Dutch newspaper it was already known that coded advertisements, containing news of the movements of British ships were being inserted in the 'Servants Wanted' columns of the press, and also that these were being wired to Berlin as soon as the English papers reached Holland. News was also being carried abroad by the following methods: 1. On a slip of paper, inserted between the sides of a match-box, and on the back of the paper covering the box; 2. In books, periodicals, newspapers and even bank notes – these things being carried ostensibly for use of the journey; 3. In shaving brushes with screw tops; 4. Stamped on the skin of a Belgian woman; 5. On toys carved by German prisoners of war; 6. Concealed in slabs of chocolate etc.

It was the use of invisible ink that would provide a breakthrough in the case of Leopold Vieyra. Vieyra, alias Leo Pickard, was a Dutch subject of Jewish extraction, born in Rotterdam, in 1881. He had enjoyed a colourful career and had worked as an acrobat, music-hall artist, cinematograph theatre manager and film dealer. He arrived in England in 1909, living, until 1914, at Sunnyholt, Acton Vale, with a Mrs Annie Fletcher; the couple passed themselves off as the married Mr and Mrs Leo Pickard. Vieyra had come to the UK from Paris as manager of a troupe known as 'The Midgets'; later he became manager of the Bijou Cinema in Finchley Road and subsequently started working as a film agent travelling between England and Holland. He left England, apparently for good, in 1914. In May 1916, however, he obtained a visa in the name of Vieyra from the British Consul in Rotterdam stating that he had business in London with one I.B. Davidson of Rupers Street. On arrival he returned home to Sunnyholt, Acton Vale. Suspicions were immediately aroused in the minds of the authorities that he was a German agent: a man, described only as 'A' – a known German agent – reported to an informant that Vieyra had been sent to England as a spy by another well-known German agent, (known as 'B'), who had given him, three days before he left Rotterdam, 2,500 florins and expenses for one month at fifty shillings a day, and had deposited another 2,500 florins in a Dutch bank to be withdrawn by Vieyra, on his return in about two months. Payments in England were to be made through Messrs Blydenstein's Bank. Prior to this information being received, Vieyra had been interrogated at Scotland Yard, and told that he would not be allowed to travel backwards and forwards, and would either have to go back at once and stay in Holland or remain in England until the end of the war. He decided that he would prefer to remain in the UK.

Vieyra's mail was intercepted and letters were seen to be passing between him and a person named S. Blom, of Amsterdam, and also between him and a woman named Jessen. Around the middle of July correspondence with Jessen indicated that Vieyra intended to return to Holland; this, it was noted, was about two months after his arrival in England, so confirming what had been stated by the German agent 'A'. The letters to and from Blom related ostensibly to the film industry but one mentioned that Vieyra kept his account at the London City and Midland Bank, and no longer at Blydenstein's, another small corroboration of 'A's' story. Another letter of Blom's ended with the sentence: 'I am very curious to hear what you bought outside of LONDON.'

Enquiries were made in Holland and from an informant it was deduced that at Blom's address resided Mrs Simon Dikker, whose maiden name was Sophia Blom. She was the sister-in-law of Philip Dikker, the man through whom money from Germany was forwarded to the convicted spy Greite. Mrs Dikker, when asked about S. Blom, said: 'S BLOM is my cousin and he does an export and import business, and he is very seldom at home. He travels to Flushing and to Belgium, and I believe he is a friend of Leopold VIEYRA.' When questioned further she excused herself and said she knew nothing about Blom's business. Enquiry into the Blom family failed to reveal any 'S Blom' except Sophia Blom; this led MI5 to think that: 'It may, therefore, be assumed that the correspondence with VIEYRA is really conducted by someone else – possibly Philip DIKKER, or his brother SIMON.'

Meanwhile, on 21 July, Vieyra, in spite of his promise to remain in England until the end of the war, appeared at the Permit Office and applied for a permit to visit Holland, which was refused. After waiting some little time longer, in the hope of intercepting some more incriminating evidence, it was decided to arrest Vieyra. Accordingly, on 24 August, he was arrested by Inspector Fitch and taken with all his papers to New Scotland Yard where he was seen by Basil Thompson, of the Metropolitan Police and Captain Carter from MI5, cautioned and interrogated.

Regarding his business in England, he said he had bought films to the amount of £164 only, and had sold them at a profit of about £80. This was confirmed by his chequebook and correspondence. During the same period he had spent about £100 in household and personal expenses. Vieyra was asked where his money came from and replied that he had a draft for £125 when he came over from Holland and since received sums of £100 and £121, and that the whole of this money was from Mr Blom, who was 'his partner'. He was questioned closely as to the identity of S. Blom and as to his connection with him. This led to the following 'astonishing story' of the man who trusted him with £300:

> He is just a café acquaintance... I have never been home with him. He is a stout, elderly gentleman, about 50 years, not very stout, height about 5ft.3inches. He has 'pepper and salt' hair; moustache, dark eyes and full face.
> I have no agreement whatever with him. Many fellows give me money. I talk to them and put a scheme before them, and if they see I make a profit they are quite willing to give me money.

Carter thought it 'somewhat significant' that although Blom's letters all referred vaguely to the film business, and he was aware that Vieyra had not succeeded in exporting many films, 'yet he has never expressed any anxiety as to the safety of his money'. Vieyra was asked if he knew a Mr Dikker and denied ever having heard of him although Simon Dikker was the occupier of the house that was the address of the mysterious 'S Blom' and the maiden name of Dikker's wife.[1]

Among Vieyra's effects were found ammonia, a packet of cotton wool, a bottle of unknown liquid resembling water and a box of ball-pointed pens. An exhaustive analysis of the mysterious liquid found in his possession showed that it contained salts of an unknown substance in such minute quantities, that a three-fold process of development was required to produce the secret writing done with it. Until this was discovered the case against Vieyra had been very weak as it depended on his relations with a man named Blom whose identity had never been satisfactorily established. Vieyra, the former acrobat turned spy, was tried by Court Martial on three counts and on the second day confessed. He was found guilty on all three charges and sentenced to be shot, but this was commuted to penal servitude for life.[2]

Often, though, MI5 were unable to prove to build a sufficient case against a suspected individual. It was in such circumstances that the power of internment was deemed to be invaluable. This was so with the case of Mrs Stanaway, a woman of French origin and a dressmaker at Folkestone, Kent. She was mixed up with one Pierre Rotheudt, a Belgian Grain Merchant of German parentage, whose arrival in England MI5 had been warned about, but he slipped in to the country unnoticed by the Bureau. The police, however, found he had gone to Mrs Stanaway's. Rotheudt, who stated he was a Corporal in the Belgian Army, after a short stay, travelled back to the Front, was wounded, and in July 1916 again came to Folkestone and to Mrs Stanaway's, but also hired a room in a house opposite the French Consulate, which was conveniently situated with a clear view of everyone who went into it.

Soon after this, the Germans shot a number of French agents on their appearance in German territory. It was suspected that Rotheudt was the informant who had identified the agents to the Germans. It was discovered that he had been in communication with and had received money from German agents and sub-agents and, in August, he was arrested by the Belgian authorities on a charge of high treason. He was tried by Court Martial in France and sentenced to death, which was commuted to penal servitude for life. From prison, Rotheudt, through an illicit channel, communicated with Mrs Stanaway and she sent him money. It became clear after much correspondence had been censored that Mrs Stanaway had aided and abetted in passing forged documents to Rotheudt's friends in Holland, that she had received money from, and corresponded with a German agent, this which brought her to the notice of MI5. It was decided to arrest her, and a number of Rotheudt's letters were found in her rooms. On being interrogated, she lied about her knowledge of the charge on which Rotheudt was convicted, and also about her communications with him in prison. She denied having received money from a German agent. MI5 was advised against prosecution, so an order was obtained for her internment under DDR 14B on the grounds of her association with Rotheudt, a spy, and of her correspondence with another known German agent.[3]

During 1916, all but one spy were detected on information received from SIS and the work of this Department grew to be of the greatest importance to the 'G' Branch of MI5. The value of the permit system, i.e. the work of 'E' Branch was very valuable in 'forming fences' through which all travellers had to pass. The records kept by the 'E' Branch were also crucially important in tracing the movements of undesirables.

These frontier controls could be used in the most elastic way, either to prevent spies from embarking in foreign ports or to allow them to embark, subjecting them to a thorough search at the ports of arrival. It could also enable their papers to be taken away on arrival and sent to Scotland Yard, where the suspect would then have to call and claim them and therefore, be subjected to examination by the Police. Concerning outgoing suspects, people possessing 'inconvenient knowledge' could be kept in the country, or those who were allowed to leave could be searched for documents or addresses. Agents abroad were used to obtain evidence with regard to the associates, employers and trading of reputed spies.[4]

Guell

During 1917, a total of five foreign agents were arrested. One of these was a Spaniard, Mario Guell, who, in March 1915, aged forty-one, had been recommended to Commandant Wallner of the French Secret Service by a French agent who had worked with Guell in the automobile trade. In the course of 1915, Commandant Wallner sent him to Germany four times – from March to May, in June, in September, and in December. After his return in June, Guell reported that he had been arrested at Loerrachm. In September he revealed he was offered work by Captain van Reschenberg of the German Secret Service; after considering this offer, he accepted in December and was sent to Antwerp for instructions. Of the two first trips he submitted reports of no great value; of the third trip in September he gave no report at all; concerning the fourth trip he told Commandant Wallner frankly about his trip to Antwerp. After some hesitation Commandant Wallner accepted him as a double agent and instructed him to write letters to an address which had been given to Guell in Antwerp: i.e. L. Florini, Entrepreneur, Hotel de l'Europe, Lugano. Without mentioning these circumstances the address was given to the British authorities who put it on check, and a letter dated 18 January 1916, addressed to Florini was intercepted and tested with iodine fumes. A secret message flashed up and disappeared after a few moments. The writer could not be traced.

After December 1915 Guell was of no further use to Commandant Wallner. Early in 1916 Guell told the Commandant that, together with

Jose Berges, he was founding a factory to make false pearls and that he had worked previously in a similar business run by the firm of Heusch. Between January and July 1916 Guell went twice to Russia in connection with this new business. In August 1916 he was brought to the attention of the Commandant as a pro-German and as a potential German agent. He was, by then, preparing for a third trip to Russia. Guell was brought to the notice of British Intelligence by Commandant Wallner who informed MI5E that two Spaniards formerly employed by the French Intelligence Service had lately undertaken to work for the Germans and were going to Russia; he asked that visas should be granted after a delay of six days and that their movements should be watched in Norway. If they went to Russia the Russian authorities were making arrangements to arrest them; if they went to Germany under pretext of working for the French, he suggested that the British authorities should arrest them on their way back. The two men arrived and were kept under observation in England but did nothing to arouse suspicion.

From the Grosvenor Hotel, Guell despatched three telegrams to two different addresses in Barcelona, addressed to a Mr Marsans and a Mr Iturmendi, announcing the safe arrival of the two men. The telegrams, in Guell's handwriting were identified as that of the writer of the Florini letter mentioned earlier. Enquiries made in Spain showed that there was no Guell at the address given; Marsans, the son of a banker, was connected with a lady who was pro-German and 'greedy of money'; Iturmendi was a doctor, and his clinic was a centre of pro-German intrigue in Barcelona. Guell and Berges went through to Russia. Care had been taken at the British ports to do nothing to arouse the Spaniards' suspicions; but in Norway they were seen conversing with Germans. The Germans noticed that the party was being watched and no doubt warned the Spaniards. In October it was thought that the men would return shortly. Towards the end of the month the French had news that they were returning from Germany in seven or eight days and would probably sail for Spain direct from Scandinavia.

Guell and Berges were not arrested in Russia. They made several journeys from Petrograd to Rostov and went also to Vitebsk. Guell also travelled to Petrozavodsk. In Rostov they bought from an English firm 288 kilos of fish scales for the manufacture of false pearls, but the Russian Government refused them permission to ship this purchase. This was on 17 November but it was not till 7 January 1917 that the two men left Petrograd for Spain via England. Instructions were issued to Newcastle that, upon landing, they were to be sent under escort to Scotland Yard. Among Guell's papers were found the address of the proprietor of boats going direct from Bergen to Spain; the record of a telegram which he had despatched from Bergen; receipts for six telegrams and two registered letters sent direct from Russia to Spain; a pass-book showing a credit of more than £2,000 and no withdrawals in an account which he had opened with a Russian Bank in 1916; and a number of addresses but no letters, for he had torn them all up. Berges had no addresses; he had a letter of credit on the Credit Lyonnais for £1,000, of which he had withdrawn only 1,000 francs for a draft in Paris. Both men carried a quantity of picture postcards, mostly of Russia, and some of these had been marked. Guell carried aspirin tablets, potassium bromide and a box of brown powder labelled 'Protargol'; Berges had a tincture of iodine and throat tablets.

In examination Berges stated that he had written two wires signed with his name and despatched from the Grosvenor Hotel, while Guell admitted that all three telegrams were in his own handwriting. Berges explained that he was by profession an actor and the director of the Teatro Novedadis, but that he wished to retire from the profession and devote his energies to business, and take a partnership in the firm of Antonio Guell, the father of Mario Guell. Both men asserted that Antonio Guell was a maker of artificial pearls and that Mario Guell was travelling for it. Guell declared that his father's business had been carried on at 14 Calle San Beltrani, Barcelona until August or September of 1916, when he moved to a place called Bardalino (or Badalona) two miles from Barcelona. Guell's account of the Florini letter was confirmed by Commandant Wallner who added the information that Guell's father, Antonio, carried on the manufacture of paper bags and tinfoil at 14 Calle San Beltrani, Barcelona and that in September 1916, Mario Guell had moved to 36 Calle Badalona, a little house in which there was no trace of any industrial undertaking. There he passed as a commercial traveller. Although Commandant Wallner had never quite trusted Guell, he was unable to formulate any definite charge against him.

Orders were given to search the General Post Office for any telegrams that Guell might have despatched from England on his various visits to this country. Meanwhile, the Spanish Ambassador was pressing for a definite charge to be brought against the prisoners. As no direct evidence of espionage was found and neutrals could not be interned on the mere grounds of hostile sympathies, the suspects were released on 30 January and sent to Spain on 10 February, and instructions were issued for their arrest should they attempt to return. After they had left, the originals of the telegrams they had despatched from Russia arrived in England; but they were not considered to be suspicious.

The opposition to Guell's release was on the grounds that he was the agent of the suspect firm of Heusch that was believed to be linked to German espionage. Subsequently the French Intelligence Service supplied the information that the firm of Heusch, manufacturers of artificial pearls, had sent Mario Guell to Russia in 1915 to buy fish scales for them. In 1916 they used him for the same purpose, but instructed him to act as though for his own account, and as he was without money or credit Mario had his business paper and cards stamped with the name of his brother's firm 'Antonio Guell y Soler'. Thanks to the help of the Spanish Consul in Russia, Guell had contrived to procure fish scales for Heusch and was engaged in efforts to get permission for their export. The credits standing to Guell's account in Russia represented funds belonging to Heusch. Although, in MI5's view, 'Guell had clearly been involved in some nefarious business, his tracks had been well covered' and they could not prove anything. Guell and Berges were released on 30 January 1917 – and were deported to Spain on 10 February.

Alfred Hagn

MI5 had better success with Alfred Hagn, a Norwegian who applied for leave to come to Britain as representative of the *Dagblad* and the *Ukens Revy* newspapers on 29 September 1916, four days after obtaining a passport at Christiania. He landed in England on 9 October and spent six weeks in London, leaving again for Norway on 19 November. His application for a permit was submitted to MI5 who had no evidence against him. Early in January he applied for leave to visit again as a correspondent for the *Dagblad* and perhaps a Bergeh and Stockholm paper. He expressed the intention of staying for the duration of the war and gave the Norwegian Legation as a reference. So swift a return being undesirable, Major Dansey issued instructions that, unless eminently satisfactory in examination at the port, Hagn should be allowed to land only on condition of signing an undertaking to remain in England during the war. Hagn signed the undertaking and landed at Hull on 11 April, travelling to London and staying at 30 Tavistock Square. On the 21st he applied at the Foreign Office for permission to visit the Front. Mr Carnegie, of the Information Department of the Foreign Office, instituted some enquiries about Hagn among trustworthy Scandinavian journalists. As none of them could vouch for Hagn or recommend him in any way, Carnegie referred to MI5, which drew attention to Hagn's signed undertaking but raised no objection to his leave being granted. Carnegie then required a recommendation from the Norwegian Legation; which proved to be immediately forthcoming.

On 7 May a report was received from SIS that Alfred Hagn was a German agent but, as the source of their information, (the Christiania police), must be kept secret, the matter would require delicate handling. In consultation with Scotland Yard it was agreed that casual observation would be unsuitable and after verifying Hagn's address William Melville (in his last year of service with MI5) was sent for a few days to stay at 39 Tavistock Square to observe. The details of the case were signalled to the GPO, MI8, MI9, to the Home Office, Permit Office, Ports and Military Permit Office. Major Carter of MI5 also communicated with Carnegie, to arrange that, in order not to arouse Hagn's suspicions, he should be allowed to participate in some trip for foreign journalists. Hagn, having run short of money applied to his Vice Consul for help. The Vice Consul lent him £5 and wired on his behalf for money to be sent care of the Consulate. The telegram was addressed to 'Synnoeve, Braaten, Loerenskog Station'. Instructions were given to the General Post Office to forward the telegram and not to stop any reply to it but to send a copy to MI5. The wire was despatched on the 14th. Meanwhile, Melville who had made friends with Hagn at the hotel, had ascertained that the *Dagblad* had another correspondent in London; that Hagn did a good deal of writing in his bedroom; and left the Hotel at 11 a.m. returning in time for dinner. On the 12th, Melville had secured from a glass-stoppered bottle in Hagn's bedroom some white liquid, which on being tested proved to 'F' ink – a secret ink. Upon this report, Major Carter obtained from the General Post Office an authorisation for a detective of MI5 to go to the nearest post office and open a letter box; a warning of the gravity of the case was sent to the Telegraphic and Postal Censor and to the General Post Office and the Censor kept special watch for communications going to the *Dagblad* and for money orders coming to the Norwegian Consulate.

On 14 May a letter was intercepted purporting to have been written by Hagn's mother to her son on the 7th and this was followed by a letter from 'Synnoeve' acknowledging receipt of a letter and card from Hagn and summoning him back to Norway at once on account of his mother's illness. The rendezvous was at the Hotel Norge, Bergen. On the 15th, Hagn was seen to post some letters; the box was cleared and a letter addressed to Frau Julie Hagn, c/o Herr W. Erikson Simonsirk, pr.Loxevaeg, Bergen was found. On the following day he posted a roll of papers to the address of an English lady in Paris. Other intercepted letters, dated 15 and 17 May, showed that Hagn had written on arrival a postcard to a Halsen and three letters subsequently to 'Synnoeve' and that an article of his writing had appeared in the Bergenstidende but that with the exception of the letter from his mother he had received no news from Norway. Letters for Halsen were addressed to Fröken Pauline Hall, c/o Herr Madssen, Tergenfrinaton 35, Christiania. Hagn's letters were tested for secret writing but none was developed; however on the letter to his mother a shred of cotton wool was found. Other letters and articles written by Hagn were intercepted and tested without result; it was known that he had been to Hampton Court, near which there were munitions factories, with a man named Fredericsen, and that he had noticed the theft of some of his secret ink.

As it was thought that he might be using some medium unknown to MI5, it was considered dangerous to leave him at large any longer and he was arrested on 24 May. Major Carter, who was present at the arrest and search, appended a note to his report to the effect that an MI5 officer 'thoroughly conversant with the ways of spies' should always attend at the search of a suspect's room. 'F' ink was found in a bottle marked 'Edinol Dentifice', in a bottle labelled 'Gargle', on a ball-pointed pen and impregnated in a sponge, three canvas collars and a scarf. Cotton wool, the use of which Hagn was unable to explain, was also found in the room. Hagn explained that he had written only three articles since his arrival and that he was to be paid £5 an article; he had come over with £5, had received no money from Norway but had borrowed £5 from the Norwegian Consul and £5 from Fredericsen. He denied that he had used secret ink but when it was made clear to him that the whole process was known and after removal in custody, he made a written confession admitting that he had secret ink in his possession.

Hagn was seen once more and from the two interrogations an account of his life was drawn up: he was born in 1882; his father died early and at the age of eight his mother took him to be educated in America. In 1895 they returned to Norway and after further study there, Hagn became a jeweller's engraver. Some years later Hagn took up painting and literature. He went three times to Paris to study art, he published a book and wrote articles and stories for the *Dagblad*. In 1916 he came to England for the purpose of journalism only and his articles on the state of England attracted the attention of the Germans and, after some resistance on his part, they engaged him to work for them. They gave him a certain sum out of which he spared all he could for his mother; but he was delayed in Norway and spent most of what he had reserved for the journey. The Germans refused further supplies until he had worked for them. The two Germans with whom he was in touch were known as Laven and Leifholt; Synnoeve Braaton to whom his letters were to be sent was said to be 'an innocent girl'. The questions on which the Germans required information were:

'was the damage done by the Zeppelins really so slight and did the population take things as calmly as was reported; did the Press Bureau keep a lot of information from the public; was it likely there would be strikes? was there a shortage of food owing to the submarines and was there any likelihood of food riots? And did the British carry troops in Hospital Ships?' The confirmation of this and the time and day of the week of the arrival and departure of these ships was also sought. The Foreign Office were informed of the question regarding hospital ships and the peculiar insistence of the Germans with regard to this point. It was thought possible that they received false reports on the subject from their agents who were known to accept pay but to remain hidden in Holland and Denmark instead of proceeding to England.

Hagn applied subsequently for another interview and confessed that he had used secret ink three times, that he was to write to two addresses and that his real mission was a naval one. Major Carter had grounds for thinking that Hagn was concealing more and that he was making an attempt to communicate with the Germans by letter in code. The usual search of telegrams was undertaken but no wires to Pauline Hall and Synnoeve Braaton were traced. Pauline Hall was said to be receiving letters from Germany and to be both a paying guest in the house of Madssen of the Norax Annoncen bureau and a worker in his office. Synnoeve Braaton was said first to be an innocent young girl, whose letters to Laven had been intercepted by the Norwegian Police; afterwards it was stated that Braaton was an assumed name: Synnoeve's family name was Gedarkvist and her father was a baker. And Frau Julie Hagn was not dangerously ill, as alleged by Synnoeve.

News of Hagn's arrest was communicated to the Norwegian Minister and to Norway. Thereupon SIS officers in Norway protested that the Christiania police had lodged information against Hagn only on condition that he would be sent back to Norway where his evidence was required against two Germans, one of whom, Erik Lawen, was believed to be the head of German spies against England. MI5G replied that the information given by the Christiania police only confirmed the suspicions already ascertained by the British authorities and that Hagn could not be released. An effort was made to procure from Norway any letters written by Hagn, but the Norwegian Government had intercepted only one letter written by Hagn to Lawen and required this piece of evidence for production in the trial of Erik Lawen. Lawen, like Hagn an artist, had been arrested at Bergen and a German named Harthern, correspondent to the *Frankfurterzeitung,* was implicated in the same case. On their part, the Norwegian Government asked for particulars of the means used to develop Hagn's secret ink and for permission to interrogate Hagn on his connection with Lawen. Neither request could be granted by the British and the Norwegians declined to give any further assistance in the trial of Hagn. After forty-five different tests the Norwegians succeeded in developing messages about the movements of ships in Hagn's letters to Synnoeve Braaten. As these, presumably, were the identical letters which MI5's own chemists had tested in vain, and as Hagn carried materials for an ink already known to the British 'it was supposed that the Germans had discovered some additional means of rendering the ink difficult to develop'. Lawen, who was implicated in the destruction of Norwegian shipping by bombs, was sentenced to five years imprisonment.

The Summary of Evidence against Hagn was completed on 15 July and the trial took place on 27 and 28 August. Hagn was charged under DRR48, 18A, and 22A on counts of having committed a preparatory act in coming to England on 11 April; of having been in communication and of having attempted to communicate with a spy address; and of being in unlawful possession of a medium for secret writing. He was found guilty on all counts and sentenced to death. The sentence was confirmed. The Norwegian Minister petitioned for mercy on the grounds that there was medical evidence of Hagn's 'reduced mentality'. A statement regarding Hagn's mental condition had been accepted by the Court and considered before passing sentence; it was therefore decided that there were no military grounds for commuting the sentence, but for diplomatic reasons and as an act of friendship to the Norwegian Government, the sentence was commuted to one of penal servitude for life. A notice of the sentence and its commutation was issued to the Press on the grounds that it would act as a deterrent and a warning to other neutrals, that it was an act of mercy and the trial was well known in Norway. When the news was received from Norway that secret writing had been found in Hagn's letters, he seemed to have been informed of the fact for, in a written statement, he confessed that after his return from England in November 1916 he had been introduced to Lawen who, with others, engaged him as a German agent. This took place in the presence of Synnoeve Braaton. By implication Hagn's first visit to Britain was innocent; MI5 noted, however, that when he left England, in November 1916, his ship was delayed and he stayed for a night or two in North Shields where he met a certain Pastor Steen, who 'knew everything there was to be known about the Tyne Docks and shipping'. By now there was little doubt that Hagn was of 'unsound mentality inclining to religious mania'. Through an 'unfortunate slip' Hagn was deported from Britain on the 19 September 1919 without any consultation with MI5.

Van der Goten

The story of Van der Goten was very obscure: 'the guiding motive of his life was cupidity but his story is essentially one of quarrels between himself and other Belgian Agents engaged in the French, Belgian and British Services and there is some suggestion that he was lured to his undoing by a Belgian for a low personal motive'. Leon Francois van der Goten, a Belgian diamond cutter by trade, fled from Belgium with his family in September 1914. The party went to Breda, where for a time Leon lived on his mother's savings and after March 1915 became a waiter at the Cavalry Barracks moving subsequently to the Café de Pool, Breda.

Together with J. Ven he endeavoured to establish a courier service for smuggling news out of Belgium on behalf of 'A. Plus', an SIS officer; they also helped young Belgians and Frenchmen to escape into Holland and conducted them to the Belgian Consulate at Breda receiving £4 for each person safely brought across. Van der Goten secured four plans of strategic points in Belgium, these he sold to Plus having previously made copies for his own future use. Dissatisfied with his remuneration Van der Goten procured from Gradon, of the Belgian Consulate at Rotterdam, an introduction to the Uranium Hotel, which was the centre of the Allied Secret Services, and there offered the services of himself and Ven to the British. After an interval of sixteen days the offer was declined.

While Van der Goten was awaiting the result of his overtures to the British he quarrelled with Ven, whose share of profits he had retained; as a result the Belgian Consul refused to pay him some 200 fr. owing for the latest batch of Belgian refugees. Then came the refusal of the British to employ him. In a rage Van der Goten vowed that as soon as the Belgian Consul paid him he would betray the Allied Services to the Germans. Unknown to him, since January 1917, Theunissen, of the French Secret Services, had been keeping Van der Goten under observation. When Theunissen learned of the quarrel with Ven and of the threat, he reported it to his superiors. Through a second intervention of Gradon, Van der Goten, had, it would seem, got into touch with an unnamed member of the British Services and had proposed and been commissioned to organise an information service on the Belgian railways. Theunissen, who had wormed himself into Van der Goten's confidence and become his partner, learned of the scheme and of Van der Goten's intention to betray the Belgians taking part in it. He informed the French and the scheme collapsed.

Van der Goten then announced that the time had come to go over to the Germans and soon after he asked Theunissen to give to the Germans certain definite information against Belgian couriers.

Theunissen then stated that the Germans were already in possession of the facts and that he himself was a German agent, whereupon Van der Goten said they would share the profits. Finally at Van der Goten's request Theunissen undertook to introduce him to a German Secret Service agent. An agent of the French Service named Gremling, who spoke German well, was put up to play the part under the alias Lieutenant Krichel. At the meeting Van der Goten produced a plan of the flying camp at St. Denys, Belgium, stating that it was the copy of an original which he had obtained from a courier working for the British; he gave other information and accepted six weeks pay and a season ticket for a month usable on the Dutch railways in order that he might visit various British agents. A trap was laid for him 'into which he fell head first'.

Between 5 and 15 May he sent in four reports giving correct information about the Allied Forces. Having found out all Van der Goten knew and seeing that he was dangerous the French determined to get him out of Holland. MI5 noted how: 'Greed was his dominating passion and he hated the British.' By playing on these motives he was induced to ask for work in England. After some apparent demur Krichel was allowed to go to England as a courier on condition the first journey was made with Theunissen. A passport and British visa were secured and, once safely on board the *Kirkham Abbey*, Van de Goten was told that he was to go to Folkestone and collect reports for a possible German bombardment of the British coast. Van de Goten accepted the mission but afterwards took fright and wished to leave the vessel; Theunissen reassured him. The two men were arrested at Hull and sent up to London. Van der Goten was interrogated at Scotland Yard and asked to see a British Secret Service official. He had 'recourse to the usual excuse, namely, that he had come to unearth and traduce a nest of spies in England'.

According to English law Van der Goten could not be tried for any offence committed in Holland; there remained the fact that on the boat he had accepted a definite mission for a person whom he believed to be a German agent. Through the courtesy of the French Intelligence Service, Gremling and Theunissen were brought over to give evidence at the Summary of Evidence taken on 10 and 11 September, and also at the Court Martial which was held on 24 September. The exhibits included the four reports which Van der Goten had furnished during May and the interrogation of 18 June, the passport showing that he had come over as a railway official, and a piece of paper giving the approximate size of the plan which Van der Goten had shown to Krichel. The Belgian Auditeur General was represented at the trial.

Van der Goten was tried under DRR48 and found guilty of

committing an act preparatory to a contravention of DRR18 with intent to assist the enemy. He was sentenced to be shot but at the 'prayer of the Belgian Government' the sentence was commuted to one of penal servitude for Life. Van der Goten's wife 'cast him off' and eventually went to live with Theunissen. This 'circumstance possibly coupled' with Van der Goten's reiterated appeals for justice induced the Belgian Government to take up his case and ask that he should be handed over to the Belgian military on the grounds that the sentence inflicted was somewhat severe and put out of date by the ending of hostilities. It was decided that the Army Council had no power to hand over the prisoner, but only to remit the remainder of the sentence. The Belgian Minister therefore appealed for this act of clemency. But the Army Council considered the crime committed by Van der Goten to be 'a particularly heinous form of espionage' and that a remission of the sentence 'was not only in itself undesirable but impolitic as it would be used as a precedent and encourage the making of similar appeals on behalf of other criminals'.[5]

Although there were other cases of German espionage – and not all spies from Germany had been detected let alone apprehended – by 1917 the Prussian threat had been, essentially, defeated. Up to the end of 1917 the number of spies captured and tried since war broke out amounted to twenty-one males and two females. Of these, thirteen males had been executed, six males sentenced to penal servitude, one to imprisonment and the two females to penal servitude; one male spy had committed suicide. Under DRR14B. 136 males and 21 females had been interned.[6] While the enemy might not have been that impressive, the organisation that was now MI5 could only confront the enemy that was before it. And it had succeeded through the sheer hard work and dedication of its staff. At the apex of the organisation sat Vernon Kell. In the summer of 1917, in recognition of MI5's work, Kell was knighted, receiving the KBE; later he was given the Belgian Order of Leopold, the Order of St. Olaf from Norway, the Order of St. Lazarus from Italy and was made Officer of the Legion of Honour, all in recognition of his work.

Endgame

Kell and his family had what one might call a good war. On the whole, with a young family, the Kells did not experience the personal sense of loss that many British families experienced as the final death toll of British and Empire war dead passed a million. The news of the death of one of Kell's cousins was probably the nearest that he came to this. It saddened him greatly; the young man had, very reluctantly, become a soldier 'for he was a genuine pacifist' but he 'had felt it his duty to join up', and trained sufficiently 'to be a really capable officer'. He fell, 'leading his men over the top', shortly after his arrival in France. 'He had a premonition would not return and told his father so.'

This was a new type of war. And an example of it was brought home to the Kells in the summer of 1917. Earlier in 1917, Constance had brought the family up to live in London; she had at last found a town house after much searching on Campden Hill:

> We came up from Weybridge on a cold snowy day, the furniture van sinking deep into the drive in front of our house. The maids got into the last van and thought it a huge joke; they brought our livestock with them, our beloved Scottie dog, the cat, and the parrot. A skid in the snowy road landed the van into a shop window on the way up, and slung the parrot cage through it, the screeching bird adding to the confusion.

Moving to London, though, provided a glimpse of the shape of thing to come. That summer Kell and Constance went off for a few days leave to Dulverton in Somerset and found that German prisoners of war were working in the garden of their hotel and in the fields helping the farmers. Kell was amused to see how happy they seemed, and that often the Germans would ride back on the farm horses while their master walked beside them, chatting gaily. Kell asked about these men and was told that the farmers liked employing them for they were good workers: 'Never a straight back all day in the field' they said. When Kell got back to London, he was just in time to see the first big daylight raid of the war. He was in his office, but suddenly hearing the warning sounded, looked up to see the sky filled with droning planes and heard explosions in quick succession. Constance was in a bus with her daughter and her cousin on their way to the Princess Theatre (to a presentation organised by many schools of the Jacques Dalcroze method of teaching concentration through rhythmic movements to music). When the bus driver realised what was happening, he pulled up his bus to the curb by Knightsbridge Barracks and 'everyone ran helter skelter... for shelter'. After about half an hour, the maroons give the all clear and Constance and her party continued on their journey through the streets where smoke was still rising from buildings hit by bombs in the Shaftsbury Avenue direction. When Constance next heard the maroons go off in London it was on 11 November and this time it was to inform that the Armistice terms had been signed. She wrote later:

Can I describe the excitement, the relief, the joy of that morning. It was greater than any pen could tell. We rushed into the streets, the crowds gathering rapidly and surging towards Whitehall, there to rejoice madly, gladly, singing and dancing to relieve the pent up feelings that oppressed us for so long. Nobody felt like work for a while, but that had to go on just the same, though now K and everyone in his office worked with light hearts after all those long years of strain and stress. There was a Victory Ball at the Albert Hall in aid of Red Cross funds and to this we all went. It was a wonderful sight, and the excitement enormous, for it still seemed almost too good to be true that we had really finished with all that the War brought with it of horror and deprivation. It took some time before the food situation eased, for it had really been a very near thing, only another two or three months' food left in the country and starvation had loomed as a stark possibility in the near future. General Foch and the grand old man Clemenceau, arrived in London on December 1st and they were given a rapturous welcome, also on December 26th, President Wilson arrived, large crowds to greet him too. Great hopes were centred on him, for if America would really take a share in solving the way to peace, we dreamed of this War being the one to end wars.

With the end, the staff at MI5 could at least relax a little – and reflect on a job well done. Some of them had the bright idea of getting up an entertainment amongst themselves, which they called the Hush Hush Show. 'It was,' recalled Constance, 'a clever take off of all the bosses of the various sections, rather merciless in some cases but all taken in very good part.' Kell was very convincingly caricatured and 'he was delighted with the thrusts at him, for they had got him walking with his familiar stoop end with all his tricks of manner. The show was followed by a dance, and the whole thing was voted a great success'.[7]

And enjoying the show was the backbone of MI5's activities throughout the war: the female staff. During the war over 650 women were employed at various times in MI5; and, in the words of the post-war report on their activities, the majority of these 'it may truthfully be said that they gave ungrudging service to what they rightly considered to be "war work" of great importance, and that in many cases they were women of particular ability. The work was exacting and continuous, the office never being shut day nor night, work going on without a break on Sundays, Christmas Days and Bank Holidays as on weekdays.' The staff worked in eight hour shifts, 'but the urgency of the work and the vital importance of tracking down the potential spy', together with the enormous mass of papers requiring to be dealt with necessitated a great deal of overtime. But the staff was not paid for overtime:

> indeed the authorities, realising the great strain involved, endeavoured to discourage it, but the extra hours were given willingly by the women from motives of patriotism and keenness in their work, and it is perhaps interesting to note, in the face of the popular belief in the leisurely existence led by Government clerks, that overtime had by September 1918 become such a matter of course with the staff that a "circular memorandum" deprecating it as prejudicial to health, was actually issued.

When MI5 went operational, in 1909, it was with one officer single-handed; but in March 1910 a confidential clerk was provided and his daughter, the first woman employed in the Bureau, was engaged as typist in January 1911. In October 1911 the first woman secretary was appointed. 'On her devolved the work of private secretary to the head of the Bureau, and the opening and acknowledging of letters, the custody of all secret and confidential documents and the formation of a card index to the records of the Bureau.' In February 1913 a second woman secretary was engaged and a third was added in January 1914. Thus on the outbreak of war – 4 August 1914 – the staff consisted of five women. Their work consisted of 'filing and indexing the records, with the resultant power of being able to produce the essential papers at the psychological moment; not to mention the importance of efficient and modifiable office organisation in speeding up the work'.

H Branch (which ultimately divided into eleven sections H to H10) took over the work formerly done by C Branch – the office organisation and the custody of MI5 records. It was in H Branch that the all-important Registry became a sub-section known as H2. A Lady Superintendent – Miss Lomax – (with an Assistant Lady Superintendent) was appointed as the officer in charge of H2 with a staff of forty-nine clerks under her. In H2 the number of women needed for the 'looking-up' and filing of papers exceeded the needs of any other section, and roughly speaking, the proportion of Registry clerks to secretaries was two to one. As the war proceeded the amount of information received from all sources and on all subjects became overwhelming. It was found necessary to divide certain Branches into sub-sections, each dealing with a different part of the world.

The qualifications which MI5 required in its women clerks and secretaries were 'intelligence, diligence and, above all, reticence'. Not only was it necessary that in accordance with the duty of all employees, the staff should not discuss the affairs of their employers, but also – especially during the earlier days of the war – it was the policy of MI5 to conceal the locality and even the very existence of a British Contre-espionage Bureau. From the earliest days, therefore, MI5 sought its clerks in the ranks of educated women, 'who should naturally be supposed to have inherited a code of honour, that is to say the women staff of MI5 consisted of gentlewomen who had enjoyed a good school, and in some cases a University education'. As it was not possible to seek such women publicly, candidates were in most instances recommended to MI5 by existing members of the staff. As the need grew for greater numbers than could be supplied in this way, the heads of the principal ladies' colleges, such as Cheltenham, Holloway, St Hugh's and Somerville Colleges, were approached and asked to nominate suitable ex-pupils for vacancies in MI5.

The hours of work as before mentioned were nominally an eight hour shift. Half a day off was given once a week, and, when possible, every alternate Sunday, and a week's holiday was given. Every effort was made 'to put the right person in the right place', while at the same time due regard was paid to the interests of the individual. Thus, instead of summary dismissal, an 'apparently rather incompetent worker' was often given another chance in a different sphere of work, and was able to show her capabilities in that particular direction. In this way the best value was obtained from the workers, and talents which might otherwise have been wasted were employed to good advantage.

As the male MI5 officer noted in his report, any account of MI5 would be 'incomplete were no mention made of the air-raids. The first Zeppelin attack was in the autumn of 1915.' The Central Special Intelligence Bureau received a warning about half an hour before the attack, 'but though the staff knew that if the German Secret Service were aware of the locality of their office it would inevitably be signalled out for destruction, there was no confusion, but everyone went on calmly with her work nor did they desist when the first bomb fell to be followed by others dropped less than a quarter of a mile away from the building'. The 'coolness of the staff' on this occasion was 'paralleled in all future raids both by daylight and at night'. There was 'never any panic', the authorities issued instructions as to procedure in raids which 'were faithfully' carried out, and a fire drill was instituted in case an incendiary bomb should strike the building.

The MI5 investigators depended heavily upon the knowledge of the female staff. The 'looker-up' had nevertheless to be for ever on the *qui vive* for possible variations; she learned to 'look-up' automatically all

Cs under K, Ph under F, V under W etc., to reverse double vowels, to divide double consonants, to transpose syllables, to translate names according to nationality, and such simple expedients; but all this was 'elementary'. A good 'looker-up' had to be intelligent, to have a wide general knowledge, and a smattering at least of foreign languages, 'but above all she must have that peculiarly feminine gift of intuition, or the faculty of not only making two and two equal four, but of realising that two and two can equal five'. Upon the 'looker-up' depended to a 'large measure the success of an Intelligence Bureau, because if the officers dealing with a suspect are not supplied by the Registry with any former papers containing incriminating information about that suspect, they are deprived of the proof necessary to bring him or her to justice'. That many spies were brought to justice during the war thanks to the intelligence and intuition of the 'looker-up' was 'an acknowledged fact'. For example, a German American who had come over to England on several occasions had succeeded in assuring the authorities that he was only a harmless commercial traveller, 'and had been completely whitewashed'. But it occurred to one of the women clerks in the Registry that, owing to a certain similarity in the names, this man might be identical with a sea captain for whom MI5 had long been on the watch. Her suggestion was at first considered much too 'far fetched', but a letter from the officer conducting the investigation shows the result in following up the clue:

Dear –
Thanks entirely to the Registry we have caught another spy. Many congratulations. Perhaps you will let them know how pleased we are with their good work in this case and I hope it will cheer them to renewed efforts.

The work of the secretaries in MI5 did not differ largely from the work of secretaries in other offices, 'but it should be mentioned that they were allowed to take more responsibility than falls to the share of the ordinary office secretary and were given more scope for individual work in the drafting of letters etc., and in keeping the bulk of the routine work from the shoulders of the officers. That this latitude was not misplaced was proved by the excellent work done by the secretaries and the responsibility taken by them with successful results.' The best secretaries were of 'invaluable service to their officers owing to the keenness with which they studied the cases with which he was dealing, and by their memory of detail they have often aided him in his investigations'. A case in point occurred with reference to the ex-German Consul Ahlers of Newcastle, who was, on the outbreak of war, removed from that prohibited area and settled at Richmond where he changed his name to Anderson. One day information came to MI5 about a certain suspect at Richmond named Anderson, who appeared to the officer to be a fresh case until, on mentioning the name to his secretary, she at once remembered the ex-Consul's change of name and residence. 'There can be no doubt that a great deal of valuable identification was done by the secretaries' recollection of apparently unimportant details, and that the officers relied upon this recollection; though it became such a matter of daily routine that it is difficult to collect instances at this date.' Another way in which the secretary 'greatly helped MI5' was by 'her knowledge of office routine, the correct style of official correspondence, and the hundred and one details of inter-departmental etiquette'.

On 1 September 1918, the two Heads of the Registry and the three original secretaries were mentioned in the London Gazette 'for valuable war services'; and in August 1919 ten other members of the staff were similarly distinguished. A letter written by Kell to the Controller of the Women's Staff summed up the opinion held by the officers of MI5 on the work of the women engaged in that Department.

MI5
18-8-19
Dear Miss Lomax
I was so pleased to see in to-days Gazette that ten of our ladies had been mentioned for valuable War Services in connection with the War. Please give them my congratulations.
  With a staff like yours, which one and all have done such splendid work, it is always very difficult to make a selection which will be small enough to be admissable and at the same time representative of the various kinds of work performed.
Yours sincerely
(ad) VGW Kell
Director Special Intelligence

Miss Lomax was made a Member of the British Empire in 1918 and received the Order of the British Empire in 1920. Miss E.L. Harrison was made an MBE in 1920.

The male officer who wrote up the account of the women's work in MI5 during the war concluded his report by asking: 'what conclusions can be drawn as to its value? Was it suited to their capacities? Or would it have been better performed had it been possible to replace the women by men?' His conclusions were:

It will be seen to what a great extent the work of MI5 depended on its women. The index (which was the work of the women) was truly the life-blood of MI5 and the intelligent use of it made by the 'lookers-up' supplied vitality to all the branches. The officers reposed such confidence in the Registry staff that they very rarely came down to 'look up' themselves, and indeed few of them had the necessary experience of 'snags' which sharpened the wits of the woman Registry clerk and enabled her to produce results from the most unpromising materials. She was equipped for the work by her two peculiarly feminine characteristics, intuition and love of detail. By the possession of these two faculties she was a more efficient instrument for the work than the majority of men. There were women in MI5 who displayed the more masculine qualities of power of organisation and decision and broad methods of work, and who did invaluable service for the Department. Still it may justly be contended that such work would have been as well done by men, even possibly – though this is more open to controversy – by the type of male clerk who (had the employment of men been either possible or desirable) would have replaced the women, i.e. of a lower social standing and fewer educational advantages. But the work of the Registry in the identification of suspects from records and indices was work for which women clerks, as women, seem peculiarly qualified and for which men, as men, have as a rule neither the patience, the interest in meticulous and tiresome detail, nor the intuition. Too much stress must not of course be laid on the last qualification, for only those who have worked in the Registry can appreciate how much of the good results obtained were due to laborious spade-work, the wading though tedious particulars with dogged endurance... that often appeared a brilliant 'brain wave'.[8]

7

Dual Threats
SIS & the General Strike 1919–1926

C's Green Ink and Eyes

In 1919, Colonel Sir Vernon Kell came up with the idea of forming a dinner club, which he called the IP. What did it stand for, he was asked: 'Well,' he would laugh, 'I suppose it stands for "Intelligent People".' There were to be two dinners a year and male members of his past and present staff were eligible to join. Kell was president, the rule being, that there should be only one short after dinner speech, that of the president, for it was to be a purely friendly gathering and some special guests were to be invited each time. The first two dinners went well; there were no ladies present but Lady Kell was allowed to peep into the large dining room at the Hyde Park Hotel:

> and see the preparations being made and enjoy the beautiful table decorations. The management took great pride in endeavouring to make these dinners the best to be had in London. I have heard it said that K's short speech was most entertaining, and the few rather spicy stories he told were greeted with much merriment and applause. He had become a good speaker, for he constantly lectured to people in the various branches of the Services interested in Intelligence, and he got the reputation of being one of the lecturers they liked best, though when they compared notes, his audiences had to confess, that interesting though he was to listen to, they had really come away with no secret information whatever – he was much too clever to give anything away.

Kell also felt that the time had come to begin to cut down the staff of the MI5 and get back to peacetime conditions. He greatly regretted saying goodbye to those who had become 'most efficient' in his department. 'At that time,' recalled Constance, 'there really was a feeling that Lloyd George's words might come true and that this was the War to end Wars – so much so, that boys leaving school had no desire to join the army or the navy – The Air Force beckoned more successfully, being so full of adventure, and was such a new branch of the fighting services.' One day, Kell smiled when Jim, 'our elder boy, said he thought it would be useless now to go to Sandhurst, he felt sure that there would be no more wars'; his father, however, considered it impossible to envisage a long period of peace, 'while the world was still so little ready to accept the League of Nations as a means of set-tling the thorny questions facing the Nations, they were too difficult to unravel. Eventually, Jim decided to try for Sandhurst, for already there was less talk of "no more wars".'

By this time Kell had become interested in the Japan Society formed to promote interchange of thought between the Japanese and British. Lectures were often given, dinners and social occasions were many, and when the Crown Prince Hirohito arrived on his state visit, the Society played a big part in entertaining him. Kell also belonged to the China Society through which he could renew his acquaintance with many of the friends who had been so hospitable while he and Constance were in Tientsin. In 1923, he joined the British Institute of International Affairs, housed in St. James's Square. Amongst others, he and Constance were lectured to by Mahatma Ghandi 'who spoke eloquently. As he concluded, several of his own countrymen got up to refute some of his remarks, and to put questions to him that he found difficult to answer. They too were eloquent, but much more realistic than Gandhi who remained perfectly calm end dignified and replied to his questioners with not a trace of irritation at their disagreement. It was most impressive.' Another fascinating lecture, was given by Dr Benes of Czechoslovakia: 'We felt,' remembered Constance, 'that if it were possible for his hopes to be fulfilled, his country could go forward peacefully and with confidence. He was to have a rude awakening!' Many years later, Constance reflected: 'Curious the way one had a sense of foreboding all through those years, the longing for peace was so great, yet the sense of unrest and frustration even greater.' Both she and Vernon worried about the future: 'Our children were too young to be involved in the first World War, but what of the next? Our two sons would certainly be fighting in that one.'[1]

But for Kell and MI5 the greatest threat to his empire came from his rival intelligence agency – the Secret Intelligence Service, commonly known as MI6, but still to acquire that title. The opportunity for SIS to make its bid to absorb MI5 was provided by the issue of money – or rather the lack of money. Peace did not usher in Lloyd George's 'Land Fit for Heroes'. Instead, after a short post-war boom, Britain experienced a severe economic depression. The financial orthodoxy of the day demanded retrenchment and so, on 22 March 1921, the Cabinet approved the appointment of a Committee 'to examine the expenditure on Secret Service by the several Departments, and, after hearing all the necessary evidence, to report their recommendations to the Cabinet for reducing expenditure and avoiding overlapping'. Sir Warren Fisher, a senior Treasury official, was appointed Chairman alongside Sir Eyre Crowe and Sir Maurice Hankey, the Chief Secretary to the Cabinet.[2] In framing the Secret Service financial estimate for the year ending 31 March 1922, the Treasury found themselves confronted by demands from the spending departments for a total sum, which, with the addition of a general reserve fund for contingencies, amounted to £475,000, as against £400,000 for 1920–1921 and a pre-war average of less than £50,000. In the belief that the presentation to the House of Commons of an estimate exceeding that for 1920–1921 'would arouse determined opposition and a demand for details which it would be most undesirable to grant, but extremely difficult to resist', the Treasury arrived at a Secret Service estimate of £300,000 hoping that it would eventually be possible to reduce the original £475,000 to this amount, or, in the worst event, to obtain the balance by a supplementary estimate later. The avoidance of the necessity for such a supplementary estimate became the principal pre-occupation of the new Committee – no one wanted Parliament sticking its nose into the Secret Service. The Departments to which Secret Service funds were ordinarily allotted, and the amount for which each had applied for 1922, was: Foreign Office £185,000; foreign intelligence £121,000; contre-espionage £31,000; Miscellaneous £28,000. The counter-espionage estimate of £31,000 was what was allocated to MI5 but the Committee recommended cutting its budget to £19,300. It could have been worse, for the Committee:

> were at first sceptical as to the necessity at the present juncture of maintaining a counter-espionage organisation, but it appears that the agents of at least four Powers are already showing activity in this country, and whereas, before the war, this branch was able to concentrate its attention on Germany, there are now several quarters which require watching. In addition to this, there is the new factor of bolshevism in the navy and army, the detection and counter-action of which fall to M.I.5, while the several Government Offices have frequent recourse to the information regarding individuals and societies compiled during the war and still available in the department. The Committee feel in the circumstances that there is justification for the continuance of M.I.5 on its present reduced scale during the current year, but that next year a further cut of £5,000 to £6,000 should be possible.[3]

What this meant in practice was that MI5 would be grossly under-funded and, consequently, undermanned for the threat that would emerge from the new Communist regime in Soviet Russia.

The serious threat to MI5 came in 1925 when the Prime Minister, Stanley Baldwin, established another Secret Service Committee, once again under the chairmanship of Sir Warren Fisher, to review the existing arrangements of the three Secret Service organisations – namely SIS, MI5, and the Special Branch based at Scotland Yard – and in particular their methods of distributing information and, when occasion arose, of taking executive action. It was a chance for SIS to attempt a palace coup and gobble up their rivals, particularly Kell's MI5.

It is the tradition of every Chief of the Secret Service, or head of SIS, to initial documents 'C', in green ink, in honour of Mansfield Cumming the first CSS who always wrote with that colour ink. When he appeared before the Secret Service Committee, Admiral Sir Hugh Sinclair, Cumming's successor as C, had eyes that were green as well as his signature, for he argued that the whole organisation of British Secret Service, by which he included all branches of it, was fundamentally wrong: all were working separately; and there was no central control of policy, but a serious lack of co-ordination and co-operation which resulted in overlapping and waste of time. An instance of this was the distance by which the various branches were separated from each other and Whitehall, which involved great expenditure of time in going to and fro; it also tended to 'excessive reliance on the telephone', which was unsatisfactory from the point of view both of the transaction of business and of the danger of compromise. Files and records were kept in different buildings, and there was great delay in consulting those in possession of another branch. C argued that all the different branches ought to be placed under one head and in one building in the neighbourhood of Whitehall, and to be made responsible to one Department of State, which ought to be the Foreign Office – this, of course, was the Department of State that C's SIS were responsible to.

C's claim was that, owing to a lack of central direction, where information or action was required by one branch of another, it was not possible to give instructions, but only to invite co-operation, with the result that in many instances such co-operation failed to mature. He also argued that it was impossible to draw the line between espionage and counter-espionage, for both were concerned solely with foreign activities, and to attempt in practice to make a distinction between the two only led to overlapping. Nor was overlapping confined to SIS and MI5: it also occurred between SIS and the secret service side of the Special Branch; indeed, he had gone to the pains of keeping record for three weeks, in the course of which twenty-five cases of overlapping had been noticed. It was known that this lack of liaison resulted in agents being paid twice for the same thing by different people. Sinclair proposed an amalgamation of SIS and MI5 under one head and one roof in the neighbourhood of Whitehall. It did not need a vivid imagination to conclude as to whom this new organisation should be under.

When Kell – referred to as K – appeared before the Secret Service Committee, he explained how MI5 was responsible for what might be described as 'home security'. The term 'counter-espionage' as a description of MI5's work was no longer entirely applicable: counter-espionage proper at present formed only a part of it. He was also responsible for the safety of the Armed Forces of the Crown, both in respect of foreign espionage and Communist interference. The dividing link between his sphere of activity and that of Scotland Yard was quite distinct: if in the course of investigating a case of tampering with the Armed Forces, K encountered an individual or a group of individuals concerned exclusively with civil disturbance, he would pass his information on to Scotland Yard and leave that department to deal with it. Scotland Yard, on its side, would at once refer to him any matter, which came its way affecting the Armed Forces. The policy of the Soviet Government, he explained, was to start 'cells' in the Armed Forces and in arsenals and dockyards; such cells, when formed, were naturally his concern. There was no overlapping between MI5 and Scotland Yard. The latter were not in a position to carry out the work, which he did with the Armed Forces. K had free and direct access to all Service commands, could see anyone he wished and give advice as to the action to be taken to deal with matters within his purview.

When it was pointed out, by Sir Maurice Hankey, that the original idea was for K and C's work to be amalgamated, Kell replied that their respective duties were not properly defined at the start. They were installed together in one room, in 1909, in Superintendent Drew's private detective agency in Victoria Street. It became essential to get some working arrangement and as a result C (Cumming) was given the foreign, and he, the home side. They then found that their methods of work were so entirely different – C's essentially secret and his own largely in the open – that their cohabitation had to be determined. This difference continued today: the present C worked entirely through secret agents, he himself mainly through the Chief Constables, Commanding Officers and other avowable channels. Foreign military attachés actually visited him in his office. Kell argued that the distinction between SIS and MI5 work lay not so much between espionage and counter-espionage as in the fact that he had 'executive' functions and C had none. By 'executive' it was agreed by Kell and the Committee that 'advisory' would more accurately describe his functions. Kell did not, for instance, have the power to give instructions to Chief Constables to take action: he would consult the Director of Public Prosecutions and address the Chief Constable concerned armed with his authority; and occasionally the Director of Public Prosecutions would communicate with the Chief Constable direct.

Kell argued that the various branches of secret service should be kept separate on the basis that it made for greater security, and because an amalgamation of the military, with the civil, side would be a mistake, especially in times of civil unrest. He was opposed even to concentration in one building: a wholly secret service ought not to be under the same roof with one, which was only partially secret. It was essential to maintain his present direct contact with Chief Constables and Commanding Officers. The former, particularly, appreciated the personal element and, if they were required to send their communications through ordinary departmental channels, they would, as sources of information, almost certainly dry up. On the other hand, the personal element did not necessarily depend on himself alone: Chief Constables would probably extend their confidence to any individual whom they felt they could trust.

Kell's arguments fell on deaf ears. A majority of the Committee took the view that MI5 and SIS would be more efficient under one leader. It seemed that C was about to get his way and absorb Kell's Service. But MI5 was saved by the intervention of Hankey who argued against this; deliverance was secured by a report, written by a senior civil servant, Sir Russell Scott, and commissioned in an effort to help resolve the split on the Committee. Scott found against amalgamation partly owing to the difficulty of correctly assigning ministerial responsibility for a single organisation and partly because such an organisation would be dangerously large in bulk. So, MI5 was saved and Sinclair's empire building halted. But SIS's relationship with MI5 remained an uneasy one.[4]

Strike

In December 1920 unemployment rose from 300,000 to 700,000 – a staggering increase. By June 1921 some 2 million men were unemployed in Britain. In January 1919, 70,000 people had gone on strike in Glasgow and the iconic image of the Red Flag flying above City Hall and tanks on the streets was burned into the minds of many people – of all classes – as a portent of things to come. Even the police were threatening to go on strike. By April 1921, 8 million working days had been lost to strikes and Lloyd George's Coalition Government of Liberals and Tories were soon faced with the prospect of ultimate industrial strike power: a General Strike by the Triple Alliance of the National Union of Railwaymen, the National Union of Seamen and the National Federation of Mineworkers. Acting together, these three Unions had the potential to paralyse the British economy and through extra-Parliamentary action challenge the basis of the British state – the rule of law through Parliament. At least this was how some in the Government saw it. The issue over which this conflict was developing centred on the coal industry. It had been nationalised during the war and the Miners Federation, representing workers who toiled in appalling conditions, resented the industry being returned to private hands. From the Government's position while some in Whitehall recognised that workers' grievances were essentially non-revolutionary but based on concerns about employment and their standard of living, others believed there was a revolutionary element that threatened Parliamentary democracy in Britain – because the world had changed, in 1917, with the Russian Revolution. And, in 1920, the Communist Party of Great Britain had been formed, led by men such as Harry Pollitt and Willie Gallagher, dedicated to creating or exploiting the conditions that would lead to the overthrow of the capitalist system.

On 1 April 1921 the Miners Federation withdrew their members from all the coal mines, specified economic and political conditions on which work would be resumed, and, in MI5's opinion, 'backed by the Communist Press and Party', endeavoured to persuade the Railway and Transport Union to strike in their support, 'compelling the rest of the nation to accede to their demands'. The Government immediately responded to the political challenge the same day: Regulations under the Emergency Powers Act 1920 were promulgated by Order in Council. On 4 April the Regulations were laid before both Houses of Parliament. It appeared likely that combined action by the Triple Alliance of labour unions would happen, and on 8 April the Prime Minister, Lloyd George, made the following statement in the House of Commons:

> It is essential that, in the face of such a widespread disturbance of the ordinary machinery of the life of the community, law and order should be effectively maintained.
>
> The Police Force, even when strengthened by the enrolment of special constables, will obviously be insufficient for this task in view of the very large number of points that require protection, and of the organised character of the interference with the Voluntary workers. They are entitled to look to the Government for protection and help from the armed forces of the Crown in their difficult task. This protection the Government has decided to afford them in whatever measure may be necessary, and therefore proposes to make a special appeal to patriotic citizens to enlist in an emergency force, recruited not for the purpose of

interfering in any wage dispute but solely to support the Police in the fulfillment of their duties to the Community.

On the same day the Army Reserves were called up and a Defence Force was constituted. Despite this the Government was unprepared for industrial action on this scale. No military intelligence organisation existed in the various Army Commands throughout Britain for the special purpose of assisting the troops to act in support of the Civil Power – ie the Government. General 'Defence Security Intelligence' duties on matters affecting foreign military operations and the efficiency for war, and the welfare, of the armed forces of the Crown (within the ground covered by the Official Secrets Act, Defence Regulations and Aliens Order) were still being carried out as normal by MI5. All Special Intelligence duties in connection with labour unrest were normally undertaken by the police at New Scotland Yard (Scotland House).

But the threat of a General Strike combined with the mobilisation of the Army Reserves and the constitution of a Defence Force necessitated a reinforcement of the military intelligence services at the War Office and in Army Commands throughout the country. Measures to strengthen military security, 'defensive, preventive, negative and precautionary', known as Intelligence B services, were set up. (Intelligence B was distinct from Intelligence A services, which were concerned with acquiring positive information required for the conduct of active military operations against an opposing force). In the War Office a Military Security and Secret Service Section (MI(B)) was organised. Officers from MI5 were temporarily transferred to it and formed the basis of MI(B). Suitable officers from the regular Army Reserve who had previous war service with MI5 were also employed as were clerical assistants from MI5. The general principles of organisation and distribution of duties were based upon those laid down (in the Manual of Military Intelligence) for the Intelligence Staff at General Headquarters of Forces in the field. The moment at which this intelligence organisation should undertake executive action and supersede the previous or normal intelligence arrangements was timed to coincide with the declaration of a general strike by the Triple Alliance, or the first demand of the Civil Power for armed assistance from H.M. Forces, whichever event should occur first. These arrangements would dissolve and revert to normal on the issue of the order for the disbandment of the auxiliary Defence Force.[5]

Directorate of Military Operations and Intelligence.
Organization for Emergency Home Defence of Sub-Section M.I.

(B) War Office.

I(B) – Room: 427; Tel: 393; General Duties: Military Security and Secret Service. Military Policy connected with the administration of the Emergency Regulations, 1921, as affecting the Military Intelligence Duties; Staff: Lt.Col.E. Holt-Wilson CMC, DSO., 1 Clerk (Mr. Strong); Drawn from MI5.

I(B) X – Room: 427; Tel: 393; General Duties: I(B) Organisation and liaison with Government Depts. and Commands. Records, reports, diary, finance and personnel; Staff: Capt.Butler, One Clerk (Miss Dunsterville); Staff drawn from MI5.

I(B)i – Room: 0047B; Tel: 622; General Duties: Military Secret Service, and liaison with the Civil Secret Service, Scotland House; Staff: Capt. A.W.C. Tomlins, Capt. Boddington, 1 Clerk; Staff drawn from MI5.

I(B)ii – Room: 427; Tel: 393; General Duties: Military Security duties amongst the Civil Population.

Military duties in support of the Civil Power in connection with the administration of the Emergency Regulations 1921, as affecting N.I. Duties; Staff: 1 Officer, 1 Legal Officer, 1 Clerk; Staff drawn from MI5.

I(B)iii – Room: 427; Tel: 393; General Duties: Military Security and Welfare duties amongst the Troops; Staff: Major W.A. Alexander, Mr. O.A. Harker, 1 Clerk (to be detailed by Major Alexander); Staff drawn from MI5. [6]

In each Army Command provision was made for the appointment of a General Staff Officer (3rd Grade), with one Assistant (an Intelligence Officer), to undertake MI(B) duties within the Command under the Command Intelligence Officer. The officer charged with MI(B) duties in each Command shared with the officer in charge of MI(A) duties the services of all Intelligence Officers appointed to lower formations (Divisional, Brigade and Battalion Intelligence Officers).

Army Command Intelligence Officers were not authorised to undertake the employment of paid secret agents to gather information. Arrangements for the acquisition of information by secret service agents, whether civil or military, were be carried out from London for military purposes under arrangements that would be made by MI(B) War Office. All cases of suspected espionage from either British or foreign agents were to be immediately referred direct to MI5 at the War Office, by telephone or telegram, in addition to transmitting full details through the prescribed military channels. Cases of persons suspected of or found committing acts of sabotage or violence were to be dealt with by the police in the ordinary course of law.[7] These were *ad hoc* arrangements, hurriedly put together – and they were not put into operation: a General Strike was adverted by the personal intervention of the Prime Minister who convinced the Miners Federation not to strike. This would not be the end of matter, for industrial relations in the coalfields remained bad. But next time the Government – and MI5 – would be ready.

The situation in the mines returned to the fore of political debate in June 1925 when the mine owners brought forward proposals to reduce miners' wages, impose a longer working day and enforce local wage agreements. By this time Stanley Baldwin was in Downing Street following the break up of the Coalition. His Conservative Government set up the Samuel Commission to inquire into the state of the coal industry. It reported in March 1926 recommending a reorganisation of the coal industry involving better working conditions, no longer working day but wage cuts. Samuel managed to upset both the mine owners and the miners. Another General Strike loomed.

At midnight on 30 April 1926, a subsidy, which had been granted by the Government to the coal industry in July 1925, expired. All efforts by the Government to arrive at an agreement with the miners' representatives on the basis of the Report of the Royal Commission having failed, the Miners Federation of Great Britain withdrew their members from all the coalmines. During the afternoon of 1 May, it was announced that the General Council of the Trades Union Congress had decided to call a General Strike, which would begin at midnight on Monday 3 May. With the exception of sanitary and health services, every form of industry was threatened with a withdrawal of union labour. Discussions between the Government and the Trades Union Congress were still taking place, and on the evening of 2 May, Baldwin, informed the representatives of the TUC that the Government required an 'immediate and unconditional' withdrawal of the instructions for a General Strike before negotiations could be resumed. Reference was also made to the action of the printers of the *Daily Mail*, who had declined to print a leading article, in consequence of which the London edition of that paper was not published on 3 May. Negotiations between the Government and the TUC ceased and at midnight on 3/4 May the General Strike began. A Royal Proclamation had already declared a State of Emergency on 1 May, which had brought Emergency Regulations into force.

This time MI5 were ready. At the end of April precautionary arrangements had been made to establish an Emergency Staff at the War Office, which involved bringing into being MI(B), now the emergency section of MI5. As well as setting up systems to organise the supply of information, preparations involved the practicalities of arranging the services of 'volunteer cars' in the event of an emergency, fully equipped offices for MI5 staff to occupy at the War Office and arrangements for the requisition of bedding, candles, petrol and stationery. As had been the case five years previously, MI5 were able to call on the services of Intelligence Officers from MI1(A). On 1 May at 12 noon MI(B) was instituted, MI5 staff moved to rooms 426, 427 and 047B in the War Office. Bedding was delivered to the War Office and MI5's HQ in Cromwell Road (which was kept under special watch by the Police). Arrangements were also made to receive regular reports from the Railway Police. A skeleton staff was left at Cromwell Road.

When the Strike began, night duty commenced and arrangements were made to transport staff to the office the next morning. On 4 May, volunteer drivers took up their duties, the volunteers included Miss Allen, Dame Adelaide Livingstone, Lady Wilson, Lady Dorothy Hope Morley, Captain Hope Morley and Admiral Heard who duly ferried MI5 officers around London in their motor cars. A clerk named Saunders brought his own wireless in to the office and, with the assistance of a shorthand writer, Tolfree, news bulletins were circulated in the offices. Colonel Haldane, with the assistance of Mr Mathy (who was from British Guiana), began compiling a 'Green List' detailing names and details of individuals whose activities were likely to cause the deployment of troops in aid of the Civil Power. Sir Vernon Kell's daughter joined the voluntary workers at the War Office and assisted with despatches and receipt of documents.

It soon became evident that the organisational structure was unsuitable for a General Strike which involved considerable movements of troops in various parts of the country and the possibility of widespread military operations; it appeared 'more rational' to mobilise a miniature GHQ Field Staff and a revised organisation was adopted on 7 May. Commands (each of which was in the charge of a GSO3 grade officer) were divided into Intelligence Areas, each of which contained a specific area of police districts, which were further divided into sub-areas. Certain larger industrial and dockyard towns and police districts, such as Birmingham and Chatham, were treated as Special Single Areas, while smaller police districts of similar interest, such as Bristol, Coventry and similar, were treated as Special Sub-Areas.[8]

Authority was given for twelve Assistant Intelligence Officers to be deployed in the London area, as it was realised that important intelligence would be found amongst the civilian population. This certainly proved to be the case: reports from MI5 agents around the country on 3 May, the eve of the strike, gave a flavour of both the general popular feeling, and also whom the agents considered likely to instigate subversion. A 'General Report' stated that the 'Pivot man' for the Communist Party 'all round' the Leamington District was a Doctor Levin who lived in Avenue Terrace. His practice was in a 'rather poor part of the town', and from observations taken he appeared to have only about twenty patients, yet managed to run a car and 'lived well', despite no other traceable source of income. Dr Levin was also, allegedly, 'very friendly' with the leading local Trade Unionists. It was also reported that agents were being sent to get into conversation with the NUR men in Birmingham on 2 May. Three separate reports were received and all were in agreement that the majority of the railway men had 'not the slightest desire to strike', and, if suitable protection were offered, they would volunteer for the emergency services established by the Government. 'Similar sentiments' were reported from many Underground Railway employees in London.

In Portsmouth, MI5 agents reported that an 'amalgamation' had occurred of the Electrician's, Fireman's and Engineman's Unions, but not of the engine drivers. This new Union was called the Power Group of Transport Workers, and had an HQ at Rotherham, with branches in most districts. 'Many employees at the Admiralty and War Office' were reported to be members. The group had 'definitely decided' to join the miners in the event of a strike, and they had reportedly been promised full strike pay for an indefinite period. In Southampton the temporary Communist Party HQ was reported as being at 100 Clarendon Road, Shirley. There were reportedly fifty to seventy-five members, the Temporary Secretary was a G. O'Dell and Town Councillor Dr Sakoschancy, a Labour Member, reportedly had 'sympathies with the Communist Party'. Salisbury Court Training College, for ex-servicemen, a government concern, was buying '10 or 12 Workers Weekly's each week'. J. Jones, a South Wales miner and a member of the Communist Party was considered to be the probable leader of this group. Sympathy throughout the area had 'increased towards the Reds, probably owing to the communists that are in prison'.

In Ipswich, the railway employees were 'mainly Left-Wing Socialists', and it was thought probable that some of them were Communists. Woodbridge Road from Warwick Road to Cauldwell Hall Road was considered to be 'a hotbed of red railwaymen'. Socialism was taught in the local schools and even the agricultural labourers were 'rather unsettled'. In Gloucester, a Mr Crammer, who was a schoolmaster at the Crypt School, was reported to be the instigator of Socialist and Communist classes, which were being held at Ruskin Hall, where one of the teachers was described as 'Wells, A Communist from

Cheltenham'. Reports from Liverpool gave names of 'people connected with the Revolutionary movements'; a Mr Blackburn, who lived in Penton Street and was a member of the Liverpool Trades Council was reportedly 'exceptionally smart at breaking up Loyalist open air meetings' and advised his audiences to carry sticks. Although he was 'on relief' – receiving assistance while unemployed – he was 'apparently always well dressed'. Mr Morgan, a 'clean shaven, almost toothless navvy' was the Chairman of the Walton Socialist party.[9]

On the evening of 4 May, a 'pouring wet night', a party of agents visited Aldershot, an army town, for the purpose of gaining general information and intelligence. Agent A of MI5 posed as a South African in England visiting Aldershot to see a friend. Agent B posed as his chauffeur. Agent C's story was that he was travelling from London to Winchester in search of work. Agents D and E's cover was that they were partners in a small motor business. A and B reported:

> that a grocer's wife told them there was a great deal of 'anti-King' feeling among the Railwaymen. A soldier's wife told them that her husband's regiment could be absolutely relied upon. At the T.U.C. Headquarters at the bottom of Victoria Road they overheard a conversation to the effect that a messenger from Eccleston Square was expected at 10 p.m., but no one was observed to arrive. The Communist Daily Herald was on sale here. An N.C.O. of Signals said the morale of his lot was rather bad. An intensive campaign of Communist propaganda has been carried on for the last 3 or 4 months, leaflets being thrown over the walls of the Barracks, distributed to the troops under the trees in the evening, pavement chalking, etc. No one knows who is responsible. A housemaid told B the chauffeur that there was a great deal of 'anti-King' feeling in the town.

Agents C, D and E operated in the lower parts of the town, in various bars and eating-houses frequented by soldiers. Political arguments were started by the agents, and it was found that the agents arguing on the subversive side were not supported by anyone. In conversation with various soldiers none were found with any disloyal feelings. In most cases, when these discussions were started, the soldiers finished their beer and left at once. The ordinary working men and labourers seemed to be 'perfectly loyal'. There seemed to be a distinct tendency to sympathise with the miners, but not with the General Strike. Communist propaganda appeared to have been going on for about a year, but was 'not very bad at the present moment'. The report went on to state that a block of barracks close to the Imperial Hotel appeared to be unguarded, as three of the agents were able to walk between the buildings and across the Parade Ground and to stand for a considerable time under the trees. As it was a pouring wet night, 'it was decided that no Communist propaganda would be spread for obvious reasons and therefore observations were discontinued at 11.45 p.m.'[10]

A report from Stratford on Avon on 5 May stated that it was 'all quiet here'. The only thing of interest was the movements of one R.H. Webb, a local Socialist employed on the Great Western Railway, who had 'expressed very advanced views during the present crisis'. On 3 May he had been observed sending off a group of four cyclists, 'destination and object unknown'. On 5 May he was kept under surveillance, although, as the report of this shows, the agents were not as discreet as they initially thought:

9.20 a.m. Left his house; proceeded via Hull Street to Co-Op. Talked animatedly with several persons, not overheard.

9.40. Left Co-Op. Stopped at Town Hall. Read Bulletin. Went up Bridge St. and talked to group at top of street.

9.55. Spoke for ten minutes to Morriss, employee of Messrs. Smiths. Spoke to photographer of Rapid Photo Co.

10.10. Went to NUR office, Wood Street, prior to entering spoke in whispers to a gentlewoman.

10.15. Went via Guild Street passage to Free Library.

10.25. Left Library and went via passage to NUR office.

10.45. Left NUR alone. Went down Rother Street, left hand side, right turned, crossed, and stopped at the corner of Greenhill Street. Talked to two respectably dressed men. Went up Greenhill St. to Station with two rough looking men. Went into Thompsons remained 5 minutes. Went across road and spoke to about 5 rough looking men.

11.15. Entered station, occupied by Station Master, 2 clerks, and refreshment woman. Remained in booking office with the 3 men, talking in undertones. Sounds as of a quarrel. Our agent got the impression that Webb had a shadow escort.

12.15. Left Station, walking along pavement under the Bridge. Next picked up on Shottery field path, where he ran and disappeared. Picked up again by chance on Shottery Rd. going towards Shottery. Opposite a farm on right he turned left into a field, disappeared among some allotment huts, finally entering first brown hut on left. Was at once joined by two men. Joined by several more. Agent did not know how they arrived at entrance of hut on the far side. Silence for 5 minutes. The two agents were lying by the roadside 75 yards away from the hut. Field with pond separated them from the hut. Two women passed agents' hiding place and entered hut. After their entrance occupants kept looking out and looking round. 5 were seen. They were obviously very ill at ease. Two women left hut on side away from agents, probably to take up posts of observation. One agent tried to crawl across field, but was half way across when someone from the hut shouted, 'Show yourself". There were then 6 men, one with field glasses, standing round hut. Two walked as if to cut off agent; others seemed to be going at right angles towards the second agent, who was still by the roadside.

First agent took to his heels, as he did not wish to be closely seen. As he reached main road someone shouted, 'What the Hell are you doing?' Agent replied, 'What's it to do with you?' He was then going towards Stratford on main road at normal pace. Second agent saw the six men cross allotment towards Evesham Road, hurriedly. Time 1.10 p.m.[11]

A more worrying report came from an informant, posing as a Communist, who told an agent that he had been told that arms could be obtained in the East End of London and that they could be bought without a police licence. When asked to explain what he meant by 'arms' he replied that he understood it meant twenty five to thirty unlicensed revolvers of various calibres and 'probably sufficient ammunition to load them once'. The agent asked him to make further enquiries, which he did, ascertaining that the arms could be obtained from a gunsmith in the Old Kent Road. Unfortunately, as the police had confiscated the gunsmith's main stock for the duration of the strike, (but had managed to keep hold of the unlicensed revolvers) the gunsmith was dubious about meeting with the agent. The agent, though, was taken by his informant to an underground hairdressers in Brixton Road, which appeared to be 'the resort of various race gangs'. He was offered a small French .22 automatic, but it was in 'bad condition' so he declined to purchase it. However, the visit was not totally in vain as he gained some information about some of the criminal gangs in the area. The Sabini gang, he was told, were 'quiet and under the control of their leaders'. The Elephant and Castle gang were probably responsible for a recent riot in the Elephant and Castle area and were now reportedly 'moving West' with the aim of 'getting their own back on the police'. Like the Sabini gang the Hackney Boys were 'quiet at the moment'; their leader was reportedly a man called 'Dave' who worked as a 'chucker out' at the Frivolity Club.[12]

This was not to be the only case foiled by the Police, as MI5's Deputy Director, Colonel Holt-Wilson, received a letter telling the 'sad story of a case that went wrong owing to an inane desire on the part of the Police to make an immediate arrest'. MI5's prime concern, during the Strike, was with Communist attempts at spreading sedition among the Armed Forces. It transpired that at 11.30 p.m. on 4 May, Major W.A. Phillips had received information that a 'Bob Stuart' wanted one of MI5's agents to find a car for him and two other people to convey an 'urgent despatch' to Fife. He had given the agent five pounds towards expenses and the car was scheduled to leave London at 12 noon the following day. Details of the car and descriptions of its occupants were to follow later. An hour later, at 12.30 a.m. on 5 May the agent reported that he had met one of the people who would be a passenger in the car and who would actually be conveying the package to Fife. The agent was then told not to drive the car himself but to find a car and driver. It was also stated that the despatches were really 'bulletins' issued by the Communist Party HQ at 16 King Street. The agent would find a car and a driver and be at Euston Station at 12 noon. The car was anticipated to leave Euston immediately and go to address in Clerkenwell, and then proceed to Fife via Newcastle and Edinburgh. The address in Fife was not yet known and neither were the names and descriptions of the persons actually conveying the despatches.

Major Philips then telephoned Scotland Yard, explained the situation and requested that Colonel Carter – formally of MI5 – telephone him with instructions at 9.30 a.m. He stated that the agent would be instructed to take no action until he had spoken to Colonel Carter. Carter duly telephoned and requested that the agent should pick up the individual and when they had collected the subversive 'documents' the agent should immediately drive the alleged Communist to the nearest police station and hand him over. Phillips disagreed: firstly he considered that it would obviously give the agent away; secondly he was doubtful that any Communist would permit himself to be driven to the police station; and thirdly, even if the car got as far as the police station, he was doubtful if an arrest could be made as the Communist would at once try to escape. He told Colonel Carter that he would be seeing the agent again that day and he would telephone him later.

At 10.30 a.m. Phillips asked the Colonel to telephone to the Metropolitan Police Commissioner, General Childs, asking him to look into the matter. Carter, apparently under instructions of Childs, later telephoned Phillips and asked if he could make any suggestions. Philips told him that a meeting was to take place as stated in the original message, at 12 noon at Euston and suggested that he might have some of 'his people' – from Special Branch – present in observation in order that they might obtain a description of the Communist. Phillips gave him a description of the agent and also said that he would have a white hand-kerchief protruding from his right hand coat pocket. He also described the car, again informing Carter that as far as he knew the Communist would not be carrying any papers at Euston as the documents had to be collected from Clerkenwell. He also suggested that the agent, having picked up the Communist should drive him to Clerkenwell to get the documents, thereby obtaining the address in Clerkenwell. Later at some convenient spot, he could stop the vehicle on a pretext of the car not being in good order and telephone for another car to be sent out to him, giving the actual position of his car and taking care himself to keep out of the way. This telephone message would be sent to a 'perfectly good garage' who would in turn inform Phillips of the message; Scotland Yard would then have been informed and could instruct the local police to take action with regard to the Communist waiting in the car. Colonel Carter agreed to this method of procedure.

Instead of this, although the police knew that it was unlikely that the Communist, when he met the agent at Euston, would have any documents in his possession, both the agent and the Communist were arrested immediately when they met at Euston. As luck would have it the Communist happened to have on him a parcel containing 1,500 pamphlets for distribution to the army but this was 'absolute luck and not judgment' on the part of the police. As the agent was 'very valuable' to Phillips, it was deemed undesirable to proceed with the prosecution; the documents were impounded and both the men were released. The Communist turned out to be James Clarke, the Secretary of the Glasgow Communist Party; therefore it was 'extremely unfortunate' that the police took the action they did, as it prevented MI5 from obtaining the address in Clerkenwell at which he was to call for the documents.

On 9 May, the agent told Phillips that the pamphlets which were taken from Clarke were only a part of a large quantity, about 20,000 in total, which were believed to have been brought from Glasgow to London for distribution to troops. These pamphlets were somewhere in Clerkenwell, at an unknown address, which the agent would do his best to obtain. Identical pamphlets had been thrown over the walls or railings of Chelsea Barracks the previous evening, which corroborated the agent's story. The agent also stated that Clarke was working in conjunction with another Glasgow Communist called Reynolds. Phillips was understandably frustrated and felt that this was 'really a good case spoilt by bad police handling', which, had it been 'discreetly handled', might have enabled MI5 to get at the source or storehouse of the pamphlets.[13] Holt-Wilson, at MI5 HQ, agreed that it was 'a pity' and sympathised that MI5 were 'always under the necessity of putting up with S[cotland]Y[ard's] choice of treatment' once their assistance was invoked. 'Twas ever thus,' he stated, and nothing MI5 could say or do would justify any complaint, as they had to work around Scotland Yard's workloads and manpower. He assured Phillips that 'this was a very fine discovery and many people (including SY) complimented us on it'.[14] As MI5 had no power of executive action, close co-operation with Special Branch was essential – and its only option.[15] It appears that while this partnership worked well at a senior level it often faltered at the lower echelons of the Police.

Despite unfounded rumours on 5 May that the army and navy were about to mutiny and reports on 11 May that Communists in Canning Town were planning to fire blank cartridges to induce troops to fire on crowds, no major incidents occurred. On 12 May the General Strike collapsed. The other members of the Triple Alliance had failed to support the miners. It was a total defeat for them and the employers would impose lower wages, longer hours and local agreements on the miners. At 11.40 a.m. on 12 May it was reported that TUC pickets were being removed. At 1.15 p.m. the BBC broadcast an official statement announcing the termination of the General Strike. On 13 May the daily reports between MI(B) and Scotland Yard were discontinued. It was decided that to locally protect personnel engaged in Government works, employees already sworn in as special constables should be utilised, with a further supply of volunteers to be available, if necessary. The Emergency Air Mail service was discontinued and on 17 May MI(B) closed. All personnel and files were returned to MI5 the following morning and business as usual resumed.[16] An exultant Kell thanked his staff effusively:

M.I.5.
War Office
16th May 1926
I desire to thank all Officers and their staffs, also the Ladies of the Office, for their splendid work and co-operation during the General Strike.
The manner in which all hands have put their shoulders to the wheel shows that the ancient war traditions of M.I.5 remain unimpaired.
Again I thank you all.[17]

Enemy Within
The Ewer Spy Ring 1924–1927

On Friday 21 November 1924 a strange advertisement appeared in the Communist newspaper, the *Daily Herald*:

NOTICE.
SECRET SERVICE. – Labour Group carrying out investigation would be glad to receive information and details from anyone who has ever had any association with, or been brought into touch with, any Secret Service Department or operation. Write in first instance Box 573, Daily Herald.[1]

MI5 immediately swung into action, making several attempts to contact whoever had placed the advertisement. At first these proved fruitless, but eventually a contact was successfully established when D, an MI5 agent, replied to the advertisement and asked for a meeting with the advertiser. He succeeded in eliciting a reply from someone who signed himself 'QX'. QX proposed that D and himself should rendezvous outside St. Georges Hospital on New Year's Day 1925. D kept the appointment, but waited for an hour in vain. On returning home D found a telegram, handed in at Fleet Street, cancelling the appointment. On 13 January, D did meet QX, by appointment, at the Vodega Wine House, Bedford Street, The Strand. QX informed D that he wanted information about the work of the Government Intelligence Services. D and QX continued to secretly meet; D, on one occasion, received £3 from QX for his expenses and on another, £3 for a Military Intelligence report, which he handed over under instructions from MI5. QX was subsequently identified as William Norman Ewer, a journalist. D reported during January 1925 that an individual whose description appeared to tally with QX had made enquiries about him at his lodgings. Possibly as a result of these enquiries, Ewer was spooked and became suspicious of D and contact was subsequently dropped.[2]

It had been expected that the MI5 agent, D, would be shadowed by the 'opposite side'.[3] The shadowing was to be carried out by a 'watcher'; on this occasion the watcher was a man later identified as Walter Dale a former Special Branch officer and known Communist. It was believed that it was Dale who succeeded in discovering D's connection with MI5.[4] In typical Secret Service style, arrangements had been made for the shadower himself to be followed by MI5's own 'watchers'. As a result of this following of the shadower, two individuals, a man and a woman, were seen going in to the Soviet Embassy in London at Chesham House. The woman was then followed to a Post Office in the Strand, where she was seen engaging in a transaction at the counter. From the Post Office she went to 50 Outer Temple and disappeared into a big block of offices situated at this address.[5] She was later identified as Rose Edwardes. Enquiries were made at the Post Office, from which it was ascertained that the she had paid a telephone bill for a telephone installed at 50 Outer Temple on behalf of the Federated Press of America (FPA). The contract for the telephone installation was signed by Ewer as manager of the FPA.[6]

MI5 already knew of Ewer. He was a journalist and a member of London West Central Branch of Communist Party.[7] Born in 1885, Ewer first came to MI5's attention in July 1915, when he made a speech, strongly pacifist in tone, in the East Finchley Wesleyan Church on behalf of the Union of Democratic Control.[8] Ewer was then working as secretary to Baron de Forest 'a virulent pro-German', prominent in the Union. On attestation [for conscription to the armed services] he received total exemption on the grounds of Conscientious Objections, but was obliged to take work on a farm at Cheltenham. From 1919 up to the present time he had been Foreign Editor of the *Daily Herald*. In July 1915 the Anti-German Union had forwarded a copy of a speech, made by Ewer, to the authorities. This speech was of a 'highly pacific and anti-British nature and was an attempted justification of the German invasion of Belgium'. As a result a Home Office Warrant was imposed on Ewer in September of that year. In January 1916 he was the speaker at a meeting on behalf of a peace movement. Throughout his early MI5 file 'there are continuous Police reports of violent speeches made both by EWER and his wife advocating revolution in this country similar to that which had taken place in Russia'. In 1917, Scotland House forwarded a book of anti-war poems by Ewer entitled 'Five Souls and other War-time Verses'; a volume which was published by the *Daily Herald*.[9] An MI5 assessment, written in 1919, described Ewer as 'pro-German principally on the ground that other Governments are not less wicked than the German… He preaches peace with Germany, followed by "revolution through bloodshed". His wife is equally rabid. EWER is a clever writer and fluent speaker… He is a dangerous and inflammatory agitator.'[10]

In January 1920, Ewer applied for a permit to work in Egypt as a correspondent of the *Daily Herald*. It transpired from intercepted communications that Ewer had been trying to arrange that the *Daily Herald* should get into personal touch with Radek 'the chief Bolshevik propagandist there'. GHQ Egypt wired that from the point of view of the situation there, facilities should be refused. Sir Basil Thompson, the Director of Intelligence, Scotland House, stated with reference to this application that Ewer, as on other visits (which included Ireland) would engage in sedition: 'On all these occasions the aim of his visits and articles had been to harass His Majesty's Government and to inflame the mind of Labour against its policy... there was no doubt that if EWER were allowed to proceed to Egypt he would not only pursue that course, but would also act as an irritant upon the Nationalist malcontents in that country.' Ewer's application was refused on 6 March 1920.[11]

As a result of Ewer's latest activities a Home Office Warrant was imposed on correspondence addressed to the FPA on 7 February 1925; the HOW bore immediate results as it was found that daily packets were sent there addressed to a 'Kenneth Milton' from an unknown individual in Paris. These packets contained four distinct kinds of documents: 1. Copies of despatches and telegrams from French Ministers in various foreign capitals; 2. Reports on the French political and financial situation; 3. Typed and unsigned covering slips in English in a plain language code; 4. Communications from the Indian Communist, M.N.Roy, or from his wife to Communists in England (these were infrequent).[12]

MI5 discovered from the FPA telephone contract that their office in London was in telephone contact with the offices of Arcos (the Soviet trading company), (roxter the official Russian news agency), and the Vigilance Detective Agency, run by a Jack Hayes. Telephone conversations were very guarded and hard to interpret. It was not until 8 May that a slip made by Ewer gave MI5 a clue to the identity of his agent in Paris. On that date there appeared in the *Daily Herald* an article on French Morocco 'from our own correspondent, George SLOCOMBE', which was practically a reprint of a note among a batch of reports addressed to Kenneth Milton at 50 Outer Temple and intercepted on 6 May. George Slocombe was at that time combining the work of foreign correspondent of the *Daily Herald* in Paris with that of manager of the Federated Press of America at 9 Rue Duhesme. A HOW was imposed on Slocombe at his private and business addresses and plain language code letters to him signed 'T' (Trilby was Ewer's nickname) were intercepted.[13]

Slocombe, born in 1894, was like Ewer, a journalist for many years, and though he served in the RAF during the 1914–1918 war, MI5 noted that 'he also held somewhat pacifist views'. After war service Slocombe became news editor of the *Daily Herald* (having worked there since 1912) subsequently becoming Chief Foreign Correspondent until 1931. He was President of the Anglo-American Press Association of Paris in 1927; was publicly commended by three British Cabinet Ministers for despatches from The Hague Conference, 1929; and mentioned in a Government White Paper, in 1930, for having initiated gaol negotiations with Gandhi which led to the Irwin-Gandhi Pact of Delhi and the subsequent appearance of Gandhi at the Second Round Table Conference, in London, concerning the constitutional future of India. Aside from his glittering journalistic career, Slocombe was also a prolific author and was mentioned in *Who's Who*.[14] A study of the correspondence between Slocombe and Ewer revealed that the latter was sending Slocombe about $1,000 a month. Slocombe was expending some Fr.8,000 on obtaining local information, from presumably well-placed sources, and the remainder was spent on obtaining from the French Foreign Office the despatches of French Ministers in Rome, Sofia, Bucharest, Belgrade and Warsaw. From the first date of the interception of the correspondence, in February 1925, it appeared that Ewer was passing on to Slocombe criticisms made by a third party on the material which Slocombe was providing; but in October 1925 it appeared from the correspondence that there was a proposal to short circuit 50 Outer Temple and to send Slocombe's material direct from Paris to Moscow. The reason given for this projected change was the arrival in Paris of an individual suitable to take over the running of Slocombe. It was clear from Slocombe's letters that he was not pleased with the new arrangement, and correspondence between Slocombe and 'Kenneth Milton' continued fitfully until June 1927, after which time no more was seen.[15]

The Home Office Warrant on the FPA had produced an almost daily supply of packages addressed to Kenneth Milton Esq., from Paris, all sent by Slocombe to Ewer. Some of these packets were accompanied by typewritten notes in plain language code. SIS advanced the theory that Slocombe had under his control: One agent in the sub-department of the Quai d'Orsay dealing with Italy; one agent in the sub-department of the Quai d'Orsay dealing with the Balkans; and one agent in an inside position in French political circles and various occasional informants. One batch of mail, on 16 March 1925, had a note in English, which read:

The babe of Bethlehem is staying in Paris at the house of a Frenchman financially interested in the French Standard Oil Group. To the babe this morning there came, on the Frenchman's recommendation, an American in close touch with the American Standard Oil Group who stated that the latter had now decided to work for the separation of Eastern Galicia from Poland, for the reason that Poland would not talk oil business with Standard.

Another batch had, on an attached slip, the message: 'Buying Polish wheat (despatches from French Minister in Warsaw) on trial. first delivery in few days. suspending spag (despatches from Italy) during this experiment, with power to renew.' On 22 September a letter from Ewer to Slocombe contained the passage: 'Can you come over and talk about the cereals and your holiday etc. There are points to be settled. I had only 30 minutes in Paris. Quant II (money) tomorrow.' On 29 September three notes for 100 dollars each were sent to Slocombe; the next day postscript to a letter, on *Daily Herald* headed paper, to Slocombe read: 'You should have the qs (money) by now delay was unavoidable. My Glasgow (Russian) friend says he doesn't want to hear any more from Bristol (Warsaw) but only from Exeter, Hereford and Gloucester. So Bristol (Warsaw) must dry up from now on.' On 2 October it was reported: 'have shut off Bristol (Warsaw) but have had to agree to take 2 weeks more i.e. half of October. first week paid for anyway before your letter arrived'. On 24 October a letter was sent from London to Slocombe, which said: 'Now all cereals are to stop – not only Bristol (Warsaw) but the Cathedral trio (Sofia, Belgrade, Bucharest.) too. Moreover, it is proposed to connect Leicester (Paris), Glasgow (Moscow), direct, chiefly for speed and efficiency reasons, there now being a flivverman of competence in Leicester (Paris) itself. All which suggest considerable advisability of your coming Londonwards for talks.' Although there was a further London–Paris note a few days later that stated: 'Cathedrals (Sofia, Belgrade, Bucharest.) close right now', eight more batches of material came in. On 18 November there was a note to Paris referring to Slocombe's new handler:

seen flivverman today. results only partially satisfactory for partly reasons intellectual partly psychological reasons. He's a thin lipped hebrew who despises politics of which d'ailleurs he's supremely ignorant and is interested only in originals of whatever value. He despises the London food service as too costly thinks you are all a lot of reckless spendthrifts is sceptical of your efficiency, and is generally jewish, but without the hebrew wit, and keenness. i am carrying on till i see where i am, but without hope or enthusiasm... It is a matter of personal equation, with some people i can work, with others i cannot. This fellow is ignorant of our past, and i am incapable of speaking for myself.

He may prove different in experience. i am willing to try. but i cannot live down instinctive suspicions and prejudices. all the others i have met, with you or otherwise, i have been willing to do anything for, but this one has the soul of a counterjumper and the incredulity of a sea-crab. i will write you later when i have had more experience.

Ewer replying to Slocombe on 19 November said: 'Got your note re the flivver. I'll talk to the chauffeur here.' A further letter on 20 November read: 'I've seen the chauffeur. He's damned angry with the Yiddisher brat whom I think he does not love, and he's filing complaint to his boss. Meanwhile you are to discuss the whole thing <u>frankly</u> with our Christian friend – the head printer I mean – and get him to put the Yid in his place. If the Yid is still difficult you'd better short circuit him and deal direct with the Christian till further developments.' A long and detailed letter was sent from Paris to Ewer, late in November, with a covering note stating: 'Im for the time being working for the Yid, without much hope though. Hes the awfullest bounder you ever saw, but I dont want to rush things and complain without due cause. Thanks for your intervention however it will be very useful.' On 26 November, Ewer wrote to Paris: 'Yid improves slightly upon acquaintance but still lacking in understanding of my past role. entirely preoccupied with first editions regardless of value. hope however to train him. our personal relations cordial enough. inferiority complex characteristic of his race responsible i think for his preliminary rudeness. have not thought it necessary to invoke the rosicrucian yet, but will keep him up sleeve.' The next day Ewer wrote to Slocombe and said: 'It is quite on the cards that the chauffeur may come over soon, and have a personal bust-up with the Yid, about whom his language is positively indecent.' The last message MI5 intercepted was on 10 June 1927; the offices at 50 Outer Temple were given up by Federated Press of America in about the middle of March, 1928.[16]

In addition to the daily packets addressed to Kenneth Milton from Paris, there were also intercepted on the check on 50 Outer Temple several letters addressed to Ewer from an individual in Berlin who signed himself 'Q'. These letters were in a plain language code similar to that used between Slocombe and Ewer, and by a process of deduction it was established that the writer was the journalist Frederick Kuh, the *Daily Herald* correspondent in Berlin and manager there of the United Press of America.[17] During the whole of the time that Ewer's organisation was located at 50 Outer Temple, no legitimate journalistic correspondence of any sort was seen going to that address; nor was the office frequented by the accredited FPA correspondent in London.

MI5 had great difficulty in observing the comings and goings at 50 Outer Temple, for their watchers found themselves in turn watched. The five persons employed there were, however, eventually identified, and a vast amount of information was obtained from observation on their movements and checks upon their correspondence. In addition to Ewer, himself a member of the West London Communist Party, there were also employed: W.M. Holmes, a well-known intellectual communist and editor of the *Sunday Worker*; a future MI5 informer, ALLEN; Walter Dale; and Mrs. Rose Edwardes, wife of a minor official in the Ministry of Health and daughter of Joe Paul, an ex-policeman and Head Detective of the Vigilance Detective Agency. With the exception of Holmes and Ewer, these persons appeared to spend the whole of their time working at or from 50 Outer Temple. Ewer usually visited the offices during the morning and then proceeded to the *Daily Herald* for his legitimate press work. Holmes did not appear to visit the offices with the same regularity as Ewer and of the whole group, Holmes was the trickiest, in that it had proved impossible to obtain any substantial direct evidence about him.

Walter Dale was found to be employed on full-time detective duties. It was he who had shadowed the MI5 agent who had first got into touch with Ewer and he was, from time to time, observed by MI5 watchers loitering outside various embassies in London. In his detective work Dale received considerable assistance from John Henry Hayes, who was at that time the head of the Vigilance Detective Agency. Hayes and his Head Detective, Joe Paul, were in constant telephone communication with the group at 50 Outer Temple and it was by arrangement with Hayes, shortly before the General Strike of 1926, that Dale was assisted by Hayes's political agent in Liverpool, Alec Griffin, in the shadowing of an individual there who was suspected of being a Special Branch agent. It was apparent that Dale, with the consent of Hayes, was able to enlist the services of Joe Paul whenever he needed to; indeed, Joe Paul was, on one occasion, seen by MI5's watcher loitering outside the offices of SIS. Other individuals who were found from time to time to be assisting Dale in his work, were James Marston, a dismissed policeman from Scotland Yard, who was subsequently employed at Arcos and George Alexander Pratt, also a dismissed policeman employed at the Arcos Bank. Dale, when engaged on detective duties out of London, was responsible to Ewer for the London activities of the group.[18]

Just what Ewer's group did, in terms of espionage activities in the UK, remained a mystery. Information received in 1928 from an informant who was a member of the group from 1921 until 1927 filled in some of the gaps in the Security Service's knowledge of the early years. Arthur Francis Lakey codenamed ALLEN was a member of Ewer's organisation who gave information to MI5. ALLEN told MI5 of his own recruitment: he had been dismissed from the police after the police strike of 1919 and was at that time in touch with Jack Hayes, who ran the Federation of Prison and police officers, as well as the head of the Vigilance Detective Agency. (Hayes later became an MP.) ALLEN was introduced by Hayes to Ewer, who had asked for someone who could make political enquiries, ostensibly on behalf of the Labour Party. After ALLEN had successfully carried out his task, probably sometime during 1921, Ewer told him that the work had really been done for the Russian Government. On agreeing to work for the Russians, ALLEN was put in direct touch with Nikolai Klishko, of the Russian Trade Delegation, on whose instructions and at whose expense he took a flat, from which his work was carried on until about 1923.

MI5 had no details of the recruitment of any other members of the group; but since Walter Dale was another dismissed policeman who was connected with the Vigilance Detective Agency, and Rose Edwardes's father worked there, MI5 assumed that Jack Hayes acted as a talent spotter in finding suitable recruits for Ewer's organisation. Slocombe and Holmes fell into a different category; both were journalists and both worked with Ewer on the *Daily Herald*. For the years from 1921 until 1924, MI5 only had ALLEN's account of the activities of Ewer's network: 'since he had knowledge of only a part of the organisation our picture is an incomplete one, but we can... regard him as a reliable source, since his story is, in part, supported by corroborated evidence'. According to ALLEN, that part of the organisation, which consisted of Dale, Rose Edwards and ALLEN himself, was originally run from the flat which ALLEN took on the instructions of Klishko. In about 1923, Ewer went to Moscow for his holiday and it was there that the decision was taken to run the organisation under the cover of a branch of a news agency, the Federated Press of America. Offices were then taken at 50 Outer Temple, and ALLEN was installed as manager. ALLEN told MI5 that Ewer, while in Moscow, had met Carl Haessler, one of the directors of the FPA in New York, and arranged with him that a fake London office should be set up. Its sole purpose would be as a front for the espionage organisation and it would do no legitimate news agency business.[19] It was, then, in 1924 that Ewer made what MI5 considered 'an error of judgment which caused the enquiries resulting in the discovery of his Organisation'.[20] According to ALLEN, as told to MI5 in 1928, the advertisement was inserted with the object of catching out an MI5 agent, 'whose endeavours on our behalf to penetrate Communist circles had aroused suspicions that he was an informer. The suspicions were confirmed when he was traced back to MI5 and he was then dropped by the FPA.' Yet, MI5 wondered why, if ALLEN's story was true, it was difficult to understand why Ewer thought it necessary to expose himself: 'He did not of course give his name, but he did meet our agent. On the other hand, it is hard to think of any other reason for the insertion of this advertisement.' The crudeness and naivety of the advertisement were totally at odds with Ewer's normal methods of operating.[21]

Of all of those involved with Ewer, Rose Edwardes was the most 'ordinary' of the group in attendance at the Outer Temple. She was a typist and office clerk, but on occasions she was observed to visit the Soviet Embassy, Chesham House, and she was known to meet up with Rose Cohen, a member of the staff of Arcos, in the middle of the day.[22] Rose Cohen was a Communist who travelled a great deal to Moscow in the 1920s. She seems to have done some work for Arcos and the Soviet Embassy in 1925, and while there was rung up several times by the Federated Press of America. Cohen was in touch with Ewer, and she wrote to him in Paris in April 1926. In the letter she wrote, cryptically: 'The situation is extremely delicate. When I told him about Geoffrey's office he wanted to know if I had said anything to Walter, and why should he know, etc. etc. So no one must know that you are acquainted with Sam.' MI5 took 'Geoffrey's office' to mean the Wayfarers Travel Agency in Paris, run by the late Geoffrey Franklin, a brother of the Communist, Olive Parsons. In 1928, Cohen was in Moscow, and then returned to England for a short holiday. She was certainly back in Moscow in 1929 and wrote fairly regularly from there to her friends Eva Reckitt and Olive Parsons. There was no sign of Rose Cohen having returned to Britain after this date. It appears that she married one Max Petrovsky, who held an important post in the heavy metal industry, in the USSR. In 1937 she was arrested on charges of espionage and conspiracy, for which she was apparently sentenced to ten years exile in 1938. It was believed that her husband had previously been shot as a Trotskyist. Cohen and her sister Nellie were friendly with Reckit; a woman of considerable wealth, most of which was derived from Reckitt's Blue and Starch Company. She had been known to MI5 since 1926 in connection with the Communist Party and there seemed to be no doubt that she was the Party's chief financial supporter. She was not an open member of the Party and her only official connection with it appeared to be confined to her post in the executive committee of the Communist run Labour Research Department, and her directorship of Collett's Holdings Ltd. and Collett's Bookshop, which were likewise under Party control. She was known to be in close touch with all the leading Party members.[23]

After a police raid on Arcos, in May 1927, there was noticeably less activity at the Outer Temple offices. Intercepted correspondence and observation showed that there were considerable difficulties around funds. In November 1927 work appeared to be practically at a standstill and ALLEN left the FPA. In March 1928 the offices themselves were vacated and the furniture sold. Mrs Edwardes left her lodgings in London and went to live in Leigh-on-Sea. Walter Dale obtained employment at the Shoreditch Town Hall. It was at this point that ALLEN became an informant for MI5 and stated that *inter alia* Ewer and his associates, while operating from 50 Outer Temple, had been in the habit of receiving bi-weekly reports from two officials at Scotland Yard which contained all the information obtainable by these officials, that they thought would be of interest to the Soviet Government. In particular, Ewer was supplied with up to date lists of persons on whose correspondence Home Office Warrants had been imposed, or with regard to whom instructions had been issued to Aliens Officers at the Ports. By the same means also Ewer was forewarned of any impending action by the authorities against Communist persons or organisations in Britain. In view of the serious nature of this information, enquiries were set on foot with a view to ascertaining whether any or all of the group previously working at 50 Outer Temple were still engaged in carrying on their secret activities. Observation was kept on Mrs Edwardes's private address at Leigh-on-Sea: she was found to be travelling regularly to London and was ostensibly running a typewriting business called the Featherstone Typewriting Bureau, at Featherstone Buildings, Holborn. Observation at this address showed that regular meetings took place between Ewer, Holmes, Dale and Mrs Edwardes. These meetings, held on Tuesdays and Fridays, usually lasted for about an hour and on occasion appeared to provide a great deal of typing for Mrs Edwardes. The greatest care was taken to ensure privacy and a visitor who happened to call during the progress of one of these meetings was immediately put into a small outer office marked 'PRIVATE' and the door locked upon him.

During the course of the enquiries at Featherstone Buildings, MI5 discovered that George Paul, Mrs Edwardes's brother, and George Pratt, a close associate of Dale, were working at the Russian Bank for Foreign Trade. It was decided to subject each of the four persons meeting at Featherstone Buildings to a short period of intensive observation. On 18 March 1929, at Lyons Café in Walbrook, Dale was seen meeting an individual who was traced back to Scotland Yard. A few days later, at the same rendezvous, Dale was seen to meet another individual who was also traced back to Scotland Yard. These meetings, which continued regularly at the same place and practically at the same hour, soon resulted in the identification of Dale's two friends as Inspector Ginhoven and Sergeant Jane of Special Branch. The shock that Communist agents had penetrated Special Branch and rendered all of MI5's surveillance redundant was only made possible by Dale's 'extraordinary lack of caution in choosing the same rendezvous for each meeting' and 'can only be put down to carelessness occasioned by long standing practice'. Since it was clear that official action would now have to be taken, the facts were immediately made known to the Home Office and to the heads of Special Branch. Ginhoven, Jane and Dale were traced to their rendezvous by specially detailed police officers of CID and, on 11 April 1929, were arrested together and searched under the provisions of the Official Secrets Act. Although ample documentary evidence was obtained of the treachery of Ginhoven and Jane, it was decided by the authorities that, for a variety of reasons (not least the bad publicity), prosecution was not the best option and that the best way to dispose of the case was by disciplinary action against the two police officers. MI5 were already aware of the existence of a diary compiled by Dale, which was alleged to contain detailed notes of his detective activities since the early days of his employment in Ewer's organisation. Special Branch officers, detailed to search Dale's house, were told of the existence of this diary and did in fact find it there. Ginhoven and Jane were accordingly dismissed from the police by a disciplinary board on 2 May 1929.[24]

Dale's diary contained detailed accounts of his activities from January 1922 until April 1929. It confirmed what MI5 had already surmised: that his activities for the Ewer organisation had fallen into two distinct categories. From 1922 until just after the ARCOS raid in 1927 he had acted as the group's private detective, and from November 1927 until his arrest as Ewer's intermediary with Ginhoven and Jane. Dale's diary also showed that he was exceedingly hard working. His duties were apparently four-fold. Firstly, he had to keep periodical observation upon the offices of the British Intelligence Services, observing both staff and whomever they came into contact with. Secondly, he was responsible for observing Russians resident in Britain who the Soviet Government considered suspicious. Thirdly, he was supplied from time to time with lists of prominent political or social personages about whom the Soviet Government required information. And, fourthly, it was Dale's duty to see that Ewer and other persons engaged on secret activities, on behalf of the Soviet Government, were not observed or shadowed by MI5 or the police while so engaged. With regard to his first duty 'there was no doubt that this was most efficiently carried out'. Throughout the five years covered by the diary, unremitting surveillance was maintained by Dale and employees of the Vigilance Detective Agency upon premises and personnel of SIS, the Code and Cipher School, MI5 and other departments of the Government. The whole itinerary of the office cars was carefully watched and laborious efforts were made to identify and trace to their homes officers and even members of the secretarial staffs. It was evidently in this way that Ewer's group became aware on 6 June 1929 of the identity of one of the subordinate staff of SIS with the result that she was approached by Rose Edwardes posing as an American intelligence agent and offered payment for the supply of regular information as to the workings of SIS. The attempt failed but MI5 noted: 'the incident gives clear indication of the lengths to which EWER was prepared to go, in order to obtain the most authentic information for the benefit of his Soviet employers.'

Dale's other papers, representing information obtained from the two Special Branch officers, 'entirely corroborated the informant's statement regarding the type of information obtained from Scotland Yard. It became abundantly clear that, for the past ten years, any information regarding subversive organisations and individuals supplied to Scotland Yard by SIS or MI5, which had become the subject of Special Branch police enquiry, would have to be regarded as having been betrayed to EWER's group.' Through his sources in the Special Branch, Ewer 'was enabled to give warning to suspects and subversive organisations of suspicions entertained or of projected police action, to nullify the effect of security measures, to cripple enquiry, and thus positively to enhance the successful operations of the Communist conspiracy in the UK and its promotion from abroad'.

Also on Dale's person, at the time of his arrest, was found a notebook in which a few names and addresses were jotted down. Under the date '2.3.29' appeared the name of Alexander Miller Feirerabend with notes as to his nationality, occupation and address. As this individual was unknown both to the Special Branch and to MI5, a Special Branch officer visited him, to try to ascertain what he was doing in Britain. Feirerabend, who was a naturalised American of Latvian birth, gave a reasonable account of his movements but apparently was not so truthful about his finances. Immediately after the visit to him by a Special Branch officer he made arrangements to leave the country. After his departure a letter arrived for him at his private address which, on preliminary examination, appeared to be an innocent private communication from Berlin. However, there were many points about this letter 'which did not ring true'; it was subjected to a number of tests for secret ink and, after considerable difficulty, a secret message was developed on the reverse of the paper used:[25]

> No. 4 4.5.29
> Dear Comrade, Did you get my letter? I am very uneasy about the form of the letter and also the 'nib' (?) happened You did not acknowledge the receipt of the money last (?) week – by the – Negro (?) 300 for this – sent 700. What happened to --- I wrote to you that it was necessary to put --- agents (?) She (?) --- address received the letters were not ----- please reply at once (?) Yours ERNST' [26]

Unfortunately, so difficult had development of this ink proved, that a great portion of the message was destroyed before the proper developer was discovered. For MI5 there was 'no doubt, however, that FEIERABEND was a Soviet secret agent in this country'.

Very shortly after the dismissal of the two Scotland Yard detectives, Mrs Edwardes's typewriting bureau at Featherstone Buildings was closed down. Ewer, who had previously been suspected of using Polish diplomatic channels for correspondence connected with his secret activities, left for Poland almost immediately. It was presumed that he visited Poland for the purpose of informing some representative of the Russian Intelligence Service personally of the check, which his organisation had received, and to obtain fresh instructions. MI5 noted that: 'Since his return from Poland in September 1929, it has not been found possible to maintain any consistent observation' upon Ewer and his associates. Both he and Dale 'take the greatest precautions to ensure that they are not followed and deliberately lay traps in order to ascertain whether they are being observed'. Ewer 'appears to spend the greater part of the time, during which he is not occupied on his legitimate journalistic work, at the flat of a wealthy woman communist in Lincoln's Inn'. The woman was Eva Reckitt and during the time that Ewer's organisation was established at Featherstone Buildings, it was observed that he or Holmes almost invariably visited this woman after each of their bi-weekly meetings. 'The woman herself is exceedingly suspicious and cautious and the location of her flat is such that observation thereon is practically impossible. MI5 are not, therefore, at present in a position to say how far EWER is still carrying on the Intelligence Organisation entrusted to him by the Soviet.'[27]

By 1930, MI5 were noting that Ewer was supposed to have been expelled from the Communist Party for refusing to retract an allegedly 'deviationist' article which he had written. After that date MI5 had conflicting reports about Ewer and it was not clear whether the severance of his connection with the Communist Party of Great Britain (CPGB) was genuine or not.[28] Ewer took up a position as the Foreign and Diplomatic editor of the *Daily Herald* and MI5 had to consider how this new role – with access to senior ministers and civil servants in the Foreign Office – gave him 'the entrée into circles which had previously not been open to him, constitutes a danger to the interests of this country'.[29] At one level the fallout between Ewer and senior members of the CPGB appeared genuine enough. R.P. Dutt, the intellectual force within the CPGB, had criticised in public Ewer's article – 'Cross Roads' – in the *Labour Monthly* stating: 'Of course we have to be ready for him finally breaking after this, and ourselves going bang, but he has asked for it, and we'll die fighting.' Another intercepted mail source, R. Burrows, writing to Moscow commented: 'So Ewer has been expelled too. That is not surprising, and he has put his own economic position before the party. I wouldn't be surprised if he joins the ILP [Independent Labour Party] that's safe enough.' In the course of a conversation, in December 1930, D.R. Jenkins was reported to have said that Ewer 'was now the tool of the British Foreign Office, and is more or less their unofficial mouthpiece through the "Daily Herald".' He added that 'this was felt so strongly at the time when the naval conference was going on, that Sir A. Willert, the head of the Press Dept of the Foreign Dept. was compelled to issue a confidential statement to other press representatives saying that Ewer's position was not an official one'. The following year, another MI5 informant reported that: 'It may be definitely assumed that W.N. Ewer, of the "Daily Herald" staff, has positively severed his connection with the C.P.G.B. as he has not the time to devote to the party.'

Indeed, the *Daily Worker* described Ewer as a 'renegade communist' while another source suggested he had 'been purged of communism'. A source close to senior British Communists was able to report to MI5 that relations between Ewer and the CPGB were definitely broken off – for now. It was reported that Ewer gave a verbal undertaking that he would return to the CPGB at a later date and that he would always be a Communist; but owing to certain articles he wrote in the *Daily Herald* criticising Communism, foreign and economic positions, the CPGB were offended and not only attacked him in the *Daily Worker* but also sent for him to meet the CPGB leaders, Harry Pollitt and Willy Gallacher. He met Pollitt, who was accompanied by J.T. Murphy and W. Robson. The meeting was arranged because Ewer objected to the tone of the *Daily Worker* article calling him a renegade. Pollitt said they had nothing to apologise for and that Ewer had actually attacked Communism in a few of his articles. Ewer demanded a withdrawal of the article and an apology in the *Worker* but Pollitt said that the Secretariat of the Party would not consent to this and 'they parted on very bad terms'. Murphy was quoted as saying that Ewer had stated that 'from now on he was going to be <u>bitterly anti-Communist</u> and would attack Communism on every conceivable occasion'. [30]

While, initially, MI5 were prepared to accept that Ewer had 'cut adrift' from the Communist Party of Great Britain, the case officer dealing with it concluded: 'I do not think, however, that we ever regarded this quarrel with the Communist Party as likely in any way to affect EWER's relations with the Soviet Government. His F.P.A. organisation worked direct with the Soviet representatives and was quite independent of the Communist Party.'[31] As MI5 continued to follow Ewer's career it became more perplexed as to the position now adopted by him with regard to Communism. One MI5 source was convinced that Ewer 'is now working in German interests'. When asked by the case officer if he meant the Nazis or the refugees: 'He said that he did not quite know but he said that he was certain that EWER was pro-German at heart.' The MI5 officer, knowing his source was pro-French and anti-German in his sympathies, was inclined to doubt his views on Ewer; however 'his statement is perhaps worth bearing in mind'.[32] Certainly Ewer was increasingly deemed to be anti-Soviet: Hugh Dalton, while Under-Secretary for Foreign Affairs in the Labour Government and one of the senior members of the Parliamentary Labour Party, attacked an article by Ewer, in the *Daily Herald*, for being pro-Nazi and anti-Russian.[33]

Postscript: the Shattered Illusions of a Soviet Spy

From this stage on there was no evidence that Ewer was involved in any form of illegitimate relationship with the Soviets – so much so that, in 1949, MI5's assessment of Ewer was that he was 'regarded as an able and distinguished journalist, and a long-standing friend of the British Labour Party. He is not at present regarded as in any way pro-Soviet'. MI5 noted that Ewer 'has not come to our adverse notice since 1929, although on occasions reports have hinted that there was more to his resignation from the Communist Party than met the eye'. Indeed, Rose Edwardes, Dale and ALLEN all appeared to have severed their connections with Soviet Intelligence. Holmes was a journalist on the

Daily Worker. George Slocombe remained in Paris until 1940, when he came to Britain – 'we have had nothing of interest on his activities since the days of the Kenneth MILTON correspondence'. ALLEN was last heard of in 1936, working as a masseur in Bournemouth. As MI5 assessed the case they were forced to admit that they had no information on the origins of the Ewer network; 'nor have we discovered with any certainty to what branch of the Russian Intelligence Service it was responsible'.[34] Having said that, MI5 were forced to admit 'there was no <u>direct</u> evidence' that Ewer himself passed on to a foreign power the unauthorised information which he received through the means of his organisation; but it was also pointed out that 'there can be no doubt that he was acting as agent for someone, and that "one" must have been the Soviet Government', because:

(a) he is a Communist.

(b) he was in daily touch with the Soviet Embassy, Chesham House.

(c) our original informant, whose other information was proved to be correct in every particular, definitely stated that all this information was passed at once to Chesham House.

(d) the circumstantial evidence in the file itself is very strong.

(e) none of the information he collected ever appeared in <u>our</u> Communist press.[35]

MI5's interest in the case had been re-awakened in 1949 with the hope that Ewer would talk to them. The legendary Maxwell Knight, Ewer's old, unseen, MI5 adversary in the shadows, was chosen to approach Ewer and seek an interview. Knight was told:

Our chief interest in what EWER may have to say is the extent to which this can help us to counter the Russian Intelligence Service today. He may be able to help by naming and describing individuals whom he knew in 1919–1929, and whom he believes to be working or likely to work for the Russians now. It would also be of great value to us to hear what he knows of Russian recruiting methods, communication methods and security methods. If he is prepared to go into details of his experiences during 1919–1929 he may well provide us with leads to follow which could bring us into the present time.

A series of questions to which MI5 wanted an answer, were given to Knight 'in the hopes that you will be able to bring at least some of them to his notice – suitably sweetened of course'. Knight met with Ewer at the Connaught Hotel, London, at 1.15 p.m. on Friday 27 January 1950:

> We did not really get down to business until about 2.15, and the intervening period was occupied giving EWER lunch and gener-ally trying to make him feel at ease. He did not inquire what I wanted to see him about until after lunch, and our conversation was most composed of trivialities about the war and the compar-ative efficiency of the German and Russian Intelligence Services. [When lunch was over, Ewer] did say to me rather facetiously, 'well now, disclose the great mystery'. I had previously given EWER no indication at all as to what I wanted to see him about, and I was reasonably satisfied that he had no inkling of the real purpose of the interview; and as he is a very highly-strung person, in spite of his experience and undoubted intelligence, I thought it might be a good idea to deal him a rapid blow at the outset. I therefore said to him that what I really wanted to talk to him about was the Federated Press of America. This certainly took him by surprise, and it was on the tip of his tongue to pretend some difficulty in recollecting what this was; but as he hesitated I took out from my despatch case a rather formidable bundle of transcript, whereupon, with a slightly self-conscious smile, he changed his tone and said, 'Oh yes, of course, I can remember the Federated Press of America very well.'

Knight then told him that he wanted him to understand quite clearly that there were no 'strings' at all attached to the interview as far as he was concerned, and that if he felt he did not wish to discuss the matter with him, 'he had only got to put on his hat and go home, and there would be no hard feelings on my side. I explained that, on the other hand, if he would be kind enough to discuss the case with me, I felt it might be extremely useful.' Knight explained that, from time to time, MI5 made a habit of going over what might be termed 'classic cases' in the light of new information or the general trend of international poli-tics, 'as by so doing we frequently not only re-educated ourselves, but also obtained new information and clearer interpretations of matters which were originally obscure'. Ewer listened very attentively to all this, and merely nodded his agreement. Knight then said that two or three cases in the last decade had seemed to indicate that there might still be persons in high Government position who would not be above giving information to the Russians; and that this, not unnaturally had been the occasion for one of these periodical revisions. Ewer then said he would do his best to help, though he might wish to have some reservations in regard to certain individuals. 'I passed lightly over this, saying that I quite understood.'

Knight commenced his questions by asking Ewer if he thought that any of the persons who had originally been associated in the secret activities of the FPA were likely still to be engaged in such operations. Ewer thought for a moment before replying and then said that to the best of his knowledge he knew of no one and he added that if he thought of anybody he would certainly let Knight know. From this Knight asked Ewer whether it was not a fact that the FPA had originally had a source in the Foreign Office, the India Office and the Colonial Office. His reply to this 'was not entirely satisfactory'. Ewer said that they had certainly used a source in the India Office but that he had been dropped before the final winding up, as it was thought that he had only supplied them with phoney information. With regard to the Foreign Office and the Colonial Office, Ewer said that he could not remember anything about these departments. Knight thought it worth while noting that at several points during the interview Ewer said that he 'could not remember', at the same time reminding the MI5 officer that these events took place twenty-eight years ago:

> Now, I am prepared to admit that any man's memory of events so long ago as these might be faulty in some respects. I am also prepared to admit that it is only human to tuck into the back of one's mind those activities of which one may not be very proud, or of which one has unhappy recollections; but I don't believe that a man of EWER's intellect and ability could possibly forget (a) whether he had a source in, say, the Foreign Office; or, (b) if he had a source, who that source may have been. There is a possible alternative to the obvious explanation that EWER was being evasive, and this is that we have been inclined to accept rather at face value some of the information which we received from our original informants. If some of this information was exaggerated or inaccurate, it is quite possible that in this lies the explanation of EWER's attitude.

Knight then told Ewer that he had provided himself with a number of questions the answers to which he would find very helpful, and thought it might be best if they started off right at the beginning with the formation of the FPA. Ewer commenced by saying that he wanted to make it quite clear that the functions of the secret organisation run by him were what he termed 'purely counter'. His instructions were to concentrate on obtaining information as to what the British authorities were doing, and what steps they were taking against Russian and Communist activities in Britain. Ewer went out of his way to emphasise that, with the exception of George Slocombe's organisation in Paris, they did not touch espionage. (A note by 'M' [Knight] at this point in the report observed: 'this I am not prepared to accept. It is quite impossible to run a counter-espionage organisation of this kind without performing acts which are to all intents and purposes espionage. Also it seems to me to be almost equally impossible to run an organisation like the FPA without obtaining information which is not purely "counter".') Ewer explained how, in 1922, he went to Moscow. While there, he was asked whether he could do anything to help the Russians on the lines indicated above. He said he thought he could, and later, when he discussed the matter with Holmes, he thought of the idea of using the FPA as a cover. Ewer stressed to Knight that the parent organisation did not know anything about the secret use that was made of the FPA, and the affair was set up by Ewer getting in touch with the Agency in the States and offering to set up a London office. He said that the only exception to this was Carl Haessler. This man did co-operate with them on several occasions, and his particular contact was with Bram Finberg, whose mistress was Gertrude Haessler, Carl's sister. Knight then asked Ewer who in the British Communist Party was aware of the enterprise. In reply to this he said that Pollitt knew a little about it, as did others such as Willy Gallagher. Knight wanted to know how contact was maintained with the Russians; Ewer's reply to this was that he or Holmes paid frequent visits to the Russian Embassy, and to the offices of the Trade Delegation, and that their principal contact was maintained on these lines. With regard to Slocombe's sources in the French Foreign Office, Ewer explained that this was really a sort of sub-department of the main organisation, and was under Slocombe's control. He had several agents who were well-paid, but Ewer thought that some of them also had ideological motives.

Knight then talked about Ginhoven and Jane. Ewer said that the whole work of the organisation in London really revolved round Ginhoven and Jane, and it was from them that they obtained most of their information. He claimed that both these men were primarily Communists and not merely mercenaries. 'This gave me a good opportunity of asking him, innocently, if he could remember what they were paid. He did not hesitate in his reply, and said that they did not receive much money, and he did not think they had ever received more than £4 or £5 a week.' Knight asked whether Ewer thought that when

Ginhoven and Jane were dismissed they left anybody behind. Ewer replied, apparently frankly, that if they had, he did not know of it. Knight suggested that it was possible that Ginhoven and Jane might have had dealings with the Russians behind his back, 'as I wanted to see how he would react to such a suggestion. He said that, of course, all things were possible, but he did not think this likely'. I asked him if he knew what had happened to them now, and I was interested to observe that Ewer 'had kept pretty closely in touch with these people throughout the intervening years. He said that he had seen GINHOVEN only last year in Copenhagen, and that he had actually met him at the British Legation. GINHOVEN had had a tiresome time during the war, and had been a prisoner of war'. Jane, Ewer thought, was living in Tooting. He was very much down and out, and on the verge of 'going off his head'. Ewer admitted to giving him sums of money from time to time 'out of compassion', and he said he regarded Jane as a sort of pensioner. Dale he had not heard of for some time.

With regard to the role of Walter Holmes, Ewer said he was his chief assistant. Ewer did not think that Holmes was doing anything now as he was so tied up with the *Daily Worker*, but he was a complete Communist fanatic and would not hesitate to give any information to the Russians if such came his way; in reply to a question as to how many of his organisation knew that information was going to the Russians, Ewer replied, 'All'. As for the 'Secret Service' advertisement in the *Daily Herald*, which had triggered MI5's prolonged interest in Ewer, he claimed that he could not remember exactly all the circumstances surrounding it, but that it had been inserted with the idea of drawing the fire of the British authorities; regarding Feierabend, Ewer professed to be puzzled about this, and did not seem to be able to recollect the man or his activities; and as for the Kenneth Milton correspondence, Knight found 'myself in a difficulty. EWER started off by saying that he really could not sort out the cover language, code names, etc., some of which I put to him on discussing this point. He claimed to be quite ignorant of such names as "Flivverman", and on all aspects of this side of the case EWER was obstinately vague, and I must confess that to me he was unconvincing.' It was at this point that Ewer provided an insight into his disillusionment with Communism and the Soviet Union that went a long way to explain his actions in the early 1930s. It was an affair of the heart. Rose Cohen, Ewer explained, was at one time a girl friend of his, and that she represented 'a very painful chapter in his life'. He intimated that her eventual fate had done more than anything else to disillusion him about the Russians and Communism. He told Knight that 'he supposed I knew that she had gone to Russia, had been framed by the Russians as a British spy, sent to Siberia for ten years, and if not actually dead, was virtually dead. He added that what he would never forgive the British[Communist] Party for, was that none of the Party leaders here, who knew what good work she had done for the Cause, made any attempt to intervene on her behalf'.[36]

Knight had the second interview with Ewer on Friday, 21 April 1950: 'It was, I fear, rather disappointing, in the sense that EWER had nothing very much to tell me beyond two amplifications on points which we discussed when I first saw him.' The first point was in connection with the original 'Secret Service advertisement' connected with the FPA case. Ewer said that he now recollected the circumstances surrounding this incident. It appeared that the insertion of the advertisement was nothing whatever to do with Ewer's organisation. The advertisement was first put into the paper by a man whose name Ewer told Knight he did not wish to disclose, as he was in no way connected with matters under discussion. This man was at the time a Member of Parliament, and he was contemplating writing a book which touched on intelligence matters. Ewer had the advertisement brought to his notice by Walter Holmes, and arranged to intercept the answers before they went to the advertiser. Among the answers was one which aroused Ewer's suspicions, as a result of which he arranged for observation to be kept. 'The rest of the story we know.'[37]

9

The ARCOS Raid

A Political Police

As had been pointed out by the Government's Secret Service Committee, MI5 did not have executive powers – it could not arrest anyone; it could only advise action. Executive power of arrest lay with the Police. And the relationship between MI5 and the police, particularly Special Branch, was necessarily a close one, as the General Strike demonstrated. But the police also had, thanks to the insistence of Sir Basil Thompson, an explicit intelligence gathering function that put a distinctive political slant on the Metropolitan Police's activities. In the imagination of the British politic the police were deemed to be, unlike their more authoritarian Continental counterparts, above politics (the exception as always being Ireland). But Special Branch always had something of a 'political' character, having been formed in 1883 in consequence of outrages committed in Great Britain by the Fenians. Since that date it had continued to 'deal with all matters of a political-revolutionary character'. In 1892 and following years the Branch was engaged largely with the Anarchist movement which grew, in the words of one head of the Branch, 'as a result of England being the asylum for foreign political agitators'. Between 1892 and 1905 the Branch was gradually augmented from twenty-five to seventy-four officers, 'owing to the increase of political intrigue'. 1908 saw the commencement of the militant Suffragette movement and about this time Indian seditionists were 'very prominent and caused trouble'. These movements necessitated a further increase in strength. During the war the Branch was mainly engaged with matters 'arising out of a state of war' – dealing with espionage and counter-espionage. And so it was, in April 1919, under pressure from Thompson, that the Government agreed to a Directorate of Intelligence being formed and the Branch was called upon to deal with political and industrial unrest, which was 'very rampant' during the transitory period from war to peace. In March 1920, the Special Irish Secret Service at the Home Office was amalgamated with Special Branch, 'owing to the enormous and alarming' development of the Irish Republican Army, both in Britain and Ireland.

Responsibilities changed somewhat when a new Assistant Commissioner responsible for Special Branch took over in 1921. He wrote:

> I found a system in vogue which I deemed to be extremely undesirable, extremely expensive, and extremely unproductive, and

that was the system under which nine men under Special Branch were out in the Provinces poaching in the preserves of Chief Constables, without their knowledge in theory, although, as a matter of fact they knew all about it and were excessively angry. This system cost roughly £5000 a year and enabled Scotland Yard to render a report on the industrial situation to the Cabinet. I suggested that it was not part of the duty of Scotland Yard to render reports on the industrial situation. My view was supported and the system was abolished.

But this did not entail the ending of investigations into revolutionary movements; during the forty odd years since the inception of the Branch there had 'been a steady increase in revolutionary political movements. Formerly such movements were controlled by men who were honest, however misguided in their opinions. Today they are taken up by men because there is money in same. Previously revolutionary movements were "self-centred". Now they are interconnected with Russian Bolsheviks as the guiding spirits.'

The Stranders case illustrates the close working relationship between MI5 and the Branch: on 31 July 1926, Sir Vernon Kell brought some papers from MI5 to Norman Kendal, the Deputy Assistant Chief Commissioner of the Metropolitan Police, relating to one Vivian Stranders who was alleged to have committed bigamy (one would assume that it was the police that had requested the file). The DACC entered a minute which ran as follows: 'I should like every effort made as soon as possible to follow up this allegation of bigamy. Apparently we need letters to Worcester and Glasgow. If prima facie evidence of bigamy can be obtained it is a case in which the D. of P.P. would probably apply for the man's extradition from Belgium if he is there.'

In the course of enquiries, Inspector Read visited, on 8 September, Mr Charles William Moorhead of 107 Frithville Gardens, Shepherds Bush, W12. This gentleman was able to give some information in regard to the allegation of bigamy. After Mr Moorhead had made his statement to Inspector Read he mentioned that he had received a letter from Stranders, which seemed to him rather peculiar and which he thought the police should have. Mr Moorhead had not got the letter on him at the moment. His statement was taken at Scotland Yard and the letter was at his home. He met Inspector Read, however, the next day by appointment and handed him the letter, which Inspector Read took to Superintendent Nicholls. At once Nicholls formed the opinion that the letter from Stranders was an attempt at espionage. He brought the letter to the Assistant Chief Commissioner and the ACC agreed. Superintendent Nicholls informed the ACC at the time that Stranders's was also wanted for bigamy. The ACC thereupon telephoned Kell telling him he had got hold of a 'funny looking letter' from Stranders, which looked to him like an attempt at espionage and he (the ACC) considered that Kell should have it at once. The letter was forwarded to Kell. Subsequently Kell asked the ACC if he could arrange for a CID officer to visit Mr. Moorhead and to ask him if he would be prepared to see an MI5 officer with a view to assisting the authorities. This was arranged and the espionage element passed out of police hands entirely as MI5 took over this aspect of the case. CID pursued its enquiries into the allegation of bigamy but owing to inability to secure satisfactory evidence the Director of Public Prosecutions, in January 1927, decided not to apply for Stranders' extradition from Belgium on a charge of bigamy.

On 6 December, Special Branch were informed by MI5 that Stranders, now resident in Germany, had been engaged on espionage on behalf of that country; that the matter had been placed by MI5 before the Director of Public Prosecutions; and that, on the facts given by MI5, the arrest of Stranders, on his next arrival in Britain, would be justified. Intelligence suggested that Stranders would arrive at one of the ports the next day. Arrangements were accordingly made by telephone, warning ports to keep Stranders under observation, and to have him detained at Victoria or any other station within the Metropolitan area. At 5.30 p.m. on 7 December a telephone message was received from MI5, stating that Stranders had gone to Paris to meet a certain suspect German named Kassinger, and it was anticipated that both would be coming to England together. All ports were immediately informed that if the other man, Kassinger, was with Stranders, he was to be similarly detained in London. Subsequently, a telephone message was received from Captain Ball, of MI5, at 3.45 p.m. on 9 December, to the effect that it was not certain that the man now in Paris was, in fact, Stranders. His name was said to be Saunders, born in London, in 1888. This man was leaving Paris at 4 p.m., 9 December, arriving in Folkestone. Ports were immediately telephoned this information. At 9.30 p.m. on 9 December, Special Branch officers at Folkestone reported the arrival by the SS *Riviera* – at 8.45 p.m. – from Boulogne, of the suspect Saunders, a note being made that there was 'great doubt' as to the man Saunders being the wanted Stranders.

Inspector Cosgrave was present at Victoria Station, and 'picked up' the man Saunders. His passport and other papers were examined and found to be in the name of Saunders. He was accompanied to his address, 4 Ely Terrace, White Horse Lane, Stepney, where it was definitely established that he was not the man wanted by MI5. During the course of the investigation Saunders informed the Special Branch officers that he had been the subject of attention by police in Paris and Boulogne, and declared that if he had been a guilty person he had ample warning to destroy any incriminating evidence. He had even overheard the correct name of the man with whose identity he had been confused in France. Ports were then informed that Saunders had arrived, and was not identical with Stranders, for whom a sharp look-out should still be kept.

That should have been the end of the affair. But what made the case interesting was that in *The Evening Standard* a paragraph appeared in the early edition, only, on 15 December and was as follows:

<u>Secret Documents</u>
Vigil at the Ports for two mysterious men.
The Channel ports were being closely watched, at the request of the Continental police, for two men who are supposed to be in possession of secret documents of great importance. The men are stated to be on their way to England. (On the other side of the Channel a strict vigil is also being kept.)[2]

It was a certainty the information had not come from MI5. So, the possibility of a leak emanating from the police with regard to an espionage case was now raised. A police officer who was authorised by the Commissioner of the Metropolitan Police to deal with the matter visited *The Evening Standard* office and found out that the author of the paragraph was a reporter named Stone, who furnished a manuscript which was inserted in the early edition of the paper on 15 December. The paragraph did not appear in the later editions, having been 'crowded out' by other matter. The manuscript was left in the possession of the sub-editors.

The officer then saw Stone, who made a statement 'which is remarkable'; he stated that on 7 December he was using a public telephone box at Trafalgar Square Tube Station with a view to speaking to a Mr Hoskins, who was a reporter employed by *The Evening Standard* and who frequently visited New Scotland Yard. This was between 7.30 p.m. and 8.30 p.m. that evening, and Stone said he believed Hoskins would be at New Scotland Yard; he called for the number, and while waiting to be connected overheard through the telephone a conversation ('this being due to two wires getting into contact; it not infrequently happens that one does hear a conversation in such circumstances' noted the police officer) which related to some instructions being given by some person to some other person ('of course he did not know who was speaking, or who was listening') to the effect that the French police were looking for two men and a strict look out was to be kept in Britain as they were believed to have important documents. There was a delay in getting a connection with New Scotland Yard, so Stone decided to abandon that call, and called instead Hoskins's private house; he got through to that address, but Hoskins was not at home. Stone then left the telephone box and thought no more about the matter until on 14 December he appeared 'to have been at a loss to provide some "copy" and bethought himself of the conversation he had heard on the 7th, and then sat down and "wrote up" the paragraph which appeared in the paper. To this statement he adhered.'

When the news was received, late on Christmas Eve, of this report the police officer concerned was instructed at once to see Kell and inquire whether between 7.30 and 8.30 p.m. on 7 December any such instructions were going over the wires, and also to see and take a statement from Hoskins. Kell reported that Special Branch had been requested by MI5 to inform ports from Harwich to Southampton that Stranders and a companion were anticipated to be coming to England from Paris, and that all proper steps should be taken to observe them, have them followed, and detained when they reached London. The telephone was accordingly utilised, and Dover, Newhaven, Harwich, Gravesend and Southampton were all spoken to between 7.20 and 8 p.m. on the night of the 7th from Special Branch, New Scotland Yard; that message, however, was not to the effect that the French or Continental police had asked British police to watch for these men, 'but that we were initiating the watching in order to catch the men ourselves'.

Hoskins, when interviewed, said that he was a close personal friend of Stone; that he attended the Press Bureau at New Scotland Yard daily morning and evening; that he had on some occasions been rung up by Stone at Scotland Yard, and also, frequently, at his private house; 'but he has no recollection as to whether he was at N.S.Y. on the evening of the 7th; further, his usual time for calling at N.S.Y. in the evening was 5.30'. The 'weak points' in Stone's statements, therefore, appeared to be '(1) that he should have waited for a week before preparing his MS, and (2) that "between 7.30 and 8.30 p.m." he should have thought it likely to be finding Hoskins at N.S.Y. – if he was so closely acquainted with him. The inaccuracies in the paragraph might however be ascribed to the week's interval and inaccurate memory.' It was 'remarkable but at the same time possible that a reporter should have been able to hear a "tapped" message from N.S.Y. to Channel Ports'. The implication was that a leak, concerning an espionage case, had originated from police at Scotland Yard. In any event, Stranders had been arrested in Paris. The Attorney General was informed:

> that while all our plans were laid to catch him on his arrival here from Brussels about the 8 or 9 December, he changed his plans and went straight to Paris, where he was caught; but our people have taken up quite the right line, I think, by giving information about Stranders to the French, so that the French should not think that a British subject was representing this country in French espionage. The French papers, I believe, have adopted this attitude towards the incident.

The Attorney General was also informed that an agent of Stranders whose correspondence had been under observation for some time, and some proceedings were being contemplated against him:

> It is quite possible that the French may think that they have not got a satisfactory case against Stranders, and that as an alien they may feel disposed to do, what I am sure Stranders would desire, that is, return him on a Channel steamer to England, and if so, it is not impossible that two or three policemen may find themselves on the same boat![3]

Special Branch was but one section of Scotland Yard which was concerned with the discovery and frustration of revolutionary activities in the United Kingdom. Few knew that this Department was subdivided into three branches, namely, SS1, SS2 and Special Branch. In general terms it might be said that the main business of SS1 was to act as a connecting link between Scotland Yard and SIS. Its role was to deal with the following:

> 1. Act... generally as the liaison office on foreign revolutionary matters between Special Branch and the Home Office on the one hand and the Secret Service section of the Foreign Office on the other.
> 2.(a) Supervision on behalf of the Home Office of propagandists of the Revolutionary experiment abroad and in or connected with Embassies, Legations, Delegations, etc., in the United Kingdom and over British subjects travelling abroad in furtherance of the Revolutionary cause.
> 2.(b) In conjunction with S.S.2. section co-ordination of foreign

and domestic information with regard to revolutionary movements and individuals.

3. Interviews suspects and persons other than agents from abroad with a knowledge of political and revolutionary affairs.

4. Examines passport applications of political and revolutionary suspects of alien origin leaving this country, and of incoming doubtfuls referred by Home Office (Immigration Department).

5. Advises Home Office re exclusion of aliens politically undesirable other than those engaged in military, naval and air espionage.

6. Exchanges communications regarding movements and conspiracies of revolutionary agitators with:

(a) <u>Self-governing Dominions and Crown Colonies.</u>

<u>Direct</u> to Canadian Mounted Police.

<u>Through High Commissioners</u> to Australia New Zealand, South Africa.

<u>Through Colonial Office or direct</u> to the Police Authorities of the Crown Colonies or Dependencies.

(b) <u>Foreign Countries</u>

<u>Through Special Branch Officers</u> to France, Belgium, Holland.

(These S.B. Officers are in liaison with the Foreign Office Secret Service abroad by special arrangement with the Under Secretary for Foreign Affairs.)

<u>Through Ministers, Legations or Consulates General</u> to other Governments hostile to revolutionary propaganda.

<u>Through Foreign Office and Foreign Office Secret Service</u> to the political police of many of these countries.

7. Conveys political information connected with foreign affairs obtained through channels in the United Kingdom to the Foreign Office; Foreign Office Secret Service; Colonial Office; India Office and other appropriate departments.

8. Examines for the Home Office foreign revolutionary literature preliminary to decision by Secretary of State as to its admission or prohibition by Home Office warrant.

9. In conjunction with M.I.1.c.[SIS] keeps observation on movements of and transactions in arms (conducted through channels other than official) at Home and Abroad.

10. In conjunction with S.I.S. investigates the sources of forged Bank of England and Treasury Notes manufactured abroad. Incidental aid to the Bank of England and C.I.D. on these and cognate subjects.

The role of S.S.2. was to collate and distribute information as to revolutionary activities and to suggest action thereon:

1. To obtain through Special Branch channels, occasional informants and Chief Constables), check, collate and distribute in the form of a weekly report to the Cabinet, a weekly report to Chief Constables and letters to Government Departments, Intelligence branches and Chief Constables, information regarding revolutionary movements (political and industrial) and individuals (other than Colonial and foreign) in England, Scotland and Wales.
2. To inform M.I.5. and N.I.D. and Air Ministry of communist activities or propaganda likely to affect H.M. Forces.
3. To pass to D[istrict].A[ssistant].C[ommissioner].S[pecial. B[ranch]. all information which may eventually lead to police action.
4. To bring to the notice of the Director of Public Prosecutions cases in which spoken, written or printed matter appears to call for legal proceedings.
5. To follow, from the British end, the contact between British and foreign revolutionary movements and individuals.
6. To institute enquiries into the activities of politically doubtful movements and individuals.
7. To keep D.A.C.S.B. informed, for the use of Officers at Ports of the passage to and from the United Kingdom of British revolutionaries.
8. To deal with queries from other Government offices and Intelligence Services regarding matters of detail connected with revolutionary movements and individuals (other than Colonial and foreign) in England, Scotland and Wales.
9. To maintain liaison with outside Intelligence Services, (other than S.I.S., with which S.S.1. deals) in regard to information dealing with revolutionary movements and individuals (other than Colonial and foreign) in England, Scotland and Wales.
10. To maintain liaison with Passport Office regarding applications from British revolutionaries and to submit doubtful cases to the Secretary of State for Home Affairs.
11. To furnish a weekly report, based on the Chief Constables' report, to the First Secretary to the American Embassy.
12. To read, and take necessary action on, revolutionary literature and periodicals printed in or affecting Great Britain.

One would think that much of this would be more suitable to what MI5 was set for but, in the aftermath of the war, its role was confined to counter-espionage and sedition in the Armed Forces.

Special Branch, in addition, was required to do the necessary police work in regard to revolutionary activities as might be necessary within the London Metropolitan area and at certain ports. Special Branch was also responsible for dealing with all manifestations of Irish revolutionary activity in Britain and provided the necessary staff for the protection of members of the Royal Family, Cabinet Ministers and other persons. The staff of SS1 and SS2 were paid from Secret Service funds. The expenses of the Special Branch, on the other hand, were chargeable to the vote for Police. SS1 consisted of two officers and two clerks; SS2 of two officers (women) and one clerk; and Special Branch of 135 police officers of various grades, headed by a Deputy Assistant Commissioner of Police. But, in a typical example of the ad hoc development of British practice, Scotland Yard's writ in such matters did not run over the whole country. Outside the Metropolitan Police area, save only at certain ports at which officers of the Special Branch were at work in co-operation with Immigration Officers, the local police authorities were responsible for dealing with 'revolutionary' matters. Constant touch was, however, maintained between these authorities and Scotland Yard, and the Assistant Commissioner Special Branch at Scotland Yard distributed about £2,000 a year among Chief Constables in other parts of the country in order to enable them to obtain such assistance as may be necessary and could not otherwise be provided. This meant:

> All police enquiries in the Metropolitan area and prosecutions of a political character are undertaken by Special Branch.
> Enquiries are made on behalf of Government Departments such as the Passport Department of the Foreign Office, Ministry of Labour, Aliens Department (Home Office), etc.
> Insane letter-writers and threatening letters are dealt with.
> 'Gun-runners' and persons connected with revolutionary organisations are kept under observation and their movements reported upon.
> Revolutionary literature is obtained.
> All revolutionary bodies are reported upon.

Open-air and indoor meetings of these organisations were covered by the Branch. They averaged twenty-five a week and many had to be attended by more than one officer, such as in Trafalgar Square, where several plinths were used, and Hyde Park, where speeches were made from many platforms. Shorthand-notes were taken in many instances and verbatim reports submitted. The 'peculiar nature' of the work of Special Branch requiring the gathering of obtaining information from an 'inside' source, for the prevention of crimes against the State, made it necessary to employ informants in the various revolutionary movements – Communist, the unemployed, Irish, Indian, Egyptian, etc. The work of Special Branch was of a highly specialised character. Officers, besides having a full knowledge of the powers and duties of the uniformed police and CID had to 'possess an intimate knowledge of world-wide revolutionary politics'. The enquiry staff was recruited from serving Metropolitan Police officers who were of 'good appearance and address, of good education, and possessing a knowledge of foreign languages or writing shorthand at a high speed in order to submit a verbatim report and give evidence on their notes in a Court of Law'. One of the key individuals involved in Special Branch was Lieutenant Colonel Carter, formally of MI5. Carter, who was not a police officer had no power of command over the personnel of the Special Branch. His duties consisted almost entirely of dealing with 'Irish Questions'. It was deemed by the Commissioner of the Metropolis 'eminently desirable' that he should have the status of a police officer so as to be able to control the discipline, administration and organisation of the Special Branch. So, on 24 October 1922, Carter was appointed a Deputy Assistant Commissioner and his position thereby regularised, although, 'as a matter of fact he had been partially performing the duties of a Police Officer without any real authority'.

Within SS1, Captain Guy Liddell and Mr Neale dealt with the study and investigation, through SIS, of revolutionary movements abroad and the control of Communist and other revolutionary aliens and literature entering the United Kingdom from the Colonies. They also co-ordinated information and prepared reports on the subject.[4] Guy Maynard Liddell was to play a significant part in the history of MI5. He was born on 8 November 1892 at 64 Victoria Street, London, one of three sons of Augustus Frederick Liddell, a retired captain in the Royal Artillery, and his wife, Emily Shinner. At the time of his birth, Liddell's father worked in the Royal Household and was comptroller and treasurer to Prince and Princess Christian of Schleswig-Holstein. Guy studied in Germany, but then served in the Royal Field Artillery during the First World War and was awarded an MC. Having abandoned a promising career as a cellist, Liddell joined Scotland Yard in 1919. He was responsible for co-ordinating the police raid on the Arcos building in Moorgate, London in May 1927 (which also housed the Soviet trade delegation), in pursuit of a missing classified RAF document.[5] The raid led to Britain breaking off diplomatic relations with the Soviet Union. Liddell was the link between Scotland Yard, MI5 and SIS as all three of these organisations exchanged intelligence on Soviet espionage activities in Britain – the focus of which was the commercial concern, Arcos Limited, and the Communist Party of Great Britain. The CPGB was part of Comintern – the Third Communist International established by the Soviet Government in 1919 (the First International was established by Marx in 1864, while the Second International, formed in 1889, was deemed unacceptable by Lenin because it was dominated by social democrat parties). Comintern was supposed to aid and guide Communist parties outside the Soviet state but, in fact, was used a vehicle to control these parties – such as the CPGB – from Moscow.

The Soviet Presence

In an edition of the *Commercial Year Book of the Soviet Union*, the Soviet Trading Agency of Arcos Ltd. was self-described as: 'The sole purchasing and selling Agency in Great Britain for the Government of the U.S.S.R.' An MI5 assessment stated that this 'naive description is typical of the child-like faith the Bolsheviks in general put in the science of auto-suggestion. They believe that if they say a thing often enough most people are bound to believe it in the long run. Hence their persistence in describing Arcos, and other Soviet Organisations as "Agencies" – as distinct from definite sub-departments of the Commissariat for Foreign Trade.' A 'similar faith in the credulity of the foreigner' was displayed by the Soviet Government when it referred to the Comintern as an independent international organisation 'granted the hospitality of the Soviet State. As a matter of fact, the People and Commissariat for Foreign Affairs and the People's Commissariat for Foreign Trade were co-dependent one upon the other.' The Trade Delegations abroad were 'official organs' of the Foreign Affairs Commissariat, and the commercial organisations 'organs' of the Foreign Trade Department; 'that was the theoretical position, but in practice the Trade Delegation was the Governing Body and was supreme in its authority over such "organs" as Arcos Ltd. Of course, the Delegation is, in turn, subject to the authority of the diplomatic representative, i.e. the Embassy; but, as the two are more or less indivisible, it is rather unnecessary to discriminate between them.'

Arcos Ltd. was the principal trading organisation in Britain. Its capital was supplied by the Soviet Trade Delegation in Britain and it was governed by that body. The staff of Arcos Ltd. was divided into three main headings: the buying, the selling and financial departments. The chief positions were held by Russians all of whom were Soviet citizens. In the majority of cases the managers were Russian Communists and where a Communist was not available, the responsible technical manager was supervised by a member of the Russian Communist Party. The Russian Communists in Arcos and the other Soviet institutions were organised in a 'bureau', which met secretly and discussed general matters of policy. This bureau was presided over by Madame Volstein, 'a notorious member' of Soviet Intelligence. The Communist bureau in addition to its other functions drew up lists for the various social and Trade Union Committees. For example, the Trade Union of Soviet and Commercial Employees (Mestkom) had an election of Committee members twice yearly. The practice of the Russian Communists was to select a list of Russian and British Communists, a majority of whom were always Russians and to add one non-party member (also a Russian). This list was then elected without fail at the General Meeting of the members of the Union. All sub-committees were selected in the same manner and, as all meetings were packed with either Communists and sympathisers or Communists, those who were 'afraid to vote' other than directed; the 'official' list was always approved. Thus the policy of the Mestkom, the Social and Sports Clubs Committees, the Cultural and Youth Educational Committees etc, 'was always a definite Communist policy'.

The All Union Textile Syndicate with offices at Imril House, King William Street 'ranked in importance' with Arcos. It did not sell anything but bought Lancashire textile machinery as well as raw wool and cotton for the Soviet Textile Trust. The Chief of the Textile Syndicate in London was Emdine: 'He is a Jew and prominent member of the Russian Communist Party.' The Bank of Russian Trade (formerly Arcos Banking Corporation) was also a part of the Trade Delegation and Hermer, who was Secretary to the Delegation, was also a Director of the Bank. Centrosojus (England) Ltd. was the English Branch of the All Russian Central Union of Consumers' Societies; and despite its 'co-operative' title was – as well as the Moscow Narodny Bank, and the Ukrainian Co-operatives – 'merely another branch of the Foreign Trade Commissariat'. The Central Association of Flax Growers 'Lnocentre'; the Russian Oil Products Company; the Arcos Steamship Company Ltd; Selosogus Ltd; Knigas Ltd; and Mosekust Ltd, were all in the same category. The names were different but they were 'all essentially organs of the Soviet State which has a monopoly of Foreign Trade and is itself the distributor of Russia's raw materials'.

In order to give some form of actuality to the Soviet system as developed by Lenin, the Trade Unions within Arcos and the other Soviet trading organisations had been granted a status, which the Bolsheviks called 'independent'. But the fact was that the Soviet Trade Unions 'are as much a part of the Soviet State Bureaucracy as the Foreign Trading Organisations. The line of demarcation is a very thin one – a modern "thin red line" in fact! All the real difference is that between one section of Russian Communists who have been appointed to the Political and Trading side of the Bolshevik organisation and another section whose efforts have been directed into the Trade Union Channel.' Naturally, the differences which were bound to crop up between two sections of the same bureaucracy, tended to strengthen that Soviet propaganda which boasted of its 'wonderful voluntary Trade Unionism; and these differences are exploited by the Soviet body Politic for the general edification of the "foreign" proletariat. Hence we have the amusing spectacle of Mr Tomsky in his role of member of the Political Bureau sitting down with Messrs Kamenev and Schmidt and laying down the policy of the Soviets; and the same Mr Tomsky, as Chief of the Trade Union Bureaucracy, going to Mr Schmidt and Kamenev – as representatives of the Council of Labour and Defence – and fighting for Concessions and Collective Agreements for his (Tomsky's) members!' The 'farce is not only amusing but it is an excellent propaganda weapon in the hands of the C.P.G.B.' In the London Soviet institutions 'the same comedy is staged for the special edification of the employees.' The directors of every trading organisation 'negotiate' a Collective Agreement with the London Mestkom. This Agreement laid down 1. hours of labour, 2. salaries, 3. holidays, 4. welfare and health work, etc. But the draft of this Collective Agreement 'is drawn up by the Russian Communists ergo: the Chiefs of the various Soviet Institutions, it then goes to Mestkom upon which sits a majority of the same people, and finally to the General Meeting of the Union Members who are told that Mestkom fought very hard for such and such a Concession or privilege but that the management were obdurate and so on.'

As a 'solid fact', Mestkom 'has the most extraordinary powers placed in its hands. It can and does decide not only upon the dismissal of members of the staff whose political views may not be to its liking; but it also decides who shall and who shall not be taken upon the staffs of the various Institutions.' Its position, therefore, 'is in no way analogous to the ordinary Trade Union. Instead, it is really a Directorate and, by virtue of the love of intrigue of the Russians, acts also as a kind of shuttlecock between the Management – whose creature it is – and the employees.' It followed that the Soviet Trade Union 'is of no real benefit to the employees. It is true that it can, and does, act as intermediary between the Management and the Employees, but this role is nothing more than a pious gesture. In every instance, the Communist (Russian) policy rules and the employee secures rather less benefit by the fact of the Union's existence than he might secure were he in a position to deal direct with the responsible Chief of the Institution.' The only time Mestkom acted was when a Communist might have a difference with his departmental Chief and in such cases it was not a Trade Union interference, but the intervention of a Communist body. Consequently, the position of the British Communists within the Soviet Trading organisation 'is a peculiar one. In theory, there is an equality between the Communists of various countries; but in actual practice the equality does not exist.'[6] The point being made here was that Soviet trading organisations and their trade union were in fact merely extensions of the Soviet state itself. And that state's intentions appeared to be far from honourable in Britain.

From their arrival in Britain, the British Secret Service used its agents to build up a picture of the Soviet presence – especially Arcos. In October 1920, MI5 was informed by SIS that: 'Our mutual friend is continuing his operations in order to discover some further particulars with regard to the ARCOS Co.;' the informant, presumably a businessman, was actually an MI5 agent and reported how 'I called on the ARCOS people again on October 5th, and as before, their waiting room was full of the most repulsive looking individuals, all Jews.' He was unable to see any of the directors named on the firm's notepaper, but had an interview with Swerdloff the head of the heavy chemical department. Swerdloff told him, 'under cross examination', about who was who in Arcos and its contacts with other Soviet trading missions in London and their relationship with British business contacts. This rather unpleasant informant – typical of the undercurrent of anti-Semitism prevalent in all classes in Britain at this time – had a minor setback by the end of the encounter:

> While I was with Swerdloff about midday, a stoutly built young Russian, rather above average height, wearing a light overcoat and Trilby hat, came in carrying a wicker basket with a lid. This basket contained cakes. Swerdloff and another Russian Jew in his room could not wait for me to finish my interview before falling upon this collation. However, to save their face, they insisted on my trying one of the cakes, explaining there was only one place in London where they could be obtained, and were made by an artist who had escaped from Moscow, and was now engaged in making Russian food in London. The cake was a hot doughnut, filled with salt white cabbage and boiled potato, and I felt very unwell after eating it.[7]

Another agent, 'P', reported, in 1925, that in April of 'this year I received a hint' that members of the feared Soviet secret police, the Cheka:

in Arcos were given a long list of Arcos employees, together with instructions that the individuals mentioned were to be very carefully watched until further orders. 'Watching' by the Cheka means that the individuals concerned are followed about day and night to see where they go, with whom they associate and what views they express, either regarding politics or concerning other members of Arcos. In many cases the one who is being watched is probably a friend of the one who is watching him. About the end of May it was known generally that the Cheka was active, with the result that everybody in Arcos was afraid to speak to anybody else. As the result of the Cheka activities 47 of the employees have been dismissed by the 13th of this month and more are likely to follow. They have all been dismissed solely on the grounds of doubtful political orientation. Of these 47, 28–30 are English and the remainder Russian. No Jews have been dismissed up to date.[8]

A picture of the internal situation in Arcos was, partly, built up by disgruntled former employees such as Miss N. Pearson, who had worked in the Arcos Timber Department. She confirmed to Special Branch/MI5, early in 1926, that Arcos were getting rid of British subjects employed as shorthand typists and replacing them with Russians from abroad. Pearson, Scotland Yard noted, had been given notice and was replaced by Mrs Ida Davis *née* Schein, a woman of Russian origin, who had recently married in Berlin the well known British Communist Edgar Davis and was employed in sending back reports on labour and revolutionary matters to Moscow, in addition to her official duties. She was formerly doing work for the Third International in Russia. The grounds given for the dismissal of Miss Pearson were those of staff reduction. In SS1, Guy Liddell told MI5 that it was difficult 'to reconcile these cases with the recent application of Marie Petrovna Koltsova, who wishes to come here as a shorthand-typist to the Trade Delegation... this application should be refused'. Although the 'granting of facilities to enable Russian subjects to join the staff of the Soviet Embassy or the Russian Consulate in the capacity of <u>confidential secretaries</u> may be justifiable, I hardly think the same view would apply in the case of a <u>shorthand-typist</u> who is to be employed by the Trade Delegation or Arcos.' The status of Soviet Delegates connected with the organisation of Mestkom:

would appear to be materially affected in the light of the information given by Miss Pearson. The only <u>raison d'etre</u> of 'Mestkom' as far as the British Authorities are concerned is in its capacity as a <u>bona fide</u> Trade Union which undertakes to investigate any cases of wrongful dismissal and to represent to the employers the grievances of its members. If therefore it fails in this respect in a case [Pearson's] where obvious injustice has been done, there is very little in our eyes to justify its existence. I think this point should be for consideration when application are submitted for the extension of visas to any Russians known to be engaged as officials of Mestkom.[9]

It was the difference in treatment between Britons (whether Communists or not) and Russians that led to an assessment, in MI5 files that, despite the alleged international aspect of Communism:

There is no more rabid Nationalist than the average Russian Communist. His cry is 'long live the World Proletariat'; but the 'World Proletariat' is only a name; a kind of exotic stimulant which plays upon his imagination and gives him an 'ideal' without which the average Russian is the merest buffoon. The Russian Communist (indeed this is true of the Communists of all nations) loves the 'Proletariat' in the mass. It is a 'meaty' expression, which includes all those who agree with his aims; but the individual proletarian is a bird of another colour! To love an intangible thing is easy; it calls for no great mental or charitable effort, but to love individuals calls for an idealism, which has to stand the greatest of all test and it is in this that the gospel of Bolshevism fails in the most remarkable manner. Your Bolshevik is no respecter of persons. He has developed a mass psychology, which is capable of thinking only by numbers. Bring him face to face with the individuals of which his 'mass' is composed and he shows himself in his true colours.

The basis of philosophical Socialism 'is a love of one's fellow-men and a sympathetic toleration of the frailties of human nature'. Yet not one member of the Soviet Communist Party 'can stand such a test'. They 'are all opportunists and demagogues'. The Russian Communist Party member sent to Britain was given a position and power, which, in the majority of cases, could never occur under a capitalist system. Few of the Russians had commercial experience, yet they were placed in positions over technicians and men of general commercial experience. 'The Russian Communist is, too, essentially a bully. He must have his own way in everything with the obvious result that he is not only feared but actually hated by those who have to work under him. He finds the English life agrees with his inherent love of luxury – this is common to all Russians. He lives up to his salary which is generally fixed at £52 per month but which he can increase by various allowances, travelling expenses and such-like.' No Russian Communist in Britain lived according to the standard of 'the average proletarian. He has his house or flat at Hampstead; his servants; his good food and clothing; and altogether is in no way different from the average businessman who is able to keep up a good home and pay visits to the theatres and other places of amusement.'

Not a single member of the CPGB employed in the Soviet Trading Organisations occupied a managerial position. 'This despite the fact that quite a few of them have sound commercial experience. The Russian Communist at heart despises the English Communist. Indeed, the most striking characteristic of the Russian Communist is his contempt for all who are not Russian.' Thus, 'while he appreciates the social amenities of England, he is anti-British. He sneers at British art, British music and British drama. It is not that he really despises these things. His horizon is limited and illimitable at one and the same time. His idea of internationalism is a hatred of everything national except it be the product of Soviet Russia.' Therefore, the British employees who happened to be members of the CPGB were expected to do as the Russian Communists dictated. 'A striking illustration of the anti-international bias of the Russian Communists is the fact that their immediate friends are always non-party Russians. The English Communists are only consulted when they may be able to do something for the Russian Communists, such as, for example, at the Mestkom Elections.' Despite the comparatively generous scale of salaries paid by the Soviet Trading Organisations, the general working conditions were bad. There was no security; no chance of commercial advancement, as all responsible posts were reserved for Russian Communists. It happened quite frequently that Englishmen who have served the Soviet Organisations well in a commercial capacity for four or five years, were dismissed on the time-honoured plea of 'reduction of staff', whereas they were usually succeeded by one or more imported Russian Communists 'Experts' whose expertness was confined 'to their undoubted capacity for a good style of living combined with general incompetence.'[10]

Documentary evidence had been obtained by MI5 that 'Johnny Walker', a secret agent of the Soviet Government and the Third International, (mentioned in Special Reports on the Russian Trade Delegation and Revolutionary Organisations in the United Kingdom, dated 30 November 1921, and 17 and 25 March 1922), was identical with Jacob Kirchenstein, a naturalised American of Lettish origin, who was employed in Britain as an official of the Arcos Steampship Company. The first record of Kirchenstein's activities in the UK dated back to December 1920, when a number of letters, the property of a Communist courier, were discovered on board the S.S. *Sterling*, which plied between South Shields and Bergen. These letters – later identified as being in Kirchenstein's handwriting – were from an individual styling himself 'John or Jack Walker', in England, and were addressed to one of the chief agents of the Third International in Western Europe and to the Lettish representative on the Executive Committee of the Third International in Moscow. They showed that John or Jack Walker was of high standing in the Third International from whose headquarters he was in immediate receipt of orders; that he was a self-confessed enemy agent residing in the United Kingdom as an unregistered alien; and that he was then engaged at the head of an organisation for distributing Bolshevik propaganda and for facilitating the passage of Bolshevik agents to and from Russia as stowaways. He was also cognisant of, though not hopeful about, the organisation of a Red Army in Britain.

In April and May 1921, through intercepted correspondence, this same individual was shown to be acting as an agent for the Third International in the despatch of propaganda and propagandists to the British Colonies. In September 1921, he received instructions, through the Moscow Foreign Office and the Soviet Trade Delegation in London, from Piatnitsky the financial secretary of the Third International, to 'refrain from liquidating his organisation'. These instructions he obeyed, though taking special precautions to sever any direct connection with the Communist Party headquarters, whom he regarded as politically unreliable. He decided in fact to build up his own organisation. In March 1922, evidence was obtained that Johnny Walker in London was still receiving both instructions and funds from the Third International by means of Lettish seamen and also through the Soviet diplomatic bag. Within a period of two or three months at the beginning of 1922, at least £700, £300 of which went to the left-wing Labour Research Department, passed through Kirchenstein's hands. In his work in Britain, Kirchenstein was, apparently, being closely assisted by the 'notorious' Peter Miller, cypher clerk to the Russian Trade Delegation, with whom he still appeared to be in the closest touch. Miller 'was known to be at the centre of Bolshevik intrigue in this country', and had been proved in the past to have been associated with the 'dubious activities' of Nicolai Klishko.

The connection between the Russian Trade Delegation and 'extremists' in the Labour Research Department, such as Page Arnot and C. Palme Dutt, was significant in the light of definite information that Moscow was inclined to regard this organisation as more fertile ground than the CPGB, which had not been giving results proportionate to the sums allowed by the Third International for propaganda purposes. 'There is no doubt that the Labour Research Department has subsequently become the real driving force of the revolutionary movement in this country. C. Palme Dutt one of its most influential members, on his own admission receives his instructions direct from Arcos and the Russian Trade Delegation.'

Kirchenstein, it seemed, did not visit Britain by legal means until 3 November 1922, when he arrived as a railroad agent from New York, accompanied by his wife, Vallie. Sometime around May 1924, Kirchenstein began to be employed with the Arcos Steamship Company, 'which had on several occasions been reported as the centre of Bolshevik intrigue in this country'. On returning to the United Kingdom on 13 October 1925, he went to reside at the address of Peter Miller who was employed in the Russo-Norwegian Steamship Company. This company worked in close touch with the Arcos Steamship Company. Residing at the same address as Peter Miller was one Jan Weiden a cypher clerk to the Trade Delegation, whose name and address were used by Kirchenstein 'as a cover for his secret correspondence'. Early in November, 1925, Kirchenstein moved into his present flat, 68a Parkhill Road, NW3.

Since February 1924, a portion of Kirchenstein's correspondence and that of his associates had been under observation. The text of the letters was in most cases 'extremely obscure.' It had, however, been possible to establish that Kirchenstein, working through the intermediary of Charles Douglas in Leith, and one 'CHARLES 'or 'KARLIS' (possibly Karl Bahn of the Arcos Steamship Company) corresponded with Russia. Communications were sent either through seamen – in the case of Russia through those working on Arcos boats – or through the diplomatic bag, or by post to cover addresses. Beyond the fact that they were of a particularly secret nature and clearly deal with revolutionary matters, nothing was known of the contents of these communications. The following facts with regard to Kirchenstein and his associates were, however apparent in his intercepted correspondence:

1. KIRCHENSTEIN'S HQ is in Moscow and he collects information regarding the activities of the British Communist Party.

Letter No. 6 – 'Harry POLLITT went to headquarters fishing on behalf of limelighters (returns next week). Please let me know all you know about him. Bob STEWART and him don't seem to agree.' Letter No. 48.

2. KIRCHENSTEIN in May 1924 took up an official position in the Arcos Steamship Company while still continuing his revolutionary activities.

Letter No. 20 – 'I am working in the City in that big building in one of the departments, but the old business partly goes on.'
Letter No. 37 – Kirchenstein signs on behalf of the Arco Steamship Company.

3. KIRCHENSTEIN is a close follower of the revolutionary movement both in the United Kingdom and in America.

Letter No. 21 – 'What is the industrial position there (USA) like now? It is getting worse here (UK) every day. Ever since the autumn of 1920 an army of about 2,000,000 unempployed. From what I am told by those who have come from Russia, not blabbers, the position there is improving daily. But, as I told you last time in the carriage, and I tell it to you again, it won't be possible for another ten years yet to apply the standard of the Russian workers to the conditions of life of the American workmen.'

4. KIRCHENSTEIN'S wife assists her husband in his revolutionary activities.

Letter No. 27 – 'Can anything sensible be written to that address? It would be of great importance to me (Vallie KIRCHENSTEIN) to know that. If not, please let me have another good address, because what I have to say has to be said in parts and I want to be able to write seriously,'

5. KIRCHENSTEIN, as far as possible, carries on his activities independently of the Delegation, who in their official capacity are afraid of disclosing any connection with the Third International.

Letter No. 33 – 'The chiefs of the society do not dare to know what and from where you receive from us.'

6. KIRCHENSTEIN was anxious that the British Authorities should not know of his connection with Arcos.

Letter No. 47 – 'I believe it is best not to bring Arcos into this mess. You might let GLUSHCHENKO (head of the Shipping Department of Arcos) know discreetly that I am obliged to delay but that he is not to take any steps. They can only do me harm, except perhaps through the Russo-Norwegian.'

7. KIRCHENSTEIN'S work is of such a secret nature that not even those in the movement and in Arcos are informed of his activities and journeys abroad.

Letter No. 47 – 'It has just occurred to me, Don't tell anyone anything about what has happened to me, except that I shall soon be back.'
Letter No. 48 – 'Other people are asking where you are. I say that I do not know, but I am inclined to think that they think that you (KIRCHENSTEIN) have gone off to the centre.' (? Moscow)

8. KIRCHENSTEIN is anxious regarding his personal safety and the possible censorship of his correspondence.

Letter No. 33 – 'As all foreigners in England are under police supervision, it is possible that they will censor our correspondence. Better write to Mr. Joseph VEIDEN (Cipher Clerk to the Russian Trade Delegation 2, St Andrew's Road, N.W.11. in an ordinary envelope.'
Letter No. 51 – 'Don't delay writing. Only make no mention of politics.'
Letter No. 56 – 'When you write, write cautiously without touching upon politics as the censorship of the letters at this end has to be reckoned with.'

9. KIRCHENSTEIN still maintains touch with Peter MILLER, with whom he has recently been staying.

Letters Nos. 45, 47, 48, 50, 52 and 56.

10. KIRCHENSTEIN, in September 1925, intended to visit this country by illegal means should he have been refused a visa in New York.

Letter No. 47 – 'If they should refuse the application, I shall be on the road, and we shall meet even if it is for a short time only.

As soon as I hear I shall set out and pay no attention to any obstructions, so you (Peter MILLER) will hear all in detail.'

11.KIRCHENSTEIN still receives reports from the British Colonies and from Moscow.

Letter No. 48 – 'I (CHARLES or KARLIS) have already sent off six telegrams and have recieved a letter from Buenos Aires. A man has already arrived from the centre. (? Moscow) I have received two letters from Australia, and all is well, and also from New Zealand.'

12. KIRCHENSTEIN appears to contemplate a visit to Palestine, possible in connection with the recent growth of Communist activity in Palestine.

Letter No. 55 – 'Perhaps you have begun to think that we have set out for Palestine.'

From the above it appeared to MI5 that Kirchenstein, under the orders of the Third International and the Soviet Government, 'is continuing his activities as an important Soviet secret agent for Great Britain and the Colonies, and for North and South America, working on more intimate lines than even the British Section of the Party itself, for the furtherance of the Muscovite policy of disturbance and dislocation'. [11]

Colonel Carter, from Scotland Yard, established from his own agents that, as Kirchenstein had 'made it his business to keep the Communist Party headquarters at arms length', he had established contact solely with former members of either the Shop Stewards Movement or the Socialist Labour Party, both of which organisations had since been 'liquidated or absorbed' by the Communist Party of Great Britain. At the beginning of March 1926, acting though Charles Douglas of Leith, Kirchenstein made enquiries as to the whereabouts of a man subsequently identified as James Messer of Glasgow. Messer was formerly connected with the old Shop Stewards Movement, which had since been absorbed by the National Minority Movement, which also had significant Communist influences within it. Although from time to time its members had fallen out with the Communist Party of Great Britain, there was 'no doubt' that, along with the Socialist Labour Party of Glasgow, now defunct, 'it contained the best, if not the only reliable, Communist elements in this country'. Douglas succeeded in locating Messer towards the end of 1926, and a meeting was arranged at Douglas's house in Leith on 4 July at which Kirchenstein, Karl Bahn and Messer were present. Details of what transpired at this meeting were unknown but with subsequent events it became evident that Messer was running a 'very secret' organisation to consist of 'specially trusted Comrades residing in certain districts'. These 'Comrades', working through shop stewards in certain factories, were to obtain information on military and economic questions, which they would then transmit to Messer, who in turn passed it on to Kirchenstein.

During September and October 1926, Messer succeeded through the agency of Tom Clark and Jack Tanner, well-known members of the left-wing Shop Stewards Movement, in getting into touch with Charles Henry of Barrrow-in-Furness, Tom Smith of Hendon and a little later with F.E. Walker of Manchester, all well-known rank and file members of the Communist Party of Great Britain. On 1 December 1926, Messer met Kirchenstein in London. Kirchenstein, in reporting this meeting to Douglas, stated that 'everything was going fine'. No definite indication as to exactly what this group were doing was obtained until 12 September 1926, when Walker informed Jack Tanner that, in connection with a previous conversation with Messer, it had been ascertained, 'after careful enquiries by reliable Comrades', that new technical designs were going through the Ordnance Department of Armstrong Whitworth's and that particulars of these, as well as of a new design of aircraft that was being manufactured by Messrs. A.V. Roe & Co would probably be obtained. On 23 January 1927, Walker reported further to Tanner that the design of A.V. Roe's new engine was proving successful and that he was 'already in possession of some interesting particulars'. By arrangement between Messer, Tanner and Walker these particulars and any further information that might be obtained were to be transmitted to a secret cover address. Two weeks later Douglas was making arrangements for a meeting between Kirchenstein and Messer, which duly took place on 18 February. 'It is significant that just about this time a report was received from an entirely different source, in which it was stated that Messer was carrying on espionage in industrial matters, on behalf of the Soviet Government and had been successful in obtaining exceptionally good information regarding scientific machinery etc.' Arrangements had since been made for the payment to Messer by Kirchenstein of a regular monthly salary and Karl Bahn had been introduced as an intermediary for further communications.

There was a 'curious development' in October 1926, when a report was received from a third independent source that W.F.R. Macartney, better known as the 'Monocle Man', was being employed by Messer 'who was a member of the Red Secret Service in this country'. It 'will be seen that he was employed in a confidential capacity by the British

Government during the war, that after the war he became associated with some of the best known gangs in this country' and that in February 1926, he was convicted of attempting to steal valuables after smashing a jeweller's window in Albemarle Street. When he came out of prison, he approached the CPGB and offered to provide the *Sunday Worker* with sensational articles on the British Secret Service. An article under his signature actually appeared in October 1926 which merely showed him as holding Labour views. It did not deal with Secret Service matters, but the heading referred to him as an 'ex-Secret Service man'. In spite of a report received in November 1926, that Macartney had been dropped by the CPGB, there was reason to believe 'that he merely went underground and that he is now an active worker on secret matters for the Soviet Government'.

These investigations appeared to show to Carter that 'there is very little co-operation between the various groups working under the Soviet Delegation in this country. There is in fact considerable risk, which leads to every form of internal intrigue. The names of certain individuals connected with these other groups are known, but beyond the fact that they are concerned in political, social and military espionage, details of their activities are not at present available. They work independently of each other and on occasions against each other. Internal dissensions have recently become so marked that higher authority in Moscow has intervened as a result of numerous denunciations and counter-denunciation that four of the most active intriguers are being recalled.'[12] MI5, however, disagreed and believed that the Russian espionage organisation in UK was 'one, and one only', controlled by Jacob Kirchenstein and divided into four sections:

1. Kirchenstein, through his assistant assisted by S.K. Melnichuk and J. Jelinsky together with Kolin, the three latter in Hamburg, would appear to be the controlling centre.

2. Kolin having a job on a boat travelling between Hamburg, Antwerp and London would appear to be in touch with Nelson of Russian Oil Products. Nelson is in touch with the underground organisation of the Communist Party and working in conjunction with Wal Hannington, D.F. Springhall and others connected with the Communist Party organisation, from the point of view of running a Courier Service for the Russian Espionage Organisation.

3. Through D.F. Springhall... contact has been established with the Irish Republican Intelligence Service.

4. The actual agents believed to be working in this country for, and on behalf of Kirchenstein would appear to be J.M. Messer, Jack Tanner, Charles Douglas, F.E. Walker and Siddal.

Despite the evidence that had been compiled, there was a reluctance to interrogate any of those suspected of espionage with a view to gaining more information on the Soviet spy ring because:

1. True it is difficult to shadow these individuals, but certain links have been established which enable us more or less to know their whereabouts and a little of their activity.

2. True nothing of any real importance is ever sent through the post and therefore the only way is to study, for two or three months, the activity of certain other individuals who are not mentioned... but who are known to be in touch with them.

3. To interrogate Walker, Siddall, Tanner and Messer it is thought would be of very little use because Tanner and Messer would probably learn far more of what we knew of their activities as a result of the interrogation than we should learn, about them. As regards Walker and Siddall, I do not think that they could help very much, other than possibly telling us that they had from time to time posted on messages and letters to some individual whose real aim and object in life they did not know.

The interrogation would... simply result in warning two of the principles, Tanner and Messer, that we were interested and had some knowledge of the organisation with which they were connected. There is no doubt that if certain individuals are left alone for a little while longer and no action is taken in regard to the activity of minors in the case, certain sources from which we are obtaining information will, before long, be in a position to link up perhaps the whole of this Russian Espionage Organisation in UK and the missing links in the Macartney case will possibly have been established.[13]

If there were any doubt (which there was not) on the part of Special Branch and MI5 about a Soviet espionage ring, on 9 February 1927 information came in from another source, Captain Nicholas Mulkaloff, Marine Surveyor and Specialist in Ice Navigation, who confirmed it. In 1922 he obtained employment with the Northern Sea Route Bureau as second in command of the Kara Sea expedition. This expedition consisted of carrying merchandise to and from Siberia, and took place annually during the months of August and September; the ships, five in all, used, were chartered from the British, under which flag they sailed, a large proportion of the crew also being British. Mukaloff revealed that the Northern Sea Route Bureau's chief was named Jelinsky – whom MI5 knew from his association with Kirchenstein; furthermore Mulkaloff revealed that the Bureau was controlled by Arcos Ltd. It was about the middle of January 1927, while in his office, that Mulkaloff was questioned by Jelinsky as to where British Men-of-War and merchantmen called and coaled. Mulkaloff also provided MI5 with a breakdown of the key personalities in the British and other European trade delegations run by the Soviets. 'JO' who had conducted the interview, noted that Mulkaloff 'who is a Russian refugee, realises the danger, particularly when out in Siberian waters, if his employers discovered he had given information, but is prepared to take the risk (without remuneration being suggested) and help the Authorities in any way possible'.[14] By this stage it had been confirmed – by the criteria of intelligence evidence – that there was a significant Soviet espionage network in Britain. But none of this evidence would, of course, stand up in a court of law. Nor was it expected to. MI5 were content to watch and learn more of the Kirchenstein organisatin. But then events took a dramatic turn.

The Arcos Raid

On 31 March 1927, C handed Kell a photostat copy of Signal Training Vol.III, Pamphlet No.II., which had been handed to one of his SIS officers, Maw, by an employee at Arcos. On 1 April, Kell sent Captain 'Jasper' Harker over from MI5 to visit C, Admiral Sir Hugh Sinclair, and saw Maw, who agreed that Harker should be put into touch with an individual 'X', who had handed this document to SIS.[15] After a great deal of discussion, it was decided that the informant should be seen by Harker and allowed to tell him: (a) who he was; and (b) all details regarding the alleged photostat at Arcos.

Harker was to interview the 'unknown mysterious individual' who would arrive under the name of Smith at the Hyde Park Hotel at a private room; he was to ask for Harker under the name of Mr Parker. The description of this individual as passed on to Harker was:

> Age about 50, height 5'9", gold-rimmed spectacles, dark ginger moustache, ginger coloured hair, Midland accent, general appearance that of a third class clerk. Believed to be drawing a salary of between £700 and £900 a year in Arcos. Has been with Arcos since the very beginning. Informant does not know whether he belongs to the Communist Party or not.[16]

The intermediary was willing to see Harker if the following conditions were guaranteed:

1. He wishes to see Mr. Harker alone. He desires his identity to remain undisclosed except to Mr. Harker.
2. His name shall not be noted down and shall not figure in any way in records or archives in connection with this case.
3. That no enquiries shall be set on foot regarding him. He, himself, will answer truthfully anything reasonable that he may be asked.
4. That he shall not be asked to conduct investigations. Anything that happens his way he will tell … Mr. Harker…
5. That his position shall not be imperilled, either directly or indirectly, nor shall he be involved in any eventual proceedings.[17]

On 6 April, Harker interviewed X and reported: 'As I expected the information in which we are really interested does not come from Mr. X but from his informant, who was formerly employed in Arcos's Photostat department. Mr. X was perfectly straightforward, and I am quite satisfied as to his genuine desire to be of assistance.' Apart from 'such general knowledge as an individual employed in the accounts branch of Arcos might normally obtain from the general talk of the office, Mr. X does not seem to me to be in a position to furnish us with any particularly useful information, unless he comes across it by accident.' After 'general conversation', Harker tackled Mr X on the subject of the individual who furnished the document 'in which we are interested. Mr. X gave me his name and expressed his willingness to try and arrange for me to be put in personal touch with this person. Mr. X did not seem to anticipate any difficulty, and he was of the opinion that this man could probably furnish us with other documents, though not necessarily of a military character, besides a great deal of detailed information regarding the work, which has been done on this photostat machine at Arcos.' Harker asked Mr X if he could explain the writing on the back of the document now in MI5's possession. He stated that the date '24.1.27' was the date on which the document was photographed, and that the name 'Dudkin' was that of the general manager of Arcos who brought the document to be photographed. As far as Harker could see 'our main hope lies in what information we can get out of the dismissed photostat hand, who really has the information that we require. I was quite favourably impressed by Mr.X, who I think is willing to help, but anxious, and quite naturally, not to jeopardise his own position in Arcos.'[18]

After a considerable delay, Mr X set up the meeting between Harker and the individual formerly employed in Arcos's Photostat Department. This individual was referred to as Y. Harker picked up X and Y, near the Mansion House and drove them to a flat in King's Bench Walk, where he had a long conversation with both. The MI5 officer was 'very favourably impressed with Y., and I see no reason at all to doubt the story which he told me himself of how he came into possession of the document'.[19] Harker gave Y an assurance that in no circumstances would his identity be disclosed, nor would any action be taken which would involve his communication with the authorities coming to light. Thus reassured, Y told Harker how, on 24 January 1927, a certain Mr Dudkin, one of the Russian Managers of Arcos, came down to the photostat room where the informant was working, handed him a pamphlet entitled 'Signal Training, Volume 3, Pamphlet No. 11' and gave him special instructions to take a photostat copy of this document. During the time that the document was photostated, Dudkin remained watching the operation. His attention, however, was distracted for a couple of minutes by some interruption and during that time, Y was able to take an extra photostat copy of the outer cover of the pamphlet in question. This copy he retained. Some two months later he was dismissed from Arcos on the grounds that his services were no longer required and his position was taken by a Russian; he then mentioned this matter to a friend, Mr X who, through a third party, passed the information together with the original photostat copy of the document to SIS then passed it on to MI5. As Harker pointed out: 'The interesting point is, of course, the fact that we here have definite proof that a military document improperly obtained, has found its way into Arcos, where, as a matter of ordinary routine, a photostat copy of it was taken.'[20] Y also informed Harker that he had managed, at various times in the past, to take copies of a number of other documents which he had photostated: 'These were still in his possession and he was quite prepared to send them to me, and is arranging to do so.' Both X and Y gave Harker a considerable amount of information regarding the personnel at Arcos and their views on the same.[21] The same afternoon Harker submitted a memorandum to Kell stating the whole case.

On 11 May, Kell consulted the Director of Public Prosecutions as to whether an offence under the Official Secrets Act had or had not been committed. The DPP was satisfied that, technically, the law had been broken. When the Secretary of War was shown the evidence and the photostat copy he said that the Prime Minister ought to see this and took it away – but was unable to find the Prime Minister and asked Kell to take the papers up to the Home Secretary's room in the House, which he did. Kell saw the Home Secretary and showed him the documents. He said at once that the Prime Minister and the Foreign Secretary ought to see them and he asked Kell to wait in his room while he went to speak to them. At 6.15 p.m. the Home Secretary came back and said: 'Raid Arcos; do you want it in writing?' After expressing his 'astonishment' that Ministers were ordering a raid, Kell asked him if the Foreign Secretary and the Prime Minister had both seen the evidence and documents. The Home Secretary said they had. Kell said that the matter was now no longer one for him but for Sir Wyndham Childs at the Metropolitan Police. Childs came over at 6.40 p.m. and the Home Secretary informed him that a decision had been made to raid Arcos as soon as the necessary arrangements could be made. Childs and Kell went back to Scotland Yard and discussed the matter.[22]

When the City of London and Metropolitan Police raided Arcos on 12 May at 4.30 p.m. they went straight to two places. They went to the photostat section, through which they had reason to believe that the document of high military importance which they were in search of had passed. In the photostat room, which was used jointly by Arcos and the Russian Trade Delegation, they came upon an individual named Robert Koling (or Kaulin). This man was interrogated. He handed over a number of envelopes addressed in name only to well known Communist individuals and organisations in Britain and in America. These letters contained information and directions from the Third International to Communist organisations in Britain including the National Minority Movement. One of the letters was addressed to the Workers' Party of America. Other letters contained applications for membership from would-be adherents to the National Minority Movement under the chairmanship of Tom Mann, the 'notorious British revolutionary', and the guidance of George Hardy, now its representative in Moscow.

Simultaneously with the raid on the photostat section of the Delegation, police Inspector Clancy noticed a light was emenating from room No. 5, on the first floor. Entering the room, Clancy found a quantity of papers burning in the fireplace and a man attempting to burn more of them. Clancy asked what he was doing. The man replied, in broken English, that he was only burning some telegrams. Noticing a deed box in front of the Russian, Clancy asked: 'Is this the box from which you took the papers that have been burnt?' There was no reply. After a few moments, the man addressed a remark in Russian to a second man: both men rushed at the deed box. During the struggle that ensued a bundle of papers dropped from the first man's jacket pocket.[23] The people in the room when the police entered were Anton Miller, the cipher clerk to the Trade Delegation (and brother of Paul Miller), a Russian named Choudiakoff and a 'lady encipherer' named Ghanovskaia. Miller had succeeded in taking from the despatch box a document, which, as he was unable to get it as far as the fireplace, he endeavoured to put in his pocket, from which it fell. This document was picked up by Clancy and was found to consist of a list of secret cover addresses for communication with the Workers' Party of America, and with the Communist Parties of South American states, Canada, Australia, New Zealand and South Africa. The list, several names and addresses of which were previously known to the Police, 'undoubtedly constituted the key to the underground movement' operated by Kirchenstein 'in the British colonies and in America'. The remaining documents in the despatch box were found to be the secret cipher between the Trade Delegation and Soviet Russia: 'The fact that the key' to Kirchenstein's underground movement was found in company with the most secret ciphers 'indicates the extreme importance which was attributed' to the Kirchenstein organisation 'by those in authority in the Trade Delegation'.

When the document containing the cover addresses was picked up by the police officer both Anton Miller and Choudiakoff 'became extremely violent in their endeavours to recover it'. Both, having committed the offence of resisting police officers in the execution of their duty, were accordingly restrained and searched. A further document was found on Miller. It consisted of three typewritten sheets of a secret cipher and decipher not adapted for telegraphic purposes, but which contained numeral ciphers for *inter-alia* the following words: 'Piatnitzky, Kuusinen Wopat, Canada, Ruthenberg, Daily Worker, in addition to ordinary vocabulary'. Piatnitzky was the financial secretary of the Third International and the head of the Kirchenstein organisation. Kuusinen was the secretary of the Third International. Wopat was the Workers' Party of America with headquarters in Chicago. Ruthenberg was the quite recently deceased chairman of the Workers' Party of America. The *Daily Worker* was the organ of the Workers' Party of America. His possession of the unofficial cipher showed that Anton Miller acted as encipherer 'both in his legitimate capacity and in an "illegal" capacity' for the Kirchenstein organisation. The final 'and most satisfactory link' between the list of addresses and cipher found on Miller with the letters found in the possession of Robert Koling of the Photostat Department was found in room No. 7 of the Trade Delegation which contained the personal files of all members of the Trade Delegation, of Arcos and its subsidiary companies, arranged in alphabetical order throughout in steel filing cabinets. The personal file of Koling/Kaulin, was found in this room. In this document, in Russian, was found the following:

ABSOLUTELY SECRET
Russian Trade Delegation.
"Departmental Memo.
From Utchraspred Dept. (Staff Allotment Department).
To Comrade Burakova, Manager of the Secret Section.
23 December 1926.
Subject. Re Comrade Koling, Robert, a carrier of the diplomatic post between Chesham House and Soviet House.
Koling has been an emigrant from Riga since 1905, by profession he was a shoemaker and afterwards he became a sailor. During the imperialist war he was mobilised into the Czar's army and was a prisoner of the Germans from 1917 to 1918. After this he again worked as a sailor and from 1923 became a member of the illegal Red Trade Union of Sailors, which carried on communist agitation and illegally engaged amongst its members in activities dealing with communications. He entered the Blaytakaya (Blyth) organisation of the British Communist Party; as a Soviet citizen he is debarred by the British Central Communist Party from membership of the London organisation. He was recommended by Comrs. Kirchenstein, Melnichuk and Bahn.
Signed ZAVUTCHRASPR (Manager of the Staff Department).
JILINSKY

The document demonstrated that Robert Koling 'is a regular diplomatic carrier between Soviet House and Chesham House'. Addressed to Burakova, Manager of the Secret Section (at Chesham House), it showed that Koling had obtained this appointment on the recommendation of Kirchenstein, Melnichuk and Karl Bahn and that recommendation had been approved by the head of the Accounts Department of the Russian Trade Delegation, Jilinsky, who was, 'till his departure for Russia the other day, the principal Soviet combined espionage and secret propaganda agent for Europe'. The document further showed the grounds upon which Koling was recommended for his confidential post, those being that from 1923 onwards he had been a member of the illegal Red Trade Union of Sailors, which was carrying on communist agitation and illegally engaged amongst its members in activities dealing with communication. Koling had, in other words, 'been a most trusted courier' in the Kirchenstein organisation. In the opinion of MI5:

the result of the raid on 49, Moorgate has accordingly furnished H.M. Government with incontrovertible evidence. This evidence is based on documents the authenticity of which is not open to dispute. They prove the operation within the walls of the principal office of the Trade Delegation of the Union of Socialist Soviet Republics in Great Britain, and in close touch with the Embassy of the Union at Chesham House, of a secret organisation in which the prime mover is PIATNITSKY, the head of the Finance Department of the Third International. The KIRCHENSTEIN organisation has been working as regards Great Britain for purposes of secret propaganda, finance, industrial sabotage and espionage from Baltic and other Northern European Ports, through seaman's groups on board Arcos boats via British ports into the Russian representation in London. From thence it has spread its tentacles again through seamen's group of the Red International of Labour Unions via New York to cover the New World and British Dominions and Colonies. It is impossible that Mr. KHINCHUK, the head of the Trade Delegation, should be ignorant of the organisation, the hub of which was in the Cipher Room next to his own. Chesham House is also involved. It had already been proved that the Commissariat of Foreign Affairs in Moscow and a former Chargé d'Affaires were also involved. The appointment of KAULIN as regular carrier of secret bags between Soviet House and Chesham House is further confirmation as regards Chesham House. The fact, ascertained in the course of the raid, that no individual is appointed to any of the Russian Trade Delegation or Arcos institutions without the express sanction of the Soviet Embassy is also conclusive. KIRCHENSTEIN, BAHN, MELNICHUK and JILINSKY have been working on espionage for years, and the Chiefs of the Soviet Mission, whether at 128 New Bond Street, Chesham House or 49 Moorgage have been cognisant of their operations throughout.

On 27 May, the Prime Minister, Stanley Baldwin, rose in the House of Commons, to inform the MPs gathered there that: 'Both military espionage and subversive activities throughout the British Empire and North and South America were directed and carried out from Soviet House.' The police in collaboration with military authorities had been investigating the activities of a group of secret agents engaged in endeavouring to obtain highly confidential documents relating to the Armed Services of the United Kingdom. Baldwin announced that, from the information received, 'it became increasingly difficult to resist the conclusions that the agents were working on behalf of the Soviet Government and that they obtained their instructions from members of the Russian Trade Delegation, working at Soviet House, who arranged for the conveyance to Moscow of photographs or copies of the documents obtained'. The Prime Minister revealed to the House that a document found in Soviet House proved that Robert Koling, or Kaulin, was engaged in subversive activities. In it Koling wrote:

> I consider the only solution to lie in making these ships of ours a base for training politically conscious seamen, who after preliminary training, could be sent to other British ships. Instruction could be given by such seamen as cannot obtain employment for Communistic agitation on any British ship. The choice of men should be carefully made, preference being given to negroes, Hindoos [sic] and other oppressed nationalists, but it would of course be necessary to investigate to what extent such material would prove appropriate to future work. As soon as a seaman is taken on he should be trained and then made to go and work amongst British sailors. This has been the practice I have so far followed and my preliminary results were apparent during the seamen's strike when those who passed through our school occupied the most prominent positions.[24]

To clinch the case against the Russians, Baldwin read from secret Soviet ciphers – and in the process revealed to the USSR that the British had cracked their codes; unsurprisingly, the Soviets soon changed their codes denying the British the access they had previously enjoyed.

Doubts

In late March 1927, before the Arcos raid, Stanley Baldwin had re-assembled his Secret Service Committee with the following terms of reference: 'To enquire into and report on existing conditions in the Secret Service side of Scotland Yard.'[25] The Permanent Under-Secretary at the Home Office, Sir John Anderson, was of the opinion that the 'Secret Service side of Scotland Yard' ought to remain where it was; but this was not the opinion of Baldwin and Sir Warren Fisher, who would chair the Committee once more, was aware that: 'The case calls for an operation; manipulation will at best be only a palliative, and I shall not feel comfortable – nor, I feel sure, will the Prime Minister – until this particular member has been amputated and grafted on to some obscure trunk' – with SS1 and SS2 being sent over to, for example, SIS.[26]

The case for keeping SS1 and SS2 where they were was set out in a memorandum entitled 'The Political Activities of the Police'. The author pointed out that it had been suggested that, if by some reorganisation of Secret Service work 'we could remove from Scotland Yard the branch of that work which is now carried on there, the Police would be clear of the imputation that they are or may be employed by the Government of the day to spy upon rival political organisations and that the importance of that result is in itself a strong argument in favour of such a reorganisation. I do not share this view.' It was 'manifestly important' that the police, like the fighting services and, if it came to that, the civil service, should be free from the suspicion of taking sides in party politics:

> But if they are open to that suspicion today, it is not because they are mixed up with secret service and the change suggested would not affect the position in that respect for better or for worse. The simple truth is that whenever the activities of a political party verge upon the unlawful it becomes the clear duty of whatever branch of the public service is concerned with the enforcement of the laws, which are in danger of being broken to take cognisance of such activities. Unfortunately the police cannot escape from this duty and they must be prepared to submit to whatever prejudice may result from its performance.
> [Their work had to be carried on under a] fierce light of publicity and the suspicious or malicious critic has plenty of material ready to his hand without bothering about secret service in the sense in which we understand the term. If he knows nothing about spies he can talk about police informers and a policeman in plain clothes is as good a target for his attacks as a secret service agent. The justification of police action – that they concern themselves solely with actual or potential crime – is equally valid whether they have or have not the assistance of secret service resources under their own control. [Finally,] if we are to assume that a Government may one day be tempted to use secret service funds for party as distinct from national purposes, the existing allocation of functions may well be regarded as a safeguard rather than a menace since the importance of not compromising the impartiality of the police can so easily be demonstrated. [27]

A separate memorandum focused not on the desirability of ending the political role of the police but on the lack of co-ordination that arose during the Arcos raid and the fact that it was actually a debacle:

To the outsider the Secret Service was vindicated by the outcome. The public were convinced by the original evidence brought forward that the authorities had no alternative but to authorise action. The raid itself was shown to have produced evidence, if not of the particular act of espionage in question, of the complicity of Arcos Ltd. in underground practices generally associated with espionage. The production of certain documents, obtained by the Secret Service previous to and independently of the raid, served to cement the somewhat loose facts leading to and resulting from the raid into a sufficiently formidable indictment, both of Arcos Ltd. and the Soviet Legation, to justify the rupture of diplomatic relations.

Nevertheless, those in a position to know the inner history of the case must be uncomfortably aware that its success was gravely threatened at more than one vital point and that it was saved from degenerating into an anti-climax, which might seriously have shaken the position of the Government, only by the eleventh hour efforts of individuals.

It is not desired to reflect in any way upon the actions or efficiency of individual Secret Service officials. They could hardly have acted otherwise than they did in the circumstances. But it is considered that the circumstances of organisation in which these officials are called upon to act in cases like the Arcos raid are such as to render confusion and misdirection of energy inevitable.

The memorandum argued that it appeared opportune, therefore, to take stock of the situation, while the lesson was still fresh, in the hope that some practical steps might now be taken to obviate the main cause of the defects, which had come to notice. That cause lay in the fact that when 'The Secret Service' was spoken of as though it were one body, in reality three separate organisations were referred to, each with its peculiar objectives, prejudices, methods and limitations, 'which own to no common authority lower than that of the Prime Minister. The remedy lies in the unification of these three bodies.' To prove this, three points only in the Arcos case were cited in which the defects of the system were most clearly exemplified.

The original information in the case was secured by SIS. Since, however, it concerned an act of espionage against the Armed Forces, SIS was not, according to the existing constitution, competent to lead it into 'concrete issues' and the matter was surrendered to MI5. The latter department naturally insisted, before proceeding to action, upon satisfying itself of the reliability of the evidence. The 'regrettable loss of time and the added risks, both of leakage and of the scaring away of valuable sources, involved in such a course is obvious'. It was, however, inevitable while the various branches of the Secret Service remained divided. 'Every Secret Service must in self-defence mistrust any but those sources to whom it can apply its own tests of reliability, and no Secret Service official should undertake responsibility for action on information received from sources which have not satisfied the standards set by his own department.' In order, however, to apply such tests, 'personal touch' must be established with the sources themselves and the latter, on being transferred to newcomers, 'are always likely to take fright and recant, or impose restrictions on the use of their information which greatly reduce its practical value'. In this particular instance the restrictions necessitated by the transfer of the sources from SIS to MI5:

> had the effect of seriously threatening the force of the Government's case. While in the hands of the officer originally responsible for finding them, the sources had imposed no restrictions upon the use of their information, but, when the proposal was made to hand them over to officers of MI5, their acquiescence was only obtained on condition that no use should be made of their information which could lead to the betrayal of their identity. Had the embargo remained, this would have proved disastrous since, in view of the fact that the raid produced no evidence confirming the alleged act of espionage, the Government would have been precluded from justifying the raid either by the circumstances leading up to it or by its results and would have been open to a not easily refutable charge of ill-considered action in authorising the raid.

Not only was the 'faulty constitution' of the Secret Service directly responsible for this complication, 'but it was chiefly due to the want of a central co-coordinating authority' that its gravity was only appreciated an hour or two before the Government's statement to the House was due, when there seemed little hope of adjusting the matter. From a Secret Service standpoint the raid took place without due consideration either of the probable issues or of the further action which might be required to deal with such issues:

> It needs no deep thinking to realise that the case, both from its nature and the action contemplated, was one, which vitally concerned the work of all three branches of the Secret Service.

Yet Scotland Yard first heard of the matter on 11.5.27., the day before the raid, when the action had already been determined upon, while S.I.S. ['s] first intimation was received only two and a half hours before the raid took place.

According to the existing system, even this late intimation was a courtesy on the part of Scotland Yard and was in no way obligatory. Even the officials of the Foreign Office (with the exception of the Secretary of State himself) were totally unaware that the raid was contemplated until informed by S.I.S. on the afternoon of 12.5.27... a state of affairs that conceivably might have led to most serious results.

Had the combined interests of the three organisations been consulted, had there been a central authority to view the matter otherwise than piecemeal and from departmental points of view, had even the three Secret Service Heads met together to determine what action should be recommended, before irretrievable steps had been taken, action would probably not have been confined to a raid on 49 Moorgate.

On grounds of expediency there were no objections to the further action, since once Ministerial approval of the principle of raiding Arcos Ltd. had been obtained, no conceivable reason appears to have existed for limiting the action to one set of premises, in view of the fact that Scotland House were fully aware of the close and even guilty connection of other premises and individuals with 49 Moorgate, and the section of Scotland House known as S.S.I. was, even before the raid, urgently insistent upon the necessity for action of wider scope.

Between the date of the raid and the publication of the seized documents by the Government there would still seem to have been time for further action. No further action was, however, taken. It was, therefore, 'difficult to believe that such omissions could have taken place had the functions of the Secret Service been unified under a central control and the plan of action been determined with a view to composite, rather than individual interests'. As Scotland House had actually carried out the seizure and examination of the documents, it devolved upon SSI to produce a written appreciation of the case. It was, however, evident that up to 18 May, i.e. the day before the Home Secretary's statement on the raid was to have been made to Parliament, that those concerned with the work of compilation appeared to have had only the vaguest idea of the object for which the report was being compiled:

As a result of this confusion, the report of the Home Secretary placed before the Cabinet on the morning of 19.5.27. as a basis both for an important decision of policy and for the Prime Minister's statement in Parliament, proved to be an unconvincing production for these purposes, and had it not been for a more suitable appreciation, hastily put together by S.I.S. at the Foreign Secretary's request, in the small hours of the 18th – 19th May, it is possible that the Cabinet might have been driven into a position of weakness unwarranted by the facts.

The memorandum finished by arguing that where almost any type of work was split up into 'separate compartments by purely artificial barriers, continuity of effort must continually falter at those barriers and dislocation or delay, which may, and frequently does, mean the breakdown of costly and conscientious effort, must occur at the very points where delicate and unchanged handling are conditions of success.' This was specially the case in the work of the Secret Service organisations, 'whose keynote is an extreme mistrust of others and with which, therefore, departmental jealousy, consciously or unconsciously, may find an easy pretext for indulgence in the plea of caution or mistrust'. Furthermore, the 'division of responsibility in homogeneous matters tends to be synonymous with evasion of responsibility, however conscientiously the divided duties are carried out according to individual views'. On general grounds alone, therefore, it was 'highly advisable' to put an end to a situation which made it possible to defend the evasion of responsibility as a departmental virtue:

It may be argued that the establishment of a cordial liaison between the departments of the Secret Service should lessen the evil. That has not been experienced in practice. A system of personal liaison has been in existence for some time. Beyond establishing personal confidence between the particular officers brought into constant touch with one another, it does not overcome the main difficulties, which are inherent in the situation itself and are, therefore, proof against personal goodwill.[28]

This would, it might have been thought, have had serious consequences for MI5 and the role it played in the run up to the raid; however, the end result – albeit not for a few years more – was that Scotland Yard lost its overtly 'political' role. MI5 would, in fact, be the beneficiary.

In the meantime it was important to try and find out what the Communists were up to now. On 4 April 1928, Captain Butler, from MI5, and Carter, Liddell and Inspector Clancy from Special Branch, met to discuss evidence from reliable informants that 'there is a recru-descence of espionage on behalf of the Russians in this country'. It was known that there were at least two organisations in existence:

1. Consists of [F.E.] Walker and Siddall in Manchester and Jack Tanner in Sheffield, Messer and probably Wal Hannington in London etc.
2. Irish Republican Intelligence Service.

MI5 and Special Branch realised that, on the evidence in their posses-sion, it would be difficult to obtain a search warrant:

1. The Point is that it is impossible to shadow these people, it has been tried and they are too clever.
2. Letter correspondence after a long trial has proved abortive and they have reason to think that their letters are being looked at.
3. There are strong reasons to believe that this spying is going on and possibly with great detriment to the State and that if the acts cannot be detected, the next best thing is to interrogate these people as a prevention.[29]

John Bankin was believed to be a courier for these men. A naturalised American citizen of Lettish origin, he worked as a ship's mate crossing the Atlantic. The Captain under whom he had worked as a first, second and third mate, from 1919 to 1924, claimed that Bankin was met reg-ularly on his arrival in Hull by Russians who brought letters and paid him frequent visits. The Captain was under the impression that Bankin 'was of Bolshevik tendencies'.[30] MI5 requested the renewal of a Home Office Warrant on Bankin's address in New York. The HOW stated, as a reason for the renewal:

This individual has been acting as a courier for a specially secret organisation of the Communist Party in this country... There is evidence that in 1922 funds were transmitted through this organi-sation to various subversive movements in this country. BANKIN is still active. Although no information has been obtained from this check for some considerable time it is known that the organisation to which BANKIN belongs is still active. It is therefore thought desirable that it should be maintained for a further period.[31]

Colonel Carter wanted to proceed with bringing the men in for ques-tioning [32] but Harker met with him and Liddell persuading them that of an interrogation of them, at this stage, would be 'undesirable, unlikely to produce any satisfactory result and possibly invalidate our present enquires'.[33]

In the meantime, MI5 had to look after the source that inadvertently triggered the sequence of events leading to the raid. On the day of the raid Jasper Harker had visited Uxbridge, after considerable difficulty, 'succeeded in running to earth our informant "Y", who was busily employed in putting in order the pub into which he is moving on Monday next'. Harker had with him one of the plain clothes officers from MI5's detective section whom Harker sent into the Public House with a message asking Y 'to meet me in a car which I had waiting some distance away'. Y 'came along at once and I explained to him that the information which he had given me was considered of such importance that it might result in immediate action being taken and that as a result of this action it was possible that the people at Arcos might come to the conclusion that he had given information to the authorities'. Y said that he did not mind what action the authorities took so long as his name was not actually dragged into the matter. He said that as far as he could see it was possible that somebody besides himself might have given information to the Police. Y added that if the authorities took any action on the information, which he had given, 'he personally would be very glad as he thought it would be a very good thing if a lot of these people were turned out of the country'. Harker explained to Y that it might possibly be necessary for him to see some high official who would like to hear his story first hand. Y had no objection to seeing any high official so long as that high official was brought down to Uxbridge to see him 'as he was much too busy getting his Public House ready to be able to spare the time to come up to London'. When Harker returned to London he reflected:

I must say that I was impressed with his truthfulness and reliability. He does not seem to be in any way afraid of any consequences of his action even if suspicion is directed against him and he told me that if anyone came down to ask any questions he would simply reply that he knew nothing about it. He made no suggestion to me that he should be given any monetary reward and expressed his willingness to help the authorities subject to the proviso that his name was not dragged into the matter. He further expressed to me his regrets that we had not met before as had he known me some few months ago he might have been able to give me a great deal of useful information. To sum up, my impression of this individual is that he is an honest reliable British subject with no particular love for the Soviet Authorities. He is extremely busy in getting into his Public House and is extremely anxious that nothing should be done to interfere with him in any way or hamper his movements in connection with this matter, which, to him, is far more important than anything else.[34]

In the aftermath of the raid, however, Y's constitution did not stand up to his initial bravado: instead he had become a nervous wreck, fearing Soviet reprisals. Y was in such a state that Harker felt it necessary to secure a firearm for him and felt he had no choice but to phone the Assistant Commissioner, 'who very kindly' arranged the necessary form, together with the licence fee, so that Harry Hunter, who ran MI5's Watchers, handed it over personally to the informer.[35] Hunter made a number of subsequent visits to Y and, on every occasion, he impressed upon Y the necessity for 'holding his tongue on any matter relative to his former employment'. While believing him to be absolutely honest in his dealings with MI5, Hunter was of the opinion that Y, inadvertently, was drawing a certain amount of attention to himself. 'The man is highly nervous' and, after reading the Prime Minister's speech in the Commons, which made special mention of Koling and the photostat room, 'he appears to have lost his nerve altogether'. To 'add to his woe a shabby individual' who Y maintained was Marsden an ex-policeman connected to Arcos, called at his house and was drinking there some time. Utterly bewildered Y, leaving his wife to carry on, rushed to the post office and sent a telegram to Harker: 'His state of mind can readily be gauged by the wording of the telegram'. He then called at the local police station and the inspector being absent, saw the sergeant in charge, telling him that Marsden was at his house and he did not know what to do. The sergeant and a detective sergeant afterwards saw the 'supposed Marsden' visit two public houses. As the supposed Marsden left the house he said apparently to Y – 'Now don't forget – Gun-barrel for next Wednesday,' which Hunter thought might refer to the Derby but Y took 'for a subtle threat and visions of a violent end flashed through his mind'; despite the fact that: 'There is not such a horse in the Derby but there is an entry Double Barrel – "Y" apparently confused the names.'

But Y was emphatic that the man who called at his house was Marsden 'in disguise'. The man was wearing a shabby coat, an old black bowler hat and a black handkerchief round his neck. Y especially noticed he had no teeth but remembered that Marsden had a complete set of false teeth about two years ago, 'and he is convinced he took out his teeth for the purpose of further disguise'. His speech and 'certain peculiarities' of manner were further points, which convinced Y that the man was Marsden. Hunter, however, disagreed: 'I think he is mistaken. In my opinion it is unlikely that Marsden, being so well known, would adopt a silly disguise to visit a public house, and draw attention to himself by loud talk in a semi-intoxicated state which undoubtedly the man was in. There must be plenty of Arcos men unknown to "Y" who could visit his house in an ordinary way, if it was desired to ascertain his whereabouts.'

On 25 May, Y appeared to be 'more normal' when Hunter left him about 9.30 p.m. 'last night. I spoke to him rather strongly and impressed upon him that there was no need for him to worry as it was extremely improbable that the Russian people would molest him in any way; moreover, if anyone connects him with the matter, it would come about solely through his own folly in not keeping his mouth shut and having more command over himself.' Y promised to follow Hunter's advice.[36] Owing to Y's nervous state of mind, Hunter kept in touch with him almost daily, and during his visits Y 'gradually became less perturbed'. The supposed Marsden had not been seen again and no other known employees of Arcos or allied companies had been observed in the vicinity.[37] When Hunter visited Y again, on 13 June, he appeared 'to have quite recovered his nerve' since the fuss over the raid had simmered down, and apart from 'Marsden', no employees or ex-employees had visited his house, and no suspicious individuals had been noticed hanging about the vicinity. 'My several visits have convinced him that he is not being neglected, and that "Cpt. H[arker]s" promise to "look after him" is being fulfilled.' This involved putting in a good word with the relevant authorities – such as the Uxbridge Magistrate Bench – so that Y was certain that he would have and retain a licence (it is unclear whether this was to run his pub or retain his gun). It was not long before Hunter was able to report to his superiors in MI5 that: '"Y" is now solely occupied with the task of running his business – he has already improved on the sales of his predecessor and has every reason to look forward to a comfortable livelihood.'[38]

In retrospect the Arcos raid was a disaster. The stolen military document that was the trigger for the raid was never found. This forced the Government to reveal that it had cracked Soviet codes. They never fully cracked the changed ones. But another long term consequence of the raid was that from a position of strength British Intelligence had lost an irreplaceable insight into Soviet espionage activities in the United Kingdom. MI5 would never recover their ascendancy. From now on they were always playing catch up. The Soviets changed tactics. The price the British state would pay for this was enormous – and it all stemmed from the Conservative Government's blunder in ordering the Arcos raid in 1927.

10

The Honey Trap
Miss 'X' & the Woolwich Arsenal Case

'Miss X'

Sample of the tempting sort of bait successfully used to catch spies by His Majesty's Government has now been on view in London's ancient, soot-blackened Bow Street Police Court for several weeks, officially tagged 'Miss X'. This slim, bobbed haired blonde, English to judge from her accent arrived curvesomely sheathed in clinging black, and kept shifting her fur-piece with the sinuosity of Mae West, as she testified before a bug-eyed judge. 'She is a lady' explained the Crown, refusing to divulge her name.[1]

The Times reported that Mr Justice Hawke, the Judge praised 'Miss X' on the grounds that she was 'possessed of extraordinary courage' and had 'done a great service to her country'.[2]

The glamorous 'Miss X's real name was Olga Grey. Born in Manchester in 1906, she lived in Birmingham, where she worked as a secretary until 'an Officer of the Intelligence Office, War Department', recruited her. This was, in fact, Maxwell Knight, known as 'M', MI5's talent spotter, who was impressed by her intelligence and patriotism.[3] Olga came from a solid middle-class background; her mother was a friend of Mrs Neville Chamberlain and her father, with whom she had a troubled relationship, was a night editor at the *Daily Mail*. Olga's father, Charles, died at Ypres in 1915 when she was nine and, from the age of eleven, she attended a boarding school. Olga had a dominant personality and assumed the role of head of the family. Striking to look at, rather than beautiful, Olga suffered from very low self-esteem and was convinced that she was unattractive and sexually unappealing. She left school at seventeen and started work for the Automobile Association, where she met a young woman called Dolly Pyle. Unbeknown to Olga, Dolly worked as a secretary for MI5 and had been asked by Knight to keep an eye out for malleable potential recruits. Dolly recognised that Olga's domineering manner masked an internal agony of insecurity and self-doubt and spotted her potential. During the summer of 1928, Olga was playing clock golf at a garden party in Edgebaston, at which Dolly Pyle was also a guest. Over high tea, Dolly asked Olga if she would like to join the 'Secret Service'. Olga at first refused to take the proposal seriously, but on realising it was genuine, agreed. However, she was to hear nothing for a further two years until 1931, when she was invited to meet with Knight in London. Within two days she was relocating to London to work as an evening volunteer at the offices of the Friends of the Soviet Union (FSU).[4]

Knight saw Olga as a long-term investment, telling her that 'she should be in no hurry to obtain results'. Olga was also required, as a matter of course, to join the Communist Party of Great Britain. In August 1932, she was approached by the League Against Imperialism (LAI), who asked her to take on a part-time post working for them, which she duly accepted, becoming friendly with Harry Pollitt, the Secretary and Leader of the CPGB and Percy Glading, a leading Communist. Glading had worked as a Grinder at Woolwich Arsenal during the First World War, and then from 1925 in the Arsenal's Navy Department as a Gun Examiner. However, in 1928 he was dismissed after being identified as a Communist and agitator; according to Glading he was called into the office of the Inspector of Naval Ordinance and told to either renounce Communism or lose his job. Glading refused to abandon his political beliefs, handing a statement to the Inspector questioning whether employers had any right to impose 'political fitness' as a requirement for employees.[5]

Born in 1893, both Glading and his wife Elizabeth were prominent Communists. Glading was highly unionised and a member of the Red International of Labour Unions. In 1925, he travelled to India under the auspices of the CPGB to study Indian labour conditions and to promote Communism, on his return attending the Colonial (Communist) Conference in Amsterdam and reporting fully on his activities in India. In 1929, Glading became a member of the Political Bureau of the CPGB and travelled to Moscow, where he studied at the Lenin School using the alias of James Brownlir.[6] He had caught the eye of SIS before the Arcos raid in May 1927[7] and had been under surveillance in 1926. SIS had concluded that 'all the military espionage reports compiled in this country and sent to Moscow' were sent via Glading and that he acted as its paymaster.[8]

Olga often found the pressure of her double life hard to bear at times, working as a secretary during the day, spending her evenings as an FSU volunteer, and establishing herself as a Communist sympathiser. She did not reveal her secret life to her family and was to later recall that the 'most terrifying ordeal' she encountered was a popular song that was regularly played on the radio during the early 1930s: 'Olga Polovsky – the Beautiful Spy'; it made her paranoid.[9]

In May 1934 Pollitt asked Olga to 'undertake a special mission' which involved carrying information 'from here to other countries'. She agreed, departing on 11 June 1934 for Paris, where she met Glading, who handed over information and instructions.[10] At MI5,

Maxwell Knight was very pleased, as he considered that Olga's mission demonstrated the extent to which she had gained the trust of the CPGB and could also provide an opportunity for SIS to gain information on Communist subversion in India.[11] Olga proceeded to Bombay, hiding the money in sanitary pads, which she handed over to Communist leaders. Knight had given her invisible ink to make a note of the numbers of the bank notes she was smuggling, but Olga was unable to make it work so she memorised some of them. She was told that she would have to take something back to England, quite what was not made clear and this prospect worried her greatly. She spent three weeks in Bombay terrified that she would be arrested, then was sent back to England empty-handed, at which point the magnitude of what she was involved in dawned on her as she realised that she 'wasn't playing spy-games any longer'.[12]

Olga arrived back in London on 28 July 1934; having completed her mission, she took a secretarial job and, in February 1935, was approached by Glading and offered a post as Pollitt's personal secretary at the CPGB's headquarters in King Street, London.[13] Olga liked Pollitt, whom she considered to be sincere and 'not particularly ambitious' and was to become extremely fond of Glading, 'a very nice man with a little daughter' whom she later remembered as a 'stimulating conversationalist'. However, a former boyfriend of Olga's arrived in London and she finally cracked under the strain of her double life. She went to Knight and told him that she could no longer work for him. Knight was horrified at the possibility of losing his double agent and tried, in vain, to reason with her; but it was all too much for Olga, who was admitted to the National Hospital for Nervous Diseases. The manipulative Knight ensured that her room was full of flowers and visited her every day. Eventually the worn down Olga reconsidered her decision and, on her discharge, she severed ties with the boyfriend, took up a post with a private advertising firm and maintained friendly contact with Pollitt and Glading.[14]

Olga wavered again in February 1937, telling Pollitt that she wanted to resign from the CPGB as her 'boyfriend did not approve'.[15] But, two days later, on 17 February, she met Glading for lunch. He asked her whether she would be prepared to find a flat, in which she could live as the nominal tenant. He explained that she could continue with her 'day job' as all that would be required was that she should live at the flat and make it available for himself and two other men to meet and talk whenever they wished. He told Olga that he would pay the rent and all bills and expenses. Olga thought that the proposal could be connected with Glading's work in the Colonial section of the League Against Imperialism. She immediately contacted Knight who asked her to agree to Glading's scheme, which she did. Glading stipulated that the flat must not be in a block, so that there was no porter. Olga found a suitable flat at 82 Holland Road, Kensington and signed the lease from 1 April. Glading told her to have three sets of keys made for the flat, two of which were to be for him. He also agreed to the hire purchase of £60 worth of furniture and he gave Olga the money to pay the monthly instalments, as well as the rent. Glading assured Olga that he would always warn her before visiting. Olga and Glading went shopping together for furnishings for the flat and years later Olga recalled that the curtains chosen for the flat had eventually ended up in her daughter's house.[16] During the evening of 21 April 1937, Glading came to the flat with a man, whom he introduced to Olga as Mr Peters. The two men stayed for about three quarters of an hour. Nothing was discussed in front of Olga and she gathered they had merely come so that Mr Peters could meet her. He was obviously a foreigner, but Olga was unsure as to his nationality.

Glading later told Olga that Mr Peters was an Austrian and had been in a monastery in Austria at the beginning of the First World War and that he had fought in the Russian Cavalry, rising to the rank of captain.[17] On 29 April, Glading again called on Olga and in the course of a conversation mentioned another man to her in connection with his work. Glading said he was 'a small man and rather bumptious in manner' and that he disliked him personally, but had to tolerate him for business reasons. It appeared that Glading both liked and respected Mr Peters, but did not care for this other man, whom SIS correctly suspected was actually one Willy Brandes.[18] Olga continued to run the flat and work at her secretarial job, until in May, Glading suggested that she should look for a new job with shorter hours, but that first she should take a fortnight's holiday for which he would pay. He told Olga that on her return she should learn from 'another comrade' something about photography so that she could work for him. He proposed that Olga should get a part time job and that he would make up her money to £5 a week.[19] Glading explained that the work would involve documents, which would be 'borrowed'. The usual procedure would be that the documents would be delivered one evening and collected the next. Olga was to take and develop the photographs but was not to print them. Glading anticipated that on average there would be some photographing to be done about once a week and that the papers and drawings would be of a 'very secret nature'.[20] Olga expressed concerns that she knew very little about photography, but Glading reassured her.[21]

Olga duly left her job and went on holiday. Before her departure, Glading arrived at the flat rather late at night and slightly the worse for wear. He told Olga that he was 'doing hardly any work for the Party now, it is mostly for other people'. He also told her that he had seen six of his 'people' that evening. On 4 August, after she had returned from her holiday, Glading visited Olga and warned her that in about a week's time some definite instructions would be given regarding the work that she was required to do. He returned a few weeks later accompanied by an individual who he introduced as Mr Stevens, telling Olga that Mr Steven's wife would come to the flat about twice a month to do the necessary photographic work and that she was to help her. Mr Stevens, said Glading, had replaced Mr Peters, who had 'gone home'.[22] The work, said Glading, would commence in October.

On 11 October, Glading told Olga to get a long refectory table as soon as possible as the gate-legged table in the flat would not be steady enough for photography. Four days later he told Olga that he had already bought a table from Maples and he would be at the flat the next morning, to take it in. The table was followed by a camera and 'complete apparatus' on 18 October, when Glading arrived at the flat in a taxi with Mr Stevens and a woman introduced as the latter's wife. Mr and Mrs Stevens were 'obviously foreigners' and Olga noticed that Mrs Stevens, whose Christian name seemed to be Mary, spoke to her 'husband' in French.[23] For three and a half hours the Stevens experimented with a complete Leica copying outfit, using maps of the London Underground. In the course of conversation, Olga was told that Mrs Steven's predecessor in the photographic work was a Russian woman who had been doing this kind of work in Britain for the last five years. She had recently become nervous and hysterical and her condition had been complicated by the fact that she had fallen in love with (the small and bumptious) Mr Stevens. This had frightened Glading and his colleagues so much that instead of having a gradual transition period during which the Russian woman would have handed over to Mrs Stevens, arrangements were made to send her back to her own country on October 15. Mrs Stevens, unfortunately, was by no means an expert photographer and she was nervous about her ability to use the apparatus effectively without much practice. This irritated Glading who found her incompetence annoying and he again told Olga he thought it would be a good thing for her to take a course in photography.[24] Olga sent a brief message to Maxwell Knight, which read:

October 11: photographic apparatus [listed] arrived. October 13: another meeting – G and Mrs S who spoke French. October 18: Mr and Mrs S experimented 3 ½ hours, photographing maps of London Underground. G very jumpy.[25]

On 21 October, Mrs Stevens arrived at the flat with a large plan of unknown content she said had to be photographed in sections, explaining that forty-two exposures would be necessary. The films were developed and left in the bathroom to dry. Mrs Stevens then left the flat at 10.35 p.m. taking the plans in a bundle of rolled newspapers and leaving the negatives. Olga had not been in the room while the actual photography was taking place but, instead, was deployed making tea. Mrs Stevens had been very 'nervous and fidgety', asking Olga for her tea in the bedroom, so that she could carry out her task unobserved.[26] Olga later found the negatives hanging in the bathroom and managed to make a note of all the markings and serial numbers, which she could read, having to stand in the bath tub to do so.[27]

On leaving the flat in Holland Road, Mrs Stevens was followed by Knight's Watchers to Hyde Park Corner, where she met Mr Stevens and a man who was later identified as George Whomack, a gun examiner for the Inspector of Naval Ordnance Department, Woolwich Arsenal.[28] Born in 1883, Whomack lived in Welling, Kent with his wife Edith and, in 1927, was an elected Bexley Urban District Councillor (as was his wife). The Whomacks were both members of the CPGB, although in 1929 (undoubtedly in the wake of Glading's dismissal), Whomack had denied to his employers at Woolwich Arsenal that he was a Communist. But it was noted that Edith Whomack visited Russia for a month in 1931. Although the Whomack's were extremely politically active locally and were known to have Communist views (which caused the Local Labour Club at one point to try and to expel them), the authorities were unable to uncover any firm evidence against them, although they were concerned at the influence the Whomacks had with 'working class' residents in their district, especially as Mrs Whomack worked as a collector for Woolwich Arsenal's Mutual Society, which brought her into frequent contact with 'the women of the neighbourhood'. Mrs Whomack was considered to have more extreme political views than her husband and apparently encouraged him to 'adopt more extreme views'; she also enjoyed talking about her trip to Russia, urging her listeners to 'support the struggle of the working classes'.[29]

So, it was to Whomack that Mrs Stevens handed the roll of newspapers containing the plan; he who took it home to Welling with him. Olga's notes were able to help identify the plan as that of a naval gun mounting of which only five copies were in existence. The plan had been issued to Vickers, the Admiralty and the Ordnance factory, Woolwich, during the week beginning 10 October. On 22 October, Olga accompanied Glading to the Ford Exhibition, returning at about 9.45 p.m. and when Glading departed at around 11 p.m. he took the negatives with him.

On 2 November, Glading told Olga that Mr Stevens and his wife were returning to Moscow immediately owing to the illness of Mr Stevens's daughter.[30] Glading did not think there would be any more work before Christmas, but it was an opportunity for he and Olga to practice with the apparatus so that they could do the photographic side of the work later themselves, as he did not like being 'dependant upon the vagaries of foreigners'. Before his departure, Mr Stevens instructed Glading to keep in touch with all his contacts while he was away. This both worried and annoyed Glading: he considered that it was exposing him to unnecessary risks and told Olga that many of the contacts were purely mercenaries who were selling information for what they could get. It would, he said, make his work even harder than ever to keep in touch with these contacts as there were 'so many of them'. By now Glading seemed to be distancing himself from the CPGB; on 12 November 1937, the following letter was sent to him signed by the Secretariat:

> Dear Comrade GLADING,
> It is now over a year since you informed us that you no longer desired to retain your membership of the Communist Party. You will remember that we immediately wrote to you then, asking that you should reconsider your decision. We again approach you to see if you have now changed your mind, and to see if you are prepared to rejoin our Party, of which you were such an active member. We will be glad to hear from you and to consider any points you may have to make.
> Yours fraternally,

In mid-November, Olga reported to Knight that Glading had to buy Christmas presents for all his and Stevens's contacts, which amounted to around ten to twelve people and Glading told her that he would have to lunch with a woman 'whom he hated'. Describing her as a 'fine figure of a woman who had done her best to impress him with her beauty, without success', he told Olga that the woman had carried out 'about one job in five years' but that she was very important and 'knew enough to be nasty'. Olga was strongly of the opinion that this woman was Jane Bennett also known as Jane Mead, and although it was later confirmed that Jane Bennett definitely worked for the same organisation as Glading, no clear proof of her activities was ever obtained.[31] Jane Bennett, was known to SIS and had been observed meeting Glading, while he was under surveillance in 1926.[32]

On 8 December, Glading called and took away the camera as he said his own camera would not fit the stands. He told Olga that he had

had to do a 'rush job' of copying and it had been difficult as he had to balance his own camera on a pile of books. During the conversation he told Olga that he did not think Mrs Stevens would ever return to Britain, and that Mr Stevens would only return for a week or so, implying that 'some other man' would replace him. On 12 January, Glading told Olga that he had a 'special job' to do at his house over the forthcoming weekend, which he thought would involve a book of about 200 pages. On 13 January, Olga reported to Knight that, quite apart from the return of Mr Stevens, who would be coming back for about a week, a new man was expected who would be the administrative chief of the organisation. Glading was worried as he had no news about the arrival of this new man. Money was running short and he was frightened that he might be forced into a difficult position. On 17 January he told Olga that his funds were almost exhausted and that 'if something did not happen in a week or so' he would have to borrow money. It was clear that Glading's aim and ambition was to 'get the whole of the executive side of the work into his own hands'. Glading was particularly anxious for the new man to arrive as he had got 'stuff parked all over London'. When Olga asked him what he meant, he replied that he had got the negatives of the various documents he had photographed 'dumped at different people's houses'.[33]

On 20 January 1938, Glading telephoned Olga at her office and told her that he wanted to lunch with her the next day, asking her to have the flat free for 'something important' in the evening. She immediately telephoned MI5 and warned them of this. Olga duly lunched with Glading at the Windsor Castle Bar the following day and he told her to return to the flat at 6 p.m. as there was 'some urgent photography to be done'. Olga thought he said that he had to return 'the thing photographed' by 8.15 p.m. during a rendezvous at Charing Cross.

Later, on arriving back at the flat, Olga realised that Glading had arrived earlier, in her absence to set up the apparatus and that he was actually intending to collect the object to be photographed at 8.15 p.m. The urgency was that he should get it photographed and return the original the same evening.[34] As soon as Glading left the flat for Charing Cross at around 7.30 p.m., Olga duly reported all of this information to MI5 by telephone. At about 8.15 p.m. a Special Branch officer at Charing Cross Station saw Glading and at 8.20 p.m. Albert Williams, an engineer in the Department of the Chief Inspector or Armaments, Royal Arsenal, Woolwich, joined him.[35] Williams, aged thirty-five, had worked at Woolwich Arsenal since 1919 when he was demobilised after serving in Flanders. He had been elected Secretary of the local branch of the CPGB and had established a reputation as a 'violent and explosive personality and an extreme Communist of the dangerous type'.

The two men went to the station yard, where Williams handed Glading a brown paper parcel. Glading and Williams were immediately arrested by Special Branch officers and taken to New Scotland Yard, where the parcel was opened in their presence and was found to contain four blue prints showing the general arrangements and details of pressure bar apparatus. Glading's home was searched and two cameras and other photographic material were discovered as well as other material relating to Glading's espionage activities. Spools of film found in the house were printed by the photographic department at New Scotland Yard, and were found to be a copy of a 1925 textbook on explosives used in the Services. Photographic plates found at the same time were revealed as negatives of five prints relating to fuses designed for use by aeroplanes against submarines. An inspection of the photograph taken from one of the photographic plates revealed on the left side a portion of patterned wallpaper, and when police officers visited Williams's house in order to search it, they found the pattern of the wallpaper to be identical with that in a room fitted up as a photographic studio and dark room at that address. During the search of Williams's house a camera, photographic materials and enlarging apparatus were also found.[36] Glading had been extremely cautious and worn gloves when using the photographic equipment but he slipped up while changing a lightbulb, taking off his glove to replace it and leaving a fingerprint. This was found by Chief Detective Inspector Birch of Scotland Yard, who later melodramatically described to the press how, using his 'powerful little pocket microscope' he found a clear impression of Glading's 'nasty fingers'.[37]

On 29 January 1938, eight days after the arrest of Glading and Williams, George Whomack and Charles Munday were arrested and charged with being concerned with Percy Glading in obtaining information calculated to be directly or indirectly useful to an enemy. Whomack's house was searched and diaries, a notebook, a camera and an attaché case with a false bottom were found. During the search of Munday's house a quantity of photographic material and documents were seized, and a pawn ticket was discovered, which indicated that on the day after the arrest of Glading and Williams, Munday had pawned a camera for £2.[38] Twenty-two year old Munday, another employee of Woolwich Arsenal, worked as an Assistant Chemist in the War Chemist's Department and had been observed meeting Glading in the public lavatories at Charing Cross Station on 16 January. He was also the lodger of Albert Williams and his wife.[39]

The case was now complete and Olga was to be the principal witness for the prosecution, a prospect that terrified her, despite Maxwell

Knight reassuring her that her real identity would not be made public. The reality of her role struck home: that she had effectively destroyed a man who had trusted her implicitly and of whom she had become extremely fond. There were also the repercussions for Glading's wife and little daughter to consider. Glading himself was deeply shocked to discover that Olga was, in fact, an MI5 agent.[40] However, in October 1939, while serving his sentence in Maidstone Prison, he softened towards her, acknowledging that he had put her in a very difficult position.[41]

Olga's fears of attack or assassination were heightened when, at the Magistrates' hearing, a piece of paper bearing her real name and address was thrust into her hand and she was asked by C.B. McClure, the Prosecuting Counsel to confirm their accuracy. Dudley Collard and Denis Pritt, the defence barristers, were known Communist sympathisers and immediately objected to Olga's identity remaining secret. However the Magistrate ruled in Olga's favour, deciding that she should remain anonymous.[42]

The trial of Glading, Williams, Whomack and Munday began at the Old Bailey in March 1938, with the accused charged on an indictment of five counts, to which they all – except Munday – pleaded guilty with no defence. Only Glading was charged on every count; he was charged with Whomack for obtaining a plan of a gun used by the navy; with Williams for obtaining part of an anti-tank mine pistol; and for obtaining plans of an anti-submarine bomb fuse and for obtaining plans, which would be useful to the enemy. With Munday, Glading was charged with obtaining information on explosives.[43] The evidence, most of which was found in Glading's house, was overwhelming and even included diary entries recording dates and times of rendezvous at Charing Cross Station, or 'CXS'. The false-bottomed attaché case was also produced. Olga, who 'spoke with a cultured voice' was clearly nervous, and at one point became distressed and was asked by McClure if she would like to sit down. She declined, replying that she would rather stand.[44]

Munday was fortunate: he was acquitted and discharged as the Attorney General, Sir Donald Somerville proposed to offer no evidence against him. On Monday 14 March, sentences were given. Glading received six years, Williams four years and Whomack three years. On passing sentence, Mr Justice Hawke told Glading, 'you were endeavouring to do anything you could to help another country and injure this. This is your own country, but I cannot quite believe that this had any effect on your mind. I am satisfied that this was done for the sole and vulgar motive of obtaining money.' He then told Williams that he 'did not see a great deal of difference between him and Glading' as he considered that they were driven by the same motive. Whomack however, was another matter. Hawke told him that he was 'the only one about whom I have felt any difficulty, having regard to the comparatively small part you have played in this case, I have considered whether I could avoid sending you to penal servitude, but I feel it is my duty to do so.'[45] Williams and Whomack were sent to Parkhurst Prison and Glading to Maidstone.

Mr Justice Hawke, however, was wrong about Glading who was not driven by financial gain; as Knight's subsequent assessment of the investigation proved, he was clearly driven by ideology, although, bafflingly, he did not like dealing with 'foreigners'.[46] Estranged from his wife he and Olga clearly enjoyed a close personal friendship.[47] Following the trial, the sensational element of the press highly dramatised Olga's background, especially Chief Detective Inspector Birch (he of the 'powerful little pocket microscope'), who stated that the bravest girl he ever knew 'was a British Secret Agent... she had forgotten more about courage than many soldiers ever learn on the battlefield'. He described Olga as 'a slender girl with dainty ankles' and a romantic aristocratic background was invented for her, including a childhood spent in an 'old English manor house'. Glading was 'dark, distinguished, suave... a reader of poetry and a dreamer of revolt under high scarlet banners'. Olga, living in genteel poverty, found all of this highly amusing. Immediately after the trial, Knight asked Olga's brother Richard, a policeman, to become her bodyguard, sending them to a hotel in Berkshire. Olga was still terrified of reprisals and hated to be left alone. Her sister Marjorie, on reading the newspaper accounts of the trial, realised just what her sister's involvement had been and was astounded. Shortly after the end of the trial, Olga, who had been paid fifty shillings a week for her work as an agent, was taken out to lunch (not dinner) at the Ritz – and not by Knight, but by an unnamed colonel – was congratulated and thanked for her loyal service. He gave her a cheque for £500, which was, in reality, a pay-off. Olga continued to work as a secretary and met a Canadian airman. They married and she moved to Canada, but feared reprisals for the rest of her life, never recovering from the double-edged hurt of firstly betraying Glading and then of being smartly dropped by Knight once she had served her purpose. As she later and bitterly recalled: 'I was dumped. In those days the adrenalin really flowed but since then the excitement has never been rekindled. That's why I feel so restless – and my abilities remain so unfulfilled.'[48]

MI5 correctly believed that although Glading was a member of the CPGB, 'the last episode' of the case was conducted and operated by Soviet Intelligence.[49] The British subjects employed in Glading's espionage organisation appeared to have been exclusively members of the CPGB, of which Glading himself was one of the most prominent members. These persons all appeared to have dropped open CPGB work, and in some cases to have resigned from the Party (as did Glading) as soon as they were recruited for espionage work. Unlike Mr Peters and Mr Stevens, Glading did not make any attempt to employ a cover story for his activities. It was clear that Whomack and Williams were aware that they were working for the Russian Intelligence Service and were not under any impression that they were simply providing information for the Communist Party. Olga was also left in no doubt as to whom the real masters of the organisation were. Glading had also been observed under surveillance, meeting with a woman named Paddy Ayriss, who was secretly employed in the Soviet Embassy, and was said to be the link between the Embassy and the underground section of the British Communist Party. It also appeared that although Glading was the organiser of his own group of sub-agents, he did not have *carte blanche* in the direction and recruitment of his agents. Aside from a period lasting around two months, Glading was always under the control and supervision of a resident foreign agent in Britain. Olga was not allowed to be allocated work, or to be told the nature of the work which she was to do until she had been twice seen, and obviously vetted.

While serving his sentence at Maidstone Prison, Glading was interviewed twice by MI5, but he did not give any information about his espionage organisation. At Parkhurst Prison, Williams and Whomack became friendly with a convict named William Parkinson. Parkinson, who was an 'intelligent man', (or possibly just a self-serving stool-pigeon), volunteered to attempt to gain their confidence and to provide information to the authorities. He had some success and was able to convince Williams and Whomack that he had Communist sympathies and he managed to obtain some information about their activities for the Russian Intelligence Service. The men working for Glading at the Arsenal had taken out plans in the evening when they left work. These plans were handed over to Glading or, in one known case, to Mrs Brandes, and immediately taken to Olga's flat, photographed and returned to the sub-agent the same evening. Presumably the sub-agent returned to work early the following morning and replaced the plans without detection. In order to avoid the usual search of workman at the Arsenal or dockyard gates, some of the agents folded their plans into newspapers, and Whomack used the famous attaché case with a false bottom.

Williams claimed to Parkinson that he had been the organiser and director of illegal operations in the Arsenal and also said that he did not personally carry out drawings, but used other members of the Party for this purpose. He also alleged that the Russian diplomatic bag was used to remove plans from Britain. Parkinson asked Williams whether this illegal work was recognised officially by the Party, and Williams replied that the kind of work that he and Whomack had been involved in was not so recognised. This kind of illegal work was under the direct control of the Soviet Intelligence Service. Williams told Parkinson that he was particularly pleased that nothing was found on him on his arrest, which could have involved the official Communist Party and which might have had the result of forcing the Government to declare it illegal, thus driving the whole of the organisation underground.

Investigation by MI5 and SIS confirmed that the mysterious Mr and Mrs Stevens were Willy and Mary Brandes. Willy Brandes also used the names, 'Mr Hoffman', William Hoffman', 'William Steinburg' and 'Nathan Green'. Born in 1902 in Romania he was described as being 5ft 8.5in. tall, with 'fair to reddish hair, blue eyes slightly crossed, sturdy build, heavy set, stout neck.' Mary Brandes, his wife was born in Romania in 1906 and was 5ft 4in. tall, with 'brown hair, grey eyes'. At the time they were introduced to Olga in September 1937, as 'Mr and Mrs Stevens', the Brandes were living at Forset Court in the Edgware Road. Brandes had been living there for about six months, but his wife had been with him for a much shorter period. Brandes introduced himself to the porter of the block of flats as a French-Canadian, and said that he was a traveller for Phantome Red Cosmetics of New York. He was also acting as an agent for another New York firm, the Charak Furniture Company. Visitors to the flat were numerous and frequent and Brandes seemed to be well supplied with money.

Brandes tried to act in accordance with his commercial cover while he was in England. In January 1937 he inserted in the *Daily Telegraph* an advertisement asking for travellers for Phantome Face Powder, and he also arranged to have certain photographs taken on behalf of the Charak Furniture Company. The Brandes left the country on 6 November 1937 and were not heard of again. Enquiries in Canada proved that their Canadian passports were obtained by a false declaration, and that they had been closely connected with a Soviet network operating in Canada and the USA during 1936. MI5 were never able, with certainty, to trace their true antecedents or to find out who they really were.[50]

From Parkinson's information, it would seem that MI5 had wrongly considered Glading to be the ringleader, when in actual fact it was

Williams. The KGB archives reveal that another member of staff at Woolwich Arsenal was involved; Melita Sirnis was an undeclared member of the CPGB, who was formally recruited in 1937. Like Glading (Soviet codename GOT), she was a committed ideological agent, however, unlike Glading, she escaped detection and was put 'on ice' until May 1938.[51]

For MI5's Maxwell Knight, the Woolwich Arsenal case brought him great kudos. It also demonstrated, in real terms, the operation of an agent on a long term basis, proving his theories around investing in and using agents as an ongoing project. MI5 considered that the 'illegal work' of Glading and his counterparts would not have been discovered without the employment of an agent such as Olga Gray, who, over a long period of time, was able to win their confidence and trust.[52] But who was the mysterious 'M' who held such a sway over Olga – and what were the principles that governed his counter-espionage work?

'M'

Charles Henry Maxwell Knight was born on 9 July 1900 at 199 Selhurst Road, South Norwood, Croydon, one of at least two sons of Hugh Coleraine Knight (d. 1914), a solicitor, and his wife, Ada Phyllis Roberts, née Handcock (d. 1925). His philandering father managed to bankrupt his legal practice. At fourteen Knight was sent to HMS *Worcester* (the Thames Nautical Training College), off Greenhithe, Kent, to be trained as an officer for the Merchant Navy. After the death of an older brother on the Western Front in 1916, Knight volunteered for the Royal Navy and served on armed merchantmen. After the war he briefly worked at the Ministry of Shipping, before taking a post as a teacher of Latin at a minor preparatory school in Putney. On 29 December 1925 he married Gwladys Evelyn Amy (d. 1934), daughter of Charles Edward Hamilton Poole, a military officer. It was not a happy marriage. There have been claims that Knight was unable to consummate it. And Gwladys had to share her husband with some unusual friends: as an obsessive naturalist, Knight had a menagerie of white mice, grass snakes, live insects, a parrot and ferrets living in the couple's Sloane Street home. Despite his marital problems Knight's social life in London remained active. Vernon Kell personally recruited him for MI5 in 1925. Kell saw in Knight someone with a perfect cover: a young gentleman about town, much in demand for débutante parties, whose new career did not interfere with his enthusiasm for the cellar clubs of Soho and Leicester Square, or his enthusiasm for American jazz and new dances like the Charleston.[53]

But, in 1935, a personal tragedy occurred that almost cost Knight his MI5 career. On 16 November 1935, Gwladys travelled to London to stay at the Overseas League Club in St. James's. After years of neglect, she was unable to endure much more. Gwladys wrote the following note to her husband: 'Sweetheart – Just arrived for a few days' shopping. Will you give me a ring in the morning to see what we can fix up – not too early, as I will be having breakfast in bed and will not be leaving here until after 10 a.m. Love, G.' On receipt of the note Knight rang the Overseas League Club and was told by the housekeeper that his wife was asleep. He rang again. And again. At almost eleven that evening Knight told the housekeeper to go up and wake her. The housekeeper reported that she could not be awakened. Panic stricken by now, Knight took a taxi to the club and found Gwladys in a deep coma. He called in a Harley Street doctor who arranged for her to be taken to a nursing home in Wilbraham Place. She had taken a massive dose of barbiturates, backed up by aspirin. A few hours later pneumonia developed and Gwladys died. Her family blamed Knight for her death. At the inquest a well known criminal counsel, Reginald Seaton, represented them. The inquest was widely reported in the press and Knight was called to give evidence in the witness box.[54] But Knight's career in MI5 survived the scandal and he was able to develop his 'M' or 'MS' organisation.

The function of MS lay in the recruitment and operation of agents who were trained for the purpose of penetrating subversive political bodies, and for the investigation of suspicious individuals or groups of individuals. Knight reflected on how, in Britain, 'for some peculiar psychological reason', there had always been a stigma attached, not only to the calling of 'secret agents', but also to the actual words. Even officials in Government departments, on whose shoulders lay the burden of responsibility in connection with national defence, had been prone to regard an 'agent' as an 'unscrupulous and dishonest person actuated by unworthy motives'. In actual fact, argued Knight, 'nothing could be more untrue; for an honest and loyal agent, whether he is working for his country in foreign lands, or at home, has often to exhibit some of the highest human qualities'. It had always been the policy of Knight's MS organisation 'to utilise as far as was humanly possible to service of persons whose personal honesty and motives were above reproach; for it must be abundantly clear to any experienced officer that not only will the eventual product of an agent be better in such circumstances, but there will also be a vast saving of time which would otherwise have to be spent in checking, not only the accuracy of the information obtained, but the truthfulness of the agent obtaining it.'

Knight considered the recruitment of agents the most important part of MS. In Knight's experience, nearly every individual officer in an intelligence department could, if he tried, find among his own circle of friends at least one person who would be suitable for employment as an agent: 'and I can claim that a very large proportion of the present total of MS agents have been recruited from amongst my own acquaintances'. It was clear that this channel for recruitment 'can be something of a snowball for many of the agents so recruited may themselves in time recommend others equally suitable'. Another possible source of supply came from among those individual members of the public who, from time to time, volunteered information to MI5. Many of these persons had to be interviewed, and if, as often happened, at the initial interview a favourable impression was created, they could 'later be exploited', after enquiries about the person being interviewed had been discreetly made. Many MS agents had been obtained in this manner.

In Knight's opinion, the best general training for an agent was 'actual and immediate work in the field, be it in ever so humble a capacity'. It was, of course, necessary to give an agent general directions on a variety of subjects, such as when, where and how to take notes, memory training and accurate description of individuals 'but in the main, the real training ground lies in the day to day of the agent'. The officer running an agent 'should set himself the task of getting to know his agent most thoroughly. He must at all costs make a friend of his agents: the agents must trust the officer as much as – if not more than – the officer trusts the agents; and a basis of firm confidence must be built up. The officer should take an interest in the agent's home surroundings, family, hobbies, personal like and dislikes; and must bear all this in mind when setting an agent to work on any particular task.' It was 'perhaps not untrue to say', believed Knight, that in dealing with an agent, the work and mental output of the officer concerned 'will be far greater than these of the agent, for the officer will have to be continually adapting himself to the agents who vary very much in character and personality'. This was one of the most important items in regard to the handling of agents, for while the officer must always adapt himself to the agent, and not the agent to the officer, the latter 'must be constantly on his guard in order to see that he does not become that terrible creature, one who is "all things to all men". Every good agent likes to think that his officer is almost exclusively concerned with him, and with him alone, even thought, the agent may know perfectly well that the officer has others with whom he deals. This is a definite and illogical kink in human nature, but it is a kink which must be featured by any officer who is going to make a success of this work.'

The exact line of training of an agent depended very much upon the objective against which the agent was to be directed. An agent who was going to be used principally for penetrating subversive organisations will require training, which was different from that of the agent who was going to be used in connection with individual suspects. The majority of MS agents were directed towards penetration of movements. Before he was introduced into the organisation, the agent should, if possible, be encouraged to attend some public meetings of the organisation: he should also be encouraged to read a certain amount of the organisation's literature available to the public. Having spent some time in attending meetings as an ordinary interested individual, it was probable that he would obtain some casual personal contact with some adherent or official of the organisation in question.

Knight highlighted the importance of endeavouring to see that approaches in connection with joining any particular body 'should if humanly possible be made by the body to the agent, not the agent to the body. In other words, it is an immense safeguard if an agent can be actually invited by some member of an organisation to join up, rather than that the agent should himself offer to join.' The importance of this lay in the future, in that if at any time some query was raised regarding the *bona fides* of the agent, 'it will nearly always be remembered by the officials of the Movement that the agent did not in any way thrust himself forward'. In many cases, 'a becoming reluctance to join a Movement which is subsequently overcome by the persuasion of the Movement propagandists will stand the agent in very good stead'. Knight was particularly interested in women agents:

Now, there is a very long-standing and ill-founded prejudice against the employment of women as agents; yet it is curious that in the history of espionage and counter-espionage a very high percentage of the greatest coups have been brought off by women. This – if it proves anything – proves that the spy-masters of the world are inclined to lay down hard and fast rules, which they subsequently find it impossible to keep to, and it is in their interests to break.

It is frequently alleged that women are less discreet than men; that they are ruled by their emotions, and not by their brains: that they rely on intuition rather than on reason; and that sex will play an unsettling and dangerous role in their work.

My own experience has been very much to the contrary... in my submission this is due to one principal factor; it is that indiscretions are committed from conceit. Taking him generally, Man is a conceited creature, while Woman is a vain creature: conceit and vanity are not the same. A man's conceit will often lead him to indiscretion, in an endeavour to build himself up amongst his fellow men, or even to impress a woman: women, being vain rather than conceited, find their outlook for this form of self-expression in their personal appearance, dress, etc.

It is not entirely true that women are exclusively ruled by their emotions, and it is to be hoped that no officer, when selecting a woman for training as an agent, will chose the type of woman who's make up is over emotional. On the other hand, the emotional make up of a properly balanced woman can very often be utilised in investigations; and it is a fact that women's intuition is a direct result of her rather complex emotions. That a woman's intuition is sometimes amazingly helpful and amazingly correct has been well established, and given the right guiding hand this ability can at times. On the subject of sex, in connection with using women as agents a great deal of nonsense has been talked and written.

The first consideration for choosing any agent, man or woman, should be that the individual in question be a normal balanced person. This means that, in connection with sex, they should not be markedly over-sexed nor under-sexed: if over-sexed, it is clear that this will play an overriding part in their mental processes, and if under-sexed, they will not be mentally alert, and their other faculties will suffer accordingly. It is difficult to imagine anything more terrifying than for an officer to become landed with a woman agent who suffers from an overdose of sex, but as it is to be hoped that no such person would be chosen for the work, there is no need to go further into this point.

It is true, however, that a clever woman who can use her personal attraction wisely has in her armoury a very formidable weapon.

Closely allied to sex in a woman, is the quality of sympathy; and nothing is easier than for a woman to gain a man's confidence by the showing and expression of a little sympathy: this cannot be done by an under-sexed woman. However, it is important to stress that I am no believer in what may be described as Mata-Hari matters. I am convinced that more information has been obtained by woman agents, by keeping out of the arms of the man, than ever was obtained by sinking too willing into them; for it is unfortunately the case that if a man is physically but casually interested in a woman, he will very speedily lose his interest in her once his immediate object is obtained; whereas, if he can come to rely upon the woman more for her qualities of companionship and sympathy, than merely those of physical satisfaction, the enterprise will last the longer.

Knight warned that the 'foregoing rather cold-blooded statements' must not lead an officer to ignore the possibility of a woman agent genuinely falling in love with an opponent; there was always an outside risk of this, but this had never happened, as far as Knight knew, and the best way to guard against such an eventuality was to hark back to the original selection of an agent. During the time when the officer was really getting acquainted with his agent, he should, in the case of a woman, 'pay particular attention to the types of men that the woman concerned likes and dislikes; and his future direction of her should, to a very large extent, be guided by the knowledge which he had obtained during this initial period'.

One of the advantages of employing women as agents was that any woman 'possessed of some secretarial ability offers unique chances for exploitation; for if it is an organisation against which the agent is to be directed, the ultimate objective should be to secure for the agent some secretarial position, either part time or permanent with the Movement concerned. No official or other single individual ever has the same opportunity for obtaining information covering a wide area as does a clerk or secretary.' A woman so placed would have a much wider grasp of the day-to-day doings in a Movement, than any of the officials of the Movement would ever dream of: 'I would state categorically that if it were possible for any business magnate or Government official to be able to see into the mind of his secretary, he would be astonished at the amount of knowledge concerning the general affairs of the business of department in question which lay in the secretary's brain.'

In an ideal world, Knight believed that one would have machinery for securing cover jobs for agents – machinery that would work smoothly and directly; but in actual practice this problem:

bristles with difficulties. It is quite possible for our own department to secure employment for an agent as cover, by utilising our liaison with firms and departments on a high level; but experience has shown me that it is seldom if ever possible to secure an agent such a cover job and yet have the confidence... lying solely with one individual: it is nearly always necessary for our official contact to call in some colleague, and this means that the colleague has to be confided in. Again, the colleague may find it necessary to confide in yet another colleague, and though it is perhaps a little sweeping to say that a secret between three persons is no secret, it is certainly bordering on the insecure to obtain cover jobs for agents under the conditions just outlined.

The ideal situation was therefore to employ persons as agents who had already an ordinary normal means of livelihood:

> for I am convinced that better work is done by agents so placed, than by an agent whose entire time is devoted to his intelligence work. Following on all this we come to the question of agents' remuneration. As a general rule, I am utterly opposed to the system of payment by results. If the precepts laid down earlier on are followed, and agents are recruited primarily for their honesty and sound motives, there should be no necessity for payment of this kind.

Knight believed that payment by results led to undue anxiety on the part of an agent to deliver the goods, with a consequent tendency – even with the most honest person – 'to "keep a little back for a rainy day", and this is the beginning of unreliable work'. He found that nearly every agent he had ever employed who required payment at all, had preferred payment of a small regular sum. This system had an additional advantage, in that it kept the agent:

> up to the mark: he feels that he is accepting money and that he must do his best to earn it. At the same time, it gives him a sense of security, when it is explained to him that the department fully understands that there will be days, weeks or even months, when not much information can be gathered, but that the rough must be taken with the smooth; and his financial position will not suffer because of circumstances which are outside the agent's control.

Another point about which Knight had often been consulted was whether was it desirable for an agent to know that he was in fact working for the British Government. With a possible margin for most exceptional cases, Knight stated:

> unhesitatingly that I think it is not only desirable, but essential that an agent should know exactly what his position is. I am

against any complicated system of cut outs; and equally against employing an agent who thinks he is working for, let us say, a news agency. If this sort of subterfuge is practised, there inevitably comes a day when the agent has to be told what his real position is, and I think this has a very bad effect on the agent himself: he feels that he has been led up the garden, and made a fool of; and worst of all that he has not been trusted; and in my submission, the disadvantages pertaining to those points far outweigh the possible risk entailed in telling an agent that he is in fact work for the British Intelligence Department [If, in the first place, the agent had been properly selected, and vetted,] he should know just where he stands; for if he cannot be trusted with the knowledge that he is an employee of the British Government, he is unlikely to be trustworthy in other respects.

With reference to the operation of agents, the question that divided intelligence officers running agents was: should these agents be operated on a centralised or de-centralised basis? The centralised running of agents was when all agents operating in a particular field of activity were 'run by one particular section of the office'. In a de-centralised system, agents would be run by individual section officers in the divisions concerned, these officers being the persons who were also dealing with the general research into the matter under investigation. For the former school of thought, it was claimed that the operation of agents was definitely specialised work, depending tremendously on the personal factor and requiring an immense amount of time to be devoted to each and every agent. Further, where investigations were being conducted into either Communist or Fascist activity, it was considered that a number of agents all being directed towards the same goal could be operated more efficiently and with better strategic and tactful success, than if they were distributed among a number of officers with other claims upon their time. Those who advocated de-centralisation took the view that the officer who was actually conducting broad research into an aspect of subversive activity had all his facts and requirements at his finger ends, and was therefore in a better position to direct and operate an agent. Knight's own view has always been that – except in very special circumstances, which will be exemplified later – far better results are obtained by having the agent run on the centralised basis. The arguments in favour of this 'appear to me to be overwhelming, and they may listed' as follows:

1. It will be agreed that the type of mind most suited to broad research is a mind which has, on the whole, the academic approach;

and experience has shown that the academic mind is not the best type of mind to direct a complex organisation of individuals, each of whom varies enormously in his personal characteristics, virtues and failings. The prime necessity for anyone who is to operate agents is that he shall be, or shall learn to be a man of very wide understanding of human nature; one who can get on with and understand all types and all classes; and it is rarely that one can find such a type allied to the academic mind.

2. The running of agents is most definitely a full time job. The officer in charge must, to all intents and purposes, be at the beck and call of the agent – not the agent at the beck and call of the officer. If, therefore, the person running the agent or agents is one who also has definite and even arduous other duties, he cannot possibly devote the amount of time necessary for the successful development of an agent.

3. While it is true that the officer dealing with a particular subject has an immense fund of information and detail available, it should not be impossible for him to brief the centralised organisation dealing with agents sufficiently well for the agents to benefit thereby. In addition, it must not be thought that those of us who have been running agents for a number of years have gathered nothing during these years, in the way of knowledge of the different political Movements in which we have been interested; and it is obvious that the liaison between the central agency and the research officers will continue to increase the knowledge of those responsible for the field investigations.

4. Finally, a peculiar kind of teamwork arises in the running of a number of agents. While it is seldom that one agent knows personally, or knows the identity of another agent, it is quite possible for the operating officer or officers to work his group of individuals as an efficient team dovetailing their activities into the general strategic plan, and organising their tactics accordingly. This again requires a particular type of mind and experience, to say nothing of an immense amount of time.

The exceptional cases where agents might be better run by individual officers not within the framework of the agent running organisations were instances where an agent required to investigate the activities of some special organisation, pertaining to a particular nationality, such as Polish or Chinese. In such a case one of the agents' principal assets would be his ability to speak the language in question, and to have some considerable knowledge of the country concerned. It was obvious to Knight that one could not have in one's centralised body officers who were familiar with all countries and with all languages; therefore in such a case it was far better for such an agent to be run by an officer of the section concerned with the relevant country, who would of course be familiar with the particular national aspects of the matter under review: 'It is therefore my considered opinion that much better results are obtained by having the agent run on a centralised basis than can ever be obtained by running agents under separate offices with purely sectional interests.'

Knight also considered the question of co-operating with the police of tremendous importance in connection with the operation of agents, 'and it is difficult to lay too much emphasis on the importance on friendly relationships being established not only between the head of the agent organisation and the senior police officers, but also between subordinates and lower ranks of police officers. Every effort must be made to get full understanding of the differences in outlook between the police and intelligence department, and a comprehension of each other's differences.' Chief Constables and police forces differed in their attitude towards the existence of agents within their territories. Some police officers were extremely understanding and cooperative, while others – 'more parochial and hide bound in their outlook – are somewhat jealous of their preserves. This sort of problem arises more in the provinces and country than in the Metropolitan area.' The circumstances in which it was likely to arise were when it had been found necessary to introduce an agent into some political organisation in a big provincial city, for instance. The question immediately arose – should the police force concerned be informed – (a) of the existence of an agent in their midst – (b) of the identity of such an agent?

In the perfect intelligence world it was Knight's contention that, except in rare cases, a secret agent should be a secret agent, and he should operate entirely unknown to, and independently of, the Police. Unfortunately, at the present time such a state of affairs 'is not universal. There are some Chief Constables who take the view that they would much rather not know about the activity of the department's agents, while there are others who insist upon knowing everything that goes on in their district. The first category is easy to deal with. In the second instance, it is necessary to make up ones mind as to exactly how much to confide in the police. This obviously depends upon the personality of the principal police officer concerned.' The most common circumstance which led to the necessity of confiding in the police was where it was feared that the activity of the agents might bring him to notice of the police force in question, thus leading to the police conducting enquires into the agent, with subsequent embarrassment both to MI5 and to the agent should the police not have full knowledge of the agent's existence. 'This situation is only likely to be really difficult where the senior police officer takes a rather narrow view of the agent's activities.' Knight found therefore, that the best thing to do was to inform the Chief Constable or the most senior office dealing with security matters that MI5 had an agent working in the district; that his name was such and such, and that he was endeavouring to investigate some named form of activity. A tactful but firm request should be made, however, that the police officer concerned should not pass this information on to any subordinate, unless the agent's identity was brought to his notice by his own officers, and that even then he should not take action without consulting MI5. 'In this way major disasters may be avoided.'[55] These were the principles that Maxwell Knight put into practice against the enemies, both internal and external, of the King.

11

Friend or Foe?
Fascism Home & Abroad 1934–1939

In 1931 the confusion over which intelligence organisation was supposed to do what was finally resolved – in favour of MI5; its functions were changed as a result of an enquiry presided over by – once again – Sir Warren Fisher (Treasury), with Sir Robert Vansittart, (Foreign Office) and Sir John Anderson (Permanent Under Secretary of State at the Home Office) and Sir Maurice Hankey. The enquiry arose from the fact that SIS had 'employed an agency' for enquiries in the UK and, as the information obtained was of value to MI5, had communicated it to them without disclosing the nature of its source. When this became apparent, 'the whole question of the functional relations between S.I.S. and M.I.5. was raised'. Sir John Anderson took the line that he could not agree to secret agents being employed inside the UK by SIS as an organisation which was not ultimately responsible to the Home Secretary. Sir Robert Vansittart felt that the opposite held good, i.e. that MI5 should not employ agents abroad. The result was that Section V was established in SIS as a counter-espionage or 'circulating section' to serve as a channel for all communications between SIS and MI5. Prior to the establishment of Section V, individual officers in SIS and MI5 had corresponded and dealt with one another 'indiscriminately'; so it was hoped that the creation of Section V with expert knowledge of the requirements of MI5 would 'conduce to greater efficiency in the despatch of the business of the two sister Services.' At the same time, it was decided that the staff employed at Scotland Yard to deal with 'intelligence duties connected with civil security' should be transferred to MI5, while Irish and anarchist matters were to remain with Special Branch. This involved the transfer of the responsibility for the work previously done in Scotland Yard in connection with Communism. MI5 thus became responsible for *all* intelligence dealing with the activities of the CPGB and therefore of the Comintern in the UK. The three organisations which had been responsible for intelligence work in this field were reduced to two, and the division as between SIS's Section V and MI5's B Branch was unofficially defined as being on the basis of the territorial 'three-mile limit' of all British countries. 'An essential factor during the period of its success was the goodwill and readiness for give and take between the officers concerned at all levels.'

Unfortunately there was a degree of initial confusion for while the change had been communicated to the police all over the country, the Directorate of Military Intelligence was only aware in a vague way that the Combined Defence Security Service – as MI5 was officially now known – had taken over 'certain civil duties from the Metropolitan Police on behalf of the Home Office' because there was no document relating to the transfer on record in the War Office. The War Office only became aware of the alteration in functions when Lieutenant Colonel Holt-Wilson, Kell's number 2, thought of preparing a memorandum on the changes.

The Combined Defence Security Service – still called, by most people, 'MI5' despite its virtual detachment from the War Office – was focussed primarily on the threat from Communist subversion: 'The Nazi threat attracted practically no attention in the Security Service between 1931 and 1933 and very little when Hitler and the Nazi Party came into power in Germany.'[1] That this was so is dramatically illustrated by the co-operation that was initiated between MI5 and the Nazi state in 1933. The biggest threat to British security and stability appeared to still be the Soviet Union and its attempts at subversion in the British Empire. With Hitler's rise to power in Germany it seemed too good an opportunity to miss for MI5 and SIS to access whatever information the Nazis had with regard to Communism in Germany and any links with subversive threats to the Empire. So, it was, that MI5's Guy Liddell, formally of SS1, was despatched to Berlin on 30 March 1933 (staying until 9 April).

On 31 March 31, Captain Foley, the British Passport Control Officer in Berlin (SIS's cover), and Liddell were introduced, by a former leader of a section of the Sturm-Abteilung of the Nazi Party, to Dr Hanfstengel, and through him to the Berlin Political police (Abteilung 1a). Dr. Hanfstengel was a Bavarian aged about thirty-five to forty. As a personal friend of Hitler, he had been associated with the Nazi movement for a number of years and had considerable influence in Party circles. Educated at Harvard University, Liddell noted that he had a 'certain reputation' as a writer and was now employed as Hitler's personal liaison officer with the foreign press. He had travelled a good deal, but, in Liddell's opinion, 'his appreciation of foreign affairs and of the psychology of foreign peoples has become somewhat warped by his enthusiasm for the present regime. He is quite unbalanced both on the question of Communism and the Jews' and genuinely believed the stories put about concerning the imminence of a Communist rising before Hitler's accession to power, the burning of the Reichstag and 'the International Jewish conspiracy' as described by Mrs Nesta Webster, 'of whose books he has made a careful study'. He was also 'under the erroneous impression that Communism is a movement controlled by the Jews' and declared to the British Secret Service men: 'If we do not unite to stamp it out and to safeguard the youth of the world against the defeatist propaganda of intellectual Communists and Socialists… before long you will find yourselves in the same position that Germany was before the Revolution.' As far as Liddell 'felt it was politic, I did my best to explain that conditions in England were very different and violent and indiscriminate action against any section of the community in Germany was bound to be misunderstood in England, and to produce unfavourable comment'. Despite this, Liddell concluded that Hanfstengel 'is on the whole an extremely likeable person. He is undoubtedly very well disposed towards us.'

Hanfstengel and another prominent member of the Nazi Party accompanied Liddell and Foley to the Karl Liebknecht Haus, formerly the headquarters of the German Communist Party (KPD), but now re-named the Horst-Wessel Haus, after another prominent Nazi who was murdered by Communists. The building was at present occupied by the major portion of Abteilung 1A. The Britons were introduced here to Kriminalrat Heller, a police official of long standing, who, Liddell learnt afterwards, was non-Party, but regarded as honest and efficient. He seemed rather worried by the sudden invasion of Party officials, but gave quite a knowledgeable survey of the Communist movement in Germany. Liddell observed that he had, evidently, been engaged on trying to produce convincing evidence that, prior to the advent of the Hitler regime, Germany had been on the eve of a Communist revolt. For this purpose a diagram had been prepared with the Karl Liebknecht Haus as its central point and dotted lines radiating outwards to bridges, power stations and other works of strategic importance. Liddell learnt that this plan had not been found on any Communist or at any Communist Headquarters in the form in which it was now presented, but had been compiled from information and documents which had come into the possession of the police from time to time: 'It was obviously intended that I should infer from this diagram that a serious Communist outbreak had just been averted.' Liddell accepted that it was, of course, quite possible and even probable, that something on the lines of the plan had been worked out by the Communists, but there was nothing to show that any immediate action based upon it was contemplated. In fact, 'all our evidence goes to show that, although the German Communist Party may have contemplated a peaceful street demonstration which might have provoked violent counter-action by the Nazis, Moscow had issued definite instructions that no overt act was to be committed which could in any way lead to the wholesale repression of the Party'.

Another Nazi leader named Burger-Neuss, who was head of the SA (Sturm Abteilung) cell organisation in the Ruhr and reputed to be one of their ablest speakers among working class audiences, now joined the company. He had been an able seaman during the war and later a miner. He was now Reichstag Deputy for one of the districts of Düsseldorf. Liddell found that his particular interest seemed to be the purity of the Nordic race 'and a fanatical hatred of the Jews'. He produced a map, which purported to show that International Jewry was being controlled from London. This, Burger-Neuss thought, was the real reason why Britain had adopted such a hostile attitude to present action against the Jews in Germany. Liddell found that the other Nazis present were inclined to believe him and were much impressed by a photograph of a Jew addressing a meeting of forty or fifty people in Hyde Park, which had been reproduced in Hitler's paper, the *Volkischer Beobachter*. Foley and Liddell explained that such meetings had little or no significance in Britain, that people of all creeds and shades of political thought ventilated their feelings in Hyde Park every Sunday, and that most of the spectators were there out of curiosity, rather than sympathy. Burger-Neuss seemed unconvinced. Liddell concluded from all this that the fact was that the SA 'have a fixed idea on these questions which has been drummed into them for the last ten years. Even the more intelligent seem to have lost their powers of reasoning on the subject.' Kriminalrat Heller, noted Liddell, took little or no part in the Jewish discussion: 'He was evidently rather embarrassed. He did not wish to offend the members of a Party on whom his future depends, but, at the same time, he did not feel able to support their childish arguments.' At the end of this discussion Liddell and Foley were passed on to Kriminal-Kommissar Sattler, who took them round the Karl Liebknecht Haus. Sattler, a young man of about thirty-five, who was a professional policeman and had been employed on political work for a number of years. There was no doubt, in Liddell's mind, that 'he knows his subject inside out. He has been and will be far the most useful contact that we have made. Secretly he has been a member of the Nazi Party since its early days. He took part in the Kapp Putsch without the knowledge of his superiors and has more than probably kept his Party informed about contemplated actions by the Social Democrats against the Nazis.'

The Karl Liebknecht Haus was a large building of three or four floors. The basement contained what appeared, to Liddell, to be a very up to date press on which a number of Communist dailies and periodicals were printed. Liddell was told that the basement had contained large numbers of pamphlets of every description. But these had mostly been removed or burnt. Liddell had noted how a good deal of 'sensational information' about the Karl Liebknecht Haus had been circulated in the press 'with the obvious intention of creating an anti-Communist atmosphere'. Mention had been made of secret passages under the Alexander Platz, of secret staircases and of secret trap doors:

> None of these in fact exist. The underground passage I was told had not yet been discovered. The secret staircase was not secret at all and had obviously been built for the sake of convenience in office administration. While the trap doors said to be concealed behind beds were reduced to one cut in the floor without any attempt at concealment, and obviously intended to facilitate the supply of paper etc to the printing press in the basement. The house and basement are certainly rather like a rabbit warren, but since the Police had already entered the building on several occasions, they must have been in possession of full details of its general layout for some considerable time prior to its final occupation. There is, therefore, nothing new or sensational in any of the recent 'discoveries'.

Before examining any documents, it was considered best that Liddell should see Staatsanwalt Diehls, who was head of the Political Section of the Police. This was arranged not by the junior ranks of the police with whom Liddell was already in touch, but by Herr Gehrt, a prominent representative of the Nazi Party who was attached to Kriminal Kommissar Sattler as liaison officer with the Sturm Abteilung. Diehls was a young man aged about thirty to thirty-five, his face scarred from the sword duels of his student days. His jet-black hair, slit eyes and sallow complexion gave him 'rather a Chinese appearance. Although he had an unpleasant personality he was extremely polite and later when he came round on a tour of inspection gave orders to all present that I was to be given every possible facility.' At their first interview Sattler told Liddell that it was his intention to exterminate Communism in its widest sense. By this he meant not only the Communist Party and its subordinate bodies but also left wing pacifist organisations. The people already arrested now numbered some thousands and the question of what to do with them was becoming a serious problem. 'Perhaps', he said, 'the British Government could set aside an island somewhere which could be jointly used as a penal settlement.' At first Liddell thought he was joking, 'but I discovered afterwards that his suggestions had been made in all earnestness'. From his contacts Liddell concluded that it was:

> quite evident that at present the Party machine is in control and that on information received from its intelligence sections, ruthless and often wholly unjustifiable acts are being committed. Communists, and other suspects are held indefinitely by the police without any charges being preferred against them. While I was at police Headquarters a man was brought in, protesting loudly that he had never had anything to do with politics. On enquiry, I was told that a letter, which had been intercepted going to his address, contained an inner envelope marked 'Please pass on'. The man was to be kept under arrest until he gave the name of the individual for whom this letter was intended.

Liddell had also discovered how, a few days before he arrived, the house of the representative of a well-known British firm had been raided by the Sturm-Abteilung. All papers had been examined and the apartment left in disorder. Two days later, the police arrived at 4.30 a.m. to arrest the man's wife, who was a German born subject. No charge was preferred against her and in spite of the intervention of a member of the British Embassy she was forced to go to police Headquarters. Her husband accompanied her and after considerable delay was informed that the arrest had been carried out on the orders of the Sturm-Abteilung. It was based on wholly unsubstantiated denunciations – one from a dressmaker who said that the lady had been making derogatory remarks about the present regime in Germany. The police official concerned was extremely embarrassed, and in the circumstances 'was bound to admit that the grounds for holding her were insufficient'. She was accordingly released at 8.30 a.m. with abject apologies.

Apart from incidents of this sort, Liddell reported 'there is certainly a good deal of "third degree" work going on, presumably with the tacit approval of certain Nazi Party officials, since much is made of the discipline of the SA. A number of Jews, Communists and even Social Democrats have undoubtedly been submitted to every kind of outrage and this was still going on at the time of my departure.' It was a matter of common knowledge in diplomatic and journalistic circles, but representations in the case of certain foreigners through von Neurath, the German Foreign Minister, seemed to be ineffective. A prominent member of the Nazi Party told Liddell that the arrest of the well-known American journalist, Knickerbocker, was imminent. A cable that he had sent to America about the ill treatment of a Jewess had been intercepted and he was to be charged with spreading false reports about the anti-Jewish activities of the Nazis. The following day, when Liddell asked about Knickerbocker's fate, 'I was told by my Nazi friend that no action could be taken' as enquiry at the hospital had shown that Knickerbocker's report was 'accurate in every detail'.

Liddell found a 'yet more sinister side' of the Sturm-Abteilung's work was centred in what was formerly known as the 'C' organisation. This body was, on the admission of Sattler and Gehrt to Liddell, responsible for the murder of one dissident:

> It was quite evident that it now undertakes the assassination of those in and outside Germany who are found guilty of unpatriotic offences. In this connection it was interesting to note how the murder of one of the Gebrüder Rotter, the well-known Berlin theatrical producers, was condoned in the Press on patriotic grounds. These brothers had absconded to Lichtenstein with huge sums of money, leaving their business in a state of bankruptcy.

On 3 April, Liddell saw Kriminal Komissar Heisig, who was in charge of the proceedings against the Dutch Communist van der Lubbe and other German and Bulgarian Communists accused of complicity in the burning of the Reichstag. No evidence was produced and Liddell's 'previous conclusions that this incident was a piece of Nazi provocation to provide a pretext for the wholesale suppression of the German Communist Party were amply confirmed'. Liddell asked Heisig how it was that van der Lubbe, who had been expelled from the Dutch Communist Party since 1931, had been employed in the vicinity and therefore allowed the opportunity 'for the outrage'. He was 'rather embarrassed by the question' but said that the Communists often publicly got rid of one of their members in order that he might be able to work underground with less risk of detection. He could not however explain why a Dutch Communist should have been employed, 'unless, as I helpfully suggested', this was an indication that the instructions for the outrage had come from the headquarters of the International in Moscow. According to the official reports van der Lubbe was found stripped to the waist with a lighted torch in his hand: 'Sceptics who are not of the Nazi Party explain the absence of his shirt by the belief that it must have been a brown one!' noted the MI5 officer.

Having made the acquaintance of the various heads of departments in the Police, Liddell and Foley were allowed access to the official files and arrangements were made whereby certain documents should be copied and forwarded, to MI5, through the SIS man. A room had been placed at Captain Foley's disposal in the offices of the Political Police. As and when further information of interest came to light, Foley would be informed by Sattler. Liddell concentrated on an examination of the files of the League against Imperialism contained in documents found in a raid in December 1931; this raid, having been carried out under the Social Democrats, was unexpected 'and much interesting material was obtained'. In particular, the files implicated the offices of the Supreme Economic Council of the USSR in Berlin in the transmission of funds and showed that the Western European Bureau of the Comintern took an active part in directing the League's affairs, particularly those affecting India. These points were of interest 'as they illustrate how intimately the Comintern has been associated with the affairs of the League both as regards finance and political direction'.

Liddell also found that the Germans 'appear to have kept themselves fairly well informed about the doings of seditious Indians in Berlin'. On requesting that he might be shown any available papers about one such Indian, Nambiar, who was recently deported, Liddell was introduced to a police Superintendent named Schulz. At first, Schulz seemed reluctant to talk. On being asked what he knew about the Indian community in Germany he replied that the British must be well-informed on this subject already as they had a number of Indian agents in Berlin. He also alleged that, about a year and a half before, two individuals whom he described as 'officers from Scotland Yard' unofficially approached him. These officers, he said, seemed to know a great deal about Indians in Berlin, and were anxious to establish an official liaison. (Nothing was known either in the Indian Police, or SIS about the identity of these people). Schulz claimed that he had also been approached by a representative of the South African police, who offered him £5,000 for full particulars about the League against Imperialism and its personnel. The atmosphere 'was now becoming rather tense', and it was clear that Schulz was not informed about the new liaison which had just been established with the full authority of his chiefs. He looked nervously at his superior, who summoned him outside. On his return he became 'extremely communicative' and confided to Liddell that Chattopadhyaya, a well-known Indian seditionist, had been his agent since 1914. Schulz told Liddell that reports had reached him, from his superiors, that the British Government had hinted at some previous date that the German Government were fostering Indian seditionist movements directed from Berlin. Schulz was anxious to repudiate this suggestion. He said that he merely wished to keep himself informed of what was going on in these circles and that whatever his intentions might be, he could not do much as his allowance for Indian informants had never been more than thirty marks a month.

When he came to assess what he had discovered in Berlin, Liddell concluded that the Germans had dealt the Third International a serious blow by liquidating its European centre. In addition, the German Communist Party had been completely broken up. Some of the arrested leaders would probably be tried and sentenced to terms of imprisonment, while others would be interned indefinitely. In some degree this action had lessened the value of the liaison which had just been established. On the other hand, the Berlin police, who had had ample opportunity for studying the working of the Communist International at close quarters, were in possession of extremely valuable records, 'which if placed virtually at our disposal will be of great assistance in establishing how the Comintern's work in Western Europe and in the Colonies is being reorganised'. There was no doubt, in Liddell's mind, that the moment chosen to establish contact with the Nazi regime had been a good one: 'Those in authority are persuaded that they have saved Europe from the menace of Communism. They are proud of what they have done, and anxious to convince the outside world that their action was fully justified. It was for this reason that they were so communicative on matters about which in more normal times they would have preferred to remain silent.' In their present mood, the German police were 'extremely ready to help us in any way they can'. It was, however, essential that constant personal contact should be maintained, particularly with Sattler, Gehrt and Schulz, 'so that when the present rather hysterical atmosphere of sentiment and brutality dies down, the personal relations established will outweigh any forms of bureaucracy which would normally place restrictions on a free interchange of information'.

Before he departed for Britain, Liddell spent 'a long and interesting' evening with Ribbentrop and two 'enthusiastic but reasonable' Nazis. Liddell found him one of the few people with whom it was possible to talk at all freely on the subject of Jews and Communists: 'I tried to explain to him as best I could the kind of atmosphere that he would find here [Britain] when discussing these questions. He put forward the orthodox Nazi point of view about the Jews, but added modifications of his own. He quite saw that the boycott movement [of Jews] had been a serious mistake, but excused the Party on the grounds that in the present atmosphere it was difficult to control excesses of this kind. He hoped that when things quietened down it would be possible to modify the various acts which prevented large numbers of Jews who were loyal citizens from practising their professions.'In discussing Communism Liddell 'rather surprised' Ribbentrop 'by saying that while we held no brief for Communists, the threat to hang those accused of complicity in the burning of the Reichstag would, if carried out, be regarded in England as a barbarous act'.[2]

Hurrah for the Blackshirts

With co-operation with the Nazis still ongoing it was, about a year later, however, that B Branch, of MI5, reported to Kell that the activities of the Nazi Party organisation established in the UK deserved 'special attention'. At the same time, although there was no knowledge of any direct connection between the two for subversive purposes, the growth of the British Union of Fascists (BUF) under Sir Oswald Mosley gave grounds for increasing interest in his movement on the part of the Home Office; and it was decided early in 1934 that the Security Service should be entrusted with the duty of watching and reporting on Fascist movements.

> There appear to have been two reasons for this. Firstly the various Police Forces were not in a position to report on these movements from such a broad point of view as the Security Service, and secondly – and this was perhaps the decisive reason – there were good grounds for believing that the British Union of Fascists was being financed to a substantial extent by the Italian Dictator [Mussolini] at the same time that it was observed to have certain contacts – apparently arising out of 'ideological' sympathies with the Nazis.

Some months elapsed before it was finally decided to institute active enquiries into the development of the B.U.F. and they were only started in April 1934.

The British Fascisti (BF) had been formed in 1923 by the eccentric Rotha Lintorn Orman, and renamed the British Fascists in 1924. The BF was viewed as largely irrelevant, and a Foreign Office minute considered that it was treated, in Britain, with 'derision and contempt'.[3] It was considered to be made up of members of the middle class, disaffected by World War I, and was seen as irritating, rather than threatening.[4] However, early in the following decade, this scenario would alter considerably with the rise, politically, of Mosley. Elected as a Conservative MP in 1918, Mosley eventually joined the Labour

Party in 1923, following a brief liaison with the Liberals. He broke away from Labour, forming the New Party, which was utterly unsuccessful and more or less wiped out in the 1931 election. Following this, Mosley became more authoritarian and founded the British Union of Fascists. Not only was Mosley charismatic and a brilliant orator, he was also extremely well connected in political circles and the BUF began to succeed where the BF had failed.

In May 1934, Kell wrote to all Chief Constables in England, Scotland and Wales (around 150 in total), explaining that MI5 had been now made responsible, by the Home Office, for the collection and collation of all information regarding the Fascist Movement in Britain. Although the Fascist Movement, which Kell believed was 'a natural reaction to Communism', was showing signs of increased activity, the programmes and policies of the various Fascist organisations in Great Britain, in Kell's view, were open, not secret, and loyalist rather than subversive. Kell felt that they probably owed their existence to foreign inspiration and enjoyed, to some extent, foreign sympathies. While the professed intention of the British Union of Fascists was to obtain power by constitutional means, Kell pointed out that the methods that brought success to their foreign counterparts should not be entirely forgotten, although he thought it 'unlikely that they will ever be imitated in this country'. MI5's immediate interest was that some of the individuals whose names had been brought forward in association with the Fascist Movement had previously been known to MI5 on account of their connection with the more extreme left wing of political thought. Undoubtedly, in some cases, they were Communist agents in Fascist circles, while some were probably 'persons of shady or eccentric character, who drift from one thing to another'.

Kell requested that Chief Constables give him their opinion as to the importance they attached to the Fascist Movement in their individual areas. He would also, he wrote, be grateful for any information, which may reach them from time to time, concerning the following: 1. The extent of the membership of local organisations; 2. The growth or decline of the movement; 3. The activities of persons of doubtful antecedents who may be connected with it; 4. The names of the principal Fascist officials; 5. Any indications of relations with foreign Fascist movements; 6. Incidents which have caused a breach of the peace.

Kell stressed the delicacy of the situation and impressed that discretion was paramount when making enquiries of this nature. He set out the addresses and chief officials of the four separate Fascist organisations with Headquarters in London, of which the most important was Mosley's British Union of Fascists, based in the Kings Road, and counted several ex-Members of Parliament amongst its members, as well as the Irishman William Joyce. British Fascists Limited was based at Westminster; the Imperial Fascists League had offices in Craven Street in the West End; and the United Empire Fascist Party had its base in Trafalgar Square and was believed to have been founded in 1933 to 'sow dissension' in the ranks of the British Union of Fascists. Kell believed that only Mosley's organisation had any influence outside London.[5]

By 29 May 1934, Kell had received responses from eighty-three Chief Constables. On a personal level it became clear that Kell was trying to work out the internal dynamics of Fascist ideology. While a detailed analysis of the Fascist principle in Europe, or of its application in different countries was beyond the scope of MI5's remit, 'certain outstanding facts' could, he noted, be emphasised. It was obvious that the position in Italy and in Germany immediately before Fascism came to power was 'very different' from that in the United Kingdom. The foundation of the 'Corporate State' was considered to be Mosley's 'most definite object'. This idea had only developed in Italy after the Fascists had seized power and MI5 considered it to be 'little more than a paper scheme' of which the actual workings had yet to be experienced. In Germany it did not appear to have been treated as a matter of immediate practical politics. Fascism in Italy and Germany had been born 'in agony and travail', while in Britain it seemed to be the product of 'doctrinaire theory', but nourished by various political and economic discontents. While Communism was international and preached class-warfare, Fascism insisted on the common interests of all classes in an 'intensified economic nationalism inspired by patriotic sentiment'.

Since Fascism was considered a reaction from Communism, MI5 thought it was important to understand the Communist view of its development, a view that was repeatedly set out in numerous Communist publications, such as *Labour Monthly*, the *Communist Review*, and *International Literature*. An important factor in the hold which Communism had on minds of 'a certain type' was the belief that Marx accurately foresaw the future developments of the capitalist system. It was in the light of this, MI5 believed, that the Communist views on the Fascist movement were to be interpreted. Every man and every movement in any way opposed to Communism could potentially be branded as Fascist. Roosevelt, Baldwin, H.G. Wells and Rudyard Kipling were all 'covered by a common opprobrium'. And the British Union of Fascists, in MI5's view, while not the first, had become the only important Fascist organisation in the United Kingdom. It had entirely eclipsed earlier formations which were now 'moribund or very insignificant'. Although ostensibly a one man movement behind Mosley were other important personages, including the proprietor of the *Daily Mail*, Lord Rothermere; W.E.D. Allen; and Major Yeats-Brown.

Rothermere's support was an important factor although, apart from selling purposes, the exact nature of the reasons which led him to lend his support were unclear. One theory was that he was using the Blackshirt Movement as a 'stick with which to beat the [Conservative]Government' and drive it on to greater activity. Another suggestion was that it was possibly connected with his friendship for Princess Stephanie Hohenlohe – on the ground that support lent to a Fascist or extreme nationalist movement by a powerful section of the English Press might prove very convenient to the 'welt-politik' of the Third Reich.

W.E.D. Allen was the Chairman of the Directors of David Allen & Sons Limited, which was a private company of printers and lithographers that owned the controlling interest in a number of subsidiaries. Under the pseudonym of 'James Drennan', Allen had published a book entitled *B.U.F. – Oswald Mosley and British Fascism*. A considerable part of the book described Mosley's political career and the steps by which he was gradually led to declare himself a Fascist. The remainder was devoted to an explanation of Fascism, which had been conceived in the light of Oswald Spengler's work. In Allen's view, Fascism not only sought to find a solution to the economic problems of the modern European world, it also challenged the inevitability of decline and looked to renew the strength and to perpetuate the cultural health of the peoples of Europe.

It was only with the development of Fascist movements that European nations began to show that they were prepared to master the formidable problems of the 'megalopolitan' civilisation of the modern world and its capitalist basis. In pursuance of the Fascist search for a solution of modern economic problems, Mussolini mastered 'the machines' and, roused the corporate consciousness of the Italian nation, organising a stable balanced people to replace the struggling city mobs and the debilitated proletariats of the countryside. Allen went on to suggest that Fascism supplied the 'Caesar-men and the legions' whom Spengler awaited. These 'Caesar-men', with their 'forceful methods', affronted the 'wincing world of intellect'. Having raised their legions from the street, they would then stride as the 'leaders of men'. 'The powers of the blood, unbroken bodily forces, resume their ancient lordship.' Fascism, as neo-Caesarism, was, to Allen, the most 'incomprehensible of movements to the cosmopolitan intellect' which could only explain the new phenomenon in the light of its own fears; 'fears which turn its thin blood into the acid of shrill hatred'. Sir Oswald Mosley's argument was that the Fascist philosophy could be expressed in clear terms and could be shown to derive both its origin and its historic support from the established thought of the past. Mosley endeavoured to demonstrate that the Nietzschean and the Christian doctrines were susceptible of a 'certain synthesis' and that a 'complete wedding of the great characteristics of both creeds' could be found in the Fascist doctrine. In effect, the Fascist principle was 'private freedom and public service'. Although Allen played no prominent part in the ordinary day to day work of the Blackshirt organisation, he was believed to have had considerable influence over Sir Oswald Mosley and was described as the 'thinker' of the movement, in contrast to Mosley who was seen as 'the man of action'.

Major Francis Yeats-Brown, with Dr Robert Forgan, Sir Donald Makgill and Captain Luttman Johnson, had founded the January Club in January 1934, as a means of contacting people who might not ordinarily be expected to join the Blackshirts, so as to influence them in favour of the Fascist Movement and Fascist policy. Among the early members of the Club were the Irish peer, Lord Middleton, Brigadier-General Spears and Sir John Squire. Middleton lent a flat in Mayfair as temporary quarters for the Club, and a series of dinners were held, mainly at the Splendide. At the dinners various well known people were guests from time to time. The *News Chronicle* tried to poke fun at one of these dinners in its issue of 1 May 1934, mentioning the names of Lord Lloyd, General Hubert Gough, Lord Middleton, Mr C.B. Fry, Mr P.G. Fender, the Earl of Glasgow, Mr Ward Price, Captain Liddell Hart, Sir John Squire and Dr Forgan as among those present. A report of another dinner of this kind appeared on 18 May when the Earl of Iddesleigh, Lord Russell of Liverpool and Sir Charles Petrie were among the 350 members and guests said to be present. 'Undoubtedly the January Club dinners brought Fascism to the notice of a large number of people who would have considered it much less favourably if its chief promoter had been the BUF.'

In short, MI5 considered that the policy of Sir Oswald Mosley and the British Union of Fascists could be summarised as combining three originally separate conceptions: 1. Economic self-sufficiency within the State (i.e. within the British Empire); 2. Occupational representation (Corporatism) and 3. Authority in politics (of Allen's Neo-Caesarism). These three conceptions were combined by the idea of complete governmental control of all economic activities within the State.

In terms of the BUF's structure and formation, MI5 identified five Provincial Regional Headquarters and three London Regional

Headquarters, thirty-eight London branches, one hundred Provincial branches, nine (British Union of Fascists) branches in Italy, three in Germany and one each in France and Spain. Special attention was directed to the Foreign Relations and Overseas Department, which was led by Dr George A. Pfister, (an Australian of German extraction). MI5 recognised that there were deficiencies in the information they held. There were three important questions arising, which, at the time, they were not able to answer: firstly, it was unclear whether the BUF had an underground organisation in place to enable them to take effective action in an emergency. Secondly, it was not known whether the BUF had any intention of attempting to influence the Armed Forces with propaganda. And finally, it was not known whether the BUF was receiving fiscal assistance from Germany or Italy.

Concerning the first question, although the official attitude of the British Union of Fascists was that the use of force had 'never been contemplated' as a legitimate means of securing power, Mosley had expressed an intention of 'using force to meet force', which had already happened 'wherever Communist violence has been encountered' at meetings or on the streets. Therefore, it seemed, Fascist theory contemplated the use of force to defeat insurgent anarchy in an emergency. To MI5 it seemed to be a 'natural precaution' to prepare plans to counter this in advance and, since the Armed Forces of the Crown would be a factor in such a situation, the Fascists would have to adopt a definite attitude towards them, directed towards securing their sympathy, or even the power to control them if and when the ultimate issue arose. The only definite information that MI5 had on this subject was a report from a reliable source to the effect that Major Yeats-Brown had been using the January Club to make contact with younger officers in the army. While the source was 'unimpeachable', the exact weight that should be attached to the information was doubtful. Just how many officers had been in touch with the January Club, or what their individual reactions had been, was unknown. The Fascists seemed to have avoided any direct approach to the rank and file of the army, air force, or navy. MI5 believed that the few isolated instances of Blackshirt papers being posted on notice boards in barracks were possibly due to the 'mistaken zeal of uninstructed subordinates'. MI5 concluded that no significance needed be attached to them.

As to the sources of money sustaining the BUF, MI5 had no certain information that any financial assistance had been received from either Italian or German sources. However, Italian Fascists and German Nazis were known to be taking a great deal of interest in

Mosley and his Movement. Signor Mussolini's interest and sympathy had extended to writing a lengthy article for the *Fascist Week*
of the 6–13 April, 1934. It was rumoured that about £50,000 had
been received from German sources, and there were also various indications that financial assistance may have been received from Italy.
MI5, though, had not been able to reach a final and definite conclusion about this. It was reported from one source of information that,
after his return from his second visit to Mussolini during the spring,
Mosley showed signs of being in command of greater resources. But,
in the absence of any certainty in the matter, it was not considered
'desirable to assume too much'.

At this stage, Kell and MI5 was not too concerned with the political
situation in Britain and Fascist prospects at a general election, or with
the political aims of Mosley and the British Union of Fascists, as long as
these aims were pursued by strictly constitutional methods. While the
Fascists maintained that they aimed at obtaining power by means of the
ballot box, MI5 could not be certain that they were not contemplating
the use of methods involving force. The political situation was, at the
time, 'very far from producing such an emergency', but warned MI5, 'its
various tendencies were developing', which seemed to be bringing Sir
Oswald Mosley and his followers 'more to the front of the stage'.[6]

Towards the end of 1934, however, Kell could be more sanguine
and noted that the Movement was 'showing signs of internal decay'
– although Mosley's filling of the Albert Hall with a largely enthusiastic audience on 28 October revived the spirits of the 'Leader' and
his chief associates. There was, also, evidence of more determined
propaganda by 'more efficient individuals'. The *Blackshirt* had
improved in tone and 'hitting power' for which A. Raven-Thompson
was largely responsible. Major-General J.C. Fuller, the military historian and strategist, who been working at National Headquarters
for the last few months had begun 'to get a grip' with the affairs of
the BUF. Without making himself in any way prominent (and behind
closed doors marked 'Political propaganda – General Fuller'), he was
gradually taking into his hands matters relating to an internal reorganisation of the movement and the co-ordination of its activities.
Kell noted that:

> a curious fact about Major-General Fuller is that he combines an
> advocacy of scientific methods and mechanization with an interest
> in the mysticism of the Yogis on which he had published a book.
> Like Mosley he perhaps has a tendency to excessive simplification
> not unconnected with concentration on a single idea. The attempt

to know the Unknowable may be an extension of the same tendency; but it is perilously near the borderline of sanity – and Major-General Fuller is a man with a grievance. Mosley is obsessed with ideas based on science and mechanics and expects human beings to react in the same simple and inevitable way as a crankshaft is driven by a piston-rod. His contact with Major-General Fuller goes back several years and they appear to have many ideas in common. The latter's obsession with the idea of mechanisation has led him into somewhat unbalanced action. He is a man with organising ability and driving power and his connection with the British Union of Fascists may have greater potentialities than are ordinarily attached to the activities of retired officers.

Major Yeats-Brown, 'the other mystically inclined soldier who adopted Fascism', was apparently dropping out of the Movement. It was understood that this was due to his forming a poor opinion of Mosley. He was interested in the idea of the Corporate State, but did not favour a dictatorship in Britain. Mosley, by this stage, had become openly anti-Semitic although he had, in one speech, said that he had not attacked Jews until they attacked him and he had nothing against the Jews who put Britain first, and Jewry second, 'etc., etc., etc.' This had not gone down well with Lord Rothermere, 'who apparently dislikes the idea of dictatorship and dropped Mosley when he attacked the Jews – as a matter of business, no doubt – and evidently still entertains a more than sneaking admiration for him'. On 19 November, the *Daily Mail*, reversing its recent policy of ignoring the Fascist Movement, devoted half a dozen short paragraphs to Mosley's speech at Bradford on 18 November, which, it said, was listened to with keen attention by an audience of more than 2,000.

By now Kell was shifting somewhat in his, and MI5's analysis of British Fascism: 'A very prevalent misconception regarding the British Union of Fascists is to regard it as mainly directed against communism. It is mainly directed against the present political and economic systems.' MI5 noted with regret that perhaps 'the most unfortunate effect of the growth of the British Union of Fascists hitherto has been the fillip which it has given to the Communist movement, but this must be attributed, to a great extent, to the propaganda and the policy directed from Moscow. In the co-ordination of its "anti-fascist" policy Moscow has been unusually fortunate and remarkably adept at seizing an opportunity'.[7]

By early 1935, Kell noted that Mosley's latest campaign in Lancashire 'must have proved a disappointment to him. It was not carried through with the energy or on the scale foreshadowed in his initial steps in that direction.' The Lancashire campaign was advertised in the *Daily Mail* – 'Rothermere is thus far supporting Mosley again at present – but does not appear to have had any resounding effect.' Nevertheless, as a result of this special effort in its neighbourhood, Manchester was alone among the important cities of England and Scotland to report that the Blackshirt movement was maintaining its position at the end of January 1935. In all the others from which MI5 had obtained details, the membership had declined, branches had been closed, sales of the *Blackshirt* had dropped and 'enthusiasm generally has cooled'.

But MI5 warned that it would be premature to rely on these indications as proof that the movement, greatly though it has lost momentum, was moribund. 'Nor is it safe to attach too much importance to the reported dissensions among fascists at National Headquarters. Such dissensions exist and they are to some extent a sign of weakness: but they will not kill the movement. Fascism represents a phase in the development of European thought: and it has roots in this country in real discontents.' National Headquarters was still actively training propagandists and the movement was still drawing recruits from the discontended elements of different classes, the extremes being typified by the ex-army officer and the ex-Communist. 'The former perhaps fail to realise the revolutionary nature of the fascist programme. They think that the country is in a bad way and that under fascism they will help to save it.' According to 'an intelligent observer' within the Fascist ranks there were many members who 'look upon the movement as a better medium than the socialist and communist parties for putting over a form of socialism'. Having won power under the Fascist banner (and destroyed the British Constitution by means of a code of laws) these elements hope to use the dictatorship to secure power and 'taking off the fascist glove to disclose the socialist fist'.

Kell thought that Mosley himself, judging by the account of his career given by his friend W.E.D. Allen, 'is probably nearer to the revolutionary outlook than to that of the somewhat naive but loyal and patriotic elements who hope that fascism may save the country from disaster.' The revolutionary nature of Mosley's position was exemplified in the frequent and bitter attacks made on existing institutions in the *Blackshirt*. Mosley, pointed out Kell, always maintained that he aimed at:

a clean cut, revolutionary change, not at gradual development. While this is, in part, conveniently demagogical, it is also based on a fundamental (if mistaken) idea – that of the nature and magnitude of the change in social and economic conditions effected by the great enhancement during recent years of the productive power of machinery. This, in turn, is perhaps partly genuine and partly convenient – genuine in so far as he is capable of obsession by a single idea, convenient in so far as he is capable of demagogic trickery.

In the face of unceasing Fascist propaganda calculated to bring Parliamentary institutions into contempt and to pour ridicule on the Conservative Party, Kell noted that the *Manchester Guardian* showed itself 'singularly ill-informed' when, on 19 January, it claimed that Sir Oswald Mosley's re-organisation of the British Union of Fascists showed that he had taken a step towards re-entering the Conservative fold. Judged at their face value all the measures of re-organisation were intended to give the Fascist Movement a broader political basis and:

> there has been no indication that Mosley has any intention of abandoning the Blackshirts. On the contrary, everything goes to show that it is intended that the division into two parts – those wearing uniform and those working in the political organisation – should facilitate the inclusion in the ranks of many who have hitherto held aloof. Simultaneously, great efforts are being made to further the formation of "cells" – after the communist manner – in the trades unions and in the professions.

The reorganisation was the work of General Fuller, and since Mosley put his imprimatur to it, they shared the unpopularity it had earned among the 'less reputable' elements among the Blackshirts. Fuller was reported to be determined to rid the movement of these same elements. These were, of course, among those inclined to a revolutionary outlook; and a struggle within the movement between those who might be conveniently, if loosely, dubbed the patriots and the revolutionaries might well develop. If such should be the case, 'the outcome will depend on the attitude of Mosley and his friends who find the money'. On this basis it was fairly safe to estimate the present rate of their total expenditure as somewhere in the neighbourhood of £40,000 a year.

This once more raised the question of contributions from the German and Italian ruling parties – which was 'still an open question' but, Kell thought 'the balance of probabilities is <u>against</u> any such subvention. Neither Mussolini, who sponsors a movement for "the universality of Rome", nor Hitler who maintained the Austrian Legion has given any evidence of being able to call the British fascist tune, unless Mosley's change of attitude to the Jews last autumn comes under this head.' If Mosley was, in fact, independent of foreign financial aid, then Kell concluded that 'fascism is something more than a mere phase in European thought'. Mosley's attention was, however, necessarily absorbed in national aims. The recent re-organisation of his movement with the division into the uniformed and political branches gave it far greater flexibility. The activities of either branch could be developed to suit the exigencies of the moment. In the immediate future effort was likely to be concentrated on the political side. The Fascist leaders would not be unwilling to split the Conservative vote. 'They – Mosley and men like Joyce and Raven-Thomson, but not perhaps General Fuller – evidently expect, and hope, that a Socialist Government will come to power and give them the opportunity to lead a reaction.' Men like Joyce – 'and there are others like him in the British Union of Fascists – are not averse from the use of force even to the extent of something like civil war. They rather enjoy a fight for its own sake'.[8]

William Joyce was certainly a very complex character. The son of Irish loyalists, he had been born and brought up in a very political atmosphere. An MI5 assessment of him described how, since his earliest days he has been what 'the Spanish refer to as "politico"'. He left school at about the age of fourteen or fifteen and more or less ran away from home to join the Black and Tans during the Irish Troubles of 1919–21. He was with them for some time until he was sent home as being too young, and he saw battle, murder and sudden death at a very tender age. He was of 'a very precocious intellectual development, with tremendous personality and energy'. His greatest failing was that his mental balance 'was not equal to his intellectual capacity'. As an Irishman he was 'naturally a person of very definite opinions and those opinions always tend towards extremes'. He was, for instance, a rabid anti-Catholic, and a fanatical anti-Semite. He had decided tendencies towards absolute monarchy, absolute government, dictatorship etc., and underlying it all was that 'romantic streak common to all Celts which makes them doubly effective and doubly dangerous'. It had been alleged that Joyce was 'a pompous, conceited little creature' although this statement should be weighed up against the fact that he had made his way in his own small world 'entirely by his own efforts and in the face of very considerable difficulties'.

Joyce was 'a very small insignificant looking little man. He had practically no early education.' He was brought face to face with desperate situations and happenings even younger than the average junior officer in the war period, yet when he returned to England after the Irish trouble he managed to educate himself and achieved 'comparatively brilliant successes'. He was as fanatical in his studies as he was 'in other directions', and several times during his scholastic career he reduced himself to the verge of a nervous breakdown. However, he secured an excellent degree with honours and other diplomas besides. Around 1927–1928 he decided to take up teaching as a profession with the object of breaking into politics, and with that aim in view he threw himself wholeheartedly into the Junior Imperial League and soon became one of their principal speakers in South London. However, his natural aptitude for intrigue, his 'abhorrence of compromise, and his rabid opinions' did not endear him to his more peaceful colleagues, and after much strife he resigned. Joyce married, in 1927, Hazel Barr, whom he met during his time with the old British Fascists 1923–1925, and had two little daughters aged eight and six. Regarding his associations with Fascism, it was felt that little needed to be said about his early efforts with the British Fascists. He was in charge of a district in Battersea, was 'untiring in his efforts and made himself so obnoxious to the Communist Party that during the election of 1924 he was "razored" at one of Mr. Hogben's meetings. (This he is not likely to have forgotten.)' it was stated with considerable understatement.

Joyce was one of the earliest to join Mosley's BUF, rising very rapidly until he occupied a seat at Mosley's right hand. He was thought likely to have had many traits in common with Mosley, though he would be 'a much more likeable character in many ways'. His political beliefs were probably very mobile, but it was considered that his fundamentals were 'quite sound'. He was violently opposed to what could broadly be described as Bolshevism. In his Fascist creed it was thought that he tended towards the 'Hitler ideal' rather than that of Mussolini. Under favourable circumstances or where he thought his own cause would benefit he would certainly not shrink from violence, but it would not be unthinking, senseless, spectacular violence. He had at times a 'very calm and cunning judgment'. He obviously had tremendous respect and admiration for Mosley himself, and it was probably Mosley's 'independence of spirit and courage' that appealed to him: 'If Fascism were to progress in this country and become more powerful, then Joyce would be a man who would undoubtedly play a very prominent part in affairs.'[9]

In September 1935, Kell received evidence which, 'now with all the circumstantial corroborative details', and the fact of Mosley's new campaign in favour of Italy in connection with its invasion of Abyssinia, 'leaves no room for doubt' that Fascist Italy was financing the BUF. With this everything changed:

Where it once seemed to have roots in this country, these roots now appear to be very much frailer and to have been kept alive only by artificial means. Thus both the Communist Movement and its re-agent, Fascism, are for all practical purposes dependent on foreign funds. Without such funds Fascism, at any rate, would probably cease to exist... In the light of the new knowledge regarding the Italian subvention it may be said that Fascism is a less important factor in English politics than it formerly appeared and that its real nature is rather that of a backwash from the main current of European affairs.

The question, then, naturally arose as to the exact nature of the relations between the leaders of the BUF and Nazi Germany. Relations between the BUF and the Nazi Party appeared 'somewhat less cordial' then they had previously been and such facts 'lead to the inference that the British Union of Fascists can hardly be in receipt of funds from Nazi sources. Nevertheless it is remarkable that there are a number of individuals connected the British Union of Fascists who have distinctly pro-Nazi tendencies and that social relations between the two have been fairly close. For instance, a number of leaders from National Headquarters have from time to time attended gatherings of Nazis in London.' MI5 knew that Joyce, 'no doubt with Mosley's cognisance', recently (in August 1935) sent to Berlin and Rome a very exaggerated account of the progress made by the BUF in Britain and its present importance to the Nazis and to the Italian Fascists. In the case of the latter, 'it is certain that the object was to encourage Mussolini to continue to pay. The question therefore arises whether the same object was intended in making the same communication to the Nazis. There is the further fact that Captain Robert Gordon Canning in consultation with Mosley, went to Nuremberg at the time of the Nazi Party Rally and that he promised the Leader that he would obtain "good results" from the Germans. We do not yet know exactly what results he had in mind, but it seems likely that they were financial.' Mosley's change of attitude with regard to the Jews, when he adopted a more hostile attitude towards them, 'might be due to German influence and perhaps German money'.

Kell summed up the position by saying that Mussolini, while convinced that Mosley was not likely to succeed as a Fascist leader, was now financing him solely to make capital out of his support of Italy in the Abyssinian crisis, and to divide British opinion. Mosley, on the other hand, was receiving Italian money as a necessary means of supporting an organisation 'whose main psychological bases were his own vanity and certain theories regarding the decadence of Parliamentary institutions'. Kell warned that Mosley would be equally ready to take German money, 'but it was very doubtful whether he was receiving any and almost certain that Hitler would regard it as an unsuitable investment'.[10]

Mussolini's payments continued into 1936 and there was no sign of the BUF being short of funds. They had, for instance, recently opened new branches in Birmingham where the Chief Constable had remarked that these signs of apparent activity were due to the organisation itself and not to any support which it had received from the public of Birmingham. In other words Mosley 'has been enabled to open new branches because he is in receipt of ample funds from abroad and not because his movement is supported by any important section of opinion in this country. The only neighbourhood in the whole country in which Fascism continued to make any headway was in the East End of London, but even there the *Blackshirt* found it necessary greatly to exaggerate their achievements.'[11] By the middle of 1936, MI5 had received information from 'an absolutely reliable source' that Mussolini's subvention to Mosley had been reduced from £3,000 to £1,000 per month. Corroboration of this was to be found in the fact that simultaneously the Movement had shown signs of having distinctly smaller funds at its disposal. There had also been intimations that Mosley was less inclined to champion the cause of Italy than he had been the previous autumn. At the same time, the remarks of Fascist speakers and their papers usually expressed some sympathy with the Fascist regimes of German and Italy.[12]

Although the Fascist movement was declining in 1936, the campaign in the East End of London continued to make more headway than elsewhere. The results of seven or eight months of intensive propaganda in the East End were brought to a head when, on 4 October, Mosley arranged for a large-scale propaganda march of uniformed Fascists into the East End, and the various sections of opinion in the population which disliked Fascism organised opposition to it. A very active part in this opposition was naturally played by the Communists and the various organisations which they have penetrated. In the midst of the wide spread attention which this affair attracted three or four points stood out. In the first place there were the immediate sequels. The counter demonstration organised the following week passed off without any serious opposition being organised by the Fascists. Mosley immediately afterwards held large meetings in the East End of London when, (the Communists having no time to organise opposition) he not only received a good hearing but the display of pro Fascist sentiments on the streets 'surprised a number of experienced observers'. MI5 noted that much was made of 'terrorism' in the East End at this time although this aspect of the matter was as usual 'exaggerated in the sensational press'. The conditions provided a good deal of scope not only for the organised hooliganism of Fascist bodies but also for that of the ordinary hooligan elements of the neighbourhood. Large numbers of extra police had to be employed in the disturbed areas and there could be no doubt that steady pressure in the shape of police action played a large part in the subsequent restoration of more normal conditions. It was, however, a significant fact that having taken advantage of the peculiar conditions of the East End, and having found in the encouragement of anti-Semitic feeling something with which to work up agitation to an extent which they had not succeeded in doing elsewhere, the Fascists, instead of keeping the situation at boiling point, allowed it to subside again during the latter part of October and November. 'It was not clear how far this failure to keep up the temperature is to be attributed to Mosley's incapacity to take advantage of a situation of this kind, or how far it was to be attributed to the announcement that fresh legislation would be adopted to deal with the situation which he had created.'

Reports on the reaction in Fascist circles to the proposed banning of uniforms, by the Government, suggested that they were prepared to 'make the best of it' and that there was a disposition to hope that it might even lead to an accession of strength. It was anticipated that a number of people might join the Movement who had been deterred by the uniforms from doing so, and that the suggestion of a persecution inspired by the Communists and Jews would also strengthen the Movement. The more drastic measures contemplated in the present Bill, took the Fascists and most other people somewhat by surprise, but was not entirely unforeseen. It was expected in some Fascist quarters that 'the result will be that the movement would tend to "go underground".'

In so far as Mosley's leadership of the Fascist movement was concerned it was thought possible that he was 'being brought to a parting of the ways'. As had been reported previously he had never been entirely successful in capturing the imagination of his followers. His name was little mentioned among the rank and file. The latter showed signs of being to a much greater extent captured by the personality of William Joyce. Joyce had played a leading part in the development of the British Union of Fascists and the National Socialists; and if 'Fascism' was to be taken more seriously than Mosley's Fascists, it seemed likely that Joyce would continue to play a prominent part. He was not considered to be above using the services of 'swashbucklers' and 'thugs', but on the other hand he lacked what Mosley possessed, namely the income of Mosley and his friend W.E.D. Allen and perhaps the capacity for obtaining a subsidy from Mussolini. Joyces's own sympathies lay with the Nazis rather than the Italian Fascists.[13]

Events came to a head in March 1937 when, after they had been removed from their paid positions in the British Union of Fascist and National Socialists, John Beckett and William Joyce took steps, in April, to develop a new movement in opposition to Mosley and gave it the title of The National Socialist League. Its general objects were similar to those of the British Union of Fascists but it was distinguished by the fact that the title 'National Socialist' apparently demonstrated that it had more in common with the German than the Italian movement, 'at any rate, so far as the sympathies of its promoters are concerned', and it 'ostentatiously avoids having any one individual leader'.[14]

New Blood

'By an accident' a German was reported to have been arrested in Switzerland in January 1934 with the London address of the Nazi Party Auslands Organisation in his possession 'in circumstances that appeared to indicate that the address was connected with the Gestapo'. The Auslands Organisation was the Foreign Organisation of the National Socialist German Workers Party (NSDAP or Nazi Party). After receiving this information Sir Vernon Kell saw Sir Russell Scott, the Permanent-Under Secretary of the Home Office, and asked him whether he expected the Security Service to take any special steps about Nazis in Britain. Scott replied that 'unless we discovered in the ordinary course of our work any case of subversive propaganda or other inimical steps against the interests of this country we were to leave them alone' and therefore no HOW should be applied 'at any rate for the time being'. Guy Liddell thereupon made further enquiries, and in June 1934, judging that a HOW on addresses in Germany would be more readily obtained than one on the address in London, applied for and obtained permission to intercept the correspondence going to two addresses in Hamburg with which he knew that the branch of the Auslands Organisation in London was corresponding. The ground for this was given as being that the headquarters of the Nazi Party in the UK was acting as an agency of the German Secret Police. 'Thus the accidental arrest in Switzerland eventually furnished a ground for getting over the Home Office reluctance to allow us to obtain intelligence about the Nazi organisations on British soil and led to the amassing of very voluminous and illuminating intelligence on the nature of the Nazi State and its aggressive tendencies.' But Home Office Warrants, although applied for by MI5, were granted on 'a few unimportant members of the British Union of Fascists, but the Home Office consistently refused to do so in the case of Mosley himself'. From the perspective of MI5 'it is obvious that not only in official but in wider circles there was a general failure to appreciate the character of the Nazi Party and the part it played in developments in Germany during the years following its accession to power'. The information 'which flowed' to MI5 as a result of the watch which was kept on the Nazi Party, 'gradually began to show how the whole power of the machinery at Hitler's disposal was used to promote goodwill in this country towards Germany, and even to encourage where possible the spirit of pacifism, while Germany was being rearmed and its people toughened in preparation for the war which he afterwards started'.

It was not until 1935 that a full enquiry commenced into the subsidiary consequences of the general Nazi policy in the shape of the Auslands Organisation as established all over the world (except, as far as the evidence went, in Russia). A report on this subject was prepared in B Branch in 1935, in the course of which it was pointed out that the objects of the Auslands Organisation were 'the welding together of all Germans abroad, and all seafaring Party members, into one great block', and that emphasis should be laid on the potentialities of the all embracing organisation of a Party which had absorbed the whole apparatus of the State. Among the results in countries outside Germany 'was to be counted the fact that, since the Nazi machine had unprecedented power over the individual, it could direct the energies of every member of the Party in any desired direction'. It was pointed out that because at that time the Führer desired British friendship, 'every German was adjured to act and speak with that end in view, but we could not lose sight of the fact that in certain eventualities the whole energy of the machine could be utilised in the reverse direction. The machine was a ready-made instrument for intelligence, espionage and ultimately for sabotage purposes.' This report formed the subject of discussion with the Foreign Office and the Home Office. The question was ultimately referred to the Cabinet, 'but it was not held that any action could be taken to curtail the activities of the Auslands Organisation on British soil'. When, however, the German Government proposed to appoint Otto Bene, the Landesgruppenleiter or head of the Organisation in the United Kingdom, to be Consul-General for Germany in London, the Foreign Office raised objections and the German Government recalled him.

In the middle of 1936, MI5 prepared a memorandum on the possibilities of sabotage by the organisations set up in British countries by the Governments of Germany and Italy. This memorandum was sent by Kell to the Joint Intelligence Sub-Committee of the Committee of Imperial Defence. The memorandum suggested that the possibilities of sabotage by the Auslands Organisation or the Fasci all'Estero were of sufficient importance to be brought to the notice of the Minister for the Co-ordination of Defence, and that information which had accumulated regarding these organisations made it desirable to review questions relating to the employment of individuals of German or Italian origin or descent, in the Armed Forces, Government establishments and firms concerned in the production of ships, aircraft and munitions. It was also suggested that measures to enable MI5 to watch these organisations satisfactorily would involve a considerable expense and an increase of staff.

After referring to the official Nazi view of the constitution of the Nazi State in which the State, the Party, and the Armed Forces, were all under the personal control and command of the Führer, the memorandum went on to mention the views put forward under the aegis of von Blomberg, the Reichskriegs-Minister and Oberbefehishaber der Wehrmacht, regarding the relations between National Socialism, the Wehrmacht, and what was described as Wehrpolitik. Wehrpolitik was explained as meaning 'in the sense of National Socialism', the co-ordination of the fighting forces of the nation, and their direction and their steeling towards the will for self-assertion and the development of all their inherent political possibilities. As head of the State, leader of the Party, and Supreme Commander of the Armed Forces, Adolf Hitler 'was the lord of Germany, with a power almost unexampled in history'. There was no longer any separation in the supreme direction of foreign policy and military strategy and the organisation of the whole people for military purposes was centralised. The new army was the creation of Adolf Hitler, and with other organisations of the Party and the State was to work, in accordance with his will to 'educate' the 'new' German people.

The memorandum went on to suggest that Hitler's intentions were indicated in his *Mein Kampf* and that his acts spoke more decisively than his words. All his acts showed that his constant aim was to secure power to promote and increase the strength of Germany until none could stand against her; that he had no conception of law as understood in British countries; and that he would shrink from no violence and no crime in order to have his way. It was in the light of these circumstances that consideration should be given to the significance for Great Britain, the Dominions and Colonies of the Auslands Organisation of the National Sozialistische Deutsche Arbeiter Partei. The memorandum also suggested that in the light of the conduct of the

Abyssinian War, it was superfluous to say that Mussolini's principle in international affairs was the use of force without restriction and without restraint. It mentioned that there was reliable information that the heads of the Partito Nationale Fascista intended to use their organisation to sabotage British aerodromes and aircraft in the Mediterranean area, when it was expected that war between Britain and Italy might break out in 1935. The nature of the official British attitude and the complete failure to recognise the real position were demonstrated by the fact that a considerable number of Italians were at that time employed in the civilian establishment of British aerodromes in the Middle East. It was believed that some of these men were members of the Italian organisation for sabotage.

This memorandum was reviewed by the Joint Intelligence Sub-Committee, (the JIC assessed from all British agencies in the security and intelligence field for senior Ministers) who recommended that attention should again be directed to the potential danger of Nazi and Fascist Party Organisations in the UK and throughout the British Empire; that the Security Service should be directed to continue to study these problems; that detailed plans should be worked out for dealing with members of the Nazi Party organisations in an emergency; that the Service Departments should take certain protective measures in regard to the Armed Forces, establishments and firms engaged in secret and general munition work; and that the Dominions and Colonies should be warned of these special dangers and advised by the Security Service regarding special measures for their own protection. But: 'No important increase in the staff of the Security Service for dealing with these matters or with espionage was sanctioned as a result of these representations.'

In 1937, B Branch prepared additional notes on the Auslands Organisation and sent them to the Home Office, the Foreign Office, and the Directors of Intelligence of the three Services. Copies were also sent to the Dominions, India and the principal Colonies; later copies were sent to the State Department in Washington and the Deuxieme Bureau – French Intelligence – in Paris. These notes dealt with the Auslands Organisation emphasised the question of principle as affecting sovereignty, which arose from the fact that it was an extension on British territory of the machinery of the Party-State; and pointed out that its branches functioned as subsidiary organs of the German police system. They mentioned that E.W. Bohle, the Gauleiter of the Auslands Organisation had been appointed to be chief of that Organisation as now incorporated in the German Foreign Office. They enlarged upon previous references to the part which it was expected that the Nazi

Party abroad might play in time of war; and the part which it was apparently intended to play in the furtherance of the general policies of the Nazi leaders. Evidence was supplied of the manner in which Germans were allowed to acquire other nationalities while retaining their German nationality, when it was considered to be in the interests of Germany that they should do so, the implications being that the loyalty to Germany was regarded as binding, while the supposed allegiance to the foreign State was an empty form. For this and other reasons it was suggested that the whole question was one of special interest to the Dominions.[15]

While this was developing, an important addition was made to the ranks of MI5. During the spring of 1935 one young man, sailing aboard the *Doric* from Liverpool to the Mediterranean, faced an uncertain future. He was escorting fifteen boys, from the Whitgift School in Croydon, on their annual Easter trip. The young man was an assistant master at the school, where he taught History, English Literature, French and German; he also helped out with the school's sporting activities. But he was unsure whether to remain in teaching (the school considered him a first-class teacher despite the fact, kept hidden from his colleagues, that he had no experience in the profession before he took up the post) or if he should pursue a career in journalism. Also on board the *Doric* was Lieutenant Colonel Malcolm Cumming, a thirty-two year old, Eton and Sandhurst educated, former soldier. The two men became friends on the trip from Gibraltar to Naples. The young teacher talked with Cummings about the 'inevitable war' to come and how he would 'cheerfully fight if it came to the crunch'. Upon the return of the *Doric* to Liverpool, the two men parted with Cumming asking that the teacher should 'keep in touch'.[16]

Unknown to him the meeting would change the young man's life forever. The meeting with Cumming had not been a chance one. It would lead to an illustrious career in the service of his country. The young teacher would, ultimately, become Director General of MI5 (1953–1956); 'C' – Chief of MI6 (1956–1968); and finally Intelligence Co-ordinator to the Cabinet (1968–1972)[17] – a position created solely for him by the Prime Minister of the time, Harold Wilson. But his career would also be tainted by the failure to uncover a major Soviet penetration of British Intelligence.

The young, uncertain, teacher was Dick Goldsmith White. He had been born on 20 December 1906 in Tonbridge, Kent, the youngest of three children. His father, Percy White, owned an ironmonger's shop, James White & Son, a family business trading since the Napoleonic Wars. Dick's mother, Gertrude, was the daughter of an architect;

she believed in the simple values of honesty and hard work. The Whites were prosperous enough to employ servants who cared for the children and the family home. Dick was a sensitive child and he was hurt by the breakdown in his parents' marriage. Percy, a bit of an old romantic, was increasingly absent. With the outbreak of the Great War, Dick dreamt of his father's valour on the Western Front; in truth, though, Percy remained in England training troops for the front. His parents decided to protect their children from local gossip as Percy spent more and more time away from home: Dick was sent to become a boarder – after failing selection for Osborne Naval School on account of he being 'too skinny' – at Bishop's Stortford College in Hertfordshire. This was a school to which non-conformists of moderate means had traditionally sent their children for fifteen guineas a term. There Dick, and his brother Alan, were both sent. Dick appeared shy and inward thinking. But he was obviously good at one thing: athletics. In his later years, Dick White was captain of cricket, athletics and rugby. His was no longer the shy child who arrived in 1917. Yet he remained a thoughtful young man who went on to study History at Oxford.

Even in July 1935, three months after his return from the Mediterranean, any thought that this young man would become a secret agent, let alone direct British Intelligence – Joseph Conrad was one of his favourite authors – would have seemed an outrageous fantasy. But now it was that White received, by post, a Government envelope. He thought it was a tax demand. It was only when he spotted a War Office address that he opened the letter rather than leaving it to one side. There was a short note inside from a Guy Liddell. It referred to a recommendation from Lieutenant Colonel Cumming and suggested a luncheon meeting. Even now White did not know that Cumming was an MI5 officer. White decided to meet with the man from the War Office. He had no idea that he was being headhunted for the intelligence work; nor that the man seeking to recruit him – Guy Liddell – was working for MI5. This would be the first meeting between the two outstanding British counter-espionage officers of the Second World War.

During the 1914–18 war, his two brothers, David and Cecil, like Guy, had demonstrated their courage under fire and won the Military Cross. All three had joined the Royal Artillery as private soldiers before receiving commissions. Guy, like his brothers, had been educated at the University of Angers and all three spoke French fluently – at least one foreign language was a perquisite for intelligence work.[18] Short, with thinning hair, Liddell appeared to be 'either very mysterious or extremely shy'. It seems that he was both. Vanity dictated an attention to his dress. Subordinates were disconcerted by his habit of avoiding direct personal contact during interviews; instead Liddell would stare into the distance at the same time plucking at an imaginary hair on his head.[19] Liddell was married to the Honourable Calypso Baring, the wealthy and eccentric daughter of the Irish peer, Lord Revelstoke. They lived at their fashionable home in Cheyne Walk, Chelsea. Calypso's choice of décor was unusual – her wallpaper, in the entrance hall, consisted of copies of *The Times* newspaper.[20] The marriage, however, was not a happy one; so Liddell consoled himself with music – as an accomplished cellist – and his work.[21] He was also a very good dancer and, occasionally, during parties, Liddell would entertain guests by offering to teach an Irish jig – he, like his wife, had strong Irish connections. Liddell's marriage, however, broke down when Calypso suddenly departed for California to live with her half-brother Larry Tailer. She took their three children with her. Alone in London, Liddell moved to a flat in Sloane Street and absorbed himself in his work.[22]

From the beginning White was impressed with Liddell who revealed the real purpose of the meeting: the latter explained that MI5's task was defensive – to protect the United Kingdom and Empire against all forms of subversion. Liddell was MI5's expert on Communist subversion but he emphasised to White that the Security Service had to prepare for an inevitable war with Germany: White's knowledge of German and French was valuable. White agreed and 'knew at once that here was a man I took to without any hesitation whatever'. Liddell warned White that he would have to learn the job from scratch 'and I'm sure it will be interesting. Forget about school mastering and freelancing for the BBC. Don't make up your mind today. Just let me know as soon as you can.' White asked about the salary; Liddell replied: 'Pretty poor I'm afraid: £350 per year. That's the bad part, but the good part is that it's tax free.' At the age of 28, White was inclined not to accept the job on account of the poor terms of employment. So, he turned Liddell down; but White had not rejected a career within MI5 out of hand: he was not sure what the offer entailed as everything Liddell said to him was by the way of hints. 'I left it that they would have to say something direct or leave it.' But Liddell had been impressed; he commented: 'This fellow White is impressive. He knows precisely what he intends to do and how to carry it out.'

At a second meeting, Liddell asked if White would be prepared to travel around Germany in order to uncover Hitler's intentions. This was outside the remit of a MI5 officer and therefore an unusual request. White held no strong views about Nazism but was lured by events in Germany and the possibility of Britain facing her in war. White 'snapped at the bait. I saw the offer as a sort of early-up war service.' White accepted and became – unofficially at this stage – MI5's thirtieth officer – formally a private secretary to Liddell. Doubts, however, surfaced as White saw out his service at Whitgift School. A teaching post arose at Wellington College and White sought advice from John Masterman his old Oxford tutor. White was concerned because not only was his security as a teacher jeopardised but he was about to enter a world that relied on secrecy and duplicity. Masterman recalled that he did not try to influence White in either direction 'but his choice of profession turned out to be of signal benefit to the country'. White also revealed his doubts to Liddell as well; the MI5 man answered with an outline of spying history from the Old Testament to the roles played by Robert Cecil and Sir Francis Walsingham in Elizabeth I's reign, countering the Jesuits and other Roman Catholics conspiring against her. The danger now came from Communists and Nazis. White was convinced: 'It seemed clear to me that fascism was a monumental threat and that something catastrophic was going to take place.' White thus joined as MI5's first graduate officer. He learnt from Liddell the rudimentary rules of the intelligence game. White was impressed by Liddell's diplomatic skills, his intellect and his personality. Liddell explained how an Intelligence Officer's task was to establish, first, what an enemy said it could do; second, what in fact that enemy was capable of doing; and, third, what in fact it intended to do. For White: 'Even the obvious had to be said.'

On 1 January 1936, Dick White formally joined the Security Service based in offices in Cromwell Road, South Kensington. At the end of his first day, White and all the officers gathered for a drink by the fire in the common room to discuss the day's business. Most of them were elderly men. The only women employees were registry clerks or secretaries, making MI5 a 'debs' coffeehouse. Romance with the male staff was forbidden. At the end of the week, a female member of the secretariat would distribute brown envelopes in which were white five pound notes. All of this, for White, emphasised MI5 as part of the Director's (Kell) 'extended family'. It was on that first day that White became reacquainted with Malcolm Cummings who said: 'So we meet again. I hope they are looking after you?' He also met T.A. 'TAR' Robertson, introduced into the Service by Kell's son in 1933. Thomas Argyll Robertson had been commissioned into the Seaforth Highlanders following his graduation from Sandhurst. At the Security Service he shared an office in HQ with Liddell and his assistant, Millicent Bagot. His initial duties had been low key, consisting of following the Japanese Military Attaché around the country and buying drinks for informers in Aldershot pub houses to gain information on potential Communist troublemakers in the military. But White would find his 'great commonsense' and directness appealing. The senior officers working with White were Robertson and Jack Curry. White also met Maxwell Knight. His eccentric interests – in the occult, as well as his suspected bisexuality, and passion for wild animals as pets – earned him a reputation as 'a bit mad'.[23] White took an instant dislike to Knight, distrusting his maverick behaviour.

It was not long before White began to stand out among the collection of ex-Indian policemen hired by Kell who had come from 'next door' (the headquarters of the Indian police was also in Cromwell Road). This, though, was on account of his academic abilities rather than his natural flair for intelligence work: he forgot his passport when applying for his German visa; TAR Robertson brought it round, in a taxi. The episode only served to convince White that: 'I wasn't really cut out to be an intelligence officer at all.' But the trip to Germany convinced White of the danger from that quarter. He was astonished by 'the extraordinary way in which ordinary Germans had swallowed Hitler's mesmeric and evil influence'. He rented a room, in Munich, from 'Jew-baiters', experiencing, first-hand, the anti-Semitic ambience within Hitler's Germany. White returned to London, signed the Official Secrets Act and was assigned to analysing German intelligence activities in the UK. So poor was the Security Service's knowledge of its potential enemy that it did not know who was directing Germany's intelligence agencies or, even more alarmingly, the name of the main German foreign intelligence service.

White, however, found no evidence of German subversion in Britain. His superiors did not accept this, although subsequent events proved that White was quite correct in his analysis. His judgement was bolstered with the recruitment of an agent within the German Embassy: Jona 'Klop' Ustinov (father of Sir Peter) the press attaché to ambassador von Ribbentrop. Ustinov, born in Tsarist Russia, had served in the German Air Force during the last war; but he was also an ardent anti-Nazi, playing host to many British Intelligence officers in his flat in Earls Court. White was promoted about this time, in 1937, to became Klop's case officer. Ustinov provided the names of anti-Nazis in Germany who might be approached by the British. White reflected, years later, that MI5 had recruited 'a natural winner who wouldn't let us down… the best and most ingenious operator I had the honour to work with'. They remained friends until Ustinov's death. Klop, it seems, found White 'odd looking, very non-Establishment. A breath of fresh air. We are united by our dislike of certain Englishmen, especially what White calls the SIS types who are "Ivory from the neck up".' Working with Ustinov allowed White to become MI5's undisputed German expert.[24]

Towards the end of 1935, with a view to obtaining information about both of these subjects, Kell placed his officers in touch with a Mr A, a British subject who, 'although not of German race', had served in the German Air Intelligence Services in the war of 1914–18 and had a number of contacts in German official and diplomatic circles. Early in 1936, Mr A informed MI5 that he had cultivated friendly relations with von Putlitz of the German Embassy in London. Von Putlitz was a German Diplomat of the 'pre-Nazi school', who had been to Oxford and Harvard. He strongly resented the Nazi methods and came to the conclusion in 1936 that the 'tendencies of Nazi policy would lead to a war which would have fatal consequences for Germany. He conceived the idea that if he could help to induce the British Government to take a "strong line" with Hitler, this might tend to prevent the disastrous consequences which he foresaw.' He believed that by giving certain information regarding Nazi tendencies to Mr A, he might to a certain extent influence the British Foreign Office in the 'right direction'.

Towards the end of 1936, during the Spanish Civil War, von Putlitz urged the view that the British Government ought to show the 'greatest energy' in insisting that German troops should leave Spain. He said that such a demand would come at the right psychological moment as the Reichswehr had been urging that they should be recalled. At about this time he also supplied some 'illuminating' facts regarding Ribbentrop's attitude towards the abdication of King Edward. He said that Ribbentrop had given orders to the German press in London to refrain from mentioning the subject. The motive was not, 'as was wrongly supposed', due to a desire to be tactful towards the British people, but to a desire to be in the 'good books' of King Edward, 'whom he regarded as a certain winner'. Ribbentrop had even attempted to have a message conveyed to the King that the 'German people stood behind him in his struggle'. When the King abdicated, Ribbentrop's report to Berlin contained the following: 'The abdication of King Edward is the result of the machinations of dark Bolshevist powers against the Führer will of the young King. I shall report all further details orally to my Führer.' He issued strict instructions that no one in the German Embassy was to make any report to the German Foreign Office on this subject. Von Putlitz exclaimed to Mr A, 'We are absolutely powerless in the face of this nonsense!'

In September, 1936, von Putlitz had told MI5, through Mr A, that a war with Russia was regarded as being 'as certain as the Amen in church', and that it was felt that developments were getting beyond the stage where the Wilhelmstrasse or the more intelligent notions of the Reichswehr could influence their course. The view in Nazi circles was that a point would be reached in the not distant future, when Germany's relative superiority in armaments would begin to decline and that the 'optimum date for war against Russia should not be missed'. These circles were convinced 'that England would not move a finger' if Hitler launched an attack against Russia.

When Ribbentrop arrived in the German Embassy in London he was accompanied by a huge staff including members of his Dienststelle, secretaries and detectives from the Schütz Staffel. Von Putlitz found that members of the Embassy staff noticed that their desks were searched at night; and he felt that he was working in what he called 'a complete madhouse'. When Ribbentrop returned to the Embassy, from an interview with the Prime Minister, Neville Chamberlain, he announced: 'the old fool does not know what he is talking about'. Ribbentrop declared to his staff that his mission in Britain was to keep this country neutral during the coming conflict with the 'Red Pest'.

Mr A encouraged von Putlitz to give him information regarding the activities of the Nazi Party as seen from the Embassy; and regarding any matters connected with improper contact with underground activities on the part of attaches and other members of the Embassy staff, in regard to which there appeared to be increasing tendencies during 1936 and 1937. During this period numerous reports were obtained from von Putlitz on matters connected with German foreign policy and were communicated by MI5 to the Foreign Office. By November 1937, he told MI5 that Ribbentrop was more anti-English than ever, and was anxious to leave his post in London. Hitler, however, said, 'he always wanted to go to London, let him stay there'. At the same time Hitler had referred to Ribbentrop as 'ein Aussenpolitischer genie' (a genius in foreign affairs).

Early in 1938, MI5 learnt from von Putlitz that, in consequence of a decision by Hitler which was thought to have been prompted by Ribbentrop, the policy of seeking British friendship had been abandoned; and Ribbentrop had issued orders to this effect to his subordinates and commented that this meant that their objective should be to work for the weakening and ultimate downfall of the British Empire. At the same time the Italian Government had decided that the Non-Intervention Committee of the League of Nations, in connection with Spain, had created an 'impossible situation' for them and that it must be brought to an end. This view was placed before the German Government and the Party leaders acquiesced in it. The Italian

Government had accordingly decided to despatch fresh Italian troops to Spain; and openly to adopt the attitude that they were taking part in the war in Spain, thus abandoning the 'farce' of the Non-Intervention Committee. It was believed that this decision was not acceptable in circles in Germany; and that this had been one of the underlying factors in a recent crisis there. This information was communicated to the Foreign Office and MI5 were informed that it agreed with information received from other sources and that the Secretary of State was impressed by it.

At the same time, early in 1938, von Putlitz told MI5 that orders had been issued to intensify arrangements for espionage against Britain. The Abwehr Abteilung – German Secret Service – had issued instructions to this effect to the Military Attaché in London, and the German Consuls in the UK had been asked to furnish reports and to supply the names of agents suitable for obtaining military secrets. In the middle of February 1938, MI5 sent, to the Foreign Office, a summary of views expressed by von Putlitz. They were to the effect that the German Army would in future be the obedient instrument of Nazi foreign policy; and a recent purge had left the Nazis in complete control of the army. Under Ribbentrop, Nazi foreign policy would be an aggressive forward policy. Its first aim – Austria – had been partly achieved: Austria 'falls to Hitler like a ripe fruit'. After consolidating the position in Austria, the next step would be against Czechoslovakia. The view in German official circles was that, in the immediate future, a block of 130 million well-organised people with armies prepared to march at order (Germany, Austria, Italy and Hungary) would face the two great Western democracies whose people did not want to fight. 'It was quite clear that a bargain had been struck between Hitler and Mussolini. This involved German support in the Mediterranean and a free hand for Germany in Central Europe.'

Von Putlitz also felt that Britain was letting 'the trump cards fall out of her hands'. If she had adopted, or even now adopted, a firm attitude and threatened war, Hitler would not succeed in this kind of bluff. The German Army was not yet ready for a major war. He emphasised again and again that the British failed to understand the 'crudity' of people like Ribbentrop and made the mistake of applying their standards of thought and diplomacy in their dealings with them. He said that in his opinion, the situation had now developed in a way that made war inevitable. It was considered in Nazi circles that 'we were now at the beginning of a Napoleonic period; there would be big events and things would move with extreme rapidity. Ribbentrop had said in the German Embassy in London, "there will be no war before we are on the Bosphorus".'

Von Putlitz also reported that it was also hoped that Yugoslavia would come under German and Italian influence. During the summer of 1938, MI5 continued to receive and to send on to the Foreign Office reports from von Putlitz and other sources, regarding Hitler's aggressive policy and German preparations for war. In the middle of August, von Putlitz, who had been transferred to the German Embassy at The Hague, sent MI5 a cryptic message to the effect that 'drastic action was contemplated'. By arrangement with SIS, the Security Service sent a representative to get in touch with him and he informed MI5 that a paper had been circulated to German Embassies and Legations abroad, dated 3 August, and signed by Ribbentrop. It covered four pages and was drafted in 'typical Ribbentrop style'. The scope and nature of the document showed that it had been issued with Hitler's authority. The sense was as follows:

> The Czech question must be settled in accordance with our views before the autumn and, though we prefer peaceful methods, war must be envisaged. I do not agree with those who maintain that France and Great Britain will interfere. The lightening speed of our action will make any such effort on their part in vain. If they should decide to be involved in a quarrel, I would point out that the German army is far stronger and better prepared than in 1914 and we shall emerge victorious from this war.

There followed detailed instructions regarding German mobilisation. The date of action against Czechoslovakia was mentioned as 'before the 20th of September'. Von Putlitz added that Schulenburg, the German Ambassador in Moscow, had reported that Russia was not in a position to come to the aid of Czechoslovakia. His reports 'stiffened Hitler's attitude'. In MI5's view: 'There was reason to believe that opinion in the Reichswehr, and particularly in the Intelligence Branch of the German General Staff, was to the effect that war was inevitable; and that in this connection Hitler was now on the same side as Ribbentrop, Himmler and Goebbels.'[25]

By now Sir Vernon Kell was the last person who needed convincing of the threat from Germany. Some friends of Kell's friends, newly arrived from Germany, gave him graphic descriptions of what they had seen and heard at meetings in Nuremburg where Hitler was greeted with particular fervour. These friends had brought back newspapers with many illustrations of young men carrying spades over their shoulders, marching and countermarching in regimental formation. They carried banners with inflammatory slogans, 'their faces expressing most unhealthy exaltation'. These friends of Kell thought Hitler was simply aiming at lifting the Germans out of the despondency they had been in since 1918; they could see no danger in the wild enthusiasm that greeted Hitler everywhere. But as Kell 'constantly listened on the wireless to the torrent of words' with which Hitler addressed these young men, 'it seemed a systematic working up to a purpose which was clear enough', but which, as Lady Kell recalled:

> such admirers as those friends of ours, only regarded as being directed to rightful and peaceful resuscitation of the German people. A handshake with Hitler, which several of them had welcomed, seemed to them a sign of great friendliness for the British, for Hitler's meetings with foreigners were certainly a clever move on his part. But it was obvious by this time that his speeches were purely incitement to a War of revenge. It was just a case of watching and waiting for the moment that he would decide to move. All those with inside information were apprehensive as to what form that action would take.

One Sunday the Kells motored to York to see the Minster, and sat close to the famous Seven Sisters Window, 'surely one of the most beautiful to be found anywhere. We listened to the music in that superb setting, and to the singing of the famous choir, glad to forget for the moment the stress and strain of the times we lived in. Curious the way one had a sense of foreboding all through those years, the longing for peace was so great, yet the sense of unrest and frustration even greater.' Hearing Vernon's comments on the many disturbing events in Germany and in other countries, not only in Europe, Constance was left in no doubt as to the probabilities of a war too horrible to contemplate:

> Our children were too young to be involved in the first World War, but what of the next? Our two sons would certainly be fighting in that one. It would take all the Nation had to give, to fight it successfully, but we knew it would be our dauntless spirit that would take us to the top. Outwardly, everything was going on just as usual. Christmas came with its gaieties, and the New Year 1938 was greeted with every sign of merriment. If we felt foreboding, it was never apparent, and what there was to enjoy, we certainly enjoyed to the full.

But the stories that Kell and his wife were hearing about the treatment of Jews in Germany were 'almost unbelievable'. Kell had a letter from an eye witness describing how bands of youths were marched through the streets and sent into Jewish houses where they smashed up everything they could lay hands on, furniture, china, pictures, household goods of sorts. At the sound of a whistle, the youths would march out of the houses and a second batch of youths would march in to complete the wreckage and destroy as much of the home itself as they could. Many Germans, it was reported to Kell, felt so disgusted that they asked the Jews into their homes to give them meals and try to help them. Kell's correspondent, who was just a visitor spending a few weeks holiday in Germany, said, that what struck her so very unpleasantly, was the look on the faces of the youths that were marched into these houses: 'their eyes looked half drugged, almost as if they were hypnotised'. She realised it would be safer not to post her letter locally, for it might never reach Kell, so she waited to post it in Belgium.

And it was around this time that Sir Vernon and Lady Constance were invited to a 'rather strange cocktail party was given by the German Military Attaché – while all this tension was growing'. It was, Lady Constance remembered, a large party, people of many nationalities were present, 'and all the time there was a sense of malaise which seemed to grow more intense as the evening wore on – there was a sort of forced gaiety, very apparent. A look of strain and dislike on the face of our host did not tend to improve matters, even the very servants, all Germans, wore most forbidding expressions. Time dragged on, at last K thought we could leave, and thankfully, we said goodbye to our host, whose veneer of social politeness barely covered up very evident hostility. A few days later, the Japanese Military Attaché gave a similar cocktail party. This was not nearly so strained, and our host was as friendly as such an occasion warranted.'[26]

With the international atmosphere deteriorating, so Kell and MI5 prepared for war. A Precautionary Index had been devised in 1921 to supply the information required at any moment on the change from peace to war. So far as the General War Book was concerned the procedure before the outbreak of war was as follows – 'assuming always that everyone concerned both understands and acts on the instructions at the right time and in the right manner':

War Office War Book: 4(v) (d).
1. The Security Service moves the Home Office to put in force an order prohibiting the embarkation of any aliens without leave of the Immigration Officers.
General War Book Chap IX.

2. The Security Service, on behalf of all the fighting services sends to the Home Office a list of (a) persons and (b) classes of potential enemy aliens whose department is undesirable for military reasons.

3. The Ministry of Labour consults the Board of Trade as to the retention for industrial reasons of specially skilled potential enemy aliens and informs Home Office of persons or classes of persons whose departure should be prevented.

4. Home Office instructs the Police to check the register of aliens of specified nationalities and verify addresse(d) and occupations.

5. Home Office consults Security Service as to the declaration of restricted areas and as to restrictions on the employment of aliens in certain occupations so as to prevent sabotage, espionage etc.

The general policy thus is to allow unimportant enemy aliens to get out of the country and prevent those of any importance leaving. There the question of 'production versus security' is considered and later those enemy aliens are either interned or employed in industry, presumably under suitable supervision. The Security Service is expected to <u>know</u> (1) which potential enemy aliens should not be allowed to leave, (2) the areas where special restrictions should be enforced and (3) the occupations from which aliens should be excluded to prevent sabotage and espionage.

Turning now to the War Office War Book the requirements from the Security Service (MI5) are as follows.

War Office War Book 1938 44(v) (b)

1. Information as to the general categories of enemy aliens <u>and other persons</u> whom they will recommend for internment.

2. A list of enemy aliens to be interned (see also 2. On page 1.)

War Office War Book 1938 44(v) (e)

3. A list of a. persons and b. categories of aliens to be deported in the event of war.

War Office War Book 1938 44 (vi) (c)

4. A list of civilian members or employees of Govt. Offices with enemy connections or suspected of hostile associations or sympathy and recommendations as to whether they should continue to be employed.

War Office War Book 1938 44 (*I) (d)

5. A list of military personnel who are known to have enemy connections or suspected to be persons of hostile sympathy or associations.

6. Lists of clubs and resorts frequented by enemy aliens and persons of hostile associations which should be closed by the police.

The Security Services are expected by the War Office to <u>know</u>.

B 1. What categories of other persons than enemy aliens should be interned.

B 2. What enemy aliens should be interned.

B 3. What aliens should be deported.

B 4. What members of civilian staffs in Govt. Offices (a) have enemy connections; (b) are suspected of hostile associations or sympathy; (c) what action should be taken.

B 5. As in 4. For military personnel.

6. (a) the names of the clubs and other resorts frequented by enemy aliens and persons of hostile association. (b) whether any of them should be closed.

The simple solution would appear to be, as proposed in 1936, to keep a separate index for each list required. This however, is no solution as no index fulfilling the requirements of the lists could possibly be kept up to date. A study of the lists required will show that in each case there is an element of <u>judgment</u> as well as of fact. Now judgment in this case means an estimate of the value of the facts in the light of existing conditions at the time the judgment is exercised. This being so judgment is only valid on the day it is made, it cannot be made 6 months in advance and 6 months after it is made it is useless for practical purposes, however valuable it may be in retrospect.

To use a simile, it is like a balance sheet which shows the state of affairs on a certain date. It cannot be made in advance and in retrospect it merely shows the position as it stood on the date the balance sheet was drawn up.

The additional duties of the Security Service in war were based on those laid down under MI5 in Part II of the War Office internal War Book. The majority of these war duties commenced in the 'Precautionary Period', because the action involved was necessary as early as possible in a national emergency. While the Security Service in peace acted as a general government security intelligence agency for all Government Departments, in war it derived special additional duties from emergency or temporary enactments administered chiefly by the Home Office and the War Office. In peace, the Security Service carried out its duties to the State 'under the direction of one head, in one building'. In war a certain amount of decentralisation might be necessary, not only on account of the increase in the number of the duties but also because of the diverse localities in which they were performed. General control of all activities connected with the Security Service were, however, to remain, in war, with the Director, in view of his responsibility at all times for the complete co-ordination of the Central Security Intelligence Records required for State purposes in connection with national security duties.

During periods of minor Civil Emergency and Partial Mobilisation the Service would continue to work on the basis of its peace organisation with certain relatively minor additions to its staff, and the provision of small detachments to work actually on the premises of the War Office or other Offices. In the case of a 'big war', however, involving the introduction and administration of extensive Emergency Regulations, Special Aliens Orders, Defence Regulations, or Martial Law, a considerable expansion of military staff would be necessary, involving corresponding extra accommodation.

While it was not possible to lay down exactly the changes that would be necessary in the working of MI5 until the particular circumstances of a war were known, it was certain that the extra duties imposed by any state of national emergency would throw a specially heavy strain on Division A of the peace establishment which was charged with all Preventative and Precautionary Measures for purposes of Security, as well as the organisation and internal administration of the Service. Division A (of the peace establishment) would therefore be split into three, which would be known as 'A', 'C', and 'D' Divisions. The general duties of the War Divisions would then be as follows:

A Division: Organisation. Administration. Finance.
B Division: Security Intelligence and Investigations.
C Division: Civil and General Security Measures.
D Division: Defence Security Measures.

The general distinction between the duties of C and D Divisions was that the duties of C Division would be based upon Civil Enactments, including the Aliens Order and other enactments administered by the Home Office or Civil Departments, while D Division would be concerned more particularly with duties arising from the administration of such of the defence or other war regulations as were administered by the army, navy or air force. For the purposes of 'official' correspondence and reference for 'military' security purposes, these War Divisions of the Security Service would be known as MI5A, B, C, and D. Within the Security Service the War Divisions would be known as AS, BS, CS, and DS.

In order that the General Staff might be fully represented in the administration and control of the important military duties and interests involved in war, the following provisional allocation was made to Divisions of the Security Service in war, of the quota of General Staff Officers envisaged in the War Book:

1. The Director of the Security Service will remain outside the military scheme.
2. The Deputy-Director of the Security Service will be charged, (in addition to his duties as Deputy to the Chief of the Service) with the special supervision of 'Defence' Security Measures; and will be graded as "G[eneral]S[taff]o[fficer][grade]1 in charge of Section MI5 War Office".
3. Division (A) will be in charge of a GSo2, with one GSo3 and attached military and civil officers as necessary.
4. Division (B) will be in charge of a Civil Officer of the Security Service, but will contain one GSo2, who will be chief military assistant and deputy to the Officer in Charge of Division B.
One GSo3 will be in charge of the section (BS.6) concerned with special duties connected with the Internal Security of the Armed Forces, and one GSo3 in charge of the Section (BS.7) which deals with Counter-Espionage and Special Investigations concerning the enemy of the day.
5. Division (C) will be in charge of a Civil Officer, with necessary attached Civil and military officers.
6. Division (D) will be in charge of a GSo2, who will act as principal military assistant to the GSo1, MI5, for Defence duties, with necessary attached officers.

In order to avoid unnecessary changes in the existing designations and duties of the permanent sections of the Peace Divisions of the Service, the existing Sections Nos.1 to 12, would be allocated under their present numbers to War Divisions as in the following list. Additional temporary War Sections Nos.13 to 20 would be formed for the duration of war and allocated to Divisions as given below. Each War Section will be subdivided into Sub-Sections, as necessary; each Sub-Section being under the charge of a Civil or Military Officer of the Service:

WAR SECTIONS
SECTION L
LS Legal Procedure and Advice. Liaison duties with DPP and Legal Advisers of Government Departments.

DIVISION A

AS 3 Security Personnel.

AS4 Security Service Finance.

AS5 Organisation, Interior Economy and Routine.

AS13 Security Records and Registry.

AS14 Overseas Security Services.

AS15 Instruction in Security Duties. War Department Constabulary. Field Security Police. Mobilisation Schemes.

DIVISION B

BS6 Internal Security of Crown Services.

BS7 Defence Security Intelligence. Counter-Espionage and Sabotage.

BS8 Defence Security Intelligence. Special Investigations.

BS9 Civil Security – (Foreign).

BS10 Civil Security – (Home).

BS11 Security Police and Inquiries.

BS12 Security Technical Research.

DIVISION C

CS1 Enemy Aliens and Hostile Persons.

CS16 Aliens in War Service.

CS17 Credentials and Security Reports for War Purposes.

DIVISION D

DS2 Defence Security Measures. Protected Places and Areas.

DS18 Port and Frontier Controls.

DS19 Military Permit Offices.

DS20 Official Passes, Permits and Documents of Identity.

Kell was convinced that he had in place a Counter-espionage organisation ready to take on the Germans as MI5 had done in the last war.[27] But he could not have been more wrong.

12

'Come Along for a Cocktail'
The Case of John King 1939–1940

Leakage from the Communications Department, Foreign Office
It is desirable to place on record at this stage the inside history of
the serious case of leakage from the Communications Department
of the Foreign Office, which has been under investigation recently
and has resulted in the conviction of a member of that Department
on a charge under the Official Secrets Act in the Central Criminal
Court, the suspension of several others, and the decision on the
part of the Under Secretary of State to discharge or transfer the
remaining members of the Communications Department.[1]

On a late spring morning in May 1946, Maxwell Knight made the short
crossing across the Solent to the Isle of Wight. His purpose was strictly
business, rather than pleasure, for his final destination was Camp Hill
prison, where he was to interview a prisoner. His aims were twofold:
firstly he wanted to 'tie up one or two loose ends'; and secondly, he
felt that, given the prisoner's anticipated release, he should reassure
him that, should any of his 'previous associates' attempt to contact
him, he would have support and assistance from the Security Service.
On his arrival he met with Dr Matheson, the prison Governor, whom
he 'knew very well' and who told him that the prisoner he intended
to visit was 'becoming prematurely senile... was suffering from bad
rheumatism and uncertain heart, and was very enfeebled'.

When Knight eventually saw the prisoner, Captain John Herbert King,
he appreciated 'the point of the Governor's remarks'. King, it seemed,
could remember very little of his former life, despite Knight's guiding
questions. The only subject that provoked an emotional response was
that of Miss Wilkie, King's beloved mistress, which inspired an 'emphatic
defence', from King, who protested her innocence. It was clear to Knight
that his impromptu visit came as a 'considerable shock' to King whom,
Knight concluded, was apparently 'speaking what he believed to be true'.
Dr Matheson, who Knight met with again after the visit, corroborated
this. Knight had not needed to employ any 'breaking' tactics, for King,
a former Foreign Office Cipher Officer, after seven years in prison, was
already a broken man.[2]

Captain John King joined the Foreign Office communications
department as a temporary clerk in 1934. Born in Ireland in 1884,[3]

King was estranged from his wife and had been involved in a relation-ship with Helen Wilkie, who was employed at the Chancery Lane Safe Deposit in London, since 1934.[4] One of King's colleagues, Raymond Oake, had been working in Geneva in 1933 as a cipher clerk for the British League of Nations delegation. Oake was introduced, by his fiancée's stepfather, Captain Harvey, the Vice-Consul of Geneva, to his friend Henri Christiaan 'Hans' Pieck, a Dutch artist and architect, who worked from a rented studio at a local pensione. Oake and Pieck soon became firm friends, and Pieck confided to Oake that he would like to 'try his luck' in exhibiting his paintings in London and asked for Oake's help. Oake pledged his support; it was clear to him from the start that Pieck was not dependent on his paintings for his income. Pieck duly moved to London, spending occasional weekends with Oake's family in the genteel seaside resort of Herne Bay, in Kent. On a train journey from London to Herne Bay with Pieck, Oake recalled a chance meeting with a man called Mr Parlanti, a decorator who specialised in shop fronts and who offered to help establish Pieck in London, inviting Pieck to visit him at his offices at 35a Buckingham Gate.[5] But, unbeknown to Oake, Pieck was actually a Soviet agent (codename COOPER). Working under the direction of the Soviet spy-master Dmitri Bystroletov, Pieck had been sent to Geneva to identify and cultivate potential agents from the British contingent there[6] and had been brought to the attention of SIS, in reports from Holland, in 1930, as a suspected Communist agent.[7]

Since 1930, another Cipher Clerk from the Foreign Office, Ernest Holloway Oldham, had been passing documents to the USSR, after walking into the Soviet Embassy in Paris in 1929 and offering to sell a copy of the British Diplomatic Cipher. He gave a false name and wanted to broker a one off deal, but Bystroletov traced him and recruited both Oldham (codename ARNO), and his wife Lucy (code-name MADAM), pretending to be a Hungarian of noble birth who had fallen on hard times and unwittingly ended up working as a Soviet agent. Bystroletov's relationship with Lucy was, apparently, on 'an inti-mate footing'. The Oldhams, however, also gravely misled Bystroletov; Oldham told him various exaggerated tales of his seniority and impor-tance at the Foreign Office and Lucy Oldham claimed that her brother was Head of the Intelligence Service at the Foreign Office (a non-exist-ent post). Naively, Bystroletov and the Soviets believed the Oldhams's unlikely tales.[8] Oldham unsuccessfully tried to extricate himself from the Soviets turning to drugs and alcohol to cope with the pressure, eventually leaving the Foreign Office in 1932, although it is unclear whether he was dismissed or resigned. Desperate for money, he continued to visit his former colleagues and to pass material to the Soviets as well as identifying who, in the Foreign Office, might be promising potential Soviet agent material. One name on the list was Raymond Oake. Travelling on a Greek passport, using the name 'Hans Galleni' Bystroletov stayed with Oldham in London and took him on holiday. Bystroletov was concerned that Oldham had attracted the attention of MI5;[9] however it appears that, despite his drinking and erratic behaviour, Oldham was never under any suspicion. The wretched Oldham continued on a downward spiral and was found unconscious in his flat in September 1933 and pronounced dead on arrival at hospital; unable to bear the weight of his double life, he had gassed himself. The Soviets were convinced that he had been murdered by British Intelligence and Bystroletov himself feared for his life.[10] This fear was behind Bystroletov's decision to send Pieck to Geneva to recruit, rather than to dangerous London, where imaginary British assassins lurked.

Undoubtedly the greatest favour that Oake did for Pieck was in introducing him to John King in 1933 or 1934 during one of the Geneva trips. Pieck actively courted King, at one stage treating King and Miss Wilkie to an all expenses paid luxury touring holiday in Spain, although Pieck's wife complained that the whole holiday had been a 'real ordeal' and that King and Wilkie were 'incredibly boring.' In 1935, however, Pieck's perseverance paid off when he asked King about the possibility of obtaining information from the Foreign Office. Within seven months of his first meeting Pieck, King (now codenamed MAG by the Soviets) was handing over information for hard cash, which he desperately needed to pay for his son's education, his estranged wife's alimony and to keep Miss Wilkie in the style to which she was accustomed.[11]

In 1937, British Intelligence became aware that there was a leak in the Foreign Office. An unknown informant, referred to only as 'X', who had established a relationship with Pieck, approached SIS. 'X' claimed that Pieck, who had visited Moscow in 1929, had become a member of the Russian Intelligence Service around the same time and was charged with the special duty of penetrating the British Foreign Office. He was established in Geneva, where for two and a half years he cultivated the British official community, which consisted mainly of Consular personnel and the members of the various Foreign Office delegations to the League of Nations. Pieck enjoyed considerable success in winning the acquaintance and even the affections of a considerable number of British officials and successfully allayed suspicion by posing as 'the prince of good fellows, habitué of the International Club, always "good" for a drink, a motor expedition, or a free meal – a histrionic effort worthy of a better cause'.

X reported that, early in 1935, Pieck, having secured the 'inside agent' he wanted in the Foreign Office, transferred his activities to London, where, though the introduction from Oake, he went into business with the decorator, Conrad Parlanti, and set up offices in Buckingham Gate. A special locked room was set apart to photograph secret documents passed to Pieck by his 'inside agent' in the Foreign Office. This continued during 1935 and 1936, after which Pieck was removed by Moscow; his contact with King was transferred to a man called 'Peters', who continued to act as Pieck's substitute until about July 1937, when he was recalled to Moscow in connexion with the Trotskyist purge ordered by Stalin – and shot. Meanwhile, Pieck himself had fallen out of favour with Moscow owing to his refusal to liquidate Reiss, a Soviet agent in Switzerland, who was subsequently murdered by Soviet thugs as a Trotskyist suspect in October 1937.

Pieck and 'Peters', X went on, were under the orders of two Soviet head agents in Europe: a controller who instructed them as to the information required (whose identity X did not know) and a paymaster from whom they received all the money required for expenses and the payment of Foreign Office personnel. This person went by the pseudonym of 'WALTHER' and, on being recalled to Moscow from Holland in connexion with the purge, deserted to France and eventually travelled to the USA. Pieck had told X that his contact in the Foreign Office was Sir Robert Vansittart (at the time the Permanent Under Secretary); Sir Robert, he went on, had a mistress named Helen Wilkie, who lived in west London and was helpful in arranging meetings and acting as an intermediary between Pieck and 'Sir Robert'. 'Sir Robert' was, apparently, very concerned when Pieck ceased to be his contact in 1937 as his finances were stretched and he needed the regular payments for his services. SIS considered that Pieck had deliberately named Sir Robert Vansittart – who was not a Soviet agent – as a safeguard to ensure that any story X might tell would be 'treated with derision', which was exactly what initially happened, although the SIS section dealing with X's statement believed that Vansittart's details and situation could well be true of another unidentified member of staff within the Foreign Office. No serious enquiries were made concerning X's information until 15 September 1937. SIS chose to ignore this early warning, which they felt, at the time, was just rhetoric from a bitter former employee.

The anonymous X, it seems, was a former MI5 agent, who, for unknown reasons, was disregarded in September 1936. Following his dismissal, X sought out Pieck again, seeking employment, and started working in Pieck's office in Holland on a profit sharing basis. X soon noticed that, despite very little work being done, Pieck was affluent and enjoyed frequent visits to London and Paris. SIS considered that X had gone to Pieck 'in a bitter frame of mind towards HMG [His Majesty's Government] on account of his discharge, which he considered to be without justification'. Pieck then welcomed this disgruntled ex-Government employee and took him into his confidence admitting that he was actually a Soviet agent. Gradually X gained a fairly detailed account of Pieck's activities and *modus operandi*, which later proved to be absolutely accurate. Pieck also told X the details of his experiences in obtaining documents from the Foreign Office. However X never came under any suspicion from SIS who believed that X 'never… wavered in his loyalty towards his own country and there has never been the slightest ground to suspect him'. SIS felt that X was working to re-establish his relationship with His Majesty's Government and that while still in the 'closest contact with Pieck and before he sensed Pieck's real quality as a high class' Soviet agent he had constantly endeavoured to vindicate himself and so to regain official British favour and employment. He had, therefore, reported 'the important and sensational part played by Pieck in suborning Foreign Office personnel and procuring Foreign Office secrets' to SIS in dribs and drabs as it was confided to him by Pieck. Valentine Vivian, of SIS, lamented later that 'the full story was therefore in the possession of the SIS nearly two years ago and, though in no consecutive form, could have been acted upon then had it been credited. It was, however, treated with coldness and even derision, largely as a result of the prejudice against "X" himself.'

While X's information was sitting on file for two years, a telegram was received in the Foreign Office on 4 September 1939 from HM Ambassador, Washington. It detailed 'certain information received indirectly from "General W G Krivitski" [sic], the self-alleged ex-member of the Soviet Military Intelligence', who had recently defected and had published a series of articles in the *Saturday Evening Post* about Stalin's purges. Krivitsky also claimed that the Soviets had two British agents, a 'King of the Communications Department of the Foreign Office, and an unknown member of the Political Committee Cabinet Office' (Committee of Imperial Defence). Astoundingly, this communication rang no alarm bells for SIS.

It was not until 15 September 1939, when Conrad Parlanti (whom X had mentioned as Pieck's collaborator) came forward, that the warning bells finally sounded. It appears that Parlanti approached British Intelligence on his own volition, possibly because the war with Germany had broken out, telling officers that he had been in business with Pieck (having been introduced to him by Oake) in 1935 at the Buckingham Gate address. Parlanti revealed there was a special locked room located there that was set apart for Pieck. Parlanti had discovered that it was set up for photographing documents. He later discovered from Pieck's wife that Pieck was obtaining documents from contacts in the Cipher Department of the Foreign Office.

Parlanti already knew that Oake and another man, Russel, also of the Cipher Department, were familiar with Pieck, but there was, he said, another person who was the main supplier of documents. Parlanti once saw him and was able to describe him, but did not know his name. One important clue to his identity was that Pieck had told Parlanti that he had met him again recently at the Brussels Conference, where he was acting as one of the two cipher officers to the British Delegation. According to Parlanti, after he had met Pieck, in 1934 the latter eventually suggested that Parlanti should leave his employment as a shop fitter and go into business with him as he was prepared to put up the capital. Parlanti agreed, suggesting that they should have offices in Holborn, but Pieck opposed this and offices were taken in Buckingham Gate. Parlanti, at first, was unconcerned that Pieck had an entire floor for his own use and kept one room locked; but later he became suspicious and found means to gain admission to the room when Pieck was away. He found that the room contained a table, three feet above which was a Leica camera, obviously arranged so as to photograph articles placed on the table. Parlanti mentioned the matter to Pieck but was, he said, unable to get a reasonable explanation.

A little later Pieck invited Parlanti to visit him at his home in The Hague where he was introduced to Mrs Pieck; Parlanti became a regular visitor. During one of his visits Pieck suddenly announced that he had to go away on urgent business. Parlanti, by this time, was extremely suspicious of Pieck. When Pieck had set off Parlanti told Mrs Pieck of his doubts and asked her to tell him the real nature of the business in which she and her husband were engaged. Mrs Pieck broke down and ultimately told Parlanti that 'she and her husband and certain other persons were engaged in financial manipulations "for big money"' and that they were able to operate as they did because they were helped by a man in the code section of the Foreign Office in London. This man, she said, was in a position to see and have temporary possession of confidential documents, which he was in the habit of taking out of the Foreign Office and lending to her husband for a short time for the latter to photograph. On Pieck's return Parlanti claimed that he confronted him and Pieck confirmed that what his wife said was true; Pieck hinted to Parlanti that the matter was no concern of his and that it would be to his advantage to keep it to himself. Parlanti 'refused to have anything to do with the matter and soon afterwards broke off his association with Pieck and the business was closed down'.

Parlanti did not know the identity of the man in the Foreign Office and did not think it could be Raymond Oake, who had first introduced him to Pieck, although he knew that Oake was a good friend of Pieck and had accepted money from him. He did think, however, that the man concerned was a colleague of Oake's and that he had seen him when he was with Pieck one evening in May 1936, in the lounge of the Victoria Hotel in Northumberland Avenue. While Parlanti and Pieck were sitting there a man entered the hotel. Pieck immediately asked to be excused and followed the man to the other end of the lounge, rejoining Parlanti about ten minutes later. Parlanti saw that Pieck was placing what appeared to be documents typed in red on a buff background in an inside pocket. When he returned Pieck asked Parlanti if he knew the man; Pieck told him that the mysterious man had 'just brought me some stuff'. Parlanti could not say whether or not he knew the man as he had only seen his back. Pieck then left the hotel very shortly afterwards, after waiting a little while. Later Parlanti noticed that Pieck's private room was lit up. He believed that Pieck had just received confidential Foreign Office documents and was busy photographing them. Parlanti was able to give a description of the man he had seen from behind at the Victoria hotel and this description was found to fit that of John Herbert King. Parlanti also said that, while in Paris in June 1937, he had met Pieck who had said that he had not seen many of his old friends except 'my other friend from the Foreign Office'.

As a result of the information given by Parlanti, enquiries were made and it was ascertained that only two men from the Code Section of the Foreign Office had attended the Brussels Conference. One of these men, Colonel Scott Elliott, was 'above suspicion' and the other was John Herbert King. The penny finally dropped, particularly for SIS, that the 'Sir Robert' of X's report, and the unknown contact referred to by Mr Parlanti were one and one the same following Krivitsky's defection although the previous failure to act was excused on the grounds that:

> It is to be noted that at the time (4th September 1939) when KRIVITSKI's denunciation of King was received, Parlanti had not come forward with his voluntary statement and 'X's' information had not been resuscitated. We had, therefore, the bare word of KRIVITISKI – at the best a person of <u>very doubtful</u>

<u>genuineness</u> and one, moreover, whose ability to speak on such a matter with authority was even more doubtful – to incriminate Captain J H King of the Communications Department, whose record appeared on the surface to be quite impeccable.

King, who was known to be suffering from ill health, was immediately given special leave until 25 September and was placed under surveillance while his post and telephone calls were intercepted and scrutinised by MI5. It was decided that, on King's return to work, he and Oake should be interrogated at the Foreign Office by officers from SIS and MI5. Oake was to be questioned first in the hope that he would yield information to use in interrogating King. An examination of King's finances, however, proved seemingly fruitless: 'nothing whatever of a material nature had been ascertained as a result of surveillance, nor had King's banking account yielded any result except to show that his small official salary of between £300 and £400 pa had been regularly paid in and that his account had consistently been in credit in a very moderate sum. This, then, was the very unpromising state of affairs when the SIS and MI5 officers met on the morning of the 25th September for an informal conference prior to interrogating Oake and King.'

At the conference, X's reports were produced which included the statement that 'Sir Robert Vansittart' was keeping a 'Helen Wilkie' in a West London flat, to act as a contact centre for Pieck. A piece of documentary evidence to support this, was a telephone installation card for 'Helen Wilkie, 218 Hamlet Gardens, Ravenscourt Park, W6', which had been clandestinely obtained from Pieck's possession. This card was the key that unlocked the puzzle giving credence to the much maligned X: 'This was immediately identified by the officer in charge of the MI5 side of this case as the name and address of a lady friend of King with whom recent surveillance over his movements has proved him to be on regular calling terms. The fact had previously had no significance whatever.' Now it drew King inextricably within the framework of Pieck's activities and proved that from X's, Parlanti's and Krivitsky's information 'we were dealing with connected statements of actual fact, upon which we could rely in pressing out examination of persons already involved in dealings with Pieck, or who might run out to be involved as a result of these interrogations. From this point onwards the investigation proceeded towards its speedy and successful completion without any real check and again, therefore, we have to give "X" the credit for the elucidation of this unsavoury case.'[12]

Upon MI5's advice, Oake was arrested by Special Branch and interrogated, on one occasion for nine hours, giving four statements during

25 and 26 September 1939. He was co-operative, describing how he first met Pieck in Geneva, and was on 'the closest terms of friendship with him' between 1933 and 1935, 'since when, according to Oake, he has not seen him'. In May 1935, Pieck and his wife were guest's at Oake's wedding, however 'they left without saying goodbye' (possibly Pieck's wife found the wedding as tedious as the trip to Spain with King and Wilkie), and Oake maintained that he had not only not seen Pieck since but had 'no explanation from him of the sudden and mysterious disappearance'.[13] He admitted taking money from Pieck, and enjoying his 'generosity' but insisted it amounted to nothing more than a few gifts, such as an all expenses paid trip to Pieck's home in The Hague, and several meals in expensive restaurants that Pieck insisted on paying for. Oake also stated that Pieck had lent him money on only two occasions; firstly one hundred Swiss francs in Geneva to save him the bother of having to change currency, and secondly, the sum of fifty pounds, of which Oake was short, to buy a car – a second hand Morris 10. Oake and his wife were 'extremely puzzled' at Pieck's disappearance, especially as he and his wife, Berny, had flown in from Holland for their wedding and given them as gifts 'a large gilt framed mirror and a large bouquet of flowers' in addition to which, Pieck took Oake aside and told him that 'as a wedding gift from him personally, he would like to "washout" his loan to me'.[14]

Pieck appears to have dropped Oake around the time that King started working for him; Oake had clearly served his purpose in helping Pieck to net a bigger fish. Oake was fortunate enough to escape prosecution, but was dismissed from his post; although SIS and MI5 considered that he was no wide-eyed innocent:

> He made a fairly good impression, but we were left with a feeling that he was withholding facts regarding monetary relations with Pieck, with whom he had undoubtedly been on terms of close intimacy until 1935. From these statements and from his demeanour we have come to the conclusion that Oake is unlikely actually to have sold Foreign Office secret telegrams to Pieck. We consider, however, that Oake obtained full value from him from the introductions he was able to obtain from him in Foreign Office and business circles.

Both SIS and MI5 considered that Oake 'must have had knowledge – or at least definite suspicions – of the real nature of Pieck's activities and we do not doubt that, in receiving monetary and other presents from Pieck, Oake knew that he was receiving payment for services rendered, though he no doubt practised some form of self-deception that prevented him from facing this fact'. Oake it seems suffered from greed, naivety and a tendency to bury his head in the sand, rather than a desire to betray his King and Country.

John King, however, was a different matter; he was initially interrogated on 25 September, following Oake's questioning:

> He made a thoroughly bad impression, pretending at first to be unable to identify the photograph of Pieck and trying desperately to maintain that his acquaintance with Pieck was confined to a few chance meetings at bars. His demeanour was furtive and guarded in the extreme. He was tripped up in a number of lies and only replied truthfully to questions of which he clearly believed his questioners to know the correct answers. Though he was several times on the point of collapse, he maintained his attitude of reserve to the end of a very prolonged interview.[15]

From the start of the interrogation, the flustered King constantly contradicted himself and had apparently 'forgotten' everything:

> Q: Do you recognise this photograph?
> A: No, I don't.
> Q: It doesn't remind you of anybody?
> A: Oh, yes it does. It's Pieck.
> Q: Who is Pieck?
> A: He was a friend of Oake's.
> Q: Where did you first meet him?
> A: Um…um…the first time I met him was in a bar in London.
> Q: Could you give me any idea when that was?
> A: I should say four or five years ago.
> Q: That would be 1935?
> A: Yes. That is the first time I ever met him. Never met me anywhere else.
> Q: Not in Geneva?
> A: Yes, he was there. I met him four of five years ago – he was in the Club.

King insisted Pieck had never invited him to dine, never visited him, nor had he ever visited Pieck. He eventually admitted meeting Pieck at the Victoria Hotel, when invited by Pieck to 'Come along and have a cocktail tonight', but professed to have absolutely no knowledge as to Pieck's occupation, or reasons for being in London.[16] During King's interview, an MI5 officer, accompanied by Special Branch officers, searched Helen Wilkie's flat and also the Chancery Lane Safe Deposit, where she was employed:

> In the flat a very large number of papers, correspondence, diaries, etc. were seized, which proved Wilkie's association with Pieck, King, Oake and other members of the Foreign Office Communications Department. At the place of business, two discoveries of the first importance were made: (a) A sum of £1,300 in various denominations of notes in Helen Wilkie's own safe deposit, which she stated was King's property and (b) Twenty-one copies of Foreign Office confidential prints, dating from 1922 to 1924, some of them marked in pencil with Major Quarry's name. These Helen Wilkie stated were the property of Major F J Quarry of the Communications Department, who had made them over to her sister, Elsie Wilkie, for safe keeping.[17]

When presented with this incriminating evidence, during the latter part of his interview, King maintained his story:

> my explanation for the possession of this money and its present location is that I have accumulated it over a course of years, commencing in the year 1935 or 1936: it is mostly the proceeds of gambling. I gave it to Miss Wilkie to keep for me in case of war. I gave it to Miss Wilkie some years ago, I think in 1935. It's my money; Miss Wilkie was merely keeping it for me. I cannot recall where I got the notes in question from, but I can remember that I did not draw them from my own banking account.[18]

Helen Wilkie was interrogated but 'maintained an attitude of reserve'[19]; when asked about the banknotes found at her workplace, she coolly replied, 'I am looking after them for Captain King.' Concerning the parcel of documents that were found, clearly marked 'Confidential' and 'Secret', she stated that 'they are papers which Major John Quarry asked me to keep for him. I packed them in the parcel and sealed them.'[20] Helen Wilkie was charged on 26 September 1939 under Section 2 (2) of the Official Secrets Act; King was charged with the same offences on 28 September, but was unaware of Wilkie's arrest. They were both brought separately to Bow Street Magistrates Court on 28 September. The wily Inspector Rogers who had questioned Wilkie and sat in on King's interrogation, 'ordered things so that King was able to have a glimpse of Helen Wilkie leaving the dock, just as he himself stepped into court. The effect on King was cataclysmic, he tried to call out to Helen Wilkie but Inspector Rogers prevented him.'

King was left reeling at the shock of seeing his beloved in court; for him this was his breaking point and he cracked spectacularly. He immediately asked to make a statement, but Rogers decided to let him 'stew in his own juice for a while'. Rogers realised that King was unwell and provided him with whiskey and 'a good meal' before interrogating him for fourteen hours, walking around the prison with him and generally 'getting on the right side of the man'. Rogers's persistence paid off; King confided several things, including that he had become estranged from his wife when she left him to become the mistress of another man.[21] Desperate to shield Helen Wilkie, King went on to make a full confession:

> I first met Henri Pieck about 1933 or 1934 in the International Club in Geneva. I was introduced to him by Mr Raymond Oake. Pieck had come there from Bari where he had been engaged on behalf of the Dutch government on work connected with a trade exhibition there. I was in Geneva as a member of the British Delegation to the League of Nations engaged on cipher work. Oake was then courting the stepdaughter of Capt. Harvey the then Principal Passport Control Officer at Geneva and has since married her. I know definitely that Pieck was a friend of Capt Harvey and I recall an evening when Pieck, Harvey, his stepdaughter, Oake and myself all motored out to a little village, 15 kilometres from Geneva, for supper and that I went on Pieck's invitation.
>
> I saw Pieck a good few times when I was at Geneva on that occasion; he was a good mixer and in fact, he knew most members of the International Club and several members of the British Delegation. As far as I can remember I only saw him in Geneva during that one session.

The next time that King met Pieck was in London, probably in 1935. During the time that King was in his company at Geneva 'he never once mentioned the subject of my obtaining for him information from the Foreign Office'. When they met in London, Pieck told King he knew a big banker in The Hague, who could make money for both of them, 'if I could get for Pieck, information passing through the Foreign Office to and from various Embassies, from which Pieck and the banker could get advance information as to the trend of political affairs thus enabling them to make profitable deals in the stock markets and the money exchanges. Pieck said that if I did this he would share his profit with me. I agreed to do so.' In his defence King pleaded: 'I am not a permanent civil servant and am not entitled to a pension. I felt that by this means I could obtain some money to provide for when I retired without in any way endangering the security of the State.' He handed to Pieck, from time to time, copies of telegrams coming in from Embassies – for example, reports of conversations between Hitler and the British Ambassador or between Kemal Ataturk and HM Ambassador in Turkey: 'They were never of any great political importance,' King added, unconvincingly. The telegrams were always decoded copies, and never in cipher. They were spare copies that were available in the room. King:

> used to meet Pieck at various places – Victoria Hotel, his own hotel in Lancaster Gate – the largest one facing the park, I think it was called Lancaster Gate Hotel, and at his office in Buckingham Gate. In one room of the office was a trestle, a lamp and a camera, but I never saw Pieck photograph anything. I used to pass the telegrams onto him to retain, there was no need to have them photographed or copied. Pieck paid me sums of money varying between £50–£200 at a time, these being according to him the profit from transactions that had taken place as a result of communication of previous telegrams.

In 1936, Pieck left but before doing so he introduced King to a man named Petersen (this was the aforementioned Peters). King believed he was a Hungarian, married, and his wife passed as an American. He was a very tall, cadaverous looking man, aged about forty. King first met him in Pieck's office in Buckingham Gate and the latter said that Petersen would 'carry on instead of him'. King kept in touch with Petersen for about eighteen months, until June or July 1937, when he told King he had to go away for a month or so. Since then King had never seen or heard of him. This last meeting was at King's flat in Chelsea. During these eighteen months King handed to Petersen copies to Foreign Office telegrams in the same way as he had to Pieck:

> I used to meet him in various places, including my flat then in Holbein House, Chelsea, my room at the Royal Court Hotel, where I stay about three weeks, and my present flat. He was very secretive and the only indication I had at any time of his address was that he once told me he was staying near Marble Arch. I met him sometimes once of twice a week, but sometimes he went

away for a period of weeks. I received various sums, generally £100 or £150.

While Pieck never asked King to obtain a Foreign Office cipher, Petersen did on many occasions.

> Looking back on things now, I realise that the money they gave me was given merely in the hope of being able to persuade me to get for them the cipher and re-ciphering tables but I always refused, and I swear on my oath I have <u>never</u> taken any ciphers or tables out of the Foreign Office. In other words, I have never transmitted to any person any cipher or re-cipher tables or in any way been party to such transaction.

All the documents from King to Pieck and Petersen 'were already decoded. Although I admit to my great regret I have been foolish and weak enough' to communicate confidential Foreign Office messages to Pieck and Petersen. 'I have not had anything to do with the communication to persons outside the Foreign Office of any ciphers or re-ciphering tables.'

While King claimed that he could not remember how much he had received from the two men he thought it was about £1,200 from Petersen and £1,300 from Pieck. He handed about £1,300 of this to Helen Wilkie 'to keep for me... I knew that she was employed at the Chancery Lane Safe Deposit and told her it was to be for her benefit if anything happens to me. I swear that she has absolutely no knowledge of the origin of that money or of the nature of my association with Pieck. Naturally I had to introduce Pieck and his wife to her but all that she knew were that they were friends of mine.' He admitted that, in 1935, Miss Wilkie and he went with Pieck and his wife on a motor tour in France and Spain but: 'It was merely a pleasure trip; we each paid our own expenses.' As for Petersen, 'Miss Wilkie has never met him and does not know of his existence.' In conclusion King put on record how greatly he regretted:

> my crass folly in ever being persuaded to commit the wrong to which I have confessed voluntarily and quite openly. During this period of tremendous mental anguish while I am not in any way trying to mitigate my actions I do believe that I have revealed all I can remember. Should anything else come to my mind I will ask for a further interview with Inspr Rogers and pass it on to him. I cannot emphasise too strongly my absolute conviction of Miss Helen Wilkie's entire

innocence. I wish finally to point out that in 1917 while serving in the army in Egypt I suffered a severe mental illness and nearly lost my life since when I have had periodic mental lapses.[22]

The search of King's flat had also revealed that he had a bank account with Lloyds Bank Ltd, Finsbury Circus. On examination it was ascertained that this account was opened in 1913 but until February 1936 there was never a balance of more than a few pounds. However, between February 1936 and June 1937 King paid no less than £3,010 in cash into the account. The payments were, in the main, in Bank of England notes. Investigations were made into the history of these bank notes and of those found in Wilkie's safe, and it was found that the majority of the notes emanated from Moscow Narodny Bank (known to have been used by a Paul Hardt), Rotterdamasche Bankvereeniging at Rotterdam and Amsterdam (also traced to Paul Hardt and Pieck).[23]

Major Francis John Quarry, whose documents Helen Wilkie claimed she was 'looking after', was also interrogated on 25 September and made a statement on 26 September. Quarry, having learned what had taken place with Wilkie, visited Scotland Yard voluntarily and made the statement in the presence of representatives of SIS and MI5. Wilkie's sister, Elsie, was his mistress and Quarry was a frequent visitor at the flat shared by the two sisters and their mother in west London. Quarry claimed that the documents found at Helen Wilkie's workplace, dated from 1922–1924, and had been kept by him for 'pathetically sentimental reasons', as some of them mentioned him by name and were signed by Lord Kilmarnock. Quarry recalled meeting Pieck at the Wilkie sisters' flat in 1935 or 1936 and understood 'that he was a Dutchman but I knew not what his business was'. A veteran of the Boer War, Quarry enjoyed a distinguished career, serving as Chief of Intelligence and Chief Political Officer of the Inter-Allied Rhineland Commission until 1929. In 1938 he obtained employment as a cipherer at the Foreign Office. He first met King in 1928 and helped him obtain a post as personal clerk to Lord Kilmarnock. From this point onwards, Quarry and King were firm friends. Quarry had met the Wilkie sisters while holidaying in Knocke, Belgium in 1931 and renewed the acquaintance on returning to London, introducing King to Helen in 1934. Quarry noted that when he joined the Foreign Office in 1938 King became noticeably cooler towards him, and Quarry was hurt by this, feeling that 'having known me for so long he might have been a little more friendly'.

Quarry enjoyed a 'close friendship' with Elsie Wilkie and stated that for the past two years or so Helen Wilkie had been addicted to 'rather heavy spirit drinking' and often came 'home at night quite "tiddly"'. He expressed concern that Helen had changed over the last few years; '... she had been quite a smart woman and took a pride in her personal appearance, but since then she has become increasingly slipshod and tended to neglect herself'. Although this could have been a result of her heavy alcohol consumption, Quarry laid the blame for this squarely at King's door: 'I do however think that in itself her friendship with King had some bearing on the matter. He is not a very entertaining companion and I know that she is quite under his domination... Elsie has from time to time mentioned her worries regarding Helen to me.' When asked about Oake, Quarry was uncomfortable, feeling that it was 'a terrible question to ask a man regarding a colleague but my candid opinion is that he is inconsequent and has no idea how to conduct his finances. He is very often "broke".' Quarry had borrowed fifty pounds from King in December 1936, when his first wife unexpectedly sued him for alimony, but stated that this was the only financial transaction that they had ever been involved in. King later wrote Quarry an unpleasant letter referring to the loan 'implying that I had no right to ask him for the money'. Quarry was adamant that he had never been approached by foreign agents, stating that during his time at the Foreign Office no one had even hinted to him that he should 'do anything not consistent with the rules of the service'. He also took the opportunity to name three men whom he personally suspected were foreign agents.[24]

Quarry found himself in the same position as his colleague, Oake, escaping prosecution, but losing his job – therefore guilty by association:

It will be remembered that twenty-one specimens of Foreign Office prints were found in the possession of Helen Wilkie and stated by her to have been made over to her sister, Elsie Wilkie, by Major Quarry for safe keeping. It was considered that Quarry was unlikely to have had any criminal connexion with Foreign Office leakages. He had, indeed, only been engaged in the Communications Department since January 1938 and the available evidence tended to show that the connexion between the Soviets and King ceased about July 1937. He might be considered liable on formal grounds to prosecution under the Official Secrets Act in respect of the papers retained by him when he ceased to be a member of the Rhineland High Commission, but the date of these papers and his clear innocence of criminal intentions in respect of them rendered a charge unsustainable. On the other hand, he is of an unsavoury type which we consider should not be engaged in a key position, such as that of a cipher officer; he has been closely associated with members of a criminal conspiracy and was in touch with Pieck through the Wilkie sisters at the time of Pieck's last visit to London in November 1937. He has been suspended and we do not consider he should be permitted to return to duty.[25]

How successful Pieck had been in penetrating the Foreign Office without any one contacting their superiors was alarming. Other employees within the Communications Department, namely Russel, Kinnaird, Captain Maling and Harvey had all been noted as knowing Pieck. All were investigated and only Russel seems to have struck a chord, although he stated that Pieck 'never on any occasion asked me questions of a political or economic nature nor did he try to extract any information from me relative to my work or any other matter'. He too, had not seen Pieck since Oake's wedding, at which he was also a guest, and corroborated Quarry's statement that 'Oake was, and is very generous and is often financially embarrassed'.[26] As SIS and MI5 considered the other associated with the case it was thought that while Russel seemed to have known Pieck 'only less well than Oake and King, and to have been on cordial terms with him during the relevant period... There must remain in our minds therefore some suspicion' that Russel 'may have known, or guessed at, Pieck's real activities, though there is no evidence that he was criminally involved'. Kinnaird, Maling and Harvey seem to have known Pieck 'only very slightly and may be acquitted of suspicion'. Maling, however, 'not only disliked, but suspected, him, and it should perhaps be placed' to Maling's 'credit that he seems to have been the only member of this circle of Foreign Office friends of Pieck's who retained his critical faculties in the face of Pieck's undoubted charm and lavish hospitality'.

Helen Wilkie was charged on 26 September 1939 under Section 2 (2) of the Official Secrets Act. However, the combined factors of King's confession exonerating her, Quarry's confirmation that he had asked her to safeguard his documents and her cool unshakeable demeanour meant that no charge was able to be sustained against her; though SIS and MI5 obviously thought she was guilty, they had no grounds or evidence to prosecute her: 'It has not, however, been found feasible to sustain this charge in view of the purely formal nature of the transgression of the act committed by Quarry in confiding these papers to her and to her sisters and, though she is deeply involved with King in the major crime, this charge would not sustainable in law owing to the fact that King's statement, upon which the prosecution have relied in the case against him, definitely, though untruthfully, exonerates her.'

There was some thought of interning her for the duration of the war under Emergency Powers, 'but for a variety of reason, including her very indifferent health, this course has not been considered feasible'.[27] On 9 October, King, probably carrying the can for his mistress, was committed to the Old Bailey, for trial under the Official Secrets Act. He was duly convicted and sentenced to ten years at His Majesty's pleasure, the first spy to be unmasked since the outbreak of World War II.

The King case changed how British Intelligence viewed Walter Krivitsky, the Soviet defector. MI5 had initially been dubious, but not now. Krivitsky had been born in Poland in 1899 as Samuel Ginsberg, but adopted his name as a revolutionary *nom de guerre* when he joined Soviet Military Intelligence around 1917, operating in Europe, until 1937, when he was sent to The Hague to co-ordinate Soviet Intelligence operations throughout Northern Europe. He was disturbed by Stalin's purges and the death of his close friend Ignace Reiss, a fellow undercover Soviet agent, who defected and was tracked down and murdered by the Soviets in Lausanne in September 1937.[28] Fearing for his life, Krivitsky defected in Paris in 1937, eventually travelling to the United States at the end of 1938. Initially, it was difficult for British Intelligence to give any credence to Krivitsky's information, but X's statement convinced them to give the matter some serious consideration, although they were still confused: 'One puzzling factor in this case was… represented by the difficulty of accounting for the accuracy of KRIVITSKI's information regarding King. Why should KRIVITSKI have ever been in a position to obtain this accurate detail?' This last missing portion of the puzzle fell into place and completed the pattern on the 6th October when 'X' was interrogated and made a 'statement of the highest value.' He was quite unaware that action had been taken against any member of the Foreign Office and in endeavouring to assist SIS and MI5 at arriving at the real identity of 'Sir Robert', he remarked: 'I believe KRIVITSKI would be able to tell you who he is if you are able to get hold of him.' X was asked why he thought Krivitsky could help and immediately replied, 'because KRIVITSKI is "WALTHER" the paymaster for Northern Europe, from whom Pieck and Peters got their funds to pay the Foreign Office agents'. While this was 'not only fully credible' but it was 'of very great importance since it shows that we must record the rest of KRIVITSKI's information as a statement of fact'.

Despite the conviction of King, the case was still considered 'disappointing'. Pieck was still at large and possibly contacting the Soviet and Nazi Secret Services. Furthermore: 'There seems no doubt that the leakage, for which King himself was responsible, ceased about July 1937, yet we have had indications that there has been leakage since then, both to the Italians and to the Germans – though there is nothing to show whether this has been taking place through a single identical channel, or through different and independent channels.' It was conceivable that, when Pieck and Petersen ceased in 1937 to operate as channels of supply to the Soviet Secret Service, 'they were replaced by other Soviet intermediaries, but, if so, it seems strange that they should not have made use of the valuable and pliable King. That they did not do so is clear from the evidence of the money found in the Chancery Lane Safe Deposit and in the banking account, Lloyds Bank, Finsbury Circus – all of which dates back to 1937 or previously'. And it was worrying, regarding other Government offices, in the testimony of Krivitsky 'that the Soviets had (or have) an agent in the "Political Committee of the Cabinet Office". This remains an ugly, unsolved puzzle, which, however, in view of the accuracy of KRIVITSKI's information as regards King, must be accepted as an equally serious statement of fact.' All that could be done in this connection was 'to continue certain incomplete lines of enquiry, suggested by the evidence, and hope that these in course of time may assist in clearing up this second point in KRIVITSKI's information'.

MI5 and SIS knew then that there were other unknown spies out there damaging Britain's national security. What, for example, of the mysterious 'Peters' or 'Mr Peterson'? Some of the money lodged in King's account, Lloyds Bank, Finsbury Circus, had been traced to Paul Hardt who had come to notice as being identical with the 'Peters' who had been involved in the Woolwich Arsenal spy ring. MI5 and SIS discovered that Hardt left England hurriedly on 24 June 1937 and there seemed no doubt whatever that the 'Peters' and 'Petersen' of the King case was Hardt. If X's story, of 'Peters' having been recalled to Moscow about July 1937 and there shot was true, 'it would account for the fact that all the elaborate enquiries, which have been made here, in France and in Holland,' regarding him, 'have entirely failed to locate him'. Subsequent information, however, discovered by SIS seemed to point to Hardt being still alive, though disgraced.[29] In fact, Paul Hardt, (Soviet codename MANN), was actually Teador Maly, a Hungarian priest turned Soviet agent, who was recalled to Moscow in 1937 and shot, on the grounds that he was a suspected German spy.

The Glading and King cases demonstrated quite clearly that there was a continuing Soviet threat. The first case revealed the role played by certain members of the CPGB. In many ways MI5 was on top of this threat and the relationship: MASK was the codename for the radio interception programme operated by the Government Code and Cipher School (GC&CS), under the control of SIS, that intercepted and read 14,000 messages of encrypted traffic between Moscow and Comintern members around the world. At it most intensive level of interception it ran from 1934 to 1937. These intercepts were, consequently, available to the British Government and proved, to it, that Comintern was controlled by the Soviet Government. MASK showed that Harry Pollitt, the CPGB's General Secretary, sought instruction from Moscow on nearly all major policy issues. He also received personal expenses from Moscow.[30] A microphone, codenamed TABLE, monitored all his office conversations in King Street. KASPAR, another microphone, recorded sound from another CPGB building in Great Newport Street.[31]

But MI5 was slow to realise the nature of the threat that was now emanating from the Soviet Union: how the ideological dimension of Communism in offering a utopian solution to the injustices of the world might appeal across class lines to idealistic men and women. Maxwell Knight had been alert to this possibility when one of his agents, Tom Driberg, gave him information about 'Café Communists' who tended to be public school and Oxford or Cambridge educated. Knight recruited Bill Younger, stepson of his friends Dennis and Joan Wheatley, to spy on Oxford undergraduates.[32] But not on Cambridge undergraduates.

Britain, and its intelligence agencies, were facing a far more sophisticated threat from espionage than it had in the war with Germany and MI5 faced two parts of that body. While MI5 was aware of the agencies of that enemy, it was only with the interrogation of Krivitsky, in 1940, that a detailed picture of it was pieced together. The Soviet Military Intelligence Department or Razvedupr was known in Russian military circles as the Fourth Department or OMS. Its function was to acquire, collate and distribute every kind of information both within and without the USSR that might be of use to the General Staff. The sections of the Fourth Department of primary importance regarding the British Empire were the second and third sections. The second section dealt with the results of the third section's activities. It collated the information obtained, and distributed it to the correct departments. The third section dealt with all matters concerning the acquisition of military information from countries outside the Soviet Union. This section was also charged with the work of 'decomposition', that was the creation in countries with which the USSR might find itself at war; and of internal situations which would be of value to the Russian Army. Subversive activities in foreign military forces was an important part of that work. Agents of the third section employed abroad were divided into main classes: legal and illegal *residents*.

Legal *residents* were members of the Fourth Department for whom places were found on the staffs of Soviet Embassies or Legations. The duties of the legal *residents* was to collect all possible military information which could be obtained through contacts made by them or by the military attaché and to assist the illegal *resident* by every means in his power; for example, acting as a postbox and arranging for the ciphering and deciphering of urgent messages for him. Illegal *resident* agents usually had a business cover. Sometimes a firm was created for a particular purpose. Often the firm would be unaware of the true character of their representative. Alongside the Fourth Department, was the foreign section of the Soviet Security Service known as the GUGB (*Glavone Upravlenie Gosudarstvennoi Bezopasnosti*) – that was the Department of State Security of the Home Office. The Russian title of the Home Office was NKVD (*Narodny Kommissariat Vnutrennich Dell*). The staff of the GUGB were known as the OGPU (*Ob'edinennoe Gosudarstvennoe Politicheskoe Upravlenie*) or Joint State Political Directorate. The OGPU had grown out of the infamous Cheka, created by Lenin in 1917 and led by the brutal Felix Dzerhinsky. There was a foreign section of the OGPU that sent its own agents abroad. Up to 1934 the OGPU representatives in the United Kingdom were concerned with the acquisition of political, economic and commercial information; the supervision of Soviet and Communist Party organisations and personnel; and the penetration of anti-Soviet and White Russian societies. After 1934, the OGPU began to usurp the role of the Fourth Department. As with the Fourth Department, the OGPU had legal and illegal *residents* in Britain.[33] And the greatest asset the Soviet Communists had was their ideology – something that appealed beyond patriotism and loyalty to the nation or class.

13

'I Want All My Girls to be Well-Bred & Have Good Legs' Joan Miller & the Tyler Kent Case 1939–1940[1]

I am in a position to prove that she has a channel of communication with Germany; that she has used that channel of communication with Germany; that she is a person of hostile association; that she is involved in pro-German propaganda, to say the least. As your Ambassador has just said, you have been found with documents in your private rooms to which he considers you have no proper title. You would be a very silly man if you did not realise that certain conclusions might be drawn from that situation... [Captain Maxwell Knight to Tyler Gatewood Kent, 20 May 1940.[2]]

On Saturday 25 May 1940, Inspector Pearson of Special Branch handed Maxwell Knight a blue-grey envelope containing two pages of newspaper covered with pencilled handwriting. Knight read the content, the details of which were sufficient to prompt him and Inspector Pearson to present themselves at 8 Ashburn Gardens, Kensington at 9.30 a.m.the next morning to interview Mrs Christabel Sybil Nicholson, in the presence of her husband Admiral Wilmot Nicholson. Knight cautioned her and asked her if she knew Anna Wolkoff and Tyler Kent. She replied that she did, explaining that she had met Kent through Anna and that he had come to her husband's birthday party.

Knight showed Mrs Nicholson a Right Club membership card and asked if the handwriting and signature shown on it were hers. She replied: 'Oh yes, rather.' Knight then produced the pencilled document and enquired as to whether Mrs Nicholson had any explanation. She told him that it was something she had copied as it looked very important. She refused to tell Knight who had shown her the 'important' original document and would only concede that it was 'someone very patriotic' who thought that it showed evidence of 'corruption in high places and also thought that Admiral Nicholson might have access to 'someone in authority' to show it to. Mrs Nicholson had apparently agreed with the unknown patriot's view, and copied the document with the intention of showing it to 'some absolutely honourable person in high quarters'; exactly whom was not made clear. When asked if Anna Wolkoff had shown her the document, Mrs Nicholson became agitated and protested that Anna had shown her nothing and that she would not implicate her as she was very fond of her. She was worried that to name Anna as the source would not only be disloyal, but also treacherous, and she accused Knight of trying to intimidate her and to get Anna 'shot'. Admiral Nicholson clearly did not share his wife's view, warning her of the seriousness of the situation and entreating her to tell the truth. The Nicholson's asked for a few minutes alone together, after which Mrs Nicholson finally admitted that Anna Wolkoff had shown her the document.[3]

The document in question was an abbreviated copy of a US Embassy telegram, the contents of which dealt with a US 'destroyer deal'. Initially, this matter was considered to be so secret that prosecution of Mrs Nicholson was 'out of the question', although she was interned under Emergency Powers Regulation 18B. However, by December 1940, it was decided that Mrs Nicholson should be charged under the Official Secrets Act and Defence Regulations.[4] She proved to be considerably luckier than some of the others involved in the case of Tyler Kent and Anna Wolkoff. At her trial, the jury despite 'overwhelming' evidence of her guilt acquitted her; prompting the Solicitor General to comment that it was the 'most astounding verdict' he had ever heard.[5]

Tyler Gatewood Kent had first attracted attention in October 1939, a mere three days after arriving in London. Kent, a descendant of Davey Crockett, was born in China, the son of an American Consul, and enjoyed a distinguished and varied education at Princeton, the Sorbonne, Madrid University and the George Washington University. He joined the diplomatic service in 1934 and was posted to the US Embassy in Moscow, where he worked as a cipher clerk.[6] It has been suggested that, while in Moscow, Kent was recruited by the Soviets, however Russian archives shed no light on whether this was the case. Knight held strong isolationist views and openly professed to hate Jews. On 5 October 1939, he arrived in London to take up a post as a cipher clerk at the US Embassy.[7]

Initially it was purely by chance that Kent attracted MI5's attention. A naturalised Swede of German extraction, Ludwig Ernst Matthias, visited London in October 1939. Matthias had been reported to MI5, by a reliable source, as being a Gestapo agent, and was under surveillance. On 8 October he was followed to the Cumberland Hotel where he met a man who was subsequently identified as Tyler Kent. The two men paid a visit to Kent's room and on leaving, Matthias was seen to be carrying a bulky envelope. Matthias and Kent then spent the rest of the evening together, finishing up at the Park Lane Hotel. Kent came to notice again in February 1940, when it was reported that Anna de Wolkoff of the Right Club regarded him as an important contact.

About a month later it was confirmed that Anna was devoting a great deal of time to this man, who she described as being 'pro-German' in his outlook and said had given her 'interesting diplomatic information of a confidential nature'.[8]

Captain Archibald H. Maule Ramsay, a Christian patriot and Conservative MP who staunchly believed that the world was threatened by a Jewish/Bolshevik/Freemason conspiracy, founded the Right Club in 1938; he was married to Ismay, the daughter of a Scottish viscount. In the view of MI5 the activities of the Right Club fell into two distinct categories: while the open and ostensible purpose of the Right Club was to disseminate political propaganda against the supposed evil influence of Jews and Freemasons, hiding behind this was the real purpose of disorganising the home front by subversive propaganda to spread fear and distress and hinder the prosecution of the war.[9] Ramsay capitalised on the existing antipathy towards Jews and Communists and enjoyed considerable support from some prominent individuals; Right Club meetings were often chaired by the Duke of Wellington. At the beginning of the war, membership had risen to around 300, but, on the declaration of war, the Club was closed to avoid any potential pro-Nazi accusations. William Joyce, one of the founder members, travelled to Germany, from where he attempted to undermine British morale by broadcasting as 'Lord Haw Haw'. Ramsay, however, decided that he would stay and educate the public towards a negotiated peace. Ramsay's aim was to organise a political coup to discredit and bring down the Churchill administration, so as to replace it with one prepared to negotiate with Hitler.[10] Ramsay created a badge for Right Club members, which featured an eagle and a snake, and had a very clear plan as to how his 'inner circle' would operate once they were 'in power'.[11] Ramsay anticipated that Hitler would eventually take over Europe, leaving Britain as a protectorate, ruled by himself. Mrs Ramsay's expectations were a little more modest; she expected that when the Nazis took over, her husband would only be Commissioner of Scotland.[12]

Ramsay sometimes described Anna Wolkoff as his 'political secretary'. Born in Russia in 1902 into a privileged family, Anna's father, an Admiral, had been serving as the Tsar's Naval Attaché in London at the time of the Bolshevik Revolution; her mother was a former lady-in-waiting to Tsarina Alexandra. The Wolkoffs settled in London in a state of permanent exile, running the Russian Tea Rooms, at the corner of Harrington Gardens, opposite South Kensington Underground Station. Anna was intelligent, determined and patriotic and fiercely resented her family's loss of wealth and influence. From its inception, she was a fervent and loyal member of the Right Club. To supplement the family income, Anna worked as a dressmaker and enjoyed some success; one of her clients was the Duchess of Windsor.[13]

Maxwell Knight had been keeping tabs on the Right Club since the summer of 1939; reports had been received, stating that, although outwardly, the Right Club professed to be unconnected with other Fascist movements, it counted amongst its members, people who were working for extreme organisations such as the British Union of Fascists, the Imperial Fascist League and the Nordic League. Captain Ramsay regularly addressed Nordic League meetings and shared its anti-Semitic views, which Knight considered to be pro-German and an 'incitement to riot'.[14] An agent was planted by MI5; referred to as 'Miss Z' she is widely thought to have been Helene Louise de Munck, a young Belgian born, British educated woman,[15] who was already acquainted with both the Ramsays and the Wolkoff family. Although no official document confirms her identity and she is referred to as 'Miss Z' one of Knight's agents, Joan Miller, in her memoirs, refers to her as 'Helen'. Miss Z had previously worked for MI5, although in what capacity is unclear. She began visiting the Russian Tearooms, reporting back to Knight. Following the outbreak of war, Miss Z's reports strongly indicated that the Right Club intended to penetrate not only anti-Semitic and anti-Communist organisations, but actually into the heart of Government Departments.[16]

Ramsay and the Right Club were clearly completely taken in by Miss Z; Ramsay told her that he had led MI5 and Scotland Yard 'quite astray by his methods' so that neither knew anything of his real activities. Miss Z was even entrusted to rent a flat at 34 Mansion Mews at the instruction of Ramsay and Anna, to be used as a venue for Right Club meetings. At the outbreak of war, Miss Z expressed her desire to help the Right Club, and was told by Ramsay that it would be useful if she could 'get into Censorship or the Foreign Office'. Miss Z replied that she had lots of contacts and would see what she could do. Knight and MI5 duly found a post in Censorship for her in October 1939. Ramsay asked her to supply details of Jews working within her department and also told her that it would be very helpful if she could establish a contact working in intelligence.[17] It also helped that Miss Z had a reputation as a mystic and was interested in the occult, a subject which also fascinated Anna. Knight reported that Miss Z had an uncanny ability to analyse peoples' characters from analysing their hand writing, a talent that he was quick to exploit. Anna quickly 'swallowed the bait' and asked Miss Z to produce a character analysis for her, which was, of course, heavily edited and embellished by MI5.

Anna was so impressed that she immediately accepted Miss Z into her inner circle of close friends.[18]

Anna clearly trusted Miss Z and was fond of her, calling her 'the little storm trooper' and telling her that they were both Ramsay's *'aides-de-camp'*, although Anna considered herself his 'chief agent'. When it came to the 'triumphant procession', said Anna, Miss Z 'would ride in the same car with Himmler'; presumably Anna would be riding with Hitler and Ramsay. Miss Z did, however, genuinely agree with Anna's anti-Semitic views. In March 1940, Anna visited Miss Z to learn the art of scrying, telling her that she had agents 'all over the place to work against the Jews', not only in England but also in America. Anna, however, took pains to point out that she was not pro-German, although she 'admired' Hitler; she wanted the English to 'do their own washing'. She was also very interested in Miss Z's regular visits to her family in Belgium, asking whether she could come too. In April and May 1940 the two women met up on most days, sometimes several times. Miss Z met all of the leading Right Club members and noticed that they appeared pleased whenever Britain 'suffered a reverse'. As Miss Z got to know Anna better she realised that her talk became increasingly pro-German, but when praising Germany, Anna was always careful to add that the Germans had 'done the right thing' in getting rid of the Jews.[19] The other agent, infiltrating the Right Club was 'Mrs Amos' (real name Marjorie Mackie), a middle-aged lady who had experience working for MI5 and about whom very little is revealed by official sources.

At this point, Knight decided that it was time to introduce another agent. Joan Priscilla Miller was a child of a broken marriage, who, on leaving boarding school, worked in an Andover tea shop, until her appalled mother ('a chorus girl from Dunbar'), who had married first Joan's Anglo-Portuguese father, then an 'impeccably middle-class engineer' who worked for the Sudan Cotton Plantation, used her contacts, while visiting her daughter, to help Joan find employment as a display assistant at Elizabeth Arden (before whisking away back to the Sudan after bestowing some hand-me-down clothes on her, which were, however 'mostly Worth and Chanel'). Like Olga Gray before her, a female friend, Janet Withers, initially recruited Joan. Janet worked for the War Office and suggested over supper that Joan might like to try for a job 'like hers' and offered to recommend her. Joan was beautiful, intelligent, articulate and had breeding, as well as impeccable references. After a successful interview with the efficient Miss Dicker, who was responsible for recruiting female staff, she was told that she would be summoned by telegram as soon as war broke out. On Sunday 3

September 1939, Joan arrived home at her flat in Chelsea, to find the fateful telegram. Next morning, as instructed, Joan set off for the Natural History Museum, and boarded the bus parked opposite the entrance, joining a crowd of girls, clad, like herself, in tweed, twin sets and pearls, and some young men in bowler hats. The bus duly arrived at Wormwood Scrubs the new headquarters of MI5; Vernon Kell had arranged this move earlier in the year in the event of war breaking out. As the new staff arrived, prisoners were still being transferred.

Joan was given a post as Lord Cottenham's secretary, replacing another girl who could not cope with the chaos caused by the relocation. Lord Cottenham had responsibility for MI5's transport section and Joan enjoyed working for him, socialising until the early hours at the Milroy and Four Hundred Clubs and meeting new and interesting people, such as the Kell's, whose son took her out several times. However, Joan felt unchallenged and hoped to obtain a transfer to a more exciting department. She soon caught Knight's eye and he invited her to lunch in the staff canteen, via Bill Younger. Joan was both flattered and intrigued; she knew Knight by sight and was aware of his engaging eccentricities, such as the hand-made cigarettes he smoked. She accepted the invitation and was bowled over by Knight's charm, dining with him again that evening at the Author's Club in Whitehall. Knight explained to her the work of his section B5(b), and set out his plan for Joan to join the two agents who were already infiltrating the Right Club. Joan started working for Knight the next day, quickly getting up to speed with Fascism. She was inspired by the 'vigilance and perseverance' of Olga Gray and enchanted by the romance of both Knight and the proposed line of work. Joan visited the Tea Rooms with Mrs Amos, who had created a cover story that Joan was a friend of her son, and worked at the War Office.

Joan took to regularly dropping in to the Tea Rooms, on one occasion, bumping into 'Helen'. The two women recognised one another and Miss Z introduced Joan to Anna, telling her that her job was 'a boring one in a filing department'. Joan found Anna 'short and unattractive' and later remembered her as having 'the intensity of manner which is often associated with those of a fanatical disposition'.[20]

Anna saw an opportunity and encouraged Miss Z to bring her 'work friend' to the Tea Rooms again, telling her that she thought Joan could be useful. Miss Z introduced Joan to Enid Riddell, Miss Van Lennep and other members of the Right Club. Anna told Miss Z that she would invite Joan to dinner to try and discover her views. Joan joined Anna for dinner, by invitation via Miss Z. Anna visited Miss Z very late that evening in extremely high spirits; she considered that the dinner had been a success and thought that Joan, whom she referred to as 'the child', had been 'quite unsuspecting'.[21] After dinner, the two women had gone to Anna's flat, where she showed Joan some dresses she had been sewing. Joan had especially admired one dress. On 3 May, Joan arrived home, to find the dress lying on her doormat. She immediately wrote Anna a note of thanks and kept a duplicate copy.[22] Anna immediately showed the note to Miss Z; unbeknown to Joan, the wily Anna had given her the dress to prompt a 'thank you' note. Anna thought that Joan could be very useful if she could convert 'her way of thinking'. Anna asked Miss Z to analyse Joan's handwriting and again, Knight was able to exploit Miss Z mystical talents, as she duly reported to Anna that Joan was a person of whom 'much use could be made'. Anna invited Miss Z to meetings at a hotel near Victoria Station, which she realised were 'Fascist in character', telling Miss Z that she had agents in Germany.

One evening in early April, Miss Z visited the Russian Tea Rooms for dinner and struck up a conversation with Admiral Wolkoff, during which she casually mentioned that she had a friend who was attached to the Russian Legation. The Admiral immediately fetched Anna, who was very interested in this piece of news, asking whether this friend was in a position to get a letter to Germany by other channels than the ordinary post. Miss Z told her that she thought it was a possibility, as he had sometimes been good enough to take letters for her to an uncle who lived in Russia. At this Anna became extremely excited, asking Miss Z why she had not told her this before. Anna then produced from her bag an envelope addressed to Herr W. Joyce in Berlin. Miss Z told her that, if her friend was to take it, she would have to have it at once, as he might well be leaving within forty-eight hours. Anna was keen to meet this 'friend', but Miss Z explained that she could not ask him to compromise himself by meeting strangers and that she thought that he would much more likely to take the letter as a personal favour to her. Anna agreed. Miss Z took the letter straight to Knight, telephoning Anna next morning and telling her that she had made the necessary arrangements for the letter to be conveyed. Anna was concerned, telling Miss Z that she wanted to add something to the contents of the letter and asking whether there was any possibility that Miss Z could retrieve it. Miss Z replied that it might be tricky, but she would do her best, arranging for Anna to visit her first thing next morning.

Miss Z collected the letter from Knight late that evening and Anna arrived at her flat bright and early next day, asking to borrow Miss Z's typewriter to amend the letter and looking carefully at the sealed envelope which 'Helen' handed to her. Miss Z commented that her 'friend' might want an idea of the letters contents before he took it out of the country; Anna then showed her the contents of the envelope which were a single sheet of paper covered with a code consisting of letters and figures. The only portion of the document which was vaguely understandable was a short passage, typed in German, a language which Miss Z did not understand. Anna explained that it contained facts relating to Jewish activities in England, which were intended for the use of William Joyce (Lord Haw Haw) in his propaganda broadcasts from Germany. In Anna's opinion the information would 'be like a bombshell' when Joyce used it. She also referred to the code, and although Miss Z could not entirely understand, Anna indicated that every fourth letter in the words at the top of the document provided the key to the code itself. Anna added a short message in German and drew an emblem of an eagle and a snake. She then resealed the letter, in a new envelope which she had brought with her, and handed it back to Miss Z, who, again, took it straight to Knight.[23]

When deciphered, the letter, written in code, proved to be a commentary on Joyce's recent broadcast with suggested improvements. Knight arranged for the letter to be sent, with a twofold purpose: firstly to see what acknowledgement Joyce would make and secondly to explore the further activities of 'these treacherous individuals'.[24] Miss Z reported to Anna that the letter was on its way and that her friend would arrange for it to be posted in a neutral country. Anna was pleased, telling Miss Z that if the mission was a success she would be 'one of ours'; however, as she was not a naturalised British subject, she could not join 'the group', but could only be an associate member. Anna had, for some time, been asking Miss Z when her next visit to Belgium would be: she explained that she wanted to send information to other agents in Belgium. Anna was concerned as she had been communicating with these agents 'through the diplomatic bag,' but had not, recently, received replies. She also said that she wanted to obtain a translation of a Russian document, which was in possession of a man, Monsieur Guy Niermans, whom she described as 'our principal agent in Belgium'. She also told Miss Z that she had been using a contact in the Belgian Embassy in London called Jean Nieumanhuys, but that recently she had developed doubts about his reliability.

On Knight's instructions, when the question was next raised, Miss Z told Anna that she hoped to be visiting her family very soon. Anna was pleased, telling 'Helen' to let her know when her travel arrangements were completed so that she could give her the necessary detailed instructions. Miss Z duly arranged to visit Belgium on 16 April. She met Anna the night before her departure and received typed instructions, written in 'bad French'. The instructions were that she was to contact Guy Niermans in Brussels, giving Anna's name as an introduction, and was to ask him whether the translation of the Russian document was finished and whether he could give her an English translation. If it was not finished she was to ask for the original Russian document, as it could be translated in England. She was also to obtain from Niermans the latest anti-Semitic and anti-Masonic publications, and she was to obtain some sort of report on the progress of 'our work' in Belgium. Miss Z would be required to obtain the names of various anti-Semitic and pro-German organisations and an estimate of their membership. Miss Z was also to go and call on the Conte and Contesse de Laubesfins (Anna told her that Conte Antoine de Laubesfins was an important official at the Foreign Office in Brussels) and to report to them that the work was 'going very well in England' and that Anna hoped to hear from them via the Belgian diplomatic bag. If they had anything to report they could confide it to Miss Z verbally. Finally, Miss Z was particularly asked to enquire whether the contact at the Belgian Embassy in London was 'absolutely trustworthy'. Although Anna 'strictly charged' her to destroy the original, Miss Z made a copy and translation, which she handed to Knight.

Miss Z flew to Belgium from Shoreham Airport on 16 April, arriving in Brussels at around 4 p.m. She immediately contacted the Contesse de Laubesfins and made an appointment for lunch two days later. She did not find Niermans so easy to track down, discovering after some considerable difficulty that he was not in Brussels but was staying at La Fenne, near Ostend. Miss Z finally managed to speak to him and arranged to meet him in Ostend. At her lunch meeting with the de Laubesfins, Miss Z found them to be 'not very open in their conversation', but it was clear from what they said to her that they had been closely concerned in pro-German and anti-Jewish activities. A remark made by the Conte during a conversation on the subject of anti-Jewish propaganda and pro-German connections, which he described as 'a dangerous game, though it would be a good game and an honourable game if there was any chance of succeeding', particularly struck Miss Z. Acting on Anna's instructions, she asked about the possibility of sending correspondence between England and Belgium via the Belgian diplomatic bag, angling the question in such a way as to ascertain whether the same method was in use between Belgium and Germany. The Conte replied: 'Yes, of course,' telling her that if anything was of sufficient importance 'we can use the bag as we have done up to now'. He also said that Miss Z or Anna could use the Belgian bag through the contact at the Belgian Embassy in London, Jean Nieumanhuys, whom they could trust 'thoroughly and entirely'.

Miss Z then moved on to enquire about anti-Jewish and anti-Masonic literature. On this subject the de Laubesfins were evasive, emphasising that they had nothing to do with any activity of this kind. After lunch it became clear to Miss Z that the Conte did not wish to leave her alone with his wife, and he asked her if there was anywhere that she would like to visit in his car. In the car Miss Z pressed him again and the Conte stopped the car at the Foreign Office. Leaving Miss Z in the car, he went inside, reappearing with a small periodical, which allegedly contained the names and addresses of Jews and Freemasons in Belgium. He also gave her the addresses of shops at which propaganda of this kind was sometimes available.

Niermans then contacted Miss Z asking her to advance the time of their appointment. She met him and his wife at Ostend at about 11 a.m. on 19 April and found Niermans 'extremely discreet'. When asked about the Russian document, Niermans replied that it was actually 'a big book', which was currently in Germany being translated by some Russians who were writing for the Germans on anti-Jewish propaganda. He promised to wire for the book and to send it to England as soon as possible via the diplomatic bag. During their conversation, Niermans discovered that he knew some of Miss Z's family quite well; he was concerned and tried to dissuade her from mixing herself up in the type of activity with which he thought she was associated. He asked her to promise him that she would 'give up this anti-Jewish work', telling her that it was 'more than anti-Jewish'. The Wolkoffs, he explained, used German agents, who 'really manipulate the whole machine'. The end result, he warned, would be that 'the Germans will be the wolves and the Wolkoffs and their agents will be the sheep. The Germans will remain unsuspected but the tools will end up in prison.' He told Miss Z to pass on a message to Anna 'to stop this stupidity' because, he considered, the Wolkoffs 'cannot come to any good in this sort of work in war time'. Being anti-Jewish now, Nierman continued, was actually being pro-Nazi. The Allies were too strong for the Germans; the Jews were too strong for the Germans. Nierman's view was that Germany could not win the war because 'she is not mistress of the seas, just as was the case with Napoleon'. He thought that the Jews should be used against their persecutors, and when the Nazis were 'done for' then it would be time to 'work sensibly'. Niermans also told Miss Z that since war broke out, he had made four visits to Germany 'on important and interesting business', and that he intended to go on 'taking as much money as he could from the Germans'. He explained that he knew the Germans well and that he could make most people do what he wanted them to, but that the Germans could not make him out; he felt that he knew too much and that he had been useful to them in the past. Miss Z and Niermans made another appointment to meet at 10 p.m. that evening. During their conversation, it transpired that there were, in the hotel where they met, five Germans, with whom Niermans had been conducting what he described as 'some important business', and for whom he had actually booked rooms in the hotel. Niermans was to spend the whole of the next week with them.

Miss Z returned to England on 20 April, arriving at 12 noon and reporting fully to Anna all the events of her trip. The only thing that Miss Z did not share with Anna was that she had asked the Conte de Laubesfins whether the diplomatic bag could be used for sending correspondence between Belgium and Germany, and he had confirmed that it could be. Anna seized on Miss Z's information, especially the reassurances about the reliability of Nieumanhuys.[25] Knight too, was extremely pleased with the outcome of Miss Z's trip to Belgium; not only had she won Anna's confidence, she had also obtained valuable information which centred around the 'undoubted fact' that Guy Niermans was an agent working for Germany, and that both he and the de Laubesfins were concerned at Anna Wolkoff's extremism. Knight considered that their concerns were probably due to a combination of, 'fear for their own safety' and 'mistrust' of Anna's 'fearful Russian temperament'.[26]

Miss Z first heard of Tyler Kent one evening in late February 1940, when she went with Anna at the Russian Tea Rooms. As Anna entered, her father spoke to her, indicating a young man sitting in the restaurant. Anna went over and spoke to him, later returning to Miss Z's table, telling her that Kent was a 'most interesting young man' working in the United States Embassy, who had been in Russia for five years and 'spoke wonderful Russian'. Anna also considered that Kent was 'of our way of thinking'. He and Anna became increasingly friendly and by the end of March were sharing Kent's car, which was very useful for the purposes of the Right Club. Anna told Miss Z that when telephoning Kent she always spoke in rapid Russian in case the line was being tapped.

In early April 1940, Anna told Miss Z that Kent was to be introduced to Ramsay that week. Ramsay was delighted at Anna's contact with Kent, telling Miss Z that he and his wife had a 'most interesting man from the United States Embassy' to dinner. He explained that their dinner guest had told them some 'interesting things about corruption at the top' and asserted that American, did not want to go into the war. It was clear to Miss Z that Ramsay hoped that America would not intervene in the war because, in his view, American intervention would 'render the defeat of Germany certain'. Mrs Ramsay too, was pleased to have made Kent's acquaintance and later revealed to 'Miss Z that Kent had become a member of the Right Club. The first indication to Miss Z that Kent was giving confidential information to Anna was on 23 April 1940, when Anna visited her after having dinner with Joan Miller. She told Miss Z that she had seen the signature of Guy Liddell on a letter concerning 'America, radio detectors and Hoovers'. She also said she had had a 'marvellous evening' with Kent at the Ritz.[27] Around the same time, another source reported that Anna had boasted that Kent had given her information about sea battles off the coast of Norway, which had been 'twisted' into 'excellent anti-British propaganda'; Anna was also claiming that Kent was telling her about confidential meetings which had taken place between the US Ambassador and Lord Halifax, the Foreign Secretary. It was also clear to MI5 that not only was Kent using the American Diplomatic Bag on behalf of the Right Club, he had also revealed to Anna details of correspondence relating to the transfer of US destroyers to the Royal Navy, which was delicately referred to as 'the purchase of certain technical apparatus'.[28]

On Saturday 11 May, Anna visited Miss Z, telling her that she 'had had a triumph'; she had had to steal a key off a watch chain and then got it copied at Woolworth's. 'Then, my dear,' Anna expanded, 'the documents had to be got out of the house.' Anna said that she had stood over 'the person' who made the copies 'while they were being copied'. Anna also mentioned that she had spent the previous evening at Kent's flat. Joan Miller and Miss Z were both invited, on 13 May, to a dinner at Anna's flat, with other Right Club members (all women as most of the Right Club's male membership were interned under Regulation 18B) during which Anna spoke at length, denouncing Jews, Freemasons and Winston Churchill.[29] Aware that she was being vetted, Joan was extremely nervous, and agreed with Anna's views, telling the group that she 'deplored' the decision to abandon the policy of appeasement.[30] After Joan left the dinner party, Anna 'executed a dance of triumph', exclaiming that not only was she sure that Joan suspected nothing, but she would also be a 'convert' who would prove 'most useful'.[31] The following day, Knight told Joan that she had passed the test, and the ladies of the Right Club had been completely taken in by her. She was invited to join the organisation, receiving a badge and attending meetings. According to Joan's memoirs, Mrs Amos told Knight that the Right Club planned to encourage Joan to obtain a transfer to another department where there would be greater scope for sabotage.[32]

Joan had been introduced to Mrs Ramsay, who told her she could visit whenever she liked. Joan arranged to visit the Ramsay residence in Onslow Square for tea on 29 May, where she was introduced to Mrs Ramsay's son. Ismay Ramsay was worried about recent arrests of Right Club members (which included Christabel Nicholson) and asked Joan whether she could find out any information. Joan left, arranging to telephone in a few days.[33] Joan, arranged to meet Mrs Ramsay at South Kensington Underground Station and took her to a flat used by SIS. Special Branch wired the sitting room and installed two officers and Knight in a cupboard, a listening system which was effective only if the windows remained closed. It was an exceptionally warm day, and, despite Joan's valiant attempts to steer the conversation, Ismay Ramsay gave nothing away.[34] She did, however, ask Joan again whether she had been able to obtain any information about recent arrests and also suggested that Joan might like to go to the cinema with her and her son.[35] She also clearly harboured suspicions about Joan's motives, telling Miss Z that as she did not know 'which side' Joan was working for, she was very careful not to tell her anything that she would not mind being repeated to 'the other side'. However, speaking again to Miss Z a few weeks later, about the recent appeal she had made to the Home Office for her husband's release, Mrs Ramsay had changed her mind about Joan and was convinced that she was genuine. She was, she said, sure that Joan was not 'working for the other side', but was afraid to openly work for the Right Club. She concluded that Joan was 'not clever, but a sweet child' who 'may yet be of use'. More alarmingly she told Miss Z that she had been visited by a member of the Right Club who was a Guards Officer and they had discussed 'the plan' for her husband's escape from prison. The plan apparently involved taking advantage of 'air raids, invasion or revolution' to organise an escape. Miss Z pointed out that breaking through the prison gates would not be easy, and Mrs Ramsay replied that when the time came, the Right Club's 'armed folk' as well as Mosley's, were armed and would fight. She longed, she said, to see 'the Home Office folk swinging and hanging from lampposts'.

Miss Z had seen Anna on Whitsunday, when she told her that she had dined, the previous Thursday, with Kent and that it was with regard to her work concerning 'Italian ships'. Anna and Ann Van Lennep (who Anna thought that Miss Z should train as an 'understudy') were going that day to Reigate to visit Enid Riddell, who was to be Anna's 'understudy'. A few days later Miss Z telephoned Anna, who invited her to visit. The two women listened to Lord Haw-Haw and the Freedom Station and then Anna asked Miss Z for some help with regard to a 'missing letter'. She said that she had posted a letter in Cadogan Square but that it had apparently not reached its destination. Anna suspected that the addressee's housekeeper had taken it. Anna told Miss Z that she wanted 'to tell me a thoroughly dirty story, then we will type it out and put it in the letter box'. Miss Z did so (though unfortunately the details of the 'dirty story' are not disclosed) and Anna addressed the envelope by hand. Miss Z did not manage to see the address, but Anna told her that the envelope was going to the man she had dined with 'the other evening', also mentioning that she, Enid Riddell and Kent had dined recently with an Italian, whose identity she did not reveal.

Anna put the addressed envelope in her handbag and the two women took the bus to Beauchamp Place and walked to Cadogan Square. At the corner Anna stopped and gave Miss Z the letter telling her that it was number 67 on the corner, 'the last house but one, you can't miss it'. Miss Z walked down to number 67 alone and posted the letter through the letterbox. She thought it best not to look at the name and address on the envelope. As they were walking home after Miss Z had put the letter in the letterbox, Anna told her that it was 'something to have a name like a tin of fruit'. Miss Z was unaware that 67 Cadogan Square, the house on the corner, was the residence of the Duco Del Monte, Assistant Naval Attaché at the Italian Embassy.

Anna went on to tell Miss Z that the documents which she had photographed on 11 May 'convicted' Churchill, then at the Admiralty, of conspiring with Roosevelt 'and leaving the neutrals out altogether'. She thought that Italy should have this information, 'because after all, my dear, one does not like to see one's country making such fantastic blunders'. Italy had received the copies of the letters and she had checked up on this through Tyler Kent, and by listening to radio broadcasts. Miss Z did not think it possible that Mrs Ramsay, despite her extreme views, was aware of how embroiled her husband and Anna were with Kent, or of what they were involved in. In early May, Anna told her that Ramsay was doing 'special Fifth Column work' with someone to whom she had introduced him. Miss Z was convinced that it was Kent. Anna had impressed upon Ramsay that this special work was a very secret matter, entirely confidential to him and to her. In spite of this, she explained to Miss Z, Ramsay had told his wife, and Anna was genuinely alarmed. She talked of the possibility of her being arrested and prosecuted and seemed to think that she would end up 'in the Tower'. Mrs Ramsay herself told Miss Z a few weeks later that her husband went to Kent's room on one occasion with Anna and had been there alone in Kent's absence. She went on to say that Ramsay knew that Kent kept documents in suitcases in his room and was horrified at his carelessness.[36]

MI5 now felt that it had more than enough evidence to approach the Americans. On 18 May, Guy Liddell approached the US Ambassador, Joseph P. Kennedy, telling him the details of the case and asking him to waive diplomatic immunity. Kennedy agreed, but was apparently furious at having been kept in the dark by MI5; this was the first time that he had been made aware of Kent and the risk to security that he posed. Hershel V. Johnson, the US Embassy's Consul General, later recalled that it was 'most regrettable' and that Kent would never have been 'left in the Code Room' if there had been even the slightest grounds for suspicion.[37]

On 20 May 1940, Kent was dismissed from the United States Government Service and detained. Anna, too, was arrested and interned under Regulation 18B. Knight led a raid with Special Branch officers, on Kent's flat in Gloucester Place, where they found him in the company of his mistress, Mrs Irene Danichevsky. Knight took possession of a huge number of official US Government documents and sheets of foolscap paper bearing codes.[38] Anna's boasts about the information Kent had given her were clearly true; as well as the documents and 'masses of confidential cables', photographic negatives were discovered. Much of the information in the documents was extremely confidential and was of great importance to the Allies diplomatic and strategic position. Much of the information contained in them corresponded with the information Anna had said she was receiving from Kent.[39] Knight then accompanied Kent to the US Embassy and interviewed him in the presence of the US Ambassador.[40] Also present were Herschel V. Johnson and P.C. Scott of Special Branch.

Kennedy opened the interview by setting out the seriousness of the situation and telling Kent that, 'from the kind of family you are from, people who have fought for the United States, one would not expect you to let us all down'. 'In what way?' replied Kent. Kennedy then asked him what he was intending to do with the information he had stolen and Kent replied that they were purely for his own information because he thought them 'very interesting'. Knight then took over, explaining that he was talking to him at Kennedy's invitation and 'not in any way in connection with matters which concern Great Britain at the moment'; he told Kent that he could prove his association with Anna Wolkoff, which Kent did not deny. Knight elaborated that he could also prove Anna had a 'channel of communication' with Germany, was a 'person of hostile associations' and involved in 'pro-German propaganda'. He then produced a leather bound locked notebook and asked Kent to identify it. Kent initially denied all knowledge, then accepted it belonged to Captain Ramsay, who had given it to him around three weeks previously. Kent admitted that Ramsay had brought the book to him at his flat, where Anna Wolkoff may have been present but claimed he had no idea of either the contents or why Ramsay had approached him, despite Knight pressing him, 'don't you think it strange that a Member of Parliament should come to you, a minor official in an Embassy and give you a locked book to take care of for him? Now seriously, doesn't it strike you as odd that a Member of Parliament should bring you a locked ledger and ask you to take care of it for him?' Kent replied that he 'did not know'. The interview was clearly frustrating for Knight: 'You are adopting a sort of naive attitude which doesn't deceive me for a moment.' he told Kent. 'You are either hiding something or… ' Kent calmly stood his ground and replied that Ramsay had simply asked him to look after the book. He said that he knew of Ramsay's association by Anna 'if by associated you mean that he knows her'.

Knight then produced a letter sent from Kent to Anna on 21 March 1940; Kent had written that he hoped to see her 'and make the acquaintance of your more interesting friends'. Who were the friends, asked Knight? Kent thought he had probably meant Captain Ramsay: 'I think I had that in mind. Then I did meet him and found him rather interesting.' Kent said, in probably the closest statement to an admission that he made during the whole interview, that he and Ramsay 'had sort of common views, to a certain extent'. Knight's patience was wearing thin and he cut to the chase telling Kent that he had first attracted attention in February 1940, 'when your friend, Anna Wolkoff, was telling people that she had made an extremely useful contact with a young man at the American Embassy. I am going to speak now extremely bluntly. I am afraid that I must take the view that you are either a fool or a rogue because you cannot possibly be in a position except that of a man who has either been made use of or who knows all these people. I propose to show you how.'

Knight continued, telling Kent that he had received a report 16 April 1940 that Anna Wolkoff was telling some of her close associates in the Right Club a story involving a meeting between Ambassador Kennedy and Lord Halifax concerning the difficulties encountered by the Royal Navy in connection with German troops landing in Norway, information which could only have come from Kent. Kent claimed that he could not recall what he had said in April. 'You have a very good memory for what you have not said, but not a very good memory for what you have said,' noted the MI5 officer. Knight then asked him about Matthias and the large envelope he had been observed with after leaving Kent's room at the Cumberland Hotel. Kent, of course, had no memory of this incident, although he did remember smuggling in a box of cigars, which were obviously what Matthias must have been carrying.

Kent did admit having dinner at the Russian Tea Rooms, but denied giving Anna confidential information about the North Sea battles, telling her that the success had been greatly exaggerated and it was British propaganda designed to cover heavy losses sustained in the air attack on Scapa Flow. He also denied giving her details of secret radio equipment. Kent admitted using the Diplomatic Bag, but claimed that he had only used it to send a few letters to his immediate family. When asked about William Joyce, Kent again denied all knowledge but said that he had heard from various sources that he was 'supposed to be some sort of Irishman'. Knight then returned to the book, but Kent coolly repeated his earlier statement that he had not opened it and had no idea of its contents, although he agreed that Ramsay asking him to look after did 'seem a bit odd'. On the matter of the documents in Kent's possession, Knight told him, 'it is not for me to discuss the question of your position with regard to these documents belonging to your Government, because that is not my affair at all. But your explanation about this appears to me to be extremely unconvincing; and your explanations of every point raised are unconvincing.' The Ambassador agreed with Knight, asking Kent: 'You don't expect me to believe for a minute that you had them for your own entertainment?' Kent pointed out that he had not said entertainment: 'I said interest.' He thought that in the future 'it would have been very interesting'.

Knight's level of frustration rose and he told Kent 'if you were English you would be in a very difficult position. You don't impress me by your cocky manner'. Kent replied that he was not trying to be cocky, but the reason he had the documents in his possession 'is what I just stated'. Knight asked in what manner the documents could be useful in the future. Kent replied that he had no definite plan, but that they were 'doubtless of importance as historical documents' and would 'throw an interesting light on what we are going though'. He also claimed he was unaware that it was illegal for him to have the documents. Ambassador Kennedy then asked Kent whether he had intended to take the documents to Germany:[41] Kent had, in late February 1940, written to Kirk, the *Chargé d'Affaires* at the American Embassy in Berlin, requesting a transfer. Kent's letter, which was eventually read at his trial, stated that he would be 'much happier' in Germany than in Britain where he had 'no particular interests' and that his knowledge of Soviet conditions and the Russian language would prove useful. Kirk had turned this request down, but Ambassador Kennedy was angry to find that Kent had written of his own volition. It also heavily implied that Kent intended to take the documents to Berlin to give to the Germans and enable them to expose Roosevelt's dual standards.[42] Kent replied that he could not have got the documents out as he was not entitled to exemptions, however Knight assured him that in reality and in regard to many countries he would have got exemption.

Knight then asked Kent about Anna Wolkoff and whether, in his opinion, she was a loyal British subject. Kent replied: 'If you mean that she holds some views that are apparently at variance with some of the ideas possibly of the British Government that is quite true; but it doesn't mean that she is not a loyal British subject.' Knight asked him whether a loyal British subject conducted secret communications. For the first time Kent's calm demeanour seems to have slipped: 'No,' he replied, 'but I have absolutely no knowledge of that. That is the first I have heard of it If you say that she is in communication with the enemy why of course she is not a loyal British subject; but when you put the question to me this morning I didn't know that.' Knight continued: 'But this morning you would not say yes or no. A person is either loyal or disloyal.' Kent was clearly rattled, stating: 'If you think that everybody that doesn't approve of what is being done by the country is disloyal that would... ' but Knight cut him off, telling him: 'Now you are merely trying to talk like a Parlour Politician, but we are dealing with fundamentals.' Kennedy then interjected, stating that if Knight had proof that Anna Wolkoff was communicating with the enemy 'she is more or less a spy'. He then asked the MI5 officer: 'If the United States government decides to waive any [diplomatic] rights [of immunity] they may have, do I understand that that might very well make Kent part and parcel of that?' Knight replied: 'Subject to the production of evidence under law, yes.' At this point Kennedy announced that he considered that there was no point in continuing the interview: 'I think honestly that at this stage nothing very useful is to be got by carrying on this conversation.'[43]

After a meeting of the War Cabinet, Ramsay was arrested on 23 May. Over the next few days most members of the Right Club, The Link and over 800 members of the British Union of Fascists were also arrested, including Oswald Mosley. When asked if he knew Tyler Gatewood Kent, Ramsay said that they had been introduced by Anna Wolkoff who had brought him to dinner about a month or so previously. Ramsay claimed that he did not have a close acquaintance with Kent, nor had he ever visited him at his flat. When asked if he knew where Kent was employed, he replied that he thought it was at the American Embassy, a statement that Ramsay later amended, saying that he knew Kent worked at the Embassy, but did not know in what capacity. Ramsay found Kent interesting because he had spent some time in Russia and was opposed to the Jews and Communism. A membership card of the Right Club had been found in a leather covered box on a table in Ramsay's study, signed by Tyler G. Kent, detailing how Kent had been had been a member of the Right Club since 2 May 1940 as a steward. Although some of the writing on the membership card was written in another hand, the signature was clearly Kent's. Ramsay was asked about the Right Club membership book and said that he had give it to Kent one night during dinner, because it contained names of many prominent and influential people to whom Ramsay had given assurances that it would be closely guarded from falling into the wrong hands.

Ramsay's claim to have never visited Kent's flat was completely refuted by statements not only from Miss Z but also from Emily King and Charlotte Durbridge, the housemaid and cook from 47 Gloucester Place where Kent resided in a serviced flat. Kent, said Emily King, had few visitors, but the most frequent were two women and a man who gave his name as Captain Ramsay, whom she was also able to identify. She had, she went on, often admitted Ramsay to the house to visit Kent at various times during the days and evenings. She did not know the purpose of Ramsay's visits, but often heard a typewriter being used in Kent's room. On occasion, Ramsay and one of the women visitors had been with Kent in his room, and she was positive that this woman was not the same one who was present when Kent was arrested on 20 May 1940 (Irene Danichevsky). Charlotte Durbridge corroborated Emily King's statement and added that the woman visitor, who she could identify, had a gruff voice and sometimes arrived with Ramsay in a 'small racing car'. Charlotte and Emily had been making King's bed one day while Ramsay was alone in the room, reading documents, often of a large size. Ramsay always called when Kent was at home, but the woman often called when he was out and went up to his room to wait for him.[44]

On 22 May 1940, Knight interviewed Enid Riddell at Scotland Yard. At first she declined to tell him with whom she was to have dined on the evening of 20 May, subsequently backing down and admitting that she had intended to dine with the Duco del Monte and Tyler Kent. Knight tried to interrogate Kent again on 21 May at Cannon Row police station, asking him why he had taken the documents. Kent replied that he considered that the document in question showed a 'dishonest discrepancy between the news which the public received and the actual trend of political affairs as was known in diplomatic circles'. He said that he considered it his duty to make these facts known, but was unable to say at what time, or by what means, he would have considered himself justified in doing so. Knight then asked Kent how he explained the fact that he had in his possession photographic negatives of the most confidential Embassy documents. Kent claimed that he had been trying out a camera he was thinking of buying from a friend, Hyman Goldstein, another Embassy employee who had left Britain several weeks before. Concerning the duplicate keys for the file room at the Embassy, Kent said that he had had them cut for his own convenience. He admitted that Anna Wolkoff had seen some 'pink telegrams', but that this had happened around two months ago. Knight saw Kent again on 27 May, when he admitted that he had not been frank. He asked for some time to consider his position and Knight arranged to visit the following day to interview him.[45]

On 28 May, Knight visited Brixton Prison to further interview Tyler Kent. This time Knight found Kent's manner 'more respectful'; Kent asked whether he could speak to Knight alone, with no other officers present, a request that Knight granted. Kent then informed Knight that he had been thinking matters over, he wished to reconsider his position and explain exactly how he came to be mixed up in what he described as 'all this'. Knight replied that he was very willing to listen to anything Kent had to say, and should Kent wish to, he could make a formal statement. Before Kent made a clean breast of it, Knight asked him if he would like to comment on the camera, which they had discussed the previous day. Kent admitted that he was lying, not only about Hyman Goldstein but about the whole incident. He stated that he had never taken any photographs of documents; neither did he know who had taken them. All he knew was that on one occasion, between 27 March and 10 April, Anna Wolkoff had taken away one of the documents which he had misappropriated from the American Embassy. He understood that she was going to make some notes from it, but did not know that she intended to photograph it. Anna, he told Knight, had returned the document the following day, and a week later had brought him round two negatives in a cardboard box and said something like 'you keep these'. Kent was insistent that there were only two negatives in the box; however the search of his room had revealed far more than two. Knight could see that Kent was finally prepared to open up, but was 'very tired at the time' so suggested that Kent run through the story verbally with him, and that he would return with a secretary the following day to formally record it. Kent agreed with this proposal and went on to describe his meeting with Enid Riddell, and their dinner at a Soho restaurant with an Italian who was introduced to Kent as 'Mr Marconi'. The three had subsequently visited the Embassy Club and then gone to 'Mr Marconi's' residence. Kent's description of the route taken to 'Mr Marconi's' residence and its location made it clear that the man Kent knew as 'Mr Marconi' was actually the Duco del Monte.[46]

Kent and Wolkoff were both remanded, and would remain so during the summer of 1940 and President Roosevelt's re-election campaign – as would Captain Ramsay and Mrs Nicholson. Mrs Ramsay would escape internment. MI5 submitted a report to the Director of Public Prosecutions, requesting that the 'desirability of conferring serious charges against five or more persons' be considered. Kent, Wolkoff, Mrs Nicholson and Ramsay and his wife were the main defendants. The substance of the case was that the five were 'both singly or jointly concerned either in espionage on behalf of the enemy or in something very closely akin to it'. The report warned of the Right Club, whose 'sayings and doings... are not merely childishly conspirational but are actually extremely dangerous' especially in a time of war. MI5 considered that the defendants were confident that, owing to the potential political explosion that publication of the documents involved would ignite, no prosecutions would be brought. However, this was not necessarily the case as 'no consideration of domestic or foreign policies need interfere with the course of justice'. The extent to which communications between the two Governments could be disclosed in court was being given 'active consideration' in London and Washington. Should prosecution go ahead, MI5 would face the loss of two, possibly three agents, who might be of value in the future. The agents in question (Miss Z, Joan Miller and Mrs Amos) would be forced to give evidence and would, therefore, face their cover being blown. MI5, however, were prepared to suffer this loss if the Director of Public Prosecutions felt that the facts of the case warranted a trial 'which would serve as a warning to other persons who are engaged or contemplating being engaged in subversive activities'.[47]

In November 1940, Kent and Wolkoff were both charged with offences under the Official Secrets Act and Defence Regulations; they were found guilty at the Old Bailey. Wolkoff received a sentence of ten years penal servitude; Kent received seven years. Captain Ramsay escaped charges, as did his wife, although he remained interned until 1944, at Brixton prison, with Kent and Admiral Wolkoff. Mrs Nicholson too escaped charges and was interned at Holloway, as was

Enid Riddell, who whiled away the days of her imprisonment knitting and cooking Cordon Bleu dishes with Diana Mosley.[48] Tyler Kent served his sentence and was deported in 1945. In 1982 he gave an interview with Robert Harris on the BBC's *Newsnight* still clinging to his belief that the Allies were wrong to go to war with Nazi Germany and stating that he had 'no moral compunction' about what he did. He felt he had been proved right by the 'results of what happened and the moral deterioration of the world position of the United States'. He ended his days living in a Texas trailer park. Anna Wolkoff, on her release in 1947, returned to the Tea Rooms, moving, on their closure, to a bohemian boarding house in Chelsea. Another resident remembered her as 'a very right-wing strident lady' who eked out a meagre living as a dressmaker and whose flat was like Miss Haversham's in *Great Expectations* 'trapped in time and full of junk'. In 1969 Anna went to Spain with a friend (anecdotally reputed to have been Enid Riddell); she later died in a car crash.[49]

Little is known of the fate of Mrs Amos and Miss Z, although Joan Miller claimed that Miss Z continued, for a while, to work as an agent. Joan Miller, her cover now blown, continued to work for MI5 in a 'back office' capacity. Her attraction to Knight was mutual and they became close, setting up home together at Camberley in Surrey.[50]

From MI5's point of view, there were four retrospective lessons to be learned from the case. Firstly, that during war time, there would come a point where an agent had to be sacrificed, and the MI5 officer in charge of the case would have to take responsibility of deciding both when and how. From his Memorandum to the Director of Public Prosecutions, Knight was clearly prepared to carry this out. Secondly, concerning agents' reports, it was learnt that it was 'impossible to overestimate the importance of distinguishing in each report which material is useless for evidential purposes', a 'lesson' that suggests some erroneous material may have been received. The other two lessons were that when a search of premises was conducted and documents taken away, that they should be 'properly listed and recorded' and that when 'proceedings are contemplated' it was essential to work closely with senior police officers in complete confidence. Knight, however considered that in the case of Kent and Wolkoff, 'the most complete co-operation existed between ourselves and Special Branch'.[51] The case had been complex, involving three agents, who were initially unaware of each another's true status and allegiance. It is still unclear as to whether Miss Z ever knew that Mrs Amos was a fellow agent.

Fifth Column

The Right Club case seemed to confirm that it was madness to allow potential collaborators with the Nazis to roam around the country. Even before the war had broken out Guy Liddell's personal view, in August 1939, was that all enemy aliens should be interned and that they should be called upon to show cause why they should be released. The suggestion that there should be a tribunal in each police district would only allow the Germans the opportunity of working on enemy aliens already in Britain and organising them into some sort of intelligence service.[52] On the day before Britain declared war on Germany, Kell suggested to the Commissioner of the Metropolis that he might call in Mosley and Harry Pollitt and ask them what was their attitude and that of their party in the present situation. The Commissioner, however, had come to the conclusion that he would wait and see if they infringed the law in any way. If they did, he would act immediately.[53] In October, Kell was staggered by the atmosphere in the Home Office: he felt 'they do not seem to think there is a war going on'. On 23 October, he arrived at the Home Office, at 9.30 a.m. and was unable to see anybody in authority – in fact, he could find no body at all, for an hour and a half, except the charwoman.[54]

In the New Year, the issue of Unity Mitford was raised with MI5.[55] Unity was a fervent admirer of Hitler and had attempted suicide in Germany after Britain declared war on the Third Reich. She returned to Britain in January but supporting the Germans in the war. Liddell, on Kell's instructions, telephoned the senior civil servant at the Home Office, Sir Alexander Maxwell, at the Home Office and suggested that Mitford and her mother should be searched, thoroughly, on arrival (although in the case of Unity this was only to be done if the medical office deemed her to be in a fit state). Maxwell was at first reluctant but agreed to sanction this. Liddell wanted Unity interned but Maxwell was reluctant even though Liddell pointed out that she had been in close and intimate contact with Hitler and his supporters for several years and was an 'ardent and open supporter of the Nazi regime'; furthermore, she had remained behind after the outbreak of war 'and her action came perilously close to high treason'. Her parents had been associated with the Anglo-German Fellowship 'and obviously supported her ideas about Hitler.' Maxwell continued to resist Liddell's suggestion 'and thought that we should make ourselves ridiculous'.[56] The Home Secretary, Sir John Anderson, backed Maxwell the next day and decided that 'nothing should be done': nobody was to be searched and no restrictions were to be imposed.[57]

Unity was close to Oswald Mosley too – her sister, Diana, was his wife. And the question for MI5 was what to do with the BUF? To Liddell it seemed that Mosley's future was 'very much bound up with the success or failure of Hitler, and his purpose would seem to be to impede the prosecution of war.'[58] When MI5 sent Francis Aiken-Sneath to have a meeting with Mosley, on 24 January 1940, he found the BUF chief standing in front of his desk and, seemingly, unperturbed by the visit. Aiken-Sneath was accompanied by Inspector Bridges of Special Branch. Mosley 'adopted at once an attitude of extreme affability and disarming frankness'. It seemed to Aiken-Sneath that he was anxious to show that 'the great Führer was as much as ease with three slow-witted policemen as with kings and presidents'. He 'expended all his charm' and explained that he had long been awaiting the opportunity of talking to the authorities. He could not understand why they should pursue a hole and corner method rather than a straight-forward man to man talk which would clear every-thing up. Mosley had always been expecting the police to tap his phone and read his letters. He offered the visitors the opportunity to see any documents they wished. It was not long before:

the leader gave the assembled company a lecture on the foreign policy of the BUF. Not however in the style of his public speeches but as one Englishman to another. He seemed to sense the ques-tion which was in the minds of his audience. 'I do not want the Germans to win', he said, 'I want peace now, before England has been reduced to a dung heap. After the politicians reduce England and the British Empire to a dung heap, they are not going to get me to take over then. I shall retire from political life.'

Among other things, Mosley said he thought Germany could with-stand a blockade for at least seven years and there was no possibility of internal upheaval since the Gestapo were the finest secret police the world had ever seen. He did not think Hitler wanted to smash the British Empire; he had had personal contact with him on two occa-sions and both he and his wife were convinced that Hitler did not want to harm England in any way.

One file produced for the visitors revealed a correspondence that made it clear that certain members of the BUF 'had an almost unbal-anced admiration of everything German'. The 'leader was asked whether he approved of this'. Mosley replied that this was a great worry to him. In fact he could produce a great list of people he had expelled because of their pro-German sentiments; he admitted that an enemy agent would find a pro-Nazi member of the BUF a good cover for his activities. When the party left the Leader's presence they had the impression that he was convinced he made a profound impression on them. Actually, Mosley struck Aiken-Sneath 'as immensely vain, a bad judge of men and extremely urbane and cunning, and entirely lacking in sincerity. His chief handicap is probably his excessive vanity which made it difficult for him to take an objective view of any situation.'[59]

Kell, Liddell and Knight attended a meeting at the Home Office from 7 p.m. to 8.45 p.m. on 21 May. Alongside Sir John Anderson, were Sir Alexander Maxwell and Sir Alan Brooke (soon to be appointed to command Home Forces). Anderson began by telling the gathering that he found it difficult to believe that any members of the BUF would assist the enemy. Mosley had been appealing to the patriotism of its members. Knight, who led the Security Service's response, explained that this was merely an example of how insincere Mosley really was and how many of his supporters simply regarded utterances of that kind as a figure of speech. He then went on to describe the underground activities of the BUF and the Tyler Kent case. Anderson acknowledged the seriousness of the Kent case but he did not think it involved the BUF. Knight replied that Archibald Ramsey and Mosley were in constant touch with one another and that many members of the Right Club were also members of the BUF. But Anderson said that he needed to be 'reasonably convinced' that the BUF might assist the enemy and that unless he could get such evidence he thought it would be a mistake to imprison Mosley and his supporters 'who would be extremely bitter after the war when democracy would be going through its severest trials'.

Liddell 'longed to say that if somebody did not get a move on there would be no democracy, no England and no Empire, and that this was a matter of days'. Instead, Liddell confined himself to stressing the urgency of the matter and said that 'surely, rather than argue the fine points of these various cases, wasn't it possible to make up our minds whether the BUF were assisting the enemy and if we came to the conclusion that it was, wasn't it possible to find some means of dealing with it as an organisation?' Anderson 'rather skated over this' and, in Liddell's view, 'seemed to have a great aversion to locking up a British subject unless he had a cast-iron case against him'; however, Liddell thought Anderson was shaken considerably by the end of the meeting and he asked MI5 for further evidence on certain points which he required for Cabinet. Liddell reflected on Anderson: 'Either he is an extremely calm and cool-headed person or he has not the least idea of the present situation. The possibility of a serious invasion of this country would seem to be no more than a vague suggestion.'[60]

A couple of days later, on 25 May, Liddell was asked to go to the Privy Council to see Clement Attlee, the leader of the Labour Party and another senior party member, Arthur Greenwood: both were now in Churchill's new Coalition Government. Liddell could not understand how they had got hold of his name. Before going up he rang up Kell to ask his permission. Liddell proposed to tell the Labour men 'exactly what I thought' and was given permission to. Attlee and Greenwood gave the impression that there was some political intrigue or graft that was holding things up. Liddell told him then that he did not think this was the case. In his view the reluctance of the Home Office to act came from an 'old-fashioned liberalism which seemed to prevail in all sections. The liberty of the subject, freedom of speech etc were all very well in peacetime but were no use in fighting the Nazis. There seemed to be a complete failure to realise the power of the totalitarian state and the energy with which the Germans were fighting a total war.' Both Attlee and Greenwood agreed and revealed that they had charged by Churchill to enquire into the matter.[61] Soon the Government moved against the BUF and interned prominent members – including Mosley (although he was released later in the war). It was only after three years of war that Dick White was able to say with certainly that the picture of German secret activities in the UK:

> which we can now construct on the basis of the past three years experience shows them to be entirely different from what is frequently alleged to have taken place in the European countries invaded and now occupied by the Germans. Reflection will, however, show that there are no good *a priori* reasons why under the very different circumstances now obtaining in this country a repetition should be expected here of what is supposed to have taken place in, say, Belgium or Jugoslavia, even if the experience of those countries had been faithfully or fully reported to us, which they certainly have not. [Indeed, it was] childish to ignore the difference in the circumstances under which the German Secret Service has to work in this country as compared with the European countries which they have invaded.

The principal difference White listed as follows:

> (a) this country has already been at war for three years. In most of the European countries, with the exception of France, invasion followed either very soon after, contemporaneously with, or even before, a declaration of war.

(b) there has been a comprehensive measure of internment: (i) of German nationals in this country, (ii) of British Fascists, which must have snapped many links with the enemy, if such ever existed.

(c) in the European countries which have been invaded, the principal instruments of German subversive activity have been the communities of Volksdeutscher, especially in the Balkans, i.e. the Germans anxious to be incorporated in the Reich. It would be absurd to assert that the German refugees in this country are analogous to such communities of Volksdeutscher.

(d) the political position in this country is entirely different from those which obtained in the invaded countries before invasion. In particular there is now no organised Fascist party in existence capable of discharging the part said to have been played... in Holland, etc.

There is of course considerable evidence showing that there exist in this country a number of individuals who for pathological or other reasons would be anxious to assist the enemy either now or if he invades. The existence of such people of course presents a problem but does not in any way affect the radical differences to which attention is drawn above.[62]

Thus it may be said that, for all the anxieties concerning a Fifth Column in Britain, willing and able to assist the Germans, there really was not one. But that takes no account of the fact that, in the dark days of 1940, the Security Service had to take the view that with invasion imminent no chances should be taken. Internment made sure that there would no collaboration on any significant scale. And the Tyler Kent case ably demonstrated what inaction might allow. With invasion feared and the country's defences in a perilous state the defence of the realm, rather than the liberty of the subject, was deemed paramount.

14

'Are the Members of
the Intellectual Type?'
The Communist Party of Great Britain
& the Formation of the Grand Alliance

The backbone of MI5 in the Second World War was the same as in the First World War: its female employees. Diana Fynn joined MI5 as a personal secretary in May 1940. Her interview was: 'very "hole and corner" and I was not at all sure what sort of job I was getting into'. Her references were supplied by relatives in the Forces and she even had one from a well-known judge, the father of a friend of hers. Diana was instructed to turn up at an office in St. James' Street but to tell no one where she was going. Signing the Official Secrets Act was daunting:

> it gave me the feeling that at any moment I might make a terrible error and be arrested. [Shortly after her arrival the 'Office' moved to Wormwood Scrubs Prison.] We were not permitted to tell anyone the name of the department or the place to which we had been moved. My father was keen to find out what I was doing and tried all sorts of trick questions, such as 'Have you met so-and-so?' and 'What's it like to work for the Army?' The fact that we did not wear uniform might have led him to make a few guesses, but I got by without too much trouble. There were a few moments when I had to cover up quickly, but it was always safe to name the Ministry of Information if I was in a tight corner.

In those days Diana had a yellow bicycle, and on the first morning, after a long and complicated ride from Sloane Square to East Acton, she arrived at the intimidating gates of Wormwood Scrubs Prison. Showing her pass to the policeman at the prison gate, she was directed to the first enormous block of cells. Catcalls and whistles followed Diana as she crossed the yard, for the cell block adjacent to the Office was still filled with prisoners. However, they were not to stay long.

On the first day there, the woman in charge of female staff spent much time pasting newspapers on the walls of the lavatories in order that the 'gels' should not see what the prisoners had written, or the crude drawings they had left behind them; but Diana and the 'gels' recalled: 'We spent some time tearing the paper off again!' Diana was allotted a cell on the first floor, next door to the one occupied by Edward Cussen, for whom she was to work. He had also only just arrived, 'so we both sat in our cells waiting for something to happen, with no idea how we were to begin working. I was dependent on work given to me by him and he had not yet discovered what he was meant to be doing.' However, 'we did at least have the opportunity to get to know each other'. Diana soon discovered that 'once you had entered your cell and closed the door it was not possible to open it again. In an emergency you had to phone up your officer to come and let you out, but at first we had no telephones so urgent shouts could be heard at intervals from along the walkways which circled the interior of the building.'

Diana found the Scrubs a disconcerting place. Wire netting had been slung between the balconies to prevent suicides amongst the prisoners. Another unnerving discovery was that each door had a peephole through which one could be observed. 'If you wanted to adjust your stockings, or something like that, the only safe position was to stand close to the left or right hand wall on either side of the door.' Diana was lucky in having a particular friend in the Office called Billie, who had been there for a few months. Through her Diana was able to discover how the Office was managed, but she was also new to Wormwood Scrubs and no one made much headway for a few weeks. A personal secretary was looked upon as being in an exalted position by the many girls who worked for MI5, especially those who were known as 'snaggers'. The snaggers, 'poor things', had to spend their lives hunting for lost files, which were either wrongly marked out to various people or were being 'sat on' by officers for different reasons. Snaggers worked from the Registry, which was housed in a large tin hut along one side of the prison block.

Later that summer Diana was told to take over the position of personal secretary to Roger Hollis, the head of Section F (Communism and subversion). Diana knew that he had a reputation for 'being difficult and exacting and I was terrified. My hand shook so much when I was taking shorthand from him that I could scarcely read it back. I don't suppose that he was really as bad as I thought, but I was very young and in my first job.'[1] Gradually, Diana got used to Hollis's way of working. He was a 'cynical, monosyllabic man who never let the slightest slip pass him by'. She began to wonder whether he was ill, 'for he was certainly worried and overtired'.

There was an occasion when a man in a flat below her family's, in Lowndes Square, was arrested. Diana was asked by her mother if she thought he was a spy, 'and had to keep a blank look on my face because in fact I knew quite a lot about him'. Her mother told Diana that a post office engineer who had come to mend her telephone had told her he had been employed to 'tap' the telephone of the man in the flat below. Diana was horrified to hear this, as such things were supposed to be strictly secret. Some time later, she told Diana that a man had come to see her about the incident and that she was afraid that 'the nice engineer' was going to get into trouble: Diana 'must have shown by my expression that I was somehow involved, because she was sure that it was I who had passed on the information. That the engineer concerned was a threat to the security of the country never seemed to enter her mind. Interestingly, it turned out that the man who had come to interview my mother was my boss Roger Hollis.'

One morning, in November 1940, at a time when the air raids on London were severe, Diana cycled to the Scrubs as usual to find firemen and hoses all over the prison yard. A bomb had fallen on the Registry during the night. This was a 'disaster for the Office and for the defence of the country'. It was, however, looked on as a 'lark' by many of the girls who worked in that department, as they all had to go home. Because Diana's part of the Office was within the prison block, they were able to remain at work, but it soon became apparent that there was no way in which MI5 could continue to work without access to the Registry. Hollis was deeply worried, and angry that so many of the staff did not realise what a catastrophe the bomb had caused. He told Diana that he had been instrumental in having MI5's entire card index photographed and sent to Canada a short while before the bomb fell. The photographs had only just reached their destination and had to be shipped straight back to London. As it turned out, the photostats of the card index returned from Canada were almost indecipherable. It was a huge blow.

The Office was moved as soon as possible to Blenheim Palace in Oxfordshire. This 'might have seemed a beneficial move for the workers in the Registry, but as secretaries we missed our little individual cells, for it was freezing in the tin huts in the yard of the Palace'. The Registry workers were much more comfortable, having left their tin shed for the interior of the Palace and a fairly warm existence. Fleets of cars and buses took the staff from London to Woodstock and they were found digs in houses around the area. Eventually Keble College in Oxford was requisitioned for female staff and about 300 of them were housed there. On a cold, grey winter night, a friend and Diana were shown to their room in the College by an elderly 'scout' who greeted them with the cheerful news that: 'The last man what 'ad this room 'anged 'imself, Miss.' Diana was 'not surprised'. There were six bathrooms in an ice cold clock tower across the quad and more than 300 women to share them. The women slept two to a unit originally designed for one person. Each unit had a small sitting- room with a single bed and a tiny fireplace, but practically no coal. A minute bedroom was screened off from the sitting room with room for another small bed, and there were lavatories, a communal kitchen and a laundry down a long passage. Men could visit the women, but had to be out by eleven o'clock at night. However, as many of the women were married this rule frequently went unobserved. 'If the man in question had not left by eleven the only option was for him to climb out over the wall, or stay all night and leave at a respectable time in the morning.' It also occasionally happened that old Keble students, on leave with nowhere to go, would climb into Keble to doss down for the night, unaware that it had suffered a wartime change. 'They must have had mixed feelings when they encountered women in flimsy nighties flitting about the ill-lit corridors.' The buses arrived every morning at seven o'clock to ferry the women from Keble to Blenheim, where they could get breakfast at the canteen. There was 'really very little secrecy as to our destination'. At Blenheim Palace 'we showed our pink identity cards to the police at the gate and were admitted to the Palace Yard. It was not unknown for those who had forgotten their passes to show the corner of a pink cheque book instead!' Hugh Astor (who had become Hollis's PA) and Diana tried to keep a light-hearted atmosphere at work:

> and in this we were helped by Roger Fulford, the historian, who was also part of the other half of our Section. He was a delightful man and a great asset to have around. Part of my work required that I should go up to a small room in the comparative seclusion of the gate-tower. I never found out how it happened, but one day the tower was discovered to be in flames and the local fire-engine arrived. Many wax cylinders were stored in the tower for use in our work and they must have burned fiercely. No one was suspected of sabotage, but this was the second time that the fire service had had to deal with those parts of the Office which were meant to be kept under strict security.

Diana found, though that her work for Roger Hollis 'was not easy, for he was not a friendly man. I dare say that he was under stresses of which I knew nothing, for things were not going smoothly at that time of the war and he was in a very responsible position.' But 'one day, when our office had been moved inside the Palace, Winston Churchill suddenly entered the Section accompanied by numerous members of his family' – the Duke and Duchess of Marlborough, who were normally resident in the other parts of Blenheim Palace, were his close relatives. Churchill's visit:

> put Roger in a dilemma, as no one was permitted in our offices without a valid reason and without having signed the Official Secrets Act. Casual visitors would never have been admitted under any circumstances. Roger leaned across his desk and, very obviously, turned all the files face downwards. Churchill, on the far side of the desk, took the hint and sent his relatives out! He then sat down and showed enormous skill as he questioned Roger on various aspects of his work. Trapped in the corner of the room behind the desk – having been taking shorthand when they arrived – I was most impressed at the knowledge shown by Churchill, who was able to discuss confidential matters in detail with Hollis.[2]

Hollis did, indeed, have a lot on his plate. What should be done with possible Communist subversives was a dilemma that preoccupied MI5 in the early stages of the war with Germany. The USSR, after all, had signed a Non-Aggression Pact with the Nazi state before the war and, after invading Finland, there was a real possibility of conflict with Britain. In April and May 1940, Kell voiced his concerns to Sir Alexander Maxwell of the Home Office. In the event of war with Russia, Kell submitted that any member of the Communist Party was open to the charge of 'hostile associations'. As Communist Party policy was dictated by Moscow, members of the Communist Party who carried out that policy could surely be ruled as carrying out the directions of the enemy. Even when, as at the present moment, Britain was not at war with Russia, 'I feel that on the basis of the evidence relating to collaboration between the Nazis and the Communists... there are strong grounds for suspecting hostile associations for a pledged member of the Communist Party. For my part, this position seems to have been reached here and now, but I can understand that while we are not at war with Russia it presents a problem which cannot perhaps be decided on a general ruling.'

Kell, therefore, felt that the case for prohibiting Communists from travelling outside the UK was a strong one. It was always difficult to decide when a particular case justified an exception to the rule but 'I feel that in times like the present we should in the national interest adopt a policy of safety first and make a general prohibition against foreign travel facilities for Communists.' Regarding Communist refugees, Kell did not advocate any measure of general internment at the present time. The particular persons whom he recommended for internment were all persons who might be regarded as potential leaders and organisers of foreign Communists in the UK. 'I should like to point out in this connection that as long as the leaders are at large, the rank and file Communists, who may very well wish to lead peaceful lives here and not to engage in political activities, may be unable to do so. Communists have a way of exacting services from the rank and file by what amounts to blackmail and by threatening denunciations.'[3] Although it might 'perhaps be academic at the moment' to discuss action in the event of war with the Soviet Union, Kell did not feel that even the Defence Regulations and the introduction of the death penalty would remove the necessity of being prepared to take action against the Communist Party as a whole; he was, therefore, anxious to make preparations and to send particulars of this plan to the Chief Constables concerned so that if the occasion should arise they would be prepared to act on receipt of a telegram; Kell, however, did not wish to take any such action until he first had Maxwell's approval of the plan.[4]

Kell did not get the Home Office's approval. On 17 May, Maxwell informed Kell that the Home Secretary, together with the Labour leadership now included in Churchill's coalition – Attlee, Greenwood and Bevin – had decided that it would be unwise at the present moment to take 'drastic action' against leading Communists – i.e. intern them. This applied to foreign Communists as well as to British Communists: 'I think, however, it would be wise to make all preparations in case at any time the Government should take the view that the immediate internment of leading Communists both British and foreign is necessary.' Maxwell suggested, therefore, that Kell should go ahead and communicate to the respective Chief Constables the names and addresses of the Communists, both British and foreign, on his lists, and tell them that while no action was to be taken at present and the communication was to be kept entirely secret, they should be prepared on the receipt of a pre-arranged code telegram to arrest, with a view to internment, the individuals on these lists.[5]

The prohibition on action meant that the Office had to reign in any enthusiastic MI5 officers in the provinces: it had been suggested by some Regional Officers that they should act as advisors to the police in matters concerning the prosecution of Communists who might be involved in disrupting war production. Hollis asserted his primacy over such matters. He was 'very anxious' that while they should be kept informed of the policy as regards Communists, MI5's Regional Officers should not let themselves advise in cases of prosecutions: individual cases for prosecutions under Defence of the Realm Regulations had to go to the DPP or Home Office, except for small breeches of the peace, which the Chief Constable could decide for himself. The question of Communists was 'not only a war issue, it is a long term matter that will be with us even more after the war is over, so that the well-intentioned but misguided handling of labour questions now may have very serious results for years ahead'. MI5's good relations with the Ministry of Labour would be seriously damaged if labour disputes were handled by Chief Constables and Regional Officers on information coming almost entirely from an employer.[6]

Circular No.50, issued by MI5 HQ, to Regional Officers, stated that although the Communist Party had shown no sign that it intended to give active aid to Hitler 'in the event of invasion it is possible that it may adopt a passive role of non-intervention in the Imperialist war'. Against this, no evidence had been collected from any of the countries already invaded that the Fifth Column had been drawn from the Communist Party or even from the working classes. This was not to say that the Communist Party had given up its aim of world revolution or even that it had not got a scheme of large-scale sabotage which it might put into effect when it considered the situation ripe for it. It was 'even possible that the Party may be prepared to suffer the rule of Hitler in this country for a time, feeling that this is a small price to pay for the overthrow of the British Empire. They certainly believe that the Hitler Regime in Germany will be overthrown from within in the fairly near future and they realise that the British Empire is a very much harder nut to crack.' But there was no evidence that revolutionary plans were going to be put into immediate effect and therefore the problem of labour was one which had also to be considered. The Ministry of Labour was of the opinion that any action against members of the Communist Party who were Trade Unionists would have 'unfortunate repercussions within the Unions, unless we were able to demonstrate the immediate danger to the country of having Communist Party members at liberty. It is to be remembered that the average Trade Unionist does not necessarily consider Left Wing political views as a danger to the country and it is clear that any evidence we might produce would have to refer to delays in production of war materials or direct assistance to the enemy.'

MI5 had, therefore, arranged with the Ministry of Labour that any case that held up production by shop stewards or other factory workers should be referred by the factory management to the area organiser of the Trade Union to which the culprit belonged. The Ministry of Labour 'says that in almost all cases these area organisers are responsible and patriotic men, and they will deal with the culprit, if the case is proved, either by dismissing him from the Union or by telling the firm to sack him'. In such a case there would be no danger of labour trouble. Regional Officers were told:

> if you should learn of any case where the area organiser is him-self a member of the Communist Party and will let us know, we should probably make other arrangements. Please, however, do not encourage Chief Constables to carry out heresy hunts among Trade Union Organisers, as this would have a most unfortunate effect. Generally the Ministry of Labour is very anxious that no action should be taken against Communist Party members and Communists, though they feel that Communists should be pros-ecuted if they commit any offence against Defence Regulations or against the bye-laws covering protected places. [There was] one other point about labour in factories. A certain number of not too scrupulous employers have tried to persuade us and the Police to get rid of troublesome employees by labelling them as Communists. It seems important to insist upon proof that the man is in fact a member of the Communist Party as, if he is not, he has not behind him the direction and finance of the Communist Party which will make him dangerous.[7]

Hollis preferred that Chief Constables write to him direct; but as one pointed out to him, it was 'a little difficult to instil into the heads of the average policeman that he must act in an entirely dif-ferent way in Communist matters'.[8]

So, Hollis set about educating them – or the Special Branch offi-cers anyway. He toured the country explaining to the Branch how the Communist Party of Great Britain was divided into sixteen dis-tricts throughout the country: each of these districts was controlled by a party organiser who was a full time paid official of the party. In some of the bigger districts there were several full time paid officials in charge of the different aspects of the party work. In spite of this fact:

> the control of the party is very strongly centralised. Every ques-tion of any importance whatsoever is referred to Headquarters in London before a decision is taken. That is why we at [MI5] Headquarters have a good opportunity of seeing all the evi-dence, and it is surprising to find how trifling are some questions referred to [CPGB] Headquarters for decision. The result of that is that the party policy is very unified simply because it is dictated by Headquarters, and that has certain advantages from our point

of view. If we find out the party is doing such and such a thing in one part of the country we can think that, given the same set of circumstances, they will do the same thing in other parts, for example, if the policy in Aircraft factories in Bristol is known to us then that in Lancashire is known too.

There was an obvious advantage in gathering information through agents – 'instead of having a large number of agents if we can have a few in key points (people who have worked up into good positions in the Communist Party) we learn the Communist Party's attitude throughout the country'.

Party membership, said Hollis, was about 20,000: 'That is, I think, a fairly accurate figure just now. It was certainly accurate at the beginning of the war and since that time we have had pointers that it has not varied in the total.' There had been a change in membership with people who did not agree with the Party's policy towards the war having resigned and several new members had joined 'and thrown their hands in after a short time'. The wastage of new members was round about 50 per cent. The Young Communist League had a fairly constant membership of some 6,000. But that 'is not the full strength of the Communist Party position'. For a number of years they had made 'a very great point of establishing a series of different organisations either set up by the Communist Party or existing organisations penetrated by the Communist Party which follow the party's instructions and its lines of policy on some particular issue. The following are examples of such organisations': the Russia Today Society 'and its more respectable cousin', the Society For Cultural Relations with the Soviet Union, The National Council for Civil Liberties, 'and more recently' The Peoples Vigilance Committee. All these bodies and many others of a similar nature existed in the Communist Party scheme 'simply to get people to think on the lines they want them to think on and be friendly disposed towards the Communist Party on some particular issue. They don't ask that the members of these various subsidiary bodies should even understand the full Communist Party programme. They don't subscribe to the Communist Party but they do want to get a very considerable body of people in this country, some in high positions, sympathetic towards the Communist Party.'

There were two reasons for this, partly as a recruiting ground for Communists and partly to gain party protection if at any time the Government should decide to attack the party. Hollis thought there was fairly good evidence of that in the recent suppression of the *Daily Worker* on the grounds of trying to undermine the war effort 'when the Home Office was inundated with letters of protest from a great number of people who were unaware that they were doing just what the Communist Party wanted'. Well-known public figures such as the Dean of Canterbury wrote to the Home Secretary '(Whom the Communist Party seem to catch at every end)', and produced a very impressive body of resistance which opposed the ban on the *Daily Worker*. 'This idea of protecting the Communist Party is one which they have been working ever since the outbreak of war because they have always felt that it is on the cards that the Communist Party would be suppressed.'

When addressing Special Branch officer in the regions, Hollis thought it was 'perhaps a good thing to say something about the aims of the party. The long terms of the party are much the same as short war aims.' The Communist Party of Great Britain was a branch of the Communist International or Comintern and it was bound by its constitution to absolute obedience to the decisions of the Comintern. The Comintern was run and controlled by the Executive Committee of the Communist International which was an elected body consisting generally of a majority of Russian members but having members of the various national bodies elected to it. A number of leading members of the British Communist Party had been members of the Executive Committee of the Communist International. It was 'a very important thing' to remember that once a decision of the Communist International was made every Communist Party had to follow the lines laid down by the Communist International, just as branches have to follow the decision of the National Central Committee. The National Central Committee merely had to rubber-stamp the policy of the Executive Committee of the Comintern. Through 'absolute obedience the Communist Party of any country may be compelled to adopt a line which is entirely opposed to the national good of their country'.

Hollis explained that the duty of the party in regard to the war with Germany was stated by what Harry Pollitt, the then Secretary of the party, described as a war on two fronts – against Hitler abroad and against the Government in Britain. Pollitt was in favour of supporting the war because he thought that the greatest menace to any social structure of society was Hitler. He wrote an 'exceedingly able' pamphlet entitled 'How to win the war' but after about three weeks instructions came from Moscow to say that the line of the Communist Party in Britain was wrong:

> and it was logically impossible for them to fight Hitler abroad and this Government at home at the same time. Fighting Hitler abroad must necessarily mean supporting this Government, which was fighting Hitler. The formulation of the party's policy

of fighting this war on two fronts was an entirely false one and the Communist Party here and every other Communist Party must follow the policy laid down by Lenin at the time of the Russian Revolution, the policy of revolutionary defeatism which is that the working class in every country engaged in an imperialist war should bring about the overthrow of its own Government and so lead to the World Revolution necessary to cause the conditions for the setting up of the World Soviet. The Communist Party of Great Britain should oppose the Government of this country, the Communist Party of Germany should oppose Hitler – the sensible view that the only Government you can oppose is the Government which is looking after you. This policy of revolutionary defeatism was employed with considerable success by Lenin in the Russian Revolution and contributed to the overthrow of the Czar and the defeat of Russia from which Communism arose.

In its application to present conditions in Britain, Hollis explained that there were three stages laid down:

1. Opposition to the grant of war credits and that was done from the beginning of the war both in the House of Commons by William Gallacher, the only Communist M.P., and throughout the country by every Communist speaker and by every article in the Daily Worker and other Communist papers.

2. The penetration of industry and the armed forces by members of the Communist Party with the aim of holding up production and thus embarrassing the Government to such an extent that the Government would be unable to carry on the war. Supposing that they were successful in this, the position would be reached when production would fall off to such an extent that the Government would have either to continue the war as best they could with inadequate supplies and then be defeated or else they would have to say that they had lost control of the country and resign and if that position is reached the only alternative will be the establishment of a People's Government. The Communist Party does not believe that a capitalist Government would be prepared to yield in that way and make way for a People's Government and believes that they would rather go down in defeat by Hitler before making way for a Government of the People.

3. Turn the imperialist war into a civil war, thinking that at the time when our war position would be desperate through lack of supplies

and the approach of defeat that revolution would break out and that the whole system of capitalist control could be broken up.[9]

Hollis warned that the penetration of industry and of the Armed Forces 'is a matter which is very much before us at the moment. Their actual methods as far as industry goes are centred very much in the establishment of the Shop Stewards Movement and it might perhaps be of some advantage to say a word or two about that'. The Shop Stewards Movement was 'a perfectly genuine Trades Union Movement in itself'. Shop stewards were very much a part of the structure, particularly of the Amalgamated Engineering Unions in which they were strongest, but their functions in the Unions were purely internal ones. 'They are simply elected by the members of the Union within the shop to represent those members to the management. They settle any complaints between the Management and the men in the establishment and see that Trades Union agreements are carried out. They have no functions whatsoever apart from the normal functions of a Trade Union member, outside the establishment where they work.'

But the Communist Party settled upon the Shop Stewards Movement as an 'admirable way' of penetrating industry, particularly the engineering industry, and they put into effect what they called a policy of 'dual unionism'. The aims of this policy of 'dual unionism' were to divert the attention of the rank and file members of the Unions from their established leaders – the Trades Union Congress and the leaders of Transport House – and to get them instead to look for guidance to the extremist shop stewards who were acting under the orders of the Communist Party. In order to bring this about they first of all instructed their members – Communist Party members and sympathisers – to put themselves forward for election as Shop stewards:

Having their actual 'cells' within these various factories the election was not a very difficult matter because they arranged in advance that one member of the 'cell' would nominate a candidate – another second him and that would put that person up at the election. The average shop stewards election is not a very well attended function. Most of the workers, probably, after they have finished work want to get home for their tea or something and as a result the Communist Party 'cell' attending in force was frequently able to get its nominee in... they have managed to get a representation among shop stewards which is out of all proportion to the total number of Communist Party members in industry. Having got these extreme shop stewards – which they are rather apt to describe as 'militant trades unionists' – they formed a body called first of all the 'Aircraft Shop Stewards National Council' and later renamed the 'Engineering and Allied Trades Shop Stewards National Council' which is entirely under Communist control and which directs the policy of these 'militant' shop stewards. Thus the policy of the various workers who look to these shop stewards is controlled by the Communist Party rather than by the Union to which they officially belong.

The result was that the Trades Union Congress and Transport House leaders were not able to command the adherence of their members to agreements, which they reached 'and as a result you get a weakening of authority at the head, and a rebellious minority – but a very vocal and dangerous minority – in the body of the membership of the Union'.

Fortunately Hollis was able to point out that the actual effects which the Communist Party had been able to produce from this revolutionary minority within the Unions and within the working class had not, as yet, been very great. But, there had been a number of serious stoppages and there had been a very much larger number of comparatively minor stoppages. In general, though, the authorities who were in a position to express an opinion about the production and labour situation were:

> very satisfied with the position. That does not, of course, necessarily mean that the Communist Party is having no effect… If we should have to suffer a fairly large series of defeats and heavy raids and various setbacks which one can be prepared to foresee it is possible that morale amongst a very large number of working people may be lowered and there is no question whatsoever if that should occur, this insidious, poisonous, Communist Party teaching would have a very much increased effect. So that the mere fact that at the moment they have failed to hold up war production to any material extent is no reason for us to feel that the Communist Party amounts to nothing.[10]

For now Hollis could be confident that: 'They have a very long way to travel before getting to the third phase.'

If there was a growing subversive influence in war production then, explained Hollis, there were two ways of dealing with the Communist Party, first on a long term and secondly on a short term 'which would be almost inevitably brought into effect' if the party were successful in delaying war production. Some sort of proscription of the party and detention of the party leaders would be necessary. But although that would be successful for a short time, it would have some obvious disadvantages, which would build up a tremendous amount of class hatred. 'The place where we would confine the Communist Party leaders would have something of the appearance of a concentration camp and the Party itself would undoubtedly say that the leaders had to follow the policy of Hitler in dealing with democratic opposition.' Naturally, then, the Government was not anxious to deal with the Communist Party on that short term policy if they could avoid it. But it 'rests with the Communist Party whether the Government's hand is forced in that manner. The long term policy is to view the problem as a social one.' A great number of the Communist Party became members:

> because there are various social injustices to which they are subject and because they feel that the Party is working for the solution of those problems. The great majority of members of the Communist Party are not revolutionaries and don't probably understand the real revolutionary programme of the Communist Party and, if the Government is allowed time to rectify these social injustices, a great number of the members will fall away from the party with the settlement of their complaint. You will have left finally a small framework of rabid revolutionaries who would belong to the Communist Party whatever any capitalist Government do simply because they don't believe in a capitalist structure of society, good, bad or indifferent. They work for a Soviet system. If these few revolutionaries are all that is left of the Communist Party in this country they will probably be ineffective, little more than theorists, but if they are effective they can be dealt with as a small body. I think, therefore, that I am safe in saying that unless the Communist Party drives the Government to some measure of suppression to get the war over the long-term policy is the one the Government will follow.

Hollis explained how the *Daily Worker*, which the Home Secretary closed down in January 1941, had 'struck a very serious blow' at the internal unity of the party. The Communist Party placed a great deal of value in its newspaper as the Russian Communist Party, when it was illegal, placed great reliance on the papers they had. They regarded it as one of the strongest links in holding members together, of great value in seeing that the rigid policy laid down centrally by the party was followed by all its members. Every day it had articles on policy questions. Every member of the party read this paper and as a result every member talked with one voice.

Since the suppression of the *Daily Worker* there had been a lack of cohesion in the party, members in different parts of the country did not know what the answer to questions were 'and fumble a bit', lacking any control which was there before. The party had believed in taking a very positive line 'when it is in a jam'. But this was the first time since the beginning of the war that the party has been caught unprepared and it was lacking drive and cohesion:

> They tried afterwards to raise an enormous campaign over the Daily Worker, then they tried to start a big campaign over the recent apprentice strikes. On the Clyde it was not entirely organised by the Communist Party but exploited by them and was reasonably successful but the Ministry of Labour dealt with it firmly and reached a settlement in the wages dispute. They have tried to carry on a similar campaign in Lancashire and it was a flop in London but it is not a big enough campaign to get the Party rallied together. They are looking for some big campaign and sooner or later they will find something. It is part of our job to find it first. An example of one of their successful campaigns which they started before we were able to prevent it was the campaign in London when the Blitz started and people began to go into Underground Stations. The Government had said they were to be kept clear for traffic but people started going down. The Government was slow and did not realise it was a mass movement which was going to go on. The Communist Party jumped into the lead, issued pamphlets and leaflets saying they would put the people down below. They got a good deal of kudos from this movement. I don't know what their next move will be but they will have something one of these days. We have to think of it first and meet it. That is where the reports from you assist us. We read them and analyse them and see the beginning of some movement... and we have the necessary evidence and can get the Government to act on it before the campaign is properly going.[11]

After delivering his talk it was the turn of the Special Branch officers to ask questions of Hollis; typical of the questions they asked him were these:

> Captain Martin: 'Are the 20,000 members known to you?'
> Hollis: 'We have an idea of 75% of them.'
> Chief Insp. Smith, Newcastle: 'Is the Party still being subsidised by Russia?'

Hollis: 'There is every indication that they are being supported by Russia but we have no proof. Some very wealthy people subscribe to the Communist Party.'

Chief Insp. Smith: 'Is the Independent Labour Party and the Communist Party the same?'

Hollis: 'No. The policy of the Independent Labour Party is not defeatist.'

Det. Supt.: 'Are the members of the intellectual type?'

Hollis: 'No, they are generally regarded as a Workers Movement, though some of them are intellectual.'

Insp. Greenwood, Scarborough: 'Do they check upon their members?'

Hollis: 'Yes, they have to be properly sponsored and they take up their past history.'

Supt. Wingfield, Newcastle: 'Is there any suggestion to counteract the Shop Stewards when taking up cases outside their work?'

Hollis: 'They have found a good deal of difficulty in combating them.'[12]

Relations between British Communists and the war effort took a sudden turn with Hitler's invasion of the USSR on 22 June 1941. Now the focus of the CPGB's loyalty and its inspiration was locked in a desperate life and death struggle. But Hollis remained unconvinced that the party could be trusted. Two days after the invasion he wrote: 'Until the attack by Germany upon the Soviet Union the Party attempted to obstruct the prosecution of the war in every way it could, and I see little sign from its new pronouncements that its present policy will be much less obstructive, whatever may be the intentions behind it.' MI5 had:

absolutely reliable evidence that the Party regards the present 'coalition Government' as a greater danger than ever, seeing a risk that the reactionaries of whom it believes the Government is composed will be prepared to do a deal with Hitler and join in the attack on the Soviet Union. The Party therefore intends to devote its whole energy to working for the establishment of a People's Government... As long as the Party continues to take this mischievous and irresponsible attitude towards the Government, I do not feel that we can possibly regard it as harmless. The main danger of the Party's previous activity has been its attacks upon industrial production. It does not seem reasonable that we should relax our attitude towards Party members, and particularly towards those in industry, until they have first given open and definite proof that they are prepared to give up their old policy and co-operate genuinely and whole heartedly in the National war effort... In considering these questions I have borne in mind that the Soviet Government in the past frequently dissociated itself from the activities of the Comintern and it is by no means certain that these two bodies may not have apparently dissimilar aims at present. I have also taken into consideration the possibility that there may be a very rapid defeat of the Red Army, in which case Communists throughout the world will be eagerly looking for some excuse. The simplest one will probably be that the British Government let down the Soviet Union and if this situation arises we may reasonably expect to find Communist Party members even more antagonistic towards the Government than they were in the past.[13]

And Hollis's scepticism was borne out as the Security Service monitored and interpreted the CPGB's reaction to Hitler's declaration of war on the USSR. MI5 noted that the invasion took the Communist Party of Great Britain by surprise. Their leaders were scattered throughout the country on their normal weekend engagements. A meeting of the party's Political Bureau was called in the course of the day and a statement was issued to the press and published before Churchill's broadcast offering support to Russia. From an agent within the CPGB, MI5 knew that when D.F. Springhall, the National Organiser, was asked in the late afternoon whether it would not have been better to await the Prime Minister's speech before the party published its statement, he replied: 'We can make up our mind without waiting to listen to that enemy of the workers.' The Political Bureau met on 23 June and issued a further statement on the Prime Minister's broadcast. It said that Churchill only offered half-measures. Technical and economic aid did not amount to immediate consultation for full collaboration in relation to the war and the peace. But the party line had definitely been changed by pronouncements on 26 June. In the provinces the speeches made on Sunday before the receipt of instructions from the Party Headquarters followed the same lines as the instructions sent out that evening. All speakers instantly linked the outbreak of war with the arrival of Rudolf Hess's mysterious solo flight to Britain and were as strongly anti-Government in their remarks as usual. The new turn of events was generally regarded as making the establishment of a 'People's Government' more urgent than previously. On 25 June, a meeting of the party's Central Committee was held in preparation for what was regarded as the promulgation of the Party's definitive line the following day when William Gallacher was to meet representatives of the press in the afternoon and Harry Pollitt was to speak in the evening.

Gallacher's statement said that the abrupt change in the international situation had led to a modification of the party's policy. The party had been fighting for a People's Government and a People's Force, but this did not mean accommodation with Hitler. The question today was collaboration between Britain and the Soviet Union in the interests of the peoples of all countries and the party would support the Government in any steps to this end. Gallacher said that the participation of the Soviet Union in the war would alter the character of the peace terms. A people's peace depended on collaboration for the elimination of Fascism. The British Government would have to modify its own policy if it collaborated with the Soviet Union. Commenting in private conversation on Gallacher's statement as it appeared in the evening newspapers, R.P. Dutt, the intellectual mainstay of the party, said that the first thing was to get the war carried through. The relative urgency of different parts of the party's programme varied at different stages. The immediate issue was not a people's peace but to get effective collaboration. The urgent thing was to push the collaboration forward and see everything else in the light of that. Speaking in the evening, Harry Pollitt took a similar line. He said that the situation demanded a review of certain domestic matters and particularly the laxity of the British war effort: 'Communists do not withdraw one word they have said against the capitalists.' No party could do more to defeat Fascism than the Communist Party but the Government was frustrating its efforts by maintaining the ban on the *Daily Worker*. Pro-fascists and reactionaries must be cleared out of the Government service and the Armed Forces. Every anti-working class element in the country was awaiting its opportunity to switch the war. 'The class enemy never gives up... It is only our mass power which changed the front.' Hess should be brought to trial. There must be unconditional recognition of the Soviet Union and an interchange of people's delegates. Much of Pollitt's speech was devoted to a criticism of the Government's domestic policy.

On 27 June, the party's Secretariat sent out to all party organisations a document of 'guiding lines' laid down by the Central Committee. This document set out as the main objectives of the Party those which were subsequently published in a manifesto of 4 July. In the former a special section was devoted to defining the attitude of the party towards the Government. Gallacher's speech in the House of

Commons on 24 June was quoted in which he said that he wanted to see a Government from which 'Municheers' and 'sell-outers' were excluded, a Government which would speak for the people and work in the closest co-operation with the Soviet Union to bring the war to an end and secure the complete elimination of Fascists. It was stated that this did not mean that the party could place confidence in the present Government. Reactionary and Fascist forces must be replaced by firm opponents of Fascism: 'While we continue to advocate a people's Government as representing the only final guarantee for the interests of the people, and a people's peace as the outcome to which we wish to reach, these slogans do not correspond to the immediate stage of the present fight which is expressed in the slogans given above.'

This attitude of the party to the Government appeared under the heading 'New Questions of Tactics'. In an accompanying document which dealt with the organisation of the campaign for the party's new line, members were urged to study again the chapters on 'Strategy and Tactics' in Stalin's *Foundations of Leninism*. Stalin defined tactics as 'the determination of the line of conduct of the proletariat in the comparatively short period of the flow and ebb of the movement... the fight to carry out this line by means of replacing old forms of struggle and organisation by new ones, old slogans by new ones'. During a given stage of the revolution tactics may change several times. Tactical leadership was defined as the mastering of all forms of struggle and organisation of the proletariat and ensuring 'that they are used properly so as to achieve, with the given alignment of forces, the maximum results necessary to prepare for strategic success'. The two principal conditions of tactical leadership were laid down by Stalin as: '1. To put in the forefront precisely those forms of struggle and organisation which are best suited to the conditions prevailing during a flow or ebb of the movement at a given moment and which therefore can facilitate and ensure the bringing of the masses to the revolutionary positions; 2. To locate at any particular moment that link in the chain and processes which, if grasped, will enable us to hold the whole chain and to prepare the conditions for achieving strategic success.'

This led to a discussion of the difference between Reformism and Revolutionism. Stalin pointed out that Leninism was not opposed to compromise as such. To reformists reforms were everything. 'To a revolutionary, on the contrary, the main thing is revolutionary work, not reforms; to him reforms are by-products of revolution. That is why, with revolutionary tactics under the bourgeois regime, reforms are naturally transferred into instruments for disintegrating this regime, into instruments for strengthening the revolution, into a base for the further development of the revolutionary movement.' A similar point was brought out at a meeting on 1 July of the Fleet Street Group of the party by Olive Page Arnot, the wife of the Principal of Marx House. In explaining the new line, and defending it against the suggestion that all the work in agitating for a People's Government was being undone, she emphasised that this was only a short term change of tactics. The two documents enabled the party in the provinces to put forward the correct line at the weekend meetings. There was, however, evidence that many of the rank and file of the party considered that the leaders were publicly not sufficiently antagonistic to the Government and that the demand for a People's Government should continue to be pressed. The party were, however, quite unanimous in believing that the change in the international situation presented great opportunities for the expansion of the party. 'Party leaders have actually said that the present situation gives the Party the greatest opportunity it has ever had.'

On 14 July the Central Committee issued another Manifesto. Almost simultaneously with the publication of this document there appeared in *World News and Views* for 5 July an article by R.P. Dutt entitled 'Battle for British-Soviet Unity'. Dutt said that unity of action could only be achieved if it was compelled, driven forward and organised by the masses of the people themselves:

> We can place no confidence in those reactionary ruling class forces who have for years shown their friendship for Fascism and their hatred for the Soviet Union; who only a little over a year ago were organising interventionist war and expeditionary forces against the Soviet Union; who still protect Hitler's emissary for the anti-Soviet campaign, Rudolf Hess; and who today even while they are prepared to utilise the present situation for their imperialist advantage (a fact of which the working class must equally not hesitate to take advantage, since in the present supreme crisis every division of imperialism is of the utmost importance); do not conceal for a moment their continued hostility to the Soviet Union; by no means wish to see a common victory of the Soviet Union and the peoples over Fascism, and therefore already seek to limit the collaboration and prepare for a rapid change of policy in the future.

The Government's policy was described as one of 'temporary collaboration', which was attributed to the sharpening of the crisis of British

Imperialism. Dutt throughout this article minimised 'the steps already taken to implement the Government's pledge to aid the U.S.S.R'.

Some of the background of the Manifesto of 4 July and Dutt's article was 'made plain' by a speech by Pat Sloan of the Russia Today Society also on 4 July. Sloan said that Britain was fighting with Russia, although not apparently fighting particularly hard. It might not be long before the capitalist Government brought off a negotiated peace with Hitler with a view to liquidating Russia. Workers must unite with Russia to fight against Fascism, whether it was German, Italian, Japanese or British. While the party 'has proclaimed that the Soviet Union is fighting a just war against aggression, it has never withdrawn its statement that Great Britain is fighting an imperialist war'. On 1 July, when the party line had already been announced, Commander E.P. Young specifically denied that Britain was engaged in the same war as the Soviet Union. These 'illuminating comments' on the background of the party's Manifesto were emphasised by remarks made by Ted Bramley, the London District Organiser, when he addressed a meeting of active party members who, it was felt, could be initiated more deeply than the rank and file into the meaning of the Manifesto. Bramley said that two wars were now being waged; the Fascist war against the Socialist Fatherland and the imperialist war between the German and British imperialists. The first war was a just war in which it was right for the peoples of every country to support the Soviet Union. But not everyone who supported it did so from the right motives. The British ruling class supported the Soviet Union with the object of weakening both their imperialist rival and the Soviet Union. If Germany suffered military reverses at the hands of Russia, the British ruling class would withdraw its aid and do its utmost to prevent an outright victory of the Soviet Union. The predominant factor in Britain was still the imperialist struggle. It was right for the British working class to collaborate with the ruling class upon one point and one point only: aid for the Soviet Union. This was a vital issue because a military defeat for the Soviet Union would be disaster for the working class.

Bramley stated emphatically that Party members should not for one moment believe that the Churchill Government had any intention of helping the Soviet Union to any extent greater than might seem expedient for their own class advantage. The public welcome given to the Prime Minister's declaration by the Communist Party was deliberately given, in order to focus the maximum possible attention upon these statements of the Imperialists' policy so as to make it more difficult when subsequently the Imperialists sought to betray the Soviet Union. The Imperialists might never openly reverse their policy, but, more subtly, they would make a show of aiding the Soviet Union and would all the time seek to limit the extent of that aid, and at the appropriate moment would cease altogether to give it. As long as the ruling class were prepared to send aid to the Soviet Union, the party would give the maximum assistance to the factories for that purpose because it was also the party's purpose. The existing situation called not for a change of party policy but for a change of emphasis.

In its analysis of all this information MI5 concluded that the main points which emerged from the Communist Party's new position were as follows:

1. Britain is still fighting an imperialist war and the Soviet Union is fighting a just war.
2. The Communist Party will support the Government so far as it assists the latter war but not to help Britain to victory.
3. The Communist Party has merely pushed its previous campaigns into the background and has not renounced them. At the appropriate moment the demand for a People's Government and a People's Peace will be renewed.
4. The Communist Party is not prepared to abate any trade union privileges in order to secure greater output. All delays in production will be blamed on the 'pro-fascists and reactionary management'.
5. The Communist Party still regards the Government as an instrument of the imperialists and pro-fascists who may try to switch the war.
6. The Communist Party regards the new turn of events as a great opportunity for strengthening its position.
7. The Communist Party is seizing a unique opportunity for obtaining the removal of the ban on the "Daily Worker" which it regards as essential for securing recruits and conducting its campaign.[14]

As far as the Security Service was concerned, the CPGB remained a clear danger to the internal security of the country. MI5 warned that, from the purely practical point of view the support of the Communist Party for the war, 'is clearly not worth the purchase' if this meant that the party was given facilities to agitate against the Government. It was essential that if the party was to join in the war effort 'it must do so on terms of absolute loyalty to this country and not by way of a bargain. In general the view of the Communist is coloured by an idealistic love of the "land of Socialism" and a hatred of its antithesis, the British Empire, the main bulwark of Capitalist Imperialism.' This 'mental attitude may be altered temporarily by a desire for our assistance in the defence of the Soviet Union against attack, but the hatred of the Communist for the British Empire is fundamental'. The Communist support of the war effort would therefore, at best, last only so long as it was to the advantage of the Soviet Union that it should be supported. Thus the Service warned:

> it is both undesirable and unnecessary to try to buy the support of the Party members by promoting them to positions of trust. If this argument is accepted there is little to be gained on the short term view by relaxing our attitude towards Party members until they have demonstrated by their actions that they are loyally and determinedly with us in the war. The whole weight of evidence in our possession goes to show that only definite present advantages should compel us to allow Party members access to information, which will inevitably be used against us in the long run.[15]

Select Bibliography

The National Archives

CAB – Cabinet Office
DEFE – Ministry of Defence
FO – Foreign Office
KV – Security Service
WO – War Office

Imperial War Museum
Lady Constance Kell Memoir
Sir Vernon Kell Diary

Bloody Sunday Inquiry
Witness Statements

Northern Ireland Political Collection
British Government–IRA exchanges

Secondary Sources
Christopher Andrew, *Her Majesty's Secret Service: The Making of the British Intelligence Community* (Viking 1987).
Christopher Andrew & Oleg Gordievsky, *KGB: The Inside Story* (Harper 1991).
Christopher Andrew Vasili Mitrokhin, *The Mitrokhin Archive: The KGB in Europe and the West* (Penguin 1999).
Christopher Andrew Vasili Mitrokhin, *The Mitrokhin Archive II: The KGB and the World* (Penguin 2005).
Tom Bower, *The Perfect English Spy: Sir Dick White and the Secret War 1935–90.*
John Bulloch, *The Origin and History of the British Counter-espionage Service MI5* (Corgi 1963).
Jason Burke, *Al Qaeda: The True Story of Radical Islam* (Penguin 2007).
Bryan Clough, *State Secrets: the Kent-Wolkoff Affair* (Hideaway Publications Ltd 2005).
Eamon Collins & Mick McGovern, *Killing Rage* (Granta Books 1998).
Andrew Cook, *M: MI5's First Spymaster* (Tempus 2006).
Philip Davies, *MI6 and the Machinery of Spying* (Routledge 2004).
Richard Deacon, *'C'. A Biography of Sir Maurice Oldfield* (London 1985).
Kevin Fulton, *Unsung Hero* (John Blake 2008).
Peter Hennessy, *The Secret State: Whitehall and the Cold War* (Penguin 2003).
Mark Hollingsworth and Nick Fielding, *Defending the Realm: Inside MI5 and the War on Terrorism* (Andre Deutsch 2003).
Oliver Hoare (ed), *Camp 020: MI5 and the Nazi Spies* (The National Archives 2000).
Ed Husain, *The Islamist: Why I joined radical Islam in Britain, what I saw inside and why I left* (Penguin 2007).
Martin Ingram & Greg Harkin, *Stakeknife: Britain's Secret Agents in Ireland* (O'Brien Press 2004).
Alan Judd, *The Quest for 'C': Mansfield Cumming and the Founding of the Secret Service* (Harper Collins 1999.
David Leigh, *The Wilson Plot: How the Spycatchers and Their American Allies Tried to Overthrow the British Government* (Pantheon 1988).
Ben Macintyre, *Agent Zigzag: The True Wartime Story of Eddie Chapman: Lover,*

Traitor, Hero, Spy (Bloomsbury 2007).

J.C.Masterman, *On the Chariot Wheel: An Autobiography.*

J.C.Masterman, *The Double-Cross System.*

Anthony Masters, *The Man Who Was 'M': The Life of Maxwell Knight* (Basil Blackwell 1984).

Joan Miller, *One Girl's War: Personal Exploits in MI5's Most Secret Station* (Brandon 1986).

Sean O'Callaghan, *The Informer* (Corgi 1999).

Sean O'Neill & Daniel McGrory, *The Suicide Factory: Abu Hamza and the Finsbury Park Mosque* (Harper 2006).

Melanie Philips, *Londonistan: How How Britain Is Creating a Terror State Within* (Gibson Square 2006).

Juan Pujol & Nigel West, *Garbo: The Personal Story of the Most Successful Double Agent Ever* (Grafton 1986).

James Rennie, *The Operators: On the Streets with Britain's Most Secret Service* (Leo Cooper Ltd 2004).

Stella Rimington, *Open Secret: The Autobiography of the Former Director General of MI5* (Arrow 2002).

Michael Smith, *The Spying Game. The Secret history of British Espionage* (Simon & Schuster 2002).

Peter Taylor, *The Guardian*, March 18 2008

Mark Urban, *Big Boys' Rules: SAS and the Secret Struggle Against the IRA* (Faber and Faber 2001).

Nigel West, *MI5: British Security Service Operations, 1909–45* (Triad 1983).

Nigel West, *A Matter of Trust: MI5, 1945–72* (Coronet 1987).

Nigel West, *MI6: British Secret Intelligence Service Operations, 1909–45* (Grafton 1985).

Nigel West, *The Crown Jewels: The British Secrets at the Heart of the KGB's Archives.*

Nigel West, *Mask: MI5's Penetration of the Communist Party of Great Britain.*

Lawrence Wright, *The Looming Tower: Al Qaeda's Road to 9/11 (Penguin 2007).*

Peter Wright with Paul Greengrass, *Spycatcher: The Candid Autobiography of a Senior Intelligence Officer* (Viking 1987).

Notes

Introduction1. *The Guardian*,
'Where the bombers struck',
Friday 8 July 2005.
2. *The Observer*, 'My 24
hours', 10 July 2005.
3. *The Observer*, 'The horror', part one,
10 July 2005.
4. *The Observer*, 'The horror', part two,
10 July 2005.
5. *The Observer*, 'The horror', part one
10 July 2005.
6. *The Guardian*, 'The rescuer's story',
9 July 2005.
7. Intelligence and Security Committee
Report into the London Terrorist
Attacks on 7 July 2005, paras. 33-35.
8. Ibid. paras. 39-40.
9. Ibid. para.41.

Chapter 1
1. Ibid. p.2.
2. John Bulloch, *The Origin and History
of the British Counter-Espionage Service
MI5* (Corgi 1963), p.24.
3. IWM, Constance Kell, op. cit. p.2.
4. John Bulloch, op. cit. p.24.
5. IWM, Constance Kell, op. cit. p.4-5.
6. Ibid. p.3.
7. Shropshire County Council Sites
and Monuments Records, reference no.
SMNO01814.
8. IWM, Constance Kell, op. cit. p.229.
9. IWM, Constance Kell, p.4-5.
10. John Bulloch, op. cit. p.25.
11. IWM, Constance Kell, p.5.
12. IWM, Constance Kell, pp.7-9.
13. John Bulloch, op. cit. p.26.
14. IWM, Constance Kell, p.10-11.
15. John Bulloch, op. cit. p.26.
16. IWM, Constance Kell. op. cit. pp.
11-19.
17. IWM, Constance Kell, p.22-26.
18. IWM, Constance Kell, pp.28-29.
19. IWM, Constance Kell, pp.32-43.
20. IWM, Constance Kell, p.53.
21. IWM, Constance Kell, pp. 66-78.
22. IWM, Constance Kell, pp.80-83.
23. IWM, Constance Kell, pp.86-95.
24. IWM, Constance Kell, pp.96, 98-99.
25. IWM, Constance Kell, pp.97-98.
26. IWM, Constance Kell, pp.101-108.
27. IWM, Constance Kell, pp.109-112.
28. John Bulloch, op. cit. p.18.
29. KV 1/1, Organisation of Secret
Service, Note prepared for DMO, 4
October 1908.
30. KV 1/2, Edmonds to DMO, 2
December 1908.
31. KV 1/8, Melville memoirs.
32. Alan Judd, *The Quest for 'C':
Mansfield Cumming and the Founding
of the Secret Service* (Harper Collins
1999), p.65.
33. IWM, Constance Kell, p.113-118.
34. John Bulloch, op. cit. p.17.
35. KV 1/2, Ewart to CGS, 31
December 1908.
36. IWM, Constance Kell, p.119.
37. WO 106/6292, Kell letter, 19
September 1909.
38. Alan Judd, Op.cit. p.94.
39. IWM, Constance Kell, p.124.
40. Judd, op. cit. p.89.
41. KV 1/53, (SS BUREAU) General
Organization.
42. Alan Judd, op. cit. p.97.
43. KV 1/53, (SS BUREAU) General
Organization.
44. KV 1/9, Report on the work done
by the Counter-Espionage Section of
the Secret Service Bureau from October
1910 to May 1911.
45. KV 1/53, (SS BUREAU) General
Organization.
46. KV 1/8, Melville memoirs.
47. Judd, op. cit. pp. 84-87.
48. Ibid. pp.102-103.
49. Ibid. pp.108-110.

Chapter 2
1. Bulloch, op. cit. p.31.
2. IWM, Constance Kell, p.120.
3. KV 1/9, IInd General Report.
4. HO 317/44, 28 April 1910.
5. IWM, Constance Kell, p.120.
6. KV 1/39, Vol 1. MI5 'G' Branch
Report. The Investigation of Espionage.
7. KV 1/16, Appendix A. Notes on the
general organization of a counter-espionage bureau.
8. KV 1/53, (SS BUREAU) General
Organization.
9. KV 1/35, para.45.
10. KV 1/9, Report on the work done
by the Counter-Espionage Section of
the Secret Service Bureau from October
1910 to May 1911.
11. KV 1/35, para.56.

12. KV 1/35, paras.60-65.
13. KV 1/9, Progress Report for the period from Nov; 23rd 1911 to Oct; 30th 1912.
14. KV 1/39, Vol 1. MI5 'G' Branch Report. The Investigation of Espionage.
15. KV 1/9 25, March 1910.
16. KV 1/9, The Frant Case, 7 March 1910.
17. KV 1/39, Vol 1. MI5 'G' Branch Report. The Investigation of Espionage.
18. KV 1/9, Kell, 21 March 1910.
19. KV 1/9, Report on the work done by the Counter-Espionage Section of the Secret Service Bureau from October 1910 to May 1911.
20. KV 1/9, Progress Report for the 6 months ending Nov: 22nd. 1911.
21. KV 1/39, Vol 1. MI5 'G' Branch Report. The Investigation of Espionage, paras.9-15.
22. IWM, Constance Kell, p.122.
23. KV 1/48, pp.207-246.
24. Judd, op. cit. p.95.
25. KV 1/35, Volume 1. MI5 'F' Branch Report. The Prevention of Espionage Parts I and II, para.22.
26. KV 1/35, Volume 1. MI5 'F' Branch Report. The Prevention of Espionage Parts I and II, paras.24-25.
27. KV 1/35, Volume 1. MI5 'F' Branch Report. The Prevention of Espionage Parts I and II, para.20.
28. KV 1/35, Volume 1. MI5 'F' Branch Report. The Prevention of Espionage Parts I and II, paras.28-31.
29. KV 1/35, Volume 1. MI5 'F' Branch Report. The Prevention of Espionage Parts I and II, para.44.
30. Progress Report for the 6 months ending Nov: 22nd. 1911.
31. KV 1/9, Report on Counter-Espionage from December 1911 to 31 July 1912.
32. IWM, Constance Kell, p.128.
33. KV 1/9, Review of the work done during the past six months, [Oct 1910-May 1911].
34. KV 1/9, Progress during the quarter ending 31st March 1911.
35. KV 1/9, Progress Report for the Quarter ending 30 June 1911.
36. KV 1/9, German Espionage in Britain.
37. KV 1/39, para.82.
38. KV 1/39, paras.84-85.
39. KV 1/8.
40. KV 1/9.
41. KV 1/39.
42. KV 1/9.
43. KV 1/39, paras.36-.
44. KV 1/9, Tenth Report on Secret Service (Counter-Espionage Bureau) April to October 1913.
45. KV 1/6.

Chapter 3
1 KV 1/35, Volume 1. MI5 'F' Branch Report. The Prevention of Espionage Parts I and II, para.68-69.
2. KV 1/35, Volume 1. MI5 'F' Branch Report. The Prevention of Espionage Parts I and II, para.72-76.
3. KV 1/35, Volume 1. MI5 'F' Branch Report. The Prevention of Espionage Parts I and II, para.80-84.
4. Nicholas Hiley 'Entering the Lists: MI5's great spy round-up of August 1914', Intelligence and National Security Issue, 1 February 2006.
5. KV 4/1, The Security Service. Its Problems and Organisational Adjustments 1908–1945, Volume 1.
6. KV 1/42, Section XXII The 'Lody' Espionage Case paras.1184-1186.
7. WO 141/82, Byrne note, 7 October 1914.
8. WO 141/82, Haldane letter, 13 August 1914.
9. WO 141/82, Beade letter, 9 October 1914.
10. WO 141/82, Simon to Haldane, 16 October 1914.
11. WO 141/82, Haldane to Brade, 16 October 1914.
12. WO 141/82, Stephenson to Simon, 17 October 1914.
13. WO 141/82, Haldane to Brade, 20 October 1914.
14. WO 141/82, Brade to GOC London District, 21 October 1914.
15. WO 71/1236, Court Martial on Carl Hans Lody otherwise Charles A Inglis. Transcript of Proceedings.
16. WO 141/82, 22nd October 1914.
17. Daily Telegraph, 31 October 1914.
18. The Times, 1 November 1914.
19. WO 71/1236, Court Martial on Carl Hans Lody otherwise Charles A Inglis. Transcript of Proceedings.
20. KV 1/42, paras. 1214-1233.
21. WO 141/113.
22. KV 1/42, para.1216.
23. WO 141/113, Letter A1.
24. WO 141/113.
25. WO 141/113. Letter B1.

26. KV 1/42, para.1217.

27. WO 141/113.

28. KV 1/42, para.1218.

29. WO 141/113.

30. WO 141/113, Kuepferle, 22 February 1915.

31. WO 141/113, Re: Spy by A.H. Bodkin, 24 February 1915.

32. KV 1/42, para.1218.

33. WO 141/113, Letter to GOC London District, 22 February 1915.

34. KV 1/42, Section XXVII Group 1 Kuepferle, Muller and Hahn, para.1219-1220.

35. KV 1/42, Section XXVII Group 1 Kuepferle, Muller and Hahn, para.1224-1229.

36. WO 141/113, Minute, 1 March 1915.

37. WO 141/113, Kuepferle-Hahn-Muller.

38. WO 141/113, Brade to Haldane, 22 March 1915.

39. WO 141/113, Letter to Brade, 24 March 1915.

40. KV 1/42, para.1230.

41. WO 141/113, American Embassy to War Office 24 March 1915.

42. KV 1/42, para.1231.

43. *Morning Post*, 19 May 1915.

44. *Morning Post*, 21 May 1915.

45. KV 1/42, Section XXVII Group 1 Kuepferle, Muller and Hahn, para.1233.

46. KV 1/42, Section XXVI German Agencies on the Continent, paras.1208-1210.

47. KV 1/42, Section XXVI German Agencies on the Continent, paras.1213-1218.

48. KV 1/42, Section XXVIII.

49. KV 1/42, Section XXVIII Group 2 Janssen, para.1237.

50. KV 1/42, para.1237.

51. KV 1/42, Section XXVIII Group 2 Janssen & Roos, paras.1237-1247.

52. KV 1/42, Section XXVIII Group 2 Breckow & Lizzie Wertheim, paras.1248-1263.

Chapter 4

1. KV 1/42, Section XXVIII Group 2 Buschman, paras.1264-1275.

2. KV 1/42, Section XXVIII Group 2 Roggen, para.1276-1279.

3. WO 141/61, To the GOC London District, 7 September 1915.

4. WO 141/61, Roggen to Court Martial, 28 August 1915.

5. WO 141/61, To the GOC London District, 7 September 1915.

6. WO 141/61, To the GOC London District, 7 September 1915.

7. WO 141/61, Uruguayan Minister to Secretary of State for War, 10 September 1915.

8. WO 141/61, BB Cubitt to the Minister of Uruguay, 15 September 1915.

9. WO 141/61, Roggen letter.

10. WO 141/61, Cubitt to GOC London District, 15 September 1915

11. WO 141/61, The General Officer Commanding, London District to the Secretary, War Office, 17 September 1915.

12. KV 1/42, Section XXVIII Group 2 Roggen, paras.1276-1281.

13. KV 1/42, Section XXVIII Group 2 Hurwitz y Zender, para.1282.

14. KV 1/42, Section XXVIII Group 2 y Zender, paras.1282-1288.

15. KV 1/42, Section XXVIII Group 2 Ries, para.1292.

16. KV 1/42, Section XXVIII Group 2 Ries, paras.1295-1296.

17. WO 71/1238, Ries Statement, 12 August 1915.

18. WO 71/1238, Proceedings of a Court Martial held at The Guildhall, Westminster, London SW on Tuesday October 5th 1915 upon the Trial of Irving Guy Ries.

19. WO 71/1238, Court Martial Verdict.

20. KV 1/42, Section XXIX Group 3, paras.1307-1314.

21. KV 1/42, Section XXIX Group 3, paras. 1315-1319.

22. KV 1/42, Section XXIX Group 3, para.1320-1325.

23. WO 71/1237, Melin Statement.

24. KV 1/42, Section XXIX Group 3, para.1326.

25. KV 1/42, Section XXIX Group 3, paras.1327-1334.

26. KV 1/42, Section XXXI Discussion of German Organisation, Methods and Agents, para.1343-1350.

27. KV 1/42, Section XXXII. Work of the Antwerp Branch of the German Secret Service, para.1351-1355.

28. KV 1/42, Section XXXIII. German Methods of Communication, para.1357-1365.

29. KV 1/39, Volume 1. MI5 'G' Branch Report. The Investigation of Espionage Part 1. Chapters 1, 2 and 3 Preface, paras I-VI.

Chapter 5
1. KV4/183, MI5 note.
2. KV4/183, Historical Sketch of the Directorate of Military Intelligence during the Great War 1914–1919.
3. KV 1/35, Volume 1. MI5 'F' Branch report. The Prevention of Espionage Parts I and II, paras.94-100.
4. KV4/183, Historical Sketch of the Directorate of Military Intelligence during the Great War 1914–1919.
5. KV 1/35, Volume 1. MI5 'F' Branch report. The Prevention of Espionage Parts I and II, paras.94–100.
6. KV 1/43.
7. KV 1/35, Volume 1. MI5 'F' Branch Report. The Prevention of Espionage Parts I and II, paras.101–111.
8. KV 1/35, Volume 1. MI5 'F' Branch Report. The Prevention of Espionage Parts I and II, para.142-145.
9. KV 1/35, Volume 1. MI5 'F' Branch Report. The Prevention of Espionage Parts I and II, para.151.
10. KV 1/35, Volume 1. MI5 'F' Branch Report. The Prevention of Espionage Parts I and II, para.159.
11. KV 1/35, Volume 1. MI5 'F' Branch Report. The Prevention of Espionage Parts I and II, paras.161-162.
12. KV 1/35, Volume 1. MI5 'F' Branch Report. The Prevention of Espionage Parts I and II, paras.165-170.
13. KV 1/39, Volume 1. MI5 'G' Branch Report. The Investigation of Espionage Part 1. Chapters 1, 2 and 3 Preface, paras.VIII-XVIII.
14. KV 1/42, Section XVIII Staff & Duties of 'G' Branch, paras.1151-1158.
15. KV 1/42, Section XX Special Contre Espionage Arrangements, paras.1168-1172.
16. KV 1/42, Section XX Special Contre Espionage Arrangements, paras.1173-1178.
17. KV 1/42, Section XXI Legislative Measures and Co-ordination of Intelligence, para.1182.
18. KV 1/43, Section XXXVII Re-organisation of 'G' Branch and Co-operation with other Government Departments, paras.1393-1413.

Chapter 6
1. KV 2/3.
2. KV 1/48.
3. KV 1/48, Section XLVI.
4. KV 1/48, Section XLIX.

5. KV 1/44.
6. KV 1/48, Chapter XIV.
7. Constance Kell, op.cit.
8. KV1/50.

Chapter 7
1. Constance Kell, op.cit.
2. CAB 127/357, Cabinet (14/21) March 22nd 1921.
3. CAB 127/357, Report of the Committee appointed by the Cabinet on March 22nd.
4. CAB 127/357.
5. KV 4/246 1(B), Summary 1, Summary of Military Intelligence action in connection with the civil emergency 1 to 18 April 1921.
6. KV 2/246 1(B), Summary 1, Appendix 1.
7. KV 4/246 I (B), Summary 1, Appendix 2.
8. KV 2/246, Civil Emergency 1-17 May 1926, Summary of Military Security Intelligence Action and Intelligence Services.
9. KV 4/246, P. Report No. 1, dated 3 May 1926.
10. KV 4/246, P. Report No. 2 continued.
11. KV 4/246, P. Report No. 6.
12. KV 4/246, P. Report No. 7.
13. KV 4/246, Letter to Colonel Holt-Wilson, 11 May 1926.
14. KV 4/246, Note to Major W.A. Phillips, 11 May 1926.
15. KV 4/246m, Extracts from a diary kept by M.I.(B)m May 1926.
16. KV 4/246, Extracts from a diary kept by M.I.(B), May 1926.
17. KV 4/246, Letter, Sir Vernon Kell, 16 May 1926.

Chapter 8
1. KV 2/1016, History of a section of the Russian Intelligence Service, operating in this country, under the management of William Norman EWER, 1919-1929.
2. KV 2/1016, William Norman EWER.
3. KV 2/1016, History of a section of the Russian Intelligence Service, operating in this country, under the management of William Norman EWER, 1919-1929.
4. KV 2/1016, Clandestine Activities of William Norman Ewer, 1919–1929, Part I Narrative, September 1949.
5. KV 2/1016, History of a section of the Russian Intelligence Service, operating in this country, under the management

of William Norman EWER, 1919–1929.

6. KV 2/1016, Clandestine Activities of William Norman Ewer, 1919–1929. Part I Narrative, September 1949.

7. KV 2/1016, Clandestine Activities of William Norman Ewer, 1919–1929, Part I Narrative, September 1949.

8. KV 2/1016, Clandestine Activities of William Norman Ewer, 1919–1929, Part I Narrative, September 1949.

9. KV 2/1016, Clandestine Activities of William Norman Ewer, 1919–1929, Part II Notes on Personalities, September 1949.

10. KV 2/1016, Ewer Profile nd.

11. KV 2/1016, EWER, W Norman, 17 November 1919.

12. KV 2/1016, Ewer Profile nd.

13. KV 2/1016, History of a section of the Russian Intelligence Service, operating in this country, under the management of William Norman EWER, 1919–1929.

14. KV 2/1016, Clandestine Activities of William Norman Ewer, 1919–1929, Part I Narrative, September 1949.

15. KV 2/1016, Clandestine Activities of William Norman Ewer, 1919–1929, Part II Notes on Personalities, September 1949.

16. KV 2/1016, Clandestine Activities of William Norman Ewer, 1919–1929, Part I Narrative, September 1949.

17. KV 2/1016, Clandestine Activities of William Norman Ewer, 1919–1929, Part III, The Kenneth Milton Correspondence, September 1949.

18. KV 2/1016, Clandestine Activities of William Norman Ewer 1919-1929, Part I Narrative, September 1949.

19. KV 2/1016, Clandestine Activities of William Norman Ewer 1919-1929, Part II Notes on Personalities, September 1949.

20. KV 2/1016, Clandestine Activities of William Norman Ewer, 1919–1929 Part I Narrative, September 1949.

21. KV 2/1016, History of a section of the Russian Intelligence Service, operating in this country, under the management of William Norman EWER, 1919–1929.

22. KV 2/1016, Clandestine Activities of William Norman Ewer, 1919–1929, Part I Narrative September 1949.

23. KV 2/1016, History of a section of the Russian Intelligence Service, operating in this country, under the management of William Norman EWER, 1919–1929.

24. KV 2/1016, Clandestine Activities

of William Norman Ewer, 1919–1929, Part II Notes on Personalities, September 1949.

25. KV 2/1016, History of a section of the Russian Intelligence Service, operating in this country, under the management of William Norman EWER, 1919–1929.

26. KV 2/1016, Clandestine Activities of William Norman Ewer, 1919–1929, Part I Narrative, September 1949.

27. KV 2/1016, History of a section of the Russian Intelligence Service, operating in this country, under the management of William Norman EWER, 1919–1929.

28. KV 2/1016, Clandestine Activities of William Norman Ewer, 1919–1929, Part I Narrative, September 1949.

29. KV 2/1016, History of a section of the Russian Intelligence Service, operating in this country, under the management of William Norman EWER, 1919–1929.

30. KV 2/1016, Clandestine Activities of William Norman Ewer, 1919–1929, Part II Notes on Personalities, September 1949.

31. KV 2/1016, William Norman EWER, 28 March 1930.

32. KV 2/1016, Minutes Sheets. 1929-1931.

33. KV 2/1016, Minute, 6 December 1932.

34. KV 2/1016, Copy Original filed in List 253 (7) S.R.Box 3111, November 1935.

35. KV 2/1016, Press Cutting W.N. Ewer Flayed By Labour Chief In *"Herald"*, June 1936.

36. KV 2/1016, Clandestine Activities of William Norman Ewer, 1919–1929, Part I Narrative September 1949.

37. KV 2/1016, Memo to DMO & I, nd.

Chapter 9

1. CAB 127/366.

2. FO 1093/70, Scotland Yard Memo. on case of Vivian Stranders, 30 March 1927.

3. FO 1093/73, Letter to Sir Douglas Hogg, 30 December 1926.

4. CAB 127/366.

5. Nigel West, DNB.

6. KV 2/818, The Soviet Trading Organisations in London.

7. KV 2/818, Morton to Farina, 9 October 1920.

8. KV 2/818, Arcos Dismissals, June 1925.

9. KV 2/818, Liddell to Mugliston, 1

March 1926.

10. KV 2/818, Memo, nd.

11. KV 3/17, The Russian Trade Delegation and Revolutionary Organisations in the United Kingdom, 7 December 1925.

12. KV 3/17, Carter Memorandum, nd.

13. KV 3/17, Comment on Carter Memorandum, nd.

14. KV 2/818, Arcos Ltd, 11 February 1927.

15. KV 3/15, SIS to Kell, 5 April 1927.

16. KV 3/15, Note, nd.

17. KV 3/15, SIS to Kell, 5 April 1927.

18. KV 3/15, Note, nd.

19. KV 3/15, Note, 10 May 1927.

20. KV 3/15, Memorandum, 10 May 1927.

21. KV 3/15, Note, 10 May 1927.

22. KV 3/15, ARCOS Ltd. A Chronological Note of Events.

23. KV 3/17, Inspector Clancy statement.

24. KV 3/17, Report on Documentary Evidence Implicating Officials of the Russian Trade Delegation and Arcos in Revolutionary Propaganda and Espionage.

25. FO 1093/73, Neville Bland letter, 28 March 1927.

26. FO 1093/73, To Fisher, 14 March 1928.

27. FO 1093/73, The Political Activities of the Police, 30 March 1927.

28. FO 1093/73, Memo to Sir William Tyrrell, 28 June 1927.

29. KV3/17, Memorandum.

30. KV 3/17, Appendix B, John Bankin.

31. KV 3/17, Home Office Warrant, 16 April 1928.

32. KV3/17, Carter to Kell, 12 April 1928.

33. KV3/17, Note, 2 May 1928.

34. KV 3/15, 13 May 1927.

35. KV 3/15, Notes, 25 May 1927.

36. KV 3/15, Re Y, 26 May 1927.

37. KV 3/15, Re the case of Y, 31st May 1927.

38. KV 3/15, Re 'Y', 14th June 1927.

Chapter 10

1. 'Miss X', *Time Magazine*, 28 March 1938.

2. *The Times*, 15 March 1938.

3. KV 2/1022, Statement of 'X', 25 January 1938.

4. Anthony Masters, *The Man Who Was 'M': The Life of Maxwell Knight*, (Basil Blackwell 1984), pp.30-32.

5. *The Daily Worker*, 7 October 1928.

6. KV 2/1021, Percy Glading: Further Observation, 21 May 1926.

7. KV 2/1020, Espionage on Behalf of Soviet Russia.

8. KV 2/1021, Percy Glading: Further Observation, 21 May 1926.

9. Anthony Masters, op. cit. p.33.

10. KV 2/1022, Statement of 'X', 25 January 1938.

11. Nigel West, *Mask: MI5's Penetration of the Communist Party of Great Britain* (Routledge 2005), p.22.

12. Anthony Masters, op. cit. p.34.

13. KV 2/1022, Statement of 'X', 25 January 1938.

14. Anthony Masters, op. cit. p.35.

15. KV 2/1022, Statement of 'X', 25 January 1938.

16. Anthony Masters, op. cit. p.44.

17. KV 2/1022, Statement of 'X, 25 January 1938.

18. KV 2/1023, Maxwell Knight's Report; 'The Woolwich Arsenal Case', 1946.

19. KV 2/1022, Statement of 'X', 25 January 1938.

20. KV 2/1023, Maxwell Knight's Report; 'The Woolwich Arsenal Case', 1946.

21. Anthony Masters, op. cit. p.44.

22. KV 2/1023, Maxwell Knight's Report; 'The Woolwich Arsenal Case', 1946.

23. KV 2/1022, Statement of 'X', 25 January 1938.

24. KV 2/1023 Maxwell Knight's Report; 'The Woolwich Arsenal Case', 1946.

25. Anthony Masters, op. cit. p.45.

26. KV 2/1022, Statement of 'X', 25 January 1938.

27. Anthony Masters, op. cit. p.46.

28. KV 2/1023, Maxwell Knight's Report; 'The Woolwich Arsenal Case', 1946.

29. KV 2/1237, George Whomack, 1938.

30. KV 2/1022, Statement of 'X', 25 January 1938.

31. KV 2/1023, Maxwell Knight's Report; 'The Woolwich Arsenal Case', 1946.

32. KV 2/1021, Percy Glading: Further Observations, 21 May 1926.

33. KV 2/1023, Maxwell Knight's Report; 'The Woolwich Arsenal Case',

1946.

34. KV 2/1022, Statement of 'X', 25 January 1938.

35. KV 2/1023, Maxwell Knight's Report; 'The Woolwich Arsenal Case', 1946.

36. KV 2/1023, Maxwell Knight's Report; 'The Woolwich Arsenal Case', 1946.

37. Anthony Masters, op. cit. p.48.

38. KV 2/1023, Maxwell Knight's Report; 'The Woolwich Arsenal Case', 1946.

39. Anthony Masters, op. cit. p.47.

40. Anthony Masters, op. cit. p.49.

41. Nigel West (Editor), The Guy Liddell Diaries Vol. 1:1939–1942 (Routledge 2005), p.35.

42. Anthony Masters, op. cit. p.49.

43. The Times, 15 March 1938.

44. Anthony Masters, op. cit. p.50.

45. The Times, 15 March 1938.

46. KV 2/1023, Maxwell Knight's Report; 'The Woolwich Arsenal Case', 1946.

47. The Times 15 March 1938

48. Anthony Masters, op. cit. pp. 52-54.

49. KV 4/227.

50. KV 2/1023, Maxwell Knight's Report; 'The Woolwich Arsenal Case', 1946.

51. Christopher Andrew and Vasili Mitrokhin, The Mitrokhin Archive: The KGB in Europe and the West (Allen Lane The Penguin Press 1999), p.153.

52. KV 4/227.

53. Eric Homberger, Oxford Dictionary of National Biography, Sept 2004.

54. Anthony Masters, Op. Cit. p.38.

55. KV 4/227, History of the Operations M.S. During the War 1939–1945.

Chapter 11

1. KV 4/1, The Security Service. Its Problems and Organisational Adjustments, 1908–1945, Volume 1.

2. KV 4/111, The Liquidation of Communism, Left Wing Socialism & Pacifism in Germany.

3. FO 371/11384/C9018, Foreign Office Minute.

4, HO 144/19069/21-3, Home Office file on the British Fascists.

5. KV 3/58, Letter: Sir Vernon Kell to all Chief Constables, May 1934.

6. KV 3/58, Report on the Fascist Movement in the United Kingdom Excluding Northern Ireland, June 1934.

7. KV 3/58, The Fascist Movement in the United Kingdom Excluding Northern Ireland, Report No.IV, Developments during October/November 1934.

8. KV 3/59, The Fascist Movement in the United Kingdom Excluding Northern Ireland, Report No. V, Developments to the end of February, 1935.

9. KV 3/59, William Joyce.

10. KV 3/59, The Fascist Movement in the United Kingdom Excluding Northern Ireland, Report No. VI, Developments from March 1935 to October 1935.

11. KV 3/59, The Fascist Movement in the United Kingdom Excluding Northern Ireland, Report No. VII, Developments from November 1935 to February 1936.

12. KV 3/59, The Fascist Movement in the United Kingdom Excluding Northern Ireland, Report No. VIII, Developments from February 1936 to July 1936.

13. KV 3/59, The Fascist Movement in the United Kingdom Excluding Northern Ireland, Report No. IX, Developments from August 1936 to November 1936.

14. KV 3/59, Note On The National Socialist League.

15. KV 4/1, The Security Service. Its Problems and Organisational Adjustments, 1908–1945, Volume 1.

16. Tom Bower, The Perfect English Spy: Sir Dick White and the Secret War 1935–90, pp.17-19.

17. Ibid. p.44.

18. Nigel West, Mask: MI5's Penetration of the Communist Party of Great Britain, p.1.

19. Ibid. p.43.

20. Ibid. p.1.

21. Ibid. p.43.

22. Ibid. pp.1-2.

23. Tom Bower, op.cit. pp.43-44.

24. Ibid. pp.20-32.

25. KV 4/170, MI5 Notes on the Aggressive Policy of Hitler and Ribbentrop and instructions to the Abwehr.

26. Constance Kell.

27. KV 4/131, General Organisation and Duties of the Security Service in War.

Chapter 12

1. KV 2/816, Valentine Vivian's Report for SIS.

2. KV 2/1009, B5/Mk/Sh, 22 May 1946.

3. Christopher Andrew and Vasili Mitrokhin, The Mitrokhin Archive: The

KGB in Europe and the West (Allen Lane, The Penguin Press 1999), p.64.

4. KV 2/816, Valentine Vivian's Report for SIS.

5. KV 2/815, Statement of Raymond Oake, 30 September 1939.

6. KV 2/814, Report on the Interrogation of Henri Christian Pieck, 12-16 April 1950.

7. KV 2/816, Valentine Vivian's Report for SIS.

8. Andrew and Mitrokhin, *Op. Cit.* pp. 58-60.

9. Nigel West, *Mask: MI5's Penetration of the Communist Party of Great Britain* (Routledge 2005) p.208.

10. Andrew and Mitrokhin, *Op. Cit.* pp. 63-64.

11. Ibid. p.65.

12. KV 2/816, Valentine Vivian's Report for SIS.

13. KV 2/815, Statement of William Rogers, Detective Inspector Special Branch, New Scotland Yard, 2 October 1939.

14. KV 2/815, Statement of Raymond Oake, 30 September 1939.

15. KV 2/816, Valentine Vivian's Report for SIS.

16. KV 2/809, Interrogation of King, 25 September 1939.

17. KV 2/816, Valentine Vivian's Report for SIS.

18. KV 2/815, Statement of John Herbert King, 25 September 1939.

19. KV 2/816, Valentine Vivian's Report for SIS.

20. KV 2/815, Statement of William Rogers, Detective Inspector, Special Branch, 25 September 1939.

21. KV 2/812, Note on Interview between Inspector Rogers, Mr Herriott and Mr Serpell on 2 January 1947 at Scotland Yard.

22. KV 2/1008, Statement of John Herbert King, 28 September 1939, at Wandsworth Prison.

23. KV 2/816, Valentine Vivian's Report for SIS.

24. KV 2/815, Statement of Francis John Quarry, 26 September 1939.

25. KV 2/816, Valentine Vivian's Report for SIS.

26. KV 2/815, Statement of James Percy Russel, September 1939.

27. KV 2/816, Valentine Vivian's Report for SIS.

28. Andrew and Mitrokhin, op. cit.

p.103.

29. KV 2/816, Valentine Vivian's Report for SIS.

30. Nigel West, *Mask,* op.cit. p.39.

31. Ibid. p.216.

32. Dictionary of National Biography (DNB), Eric Homberger, (Sept.2004).

33. Nigel West, *Mask,* op.cit.

Chapter 13

1. Anthony Masters, *The Man who was 'M': the Life of Maxwell Knight* (Basil Blackwell 1984), p.77.

2. KV 2/543, Interrogation of Tyler Kent by Captain Maxwell Knight, 20 May 1940.

3. KV 2/543, Statement of Captain Maxwell Knight to Special Branch, 24 May 1940.

4. Nigel West (ed), *The Guy Liddell Diaries: 1939-1942* V. 1 [hereafter Liddell's Diary], 19 December 1940.

5. KV 4/227, Report by Captain Maxwell Knight on the work of agents during the War, 1945.

6. Anthony Masters, op. cit. p.82.

7. Anthony Masters, op. cit. p.83.

8. KV 2/543, Extract relating to Tyler Kent, 26 September 1940.

9. KV 2/543, Supplementary proof of (censored).

10. Anthony Masters, op. cit. pp.80-81.

11. KV 2/543, Supplementary proof of (censored).

12. KV 2/543, Memorandum on Tyler Kent, Archibald Maule Ramsay and others, 1946.

13. Anthony Masters, op. cit. p.82.

14. KV 4/227, The Case of Anna Wolkoff and Tyler Kent, Captain Maxwell Knight's report, 1946.

15. Bryan Clough, *State Secrets: the Kent-Wolkoff Affair*, (Hideaway Publications Ltd 2005), p.184.

16. KV 4/227, The Case of Anna Wolkoff and Tyler Kent, Captain Maxwell Knight's report, 1946.

17. KV 2/543, Supplementary proof of (censored).

18. KV 4/227, The Case of Anna Wolkoff and Tyler Kent, Captain Maxwell Knight's report, 1946.

19. KV 2/543, Supplementary proof of (censored).

20. Joan Miller, *One Girl's War: Personal Exploits in MI5's Most Secret Station* (Brandon Book Publishers Ltd 1986) pp.8-12.

21. KV 2/543, Supplementary proof of (censored), 1940.

22. Joan Miller, op. cit. p.22-24.

23. KV 2/543, Supplementary proof of (censored), 1940.

24. KV 2/543, Statement of Joan Priscilla Miller, 1940.

25. KV 2/543, Supplementary proof of (censored), 1940.

26. KV 4/227, The Case of Anna Wolkoff and Tyler Kent, Captain Maxwell Knight's report, 1946.

27. KV 2/543, Supplementary proof of (censored),1940.

28. Extract from Report on the Right Club, 26 September 1940.

29. KV 2/543, Supplementary proof of (censored),1940.

30. Joan Miller, op. cit. p.25.

31. KV 2/543, Supplementary proof of (censored),1940.

32. Joan Miller, op. cit. pp.26-27.

33. KV 2/543, Statement of Joan Priscilla Miller, 1940.

34. Joan Miller, op. cit. pp.28-29.

35. KV 2/543, Statement of Joan Priscilla Miller, 1940.

36. KV 2/543, Supplementary proof of (censored),1940.

37. Anthony Masters, op. cit. p.88.

38. KV 4/227, The Case of Anna Wolkoff and Tyler Kent, Captain Maxwell Knight's report, 1946.

39. KV 2/543, Memorandum on Tyler Gatewood Kent, Captain Archibald Maule Ramsay and others, nd.

40. KV 4/227, The Case of Anna Wolkoff and Tyler Kent, Captain Maxwell Knight's report, 1946.

41. KV 2/543, Preliminary Interrogation of Tyler Kent, 20 May 1940.

42. Anthony Masters, op. cit. p.88.

43. KV 2/543, Preliminary Interrogation of Tyler Kent, 20 May 1940.

44. KV 2/543, Special Branch Report on the arrest of Ramsay, 30 May 1940.

45. KV 2/543, Statement of Captain Maxwell Knight, nd.

46. KV 2/543, Interview with Tyler Kent: Captain Maxwell Knight's record, 29 May 1940.

47. KV 2/543, Memorandum on Tyler Gatewood Kent, Captain Archibald Maule Ramsay and others, nd.

48. Charlotte Mosley (ed.), The Mitfords: Letters Between Six Sisters (Fourth Estate 2007), p.164.

49. Anthony Masters, op. cit. pp.105-106.

50. Joan Miller, op. cit. pp.48-67.

51. KV 4/227, The Case of Anna Wolkoff and Tyler Kent, Captain Maxwell Knight's report, 1946.

52. Liddell, Diary, 30 August 1939.

53. Ibid. 2 September 1939,

54. Ibid. 24 October 1939.

55. Ibid. 1 January 1940.

56. Ibid. 2 January 1940.

57. Ibid. 3 January 1940.

58. Ibid. 25 September 1939.

59. Ibid. 30 January 1940.

60. Ibid. 21 May 1940.

61. Ibid. 25 May 1940.

62. KV 4/170, DG White lecture.

Chapter 14

1. Diana Fynn, On the Turn of the Tide: MI5, London Blitz, Turmoil in Africa, Dreams, Mediums and Poetry. The Autobiography of Diana Fynn, pp.31-32.

2. Ibid. pp.49-52.

3 KV 4/265, Kell to Maxwell first letter 16th, May 1940.

4. KV 4/265, Kell to Maxwell.

5. KV 4/265, Maxwell to Kell, 18 May 1940.

6. KV 4/265, Minute on Regional Officers.

7. KV 4/265, Circular No.50, 3 July 1940.

8. KV 4/265, Letter to Hollis.

9. KV 4/265, Address By R.H. Hollis, Esq., M.I.5 Headquarters on "Communism And The Position Of The Communist Party".

10. KV 4/265, "Communism." Lecture By Mr. Hollis (M.I.5) At a Conference Of Special Branch Officers At Manchester City Police Headquarters on Friday, 2nd May, 1941.

11. KV 4/265, Address by R.H. Hollis, Esq., M.I.5 Headquarters on "Communism and the Position of the Communist Party".

12. KV 4/265, Hollis to Forrest, 6 May 1941.

13. KV 4/265, Hollis to Hutchinson, 24 June 1941.

14. KV 4/265, The Communist Party Of Great Britain And The Attack On Russia.

15. KV 4/265, Memo, 24 June 1941.

Available from July 2010 from Amberley Publishing

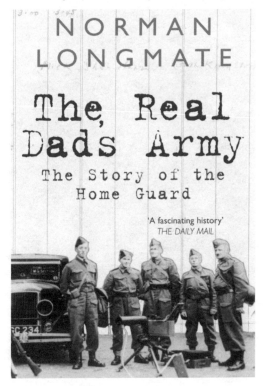

NORMAN
LONGMATE

The Real
Dads Army
The Story of the
Home Guard

'A fascinating history'
THE DAILY MAIL

*A narrative history of the Home Guard from its creation in May 1940
to the end of the Second World War*

'A fascinating history' THE DAILY MAIL
'Wonderful stories... a well-written account of the last line of defence' THE DAILY MIRROR

The enduring popularity of the BBC tv series *Dad's Army* has focused attention on one of the strangest and least
military armies ever formed — The British Home Guard. Norman Longmate, an ex-member of the Home
Guard and an authority on wartime Britain, has collected together a wealth of hilarious anecdote as well as all
the unlikely facts to produce the first popular history of the Home Guard to be written since the war.

£18.99 Hardback
50 illustrations
160 pages
978-1-84868-914-5

Available from July 2010 from all good bookshops or to order direct
Please call **01285-760-030**
www.amberley-books.com

Also available from Amberley Publishing

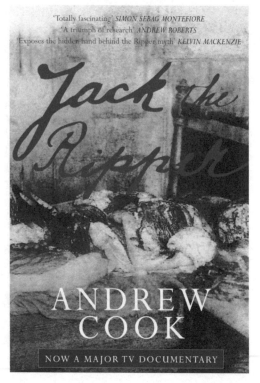

Finally lays to rest the mystery of who Jack the Ripper was

'Totally fascinating' SIMON SEBAG MONTEFIORE
'A triumph of research' ANDREW ROBERTS
'Exposes the hidden hand behind the Jack the Ripper myth' KELVIN MACKENZIE

The most famous serial killer in history. A sadistic stalker of seedy Victorian backstreets. A master criminal. The man who got away with murder – over and over again. But while literally hundreds of books have been published, trying to pin Jack's crimes on an endless list of suspects, no-one has considered the much more likely explanation for Jack's getting away with it... He never existed.

£9.99 Paperback
53 illustrations and 47 figures
256 pages
978-1-84868-522-2

Also available from Amberley Publishing

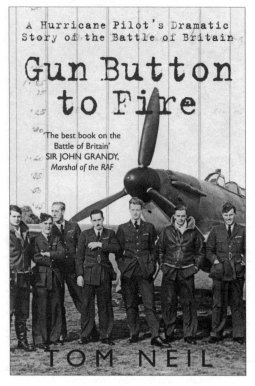

The amazing story of one of the 'Few', fighter ace Tom Neil who shot down 13 enemy aircraft during the Battle of Britain

'A thrilling new book... Tom Neil is one of the last surviving heroes who fought the Luftwaffe'
THE DAILY EXPRESS

'The best book on the Battle of Britain' SIR JOHN GRANDY, Marshal of the RAF

This is a fighter pilot's story of eight memorable months from May to December 1940. By the end of the year he had shot down 13 enemy aircraft, seen many of his friends killed, injured or burned, and was himself a wary and accomplished fighter pilot.

£20 Hardback
120 Photographs (20 colour)
320 pages
978-1-84868-848-3

Available from all good bookshops or to order direct
Please call **01285-760-030**
www.amberleybooks.com

Available from November 2010 from Amberley Publishing

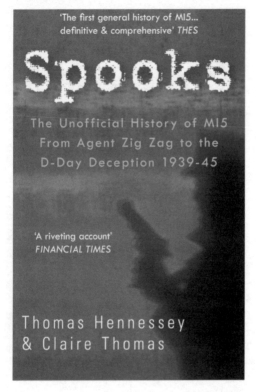

'The first general history of MI5...
definitive & comprehensive' *THES*

Spooks

The Unofficial History of MI5
From Agent Zig Zag to the
D-Day Deception 1939-45

'A riveting account'
FINANCIAL TIMES

Thomas Hennessey
& Claire Thomas

The history of MI5 during the Second World War

During the Second World War, the Security Service, through brilliant officers such as Guy Liddell, Dick White and the fearsome spy-breaker, 'Tin-eye' Stephens, commandant of MI5's interrogation centre, Camp 020, successfully ran the Double Cross (XX) system. XX agents such as the dynamic, womanising petty criminal ZIGZAG, the suave TRICYCLE and the aptly named CARELESS laid the basis for Operation FORTITUDE in which MI5's agents BRUTUS and GARBO were central to the success of the greatest deception in modern military history: convincing Hitler that the D-Day landings in Normandy were an elaborate diversion to the 'real' Allied landings at Calais. It was MI5's finest hour.

£9.99 Paperback
384 pages
978-1-4456-0184-7

Available from November 2010 from all good bookshops or to order direct
Please call **01285-760-030**
www.amberleybooks.com

Available from February 2011 from Amberley Publishing

'The first general history of MI5...
definitive & comprehensive' THES

Spooks

The Unofficial History of MI5
From the First Atom Spy to 7/7
1945-2009

'A riveting account'
FINANCIAL TIMES

Thomas Hennessey
& Claire Thomas

*The history of MI5 during the era of the Cold War, the IRA
and international terrorism*

Despite an outstanding record against German and Soviet espionage, the book reveals MI5's greatest failure: how
and why it failed to prevent Soviet agents like Anthony Blunt, penetrating the heart of the British
establishment, including MI5 itself. The authors look in detail at MI5's role in the post-Cold War world; in
particular, they consider its changing role as it took on the main responsibility in countering terrorist threats to
Britain. Controversy has never been far away during MI5's battle against the IRA, which included sending deep
penetration agents into the heart of Northern Ireland's terrorist organisations. And in the twenty-first century,
MI5 has had to face the deadliest terrorist threat of all – from Al Qaeda. The book looks at MI5's attempts to
prevent mass murder on the streets of Britain, including the failure to stop the 7/7 bombings in London in 2005.

£9.99 Paperback
384 pages
978-1-84868-050-0

Available from February 2011 from all good bookshops or to order direct
Please call **01285-760-030**
www.amberleybooks.com